THE ECONOMICS
OF INEQUALITY

The Economics of Inequality

SECOND EDITION

BY

A. B. ATKINSON

CLARENDON PRESS · OXFORD

1983

Oxford University Press, Walton Street, Oxford OX2 6DP

London Glasgow New York Toronto
Delhi Bombay Calcutta Madras Karachi
Kuala Lumpur Singapore Hong Kong Tokyo
Nairobi Dar es Salaam Cape Town
Melbourne Auckland
and associated companies in
Beirut Berlin Ibadan Mexico City Nicosia

Oxford is a trade mark of Oxford University Press

Published in the United States
by Oxford University Press, New York

First published 1975
Second edition 1983

British Library Cataloguing in Publication Data
Atkinson, A.B.
The economics of inequality. – 2nd ed.
1. Wealth
I. Title
339.4'1   HB771
ISBN 0-19-877209-2
ISBN 0-19-877208-4   Pbk

Library of Congress Cataloging in Publication Data
Atkinson, A.B. (Anthony Barnes)
The economics of inequality.
Bibliography: p.
Includes index.
1. Income distribution.   2. Wealth.   3. Income
maintenance programs.   I. Title.
HC79.I5A8 1983   339.2   83-4153
ISBN 0-19-877209-2 (Oxford University Press)
ISBN 0-19-877208-4 (Oxford University Press: pbk.)

Typeset by Hope Services, Abingdon
and printed in Great Britain by
Billing & Sons Ltd
London and Worcester

PREFACE TO THE SECOND EDITION

Since the first edition of this book was written eight years ago, a great deal has happened. A succession of events has sent the world economy into recession. Most advanced countries have suffered higher levels of unemployment than at any time since the 1930s. Several, including Britain and the United States, have elected governments pledged to reduce the size of the public sector, and redistributional policy has been given a low priority. At an international level, initiatives to tackle world poverty have met with singularly little success. Against this background, the problems of inequality are more pressing than ever before. The cost of the recession is not borne equally by all; the dismantling of social security programmes has severe consequences for low-income groups; and transfers to poor countries have diminished.

Also, much more has been written on the distribution of income and wealth, and in revising the book I have attempted to incorporate this new material. The empirical sections have been brought up to date, although it should be emphasized that one of the casualties of cuts in government spending has been the provision of information on the distribution of income, and in some cases recent figures are not available. At the theoretical level, there have been advances in understanding such issues as the measurement of inequality, the determinants of earnings, and the causes of concentration of wealth. These developments have been incorporated as far as seemed possible without upsetting the balance of the book and without making the analysis too technical. The one major omission is that I have dropped the chapter on the world distribution of income (although some of the empirical material is included in Chapter 2). This seemed the only way of keeping the book within a reasonable length, but it does not mean that I believe that this subject is of any lesser importance.

In preparing the revised edition, I have been considerably aided by the research assistance of Celia Rhodes, who prepred a detailed bibliography. I should also like to take this opportunity of thanking Judith Atkinson, Frank Cowell, Ettie Curley, Jane Dickson, Prue Hutton, Laura O'Leary, Anne Robinson, Tony Shorrocks, Ruth Singh, Angela Swain, Chris Trinder and Michael Wagner, who have helped in a variety of ways, and the students at University College London and the London School of Economics, who have attended — and criticized — my lectures on this subject.

London School of Economics
September 1982   A.B. ATKINSON

PREFACE TO THE FIRST EDITION

This book has grown out of a course of lectures given for third-year students of economics, but it has been written with a wider readership in mind. The book assumes very little in the way of prior knowledge of economic analysis and I hope that it can be used by first- or second-year students as a supplement to introductory textbooks, which typically do not cover this ground. Nor is it intended solely for economists. The lectures were attended by students of sociology and politics, and I have tried to make the book intelligible to them. To this end, the more technical passages have been clearly marked. The fact that the issues discussed are topical and controversial may mean that the general reader will also find it of interest.

My first debt is to the students of the University of Essex who attended the lectures. Their interest in the subject encouraged me and their criticism led to substantial improvements in the exposition. Secondly, I would like to thank the friends and colleagues with whom I have discussed different aspects of the book, particularly Judith Atkinson, Christopher Bliss, Alan Harrison, Klaus Heidensohn, James Meade, Joy Skegg, M. Taussig and Peter Townsend. I owe a great deal to Christopher Trinder, who not only made valuable comments on the draft manuscript, but also prepared and checked many of the statistical tables and references. I am grateful to Adrian Sinfield for arranging for the draft to be read by two members of his course on social policy, Janet Gillinder and Jef Collingwood, whose comments from the perspective of non-economist students were most helpful. The manuscript was typed and retyped by Jill Adlington and Sheila Ogden with great accuracy and patience. Finally, Michael Shaw of Shaw Maclean and the staff of the Clarendon Press have been most helpful in making the arrangements for publication.

Lastly, I should explain about the system of references. In the text sources are indicated by the author's name and the date of publication: for example, Smith (1776). Where there are two works by the same author in one year, they are distinguished as Smith (1976a) and (1976b). The full citation may be found in the References at the end of the book. I have also given, in the sections, 'Notes on sources and further reading', suggestions in case readers wish to explore further the issues discussed in this book. I hope that they do.

A.B.A.

University of Essex
August 1974

CONTENTS

LIST OF FIGURES

LIST OF TABLES

1

INTRODUCTION

The two greatest ends of economic inquiry seem to me to be the furnishing of general answers to the two questions, first, why whole communities are rich or poor, and, secondly, why inside each community some individuals and families are above, and others below the average in wealth. . . Economists sometimes vaguely wonder why economic theory is so unpopular. . . Is there anything in this to excite surprise, if we reflect for a moment on the inadequacy of the answer furnished by the theory of distribution, as at present taught, to the questions in which the ordinary person is interested?

(Edwin Cannan, 1905)

1.1 Economists and the distribution of income and wealth

The subject of this book is the distribution of income and wealth. It is concerned with incomes and needs, wages and profits, wealth and poverty. These are important topics, and the questions they raise are both difficult and controversial. Why is it that a doctor can earn in a week what the average worker takes home in a month? Is it true that wealth is concentrated in a few hands? Should governments still be concerned about poverty, and would a negative income tax be the answer? Does the average Indonesian really live on US $1 a day, or are such comparisons between countries meaningless?

Despite the profound implications of questions such as these, the subject of income and wealth has not occupied the central position in economics that one would expect. A glance at the titles in the economic section of any bookshop will show that there are still relatively few books devoted principally to this topic. And it is probably fair to say that most textbooks on economics give more prominence to economic efficiency and macroeconomic problems than to the issues with which this book is concerned. There has been a revival of interest in distributional questions by economists in the 1970s, but nevertheless the situation is not so very different from that described by Cannan at the start of the century.

The subject of distribution was of course given a great deal of prominence by classical economists. Ricardo, for example, wrote to Malthus that 'Political Economy you think is an inquiry into the nature and causes of wealth. I think it should rather be called an inquiry into the laws which determine the division of the produce of industry among the classes who concur in its formation.' But the classical writers, including Marx, were primarily concerned with the distribution among *factors of production* (land, labour, and capital); the distribution among *persons* received relatively little attention. How national income is divided between land, labour and capital is important in understanding the distribution between persons, but it is not by itself sufficient to explain all the aspects in which we are interested. At one time it may have been adequate to identify social classes with the ownership of particular factors of production, and to focus on the distribution between capitalists, landlords and workers. Today this identification does not necessarily hold, and the link between the shares of factors of production in national income and the personal distribution of income is more complex. An explanation as to why wages and salaries represent three-quarters of total income does not help us understand why a managing director may earn fifty times as much as a labourer. The implications of a rise in profits may be quite different if it accrues to widows and orphans rather than to industrial milionaires. It is therefore important to go beyond the question of factor shares with which classical writers were concerned and to consider the distribution among persons.

The purpose of this book is to examine what economic analysis can contribute to understanding the nature and causes of the differences between people in their income and wealth.

1   *How are income and wealth distributed?* This may appear at first sight to be a relatively easy question, but in fact it is far from straightforward. The amount of information available about the distribution of income, wealth and other resources is very limited. We know much less about this than about macroeconomic aspects of the economy. Our knowledge of the extent of inequality consists mainly of information pieced together from sources that were not explicitly designed for the purpose, such as tax returns, and it may need careful interpretation.

2   *How can the differences in income and wealth that we observe be explained?* Having assembled the available evidence about the distribution of income and wealth, we need to examine the causal factors involved. What, for example, explains top salaries? Is it differences in training or in skill? Is it bargaining power? Is it having had fathers with high incomes? Is it simply luck? In discussing such questions the primary emphasis of this book is on the role of economic factors, but this should not be taken as reflecting the view that economists' explanations are the sole ones that should be considered. The aim is rather to allow the reader to assess the relevance of economic explanations of inequality,

which can then be viewed in the light of broader considerations. In asking, for example, how far the earnings of doctors can be explained by their long training period, there is no presumption that this is the only factor of importance: to obtain a complete picture one would certainly have to examine the social and political role of the medical profession.

3 *What is the impact of government measures to redistribute income and wealth?* In any explanation of the patterns observed, an important consideration is the effect of government policy. For example, in explaining the persistence of inequality in wealth-holding, account has to be taken of the laws regarding the ownership of property and of the taxes levied on the transfer of wealth. In the same way, we can examine the effect of changes in policy. Would, for example, an alternative system of inheritance taxation lead to a reduction in concentration? In the course of the book a selection of policy measures is discussed. This discussion cannot be exhaustive, for the book would otherwise reach an inordinate length, but it covers a range of measures including progressive income taxation, minimum wage legislation, and income maintenance.

Why are these questions of interest? First, the distribution of income and wealth is a major feature of any social system and is therefore a phenomenon that requires explanation. There is an intellectual challenge in answering the questions outlined above which is parallel to that provided by explaining the origins of the universe or of the Second World War. It is, however, unlikely that intellectual curiosity is the only reason people have for reading this book, and concern about measures for redistribution is probably an important stimulus. Some people feel that present policies are inadequate, others that they go too far. The subject is controversial, and for this reason it is essential that the issues should be fully debated.

1.2 The meaning of inequality

A major source of disagreement is indeed over the meaning of 'inequality'. The term may be applied quite generally to cases where incomes or wealth are simply different, just as we might refer to two people being of unequal height, or it may be restricted to cases where there is a moral content (i.e., a presumption that equality would be desirable). This may be seen as parallel to the distinction drawn in the *Oxford English Dictionary* between inequality meaning disparity in magnitude or quantity and inequality meaning 'the fact of occupying a more or less advantageous position' (see Wilson, 1966). The two uses of the term are clearly different. One person may have a higher income than another, but this may not be considered unjust because he will have a correspondingly lower income next year. The use of the term in its general sense of income differences is widespread. To take one example, Kuznets, in his pioneering study of incomes in the United States, set out by stating that 'When we say "income inequality", we mean simply differences in income, without regard to their desirability as a system of reward or undesirability as a scheme running counter to some ideal of equality' (1953, p.*xxvii*). The statistical evidence is typically of this type: the World Bank's *Development Report*, for example, shows the differences in the shares of income received by different groups in the population. But the mere existence of differences in income or wealth is not, of course, a sufficient basis for statements about justice or injustice. For this reason, as noted by Bauer and Prest (1973), it may be preferable to refer to 'differences' or 'disparities' in income when all that is meant is that they are not the same, rather than to 'inequality', although the authors note that 'existing usage is so firmly established that it would be pedantic to insist on avoiding it completely' (1973, p. 23).

In order to assess the implications of differences in incomes, we need first to establish that the people involved are comparable in other relevant respects. The definition of 'relevant' is a matter for social judgement, and we do not discuss this at any length. However, it may be useful to indicate some of the important factors that are likely to have to be taken into account.

Resources and needs The flow of income received by an individual or the amount he consumes has to be viewed in relation to his needs, as represented by such considerations as his age, the size of his family, and his health. What is generous for a single man may be felt to be inadequate for a family of six. What is enough for a child may not be enough for a working man. The distribution of income and wealth has therefore to be assessed in the light of individual differences in needs.

Tastes and choice Individuals differ in their tastes with regard to work, to saving and to risk-taking. As a result, people with the same opportunities may make different decisions, leading to disparities in observed incomes or wealth. One person may prefer a job with low earnings but short working hours and little responsibility. A person who prefers to save while working to provide for old age may have more wealth when he retires than those who preferred to consume when they were younger.

Age and the life-cycle The distribution may be influenced by the systematic variation of income and wealth over a typical person's life. One person may be richer than another because he is older and has had longer to save. Individuals may differ in the time when they receive their peak incomes. One person may choose to forgo earnings when young to train for a skilled job, whereas another may not.

Opportunity and outcome The impact of random chance factors on the distribution means that people who start out with the same opportunities ahead of them may still end up with very different incomes.

Once we have established that people have comparable circumstances, the inferences drawn depend on the underlying principles of social justice. The theory of justice is an area of moral philosophy that has received a great deal of attention in recent years, stimulated particularly by the writing of John Rawls and Robert Nozick. No attempt is made to review the controversies here, but it is evident that different principles of justice lead to quite different views about inequality. A principle based on fair exchange starting from just entitlements directs our attention to procedures rather than outcomes. In terms of the material covered in this book, the statistical evidence on actual incomes is, on this basis, of little interest; it is on the causes of differences in incomes that we should concentrate. Can the processes by which incomes are determined be justified as 'fair'? In contrast, an egalitarian theory of justice may be concerned with the actual differences that are observed in living standards and may see the causes as relevant only in so far as they cast light on possible means of reducing inequality.

It is not therefore easy to move from statements about differences in income and wealth to statements about justice and injustice. There are many difficulties in reaching social judgements about (say) the allowance for differing needs, or in deciding between opportunity and outcome. The fact that these problems are hard does not mean, however, that we should give in. Sen has drawn attention in this context to 'the danger of falling prey to a kind of nihilism [which] takes the form of noting, quite legitimately, a difficulty of some sort, and then constructing from it a picture of a total disaster' (1973, p. 78). Just as we should not assume that any difference implies injustice, so too we should not conclude that the difficulties of comparison mean that distributional questions should be ignored.

1.3 Plan of the book

The principal part of the book is concerned with different aspects of the distribution of economic resources — earnings, wealth, the shares of wages and profits, and the incidence of poverty — but before embarking on these subjects two preliminary chapters provide some of the necessary background. The first of these (Chapter 2) is intended to provide an overall view of different features of the distribution of income and wealth, which will allow the reader to see the problem in its perspective and to understand the kind of issues with which the book is concerned. Following this broad survey, Chapter 3 deals with some of the conceptual problems that recur in the fields considered. These two introductory chapters also provide some of the tools needed to understand subsequent chapters. They explain what is meant, for instance, by a Lorenz curve, by the discounted value of lifetime income, and by different measures of the dispersion of incomes.

The first of the main topics considered (Chapter 4) is the evidence about incomes in Britain, the United States, and other advanced countries, and how the distribution has been changing over time. The sources of information about this important topic are limited. Surveys of incomes carried out by the tax authorities, for example, exclude a substantial number of people at the lower end of the distribution, and provide little information about the needs of different people. Data collected from inquiries in which participation is voluntary typically understate the income from investment and certain other sources. For such reasons, the official statistics must be treated with caution, and Chapter 4 examines their reliability as a guide to how the distribution of income has altered over the postwar period. It also considers the need to interpret this evidence in the light of changes in the underlying economic and social structure, taking account of factors such as the level of unemployment, the age composition of the population, and the rate of inflation.

Most people derive their major source of income from work. Chapters 5 and 6 discuss the evidence about the distribution of earnings and the theories that have been put forward to explain the observed differentials. In practice these differentials represent the outcome of a number of forces, working quite possibly in opposite directions. A model based on training costs might indicate that clergymen would be paid more than the average industrial worker, whereas a model of bargaining power might suggest the reverse. A range of factors is considered in detail in Chapters 5 and 6: education and training costs, ability (IQ), parental background, trade union bargaining power, the structure of the labour market, and segmentation. After this general review of different theories, the last part of Chapter 6 examines their application to the problem of low pay. It considers a number of possible explanations for low pay and their implications for government policy, particularly the effectiveness of minimum wage legislation.

The difference between income and wealth may be expressed most simply as being that income represents a *flow* of resources over a period, whereas wealth is a *stock* at a point in time. A person may have £1000 invested on 1 January. This represents wealth, whereas the £80 received in interest during the next year represents income. The distribution of wealth is the subject of Chapters 7 and 8. In the first, the evidence about the present situation and about the long-run trends in Britain and the United States is examined in detail. The aim of this examination is to establish what conclusions can be drawn from the limited available data about the extent of concentration, and how far it can be attributed to factors such as differences in age. In order to throw light on the changes over time, Chapter 8 examines the underlying processes of wealth acquisition: thrift, differential returns to investment, patterns of inheritance, and marriage. How do people get to be rich? What is the effectiveness of government policies, particularly the use of taxation as an instrument for redistribution?

The distribution between factor shares is not the central concern of the book, as explained earlier, but it is clearly an important ingredient in determining the distribution among persons, and Chapter 9 provides a brief survey of the literature on this subject. This literature is in part theoretical and in part empirical. The first part of the chapter presents some of the evidence about the behavior of factor shares over time and in particular whether, as Keynes believed, they remain broadly constant, or whether, as others assert, there has been a steady rise in the share of labour. The second part of the chapter describes the leading theories put forward to explain the distribution between labour, capital, and other factors. These include the 'orthodox' competitive theory, those based on bargaining power and the accumulation of capital, and the Marxist theory of exploitation.

In Chapters 10 and 11, attention is focused on the problems of poverty and the reform of income maintenance. 'Poverty' is a term that is used in many different ways, and the first part of the analysis is concerned with defining more precisely what is meant. Chapter 10 goes on to analyse the evidence about poverty, particularly in Britain and the United States. How many people live below the official poverty line, and who are they? Is poverty associated with exceptional circumstances, such as sickness or losing one parent, or is it the normal expectation for many people at certain stages of the life-cycle? What is the relationship between poverty in the United States and racial discrimination? The persistence of poverty according to the official standards demonstrates a basic inadequacy in present policies for income maintenance, and Chapter 11 leads on to examine the shortcomings of the present system and to consider proposals for reform.

The final chapter does not attempt to summarize the findings of the book, or to draw any grand conclusions. Indeed, the main aim of the book is not to provide definite answers to the questions raised, but rather to show how they may be investigated using the tools of economic analysis. The function of Chapter 12 is to draw attention to features of the approach adopted which are distinctive and may therefore be controversial.

1.4 Some qualifications

A book covering such a wide range of subjects must inevitably leave many avenues unexplored. The expert reader will be aware that in places there are difficulties of a theoretical or statistical nature that warrant fuller discussion than space here permits. The aim has been to provide as balanced an account as possible of the existing state of the art, while not losing sight of the readership for which the book is intended. The references, and the notes on further reading, do however go some way towards guiding the reader in the more technical areas.

A further limitation is that of geographical coverage. The book does not analyse the reasons for inequality between nations (although the dimensions of the world distribution of income are described in Chapter 2), and it is concerned essentially with Western advanced countries. Within this group, the main focus of the book is on Britain and the United States. Indeed, it attempts in a number of places to provide a comparative treatment of the experience in these two countries, for example in the policies adopted to combat poverty. However, reference has also been made wherever possible to other countries, and it is hoped that the theoretical analysis is of wider applicability.

Finally, it should be re-emphasized that this book is concerned with *economic* inequality. Questions of equality before the law or in politics, of inequalities in social status or power, are not considered; nor is any attempt made to discuss the relationship between these dimensions of social inequality and the distribution of income and wealth.

Notes on sources and further reading

The aim of these notes (which appear at the end of Chapters 1-11) is to provide fuller details of the main sources, and to suggest further reading. No attempt has been made to be exhaustive.

There is very little in this book that is original, and it has drawn heavily on the work of others. This has, however, involved assembling material from different sources, since there have been few books in recent years covering the same wide range of topics. The classic studies of Cannan (1914), Dalton (1920a), and Dickinson (1932) have no modern counterparts. Pen's book on income distribution (1971) covers similar ground to our Chapters 1–6 and 9. His clarity of exposition is remarkable (and I have borrowed from him in Chapter 2), although the housewives to whom his book is partly addressed may be put off by there being considerably more mathematics than here (although fewer statistics). Meade's *The just economy* (1976) covers the theory of the distribution of earnings and of capital income, corresponding to Chapters 5–9. (Books on the determination of earnings alone are referred to in Chapter 5). The same broad coverage of income distribution is provided by Thurow (1976), Taubman (1978a), and Part III of Lydall (1979). More technical are the books by Blinder (1974) and Beach, Card and Flatters (1981).

The volume of readings Atkinson (1980b) is designed to accompany the present book. It contains twenty-five articles or extracts from books and is organized in five sections: the concept of inequality, the distribution of income, the determination of earnings, the distribution of wealth, and poverty, low pay, and discrimination. Other books of readings on specific topics are referred to in the relevant chapters.

For an excellent introduction to some of the issues involved in the definition of inequality, and further reference to the literature, see Sen (1973). The theories of justice of Rawls (1972) and Nozick (1974) are discussed in Barry (1973), Daniels (1975), Gordon (1980), Gutmann (1980), and Paul (1981).

A small selection from the many sources dealing with the relationship between economic inequality and wider social inequality are Tawney (1964), Miller and Roby (1970), Runciman (1966), Goldthorpe (1974), Dahrendorf (1979) and Matras (1975). The Open University unit by Blowers, Braham, and Woollacott (1976) is a useful introduction.

2

AN OVERALL VIEW

Obviously not everybody in the world has two very nice houses, a couple of boats, a tennis court, a swimming pool, and a Rolls Royce or two in the family.

(Rose Fitzgerald Kennedy)

The aim of this chapter is to provide an introduction to some of the main questions with which we are concerned in this book. The intention is to give the reader an overview of the field and to indicate the way in which the material will be developed in later chapters.

2.1 The distribution of income in Britain

One of our principal concerns in this book will be with the distribution of income, and this first section examines the evidence about incomes in Britain today. Later in this chapter we consider how the situation compares with that in other countries. For this purpose, we have taken the estimates of the distribution of before tax income published in the *National Income Blue Book*. These official statistics have enjoyed a somewhat chequered history. In 1970 it was announced that the relevant table had been dropped on the grounds of 'the increasing amount of estimation required'. Five years later, the Royal Commission on the Distribution of Income and Wealth was responsible for the re-introduction of the series, the results being published both in their reports (see the notes on sources at the end of the chapter) and annually in the official statistical publications. When the Royal Commission was abolished by the Conservative government in 1979, the Secretary of State for Employment stated that 'As a consequence of the Commission's recommendations the Government's own regular statistics on income and wealth are now providing more and better information.' However, within two years the Rayner Review of the Government Statistical Service led to a substantial reduction in the availability of statistics on income and wealth, the production of annual estimates of the size distribution of income being once more dropped.

As a result, the most recent official figures for the distribution of income in Britain relate to the year 1978/9 (i.e., the period ending just before the Conservative government of Mrs Thatcher took office). These figures for Britain are set out in Table 2.1. (Throughout the book, the

TABLE 2.1

Incomes in the United Kingdom, 1978/9

Range of income before tax (£ per year)	Number of income units (thousands)	Average incomes (£ per year, rounded)		% of total income units*	% of total income before tax*
		Before tax	After tax		
Under 1000	1 411	700	700	4.9	0.8
1 000–	3 670	1 320	1 310	12.6	4.0
1 500–	2 974	1 760	1 690	10.2	4.4
2 000–	2 701	2 250	2 070	9.3	5.1
2 500–	2 263	2 750	2 440	7.8	5.2
3 000–	1 975	3 250	2 800	6.8	5.4
3 500–	1 815	3 750	3 200	6.2	5.7
4 000–	1 698	4 240	3 580	5.8	6.0
4 500–	1 652	4 740	3 970	5.7	6.5
5 000–	2 855	5 460	4 540	9.8	13.0
6 000–	2 173	6 460	5 310	7.5	11.7
7 000–	1 460	7 460	6 050	5.0	9.1
8 000–	1 394	8 880	7 040	4.8	10.4
10 000–	458	10 930	8 360	1.6	4.2
12 000–	310	13 200	9 740	1.1	3.4
15 000–	160	17 160	11 810	0.6	2.3
20 000–	76	23 970	14 280	0.3	1.5
30 000–	31	45 870	18 810	0.1	1.2
TOTAL OR AVERAGE	29 076	4 110	3 420	100	100

* The totals do not necessarily add to 100% because of rounding.
Source: National Income and Expenditure, 1981, Table 4.9.

term 'Britain' is used as a shorthand; the sources make it clear whether the data refer to Great Britain or to the United Kingdom, where the latter includes Northern Ireland.)

Before considering what the official estimates can tell us about the distribution, we should explain what is being measured. (The precise definitions are discussed further in Chapter 4). The estimates are derived from income tax returns, and therefore relate to family units as assessed for income tax purposes. In broad terms, an *income unit* in Table 2.1 comprises a man, wife and dependent children: i.e., the 'nuclear family'. It would not normally include other adults resident in the same household, such as grandparents or grown-up children. The distinction between income units, households and individuals is an important one; some idea of the difference is provided by the fact that, according to Table 2.1, there were some 29 million income units in the United Kingdom in 1978/9, whereas at that date there were around 20 million households and some 40 million adults. The second point that requires clarification is the *definition of income*. The figures for income before tax in the table cover in general terms wages, salaries, interest income, rents, dividends, and professional fees. This does not necessarily constitute a comprehensive definition of income, a point that will be taken up in later chapters. It should also be noted that it includes items not always considered part of original income, most importantly transfer payments such as pensions, child benefits, and student grants. In other words, part of the activity of the government in redistributing income through cash transfers has already been taken into account in these figures. Finally, the *time period* covers the tax year, i.e., the twelve months ending on 5 April 1979 in the present case. (The conceptual issues underlying the choice of income unit, definition of income, and time period are considered in Chapter 3.) We must also bear in mind that the official estimates of the distribution of income have been severely criticized by Titmuss (1962), Townsend (1979, Ch. 4), and others. These criticisms are discussed at length in Chapter 4; for the present we simply take the official figures at face value.

What do these official estimates of the distribution tell us about the dispersion of incomes? The most striking point at even a casual glance is the distance between the top and the bottom of the distribution. At the bottom there were nearly 1½ million income units with incomes of less than £1000 a year in 1978/9. Many of these were probably old age pensioners, the pension for a single person being £17.50 a week at the start of the year. At the top of the scale, there were 31 000 income units with before-tax incomes of over £30 000. Indeed, from the Inland Revenue *Survey of Personal Incomes 1978/9* (Table 5) we can see that 1000 had incomes of £100 000 or over, with an average of £156 000 –

or more than 200 times the average for the lowest income group. According to the 1979 *Annual Report* of ICI Limited, the emoluments of the Chairman in that year were £124 380; for British Petroleum the remuneration of the Chairman was £120 385.

A second feature of the distribution is that most income units are bunched around the middle, approaching half of the 29 million being found in the range £1000–£3000, with a long tail spread out over the upper income ranges. One way in which this can be presented is in the form of a frequency distribution, as in Fig. 2.1, which shows the number

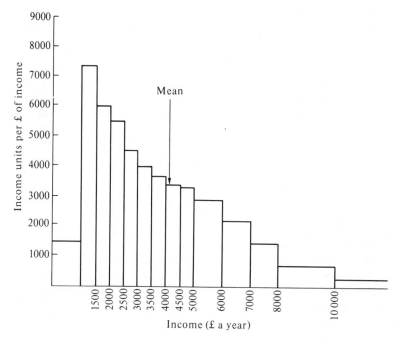

Fig. 2.1. Frequency of Incomes, United Kingdom, 1978/9. (*Source*: Table 2.1)

of income recipients in each income range. For this purpose, the figures have to be standardized so that they correspond to income ranges of the same length. The range £5000–£6000 includes more income units than the range £4500–£5000, but the former range is clearly wider than the latter and the frequency of incomes per pound sterling of the income scale is in fact greater in the range £4500–£5000. The frequency distribution brings out clearly the bunching at the lower end of the income range. The most popular frequency (the mode) is considerably less than the mean income (£4110). Moreover, it shows how the distribution spreads out above the mean, with the tail stretching away to the right.

The frequency distribution is a useful presentational device, but it does not do full justice to the tails of the distribution. To the left, there should be people with negative incomes, that is, people, typically in business on their own account, who have made losses during the year. These people are not covered adequately by the statistics. To the right, Fig. 2.1 is cut short, whereas the frequency distribution should really be continued until we have reached the richest man in the country. To do this, however, we would need a much larger page. The very size does indeed provide some indication of the extent of the gap. As we have seen, there are people with incomes in excess of £100 000, and a graph incorporating them would stretch in fact for approximately 10 pages of this book.

The frequency diagram may, therefore, represent the middle, but it fails to bring out the full extent of differences in income, and in view of this Pen (1971) has suggested an alternative way of depicting the distribution of income. The device used is to imagine a parade in which every person (in our case, every income unit) marches past in an hour and where his height in the parade corresponds to his before-tax income. A person with the average income would therefore appear as being 5'10" tall and everyone else would be correspondingly taller or shorter. The attraction of this presentational device is that it not only brings out the relative positions of different people, but also allows one to identify who appears where in the distribution.

The highlights of Pen's parade may be summarized briefly. (The heights have been adjusted to fit data for 1978/9 as shown in Table 2.1.) Right at the beginning come those who are walking upside down: businessmen and others who have made losses and therefore have negative incomes. Next, as we have seen, come old age pensioners dependent on the state pension. The height of the pensioners is not much over a foot. After them come low paid workers, with, as Pen says, the rule of women first for each occupation. In April 1978, 10 per cent of all full-time adult women workers earned less than £35.80 a week. Their height begins at about 2'9" and rises very slowly. The slowness with which height increases is one of the striking features of the parade, although it is exactly what we would have expected, given the bunching together of incomes indicated by the frequency distribution. It is only when we pass the average income (with twenty-four minutes to go) that events begin to speed up, but even when we enter the last quarter of an hour (the top 25 per cent), the height of the marchers is only some 7'. But then they begin to shoot up. Police superintendents are 11' tall. The average doctor or dentist is some 14'. Around 20' come senior civil servants, admirals and generals. The chairman of a medium-size company might be about 35' and for larger companies his height could be 35 *yards* (some £100 000 in 1980). Indeed, the highest-paid directors of companies such as Shell and Lonrho are over 70 yards tall. They are not, however, the last, since the final part of the parade is made up of people of whom Pen says 'their heads disappear into the clouds and probably they themselves do not even know how tall they are'. The last man in the parade at the time Pen wrote was J. Paul Getty, whose height he reckoned to be at least 10 miles and perhaps twice as much. It is in fact important to watch the last few seconds of the parade carefully, since there is a great deal of difference between those who arrive at the beginning of the last minute (the top 1.7 per cent) and those who arrive at the very end. This difference is partly one of height, from a mere 7 yards at the beginning to 10 miles at the end, but there is also a difference in the nature of their incomes. Those at the *beginning* of the last minute are the top salary earners, managers with possibly some £100 000 in savings, whereas those at the very end derive nearly all their income from wealth.

The differences in before-tax incomes are clearly reduced by the taxation of income. Table 2.1 showed that in 1978/9 income after tax for the top income range was less than half of income before tax. The income tax, and the transfer payments already taken into account, are however the most important in cash terms of the redistributive elements of the government budget. Other taxes, notably indirect taxes and social security contributions, may be regressive in their incidence, forming a declining proportion of income as we go up the scale. (Redistribution in kind has not been discussed, but neither have important elements of income in kind, such as fringe benefits; both are considered in Chapter 4.)

An alternative way of presenting data about the distribution of income is through what is called a Lorenz curve. Although less dramatic than Pen's parade, it is in many respects more useful and will be used at a number of points in later chapters. The Lorenz curve corresponding to the data given in Table 2.1 for before-tax incomes is shown in Fig. 2.2 and indicates the share of total income that is received by the bottom *x* per cent of income units. From the dashed lines we can, for example, read off that the bottom 40 per cent of income units received around 16 per cent of total before tax income. The construction of the Lorenz curve from Table 2.1 is straightforward. The last two columns in the table show the percentages of total tax units in the different income ranges and the percentage of total income they receive. The bottom group (those in the range £1000) make up 4.9 per cent of tax units and receive 0.8 per cent of total income. This gives the first point on the Lorenz curve (because their share is so small, the point is close to the

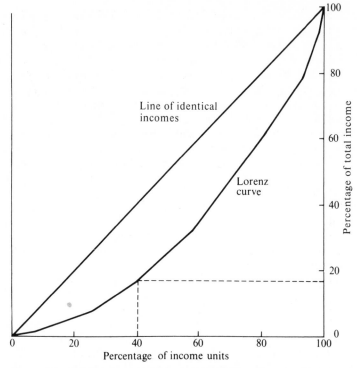

Fig. 2.2 Lorenz curve of income, United Kingdom, 1978/9.

horizontal axis). We now add the next group and find that the bottom
17.5 per cent (4.9 + 12.6) receive 4.8 per cent (0.8 + 4.0) of total
income, which gives the next point on the Lorenz curve, and so on.

The Lorenz curve is useful because it shows very graphically the
degree of dispersion of incomes. If all incomes are equal, so that every
10 per cent of the population receives 10 per cent of the total income,
the Lorenz curve follows the diagonal 'Line of identical incomes' in
Fig. 2.2. If the bottom 10 per cent receives less than 10 per cent of
total income, then the Lorenz curve lies below the diagonal. In the
extreme case where all the income is received by one person, the Lorenz
curve follows the horizontal axis until we reach the last person and then
rises steeply, so that it has an ⌐ shape. The closeness of the Lorenz curve
to the diagonal, therefore, provides a means of assessing the extent of
income differences. If, just to illustrate the working of the Lorenz curve,
we look at the distribution of height, IQ, and income, we can see (Fig.
2.3) that measured IQ scores are more dispersed than height and that
income in turn is more dispersed than IQ.

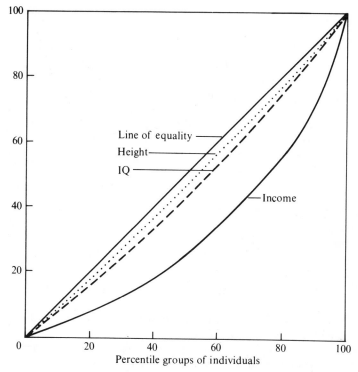

Fig. 2.3 Lorenz curves for height, intelligence, and income. (*Source:* Brown, 1970, p. 114)

As was emphasized in the previous chapter, differences in income do not necessarily imply the existence of injustice. It is possible that differences in income may reflect differences in needs. It is possible that they may be offset by non-pecuniary factors, such as longer hours of work. It is possible that they correspond to differences in age, as where people have saved for their retirement, or to longer periods of training. A hospital consultant who was 20' tall in Pen's parade may have been only 2'6″ tall as a medical student. On the other hand, it is also quite possible that none of these factors can explain the full extent of income dispersion. One of the aims of this book is to examine how far this is the case.

2.2 The sources of income

One of the features of the parade of incomes was that it brought out the differences in the sources of income. In this section we examine two of the main sources: earning and wealth.

Earnings

For most people, earnings are the single most important, if not the only,
source of income, and a view of the distribution of earned incomes is
essential to an understanding of the nature of inequality in any advanced
economy. The findings of the *New Earnings Survey*, a sample survey of
those in employment, in April 1980, are set out in Table 2.2. Since

TABLE 2.2
Distribution of earnings in Great Britain, April 1981

	Gross weekly earnings of full-time adult employees			
	Men (21 and over)		Women (18 and over)	
	£ per week	% of median	£ per week	% of median
Lowest decile	82.9	66	55.9	68
Lower quartile	100.9	80	66.3	81
Median	126.5	100	82.2	100
Upper quartile	163.8	130	106.7	130
Highest decile	212.1	168	141.9	173
Mean	140.5	111	91.4	111

Source: Department of Employment, *New Earnings Survey 1981*, Table 15.

earnings may vary for a large number of reasons, depending on the hours
worked, age, sex, and other factors, the figures in the table are based on
adult workers employed full-time, both wage- and salary-earners, and
show separately the distribution for men and women.

The table presents the distribution in the form of the earnings at
different *deciles* and *quartiles*. Their meaning may be understood as
follows. Suppose that we were to line up workers in ascending order of
earnings and to count off those making up the bottom 10 per cent;
then the person just completing the bottom 10 per cent would be at the
lowest decile, and his earnings are those shown in the first line of the
table. The lower quartile is a quarter of the way along the line from the
bottom; and the median is the man in the middle. The table shows

Lowest decile	Lower quartile	Median	Upper quartile	Highest decile	
├——┼————┼————┼————┼———┤					100% of employees
10%	25%	50%	75%	90%	

earnings both in cash terms in 1981 and as a percentage of the median
person's earnings. To take one example, the earnings at the lower quartile
for men are only 80 per cent of those of the median.

These figures demonstrate once again the gap between the top and
the bottom of the scale. The bottom 10 per cent of workers have earnings

that are less than two-thirds of those of the median. On the other hand, earnings at the top decile are some 70 per cent higher than those of the median, and as we have seen in Pen's parade there are considerable differences within the top 10 per cent. A further feature of the distribution brought out by Table 2.2 is the difference between the median and the mean (or average). The median is only 90 per cent of the average. This reflects the bunching of the earnings distribution to the left, just as we observed in the case of income, with the average being pushed up by the long upper tail. Since the average earnings figure is one commonly quoted in popular discussion, it is important to remember that more than half of all workers earn less than the average.

The right-hand part of Table 2.2 shows the weekly earnings of women at the same date. The restriction to full-time workers is much more important in this case, since many women work part-time, and it has to be borne in mind that average hours are lower even for women working full-time. The figures demonstrate the large gap that exists between the sexes. The median earnings for women are only 65 per cent of those for men, and more than 50 per cent of women earn less than the lowest decile of men. Even adjusted for the difference in hours worked, the median earnings of women are only 73 per cent of those of men. A less expected finding is that the shape of the distribution of earnings among women is very close to that for men. The ratios to the median of the lowest decile and the quartiles are almost exactly the same.

It may be very helpful to put some flesh on to the statistics presented in Table 2.2, by examining just who appears at different points on the earnings scale. In the introduction to *The social foundations of wage policy*, Barbara Wootton (1962) says that one of the incidents that led to her writing the book was the discovery just before the Second World War that the elephant giving rides at Whipsnade Zoo earned £600 a year, which was precisely the same salary as she drew as a senior university teacher. As a result she started wondering what other occupations stood on the same rung of the ladder as the elephant and herself.

In Fig. 2.4 we have set out an earnings 'tree' giving some idea of relative positions. Two points should be noted about this diagram. First, the scale is measured not in pounds sterling but relative to the earnings of the person with the lowest earnings shown — the farm labourer. This presentation avoids the need to update the earnings with every general increase in money wages. Second, the vertical distances are measured on a logarithmic scale, which means that the gap between 1 and 2 is the same as that between 2 and 4, as that between 4 and 8, etc. This compresses the top part of the earnings scale so that we can get the very top earners on to the graph. Even so, we have had to squash most of the population into the bottom quarter of the diagram. The occupations

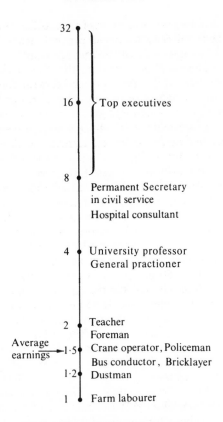

Fig. 2.4 The earnings tree (men only).

shown in Fig. 2.4 are only a selection, but they give some indication of the relativities. The reasons why different people appear where they do are discussed in Chapters 5 and 6.

Wealth

We have seen earlier that the managing directors who appear at the top of the earnings ladder are not at the very top of the income distribution. This position is reserved for those with unearned incomes, that is, incomes from wealth. This source of income is less important than earnings in absolute terms, since the share of property income in total income is only about a quarter or less, but it is highly concentrated and hence may add more to the differences in incomes.

The extent of concentration of wealth in Britain can be determined only within rather broad limits. As is explained in Chapter 7, the statistical sources need to be interpreted carefully. It also depends on what one means by wealth and how it is valued. If one values assets at what they could be sold for, then the official estimates (*Inland Revenue Statistics 1982*, Table 4.8) suggest that at the start of the 1980s the top 1 per cent of adults owned around a quarter of total personal wealth and the top 5 per cent around 45 per cent. These figures may be contrasted with an estimated share of 5 per cent of total income for the top 1 per cent of income units and 16 per cent of the total for the top 5 per cent of income units (based on the data in Table 2.1). The Lorenz curve for wealth appears, at least at the top, to be outside that for incomes. If in the estimates of wealth one includes assets, such as state and occupational pension rights, which have no market value but are worth something to the individual, the share of top wealth-holders is reduced, but the Lorenz curve still lies well outside that for incomes.

As in the case of incomes, the existence of differences in wealth-holding does not necessarily imply the existence of inequality. It has been pointed out that part may be explained by age differences and by people saving for retirement. The person who has paid off his mortgage on a London suburban house would not need a lot in the bank to qualify for a place in the top 5 per cent (although he might well be surprised to learn that!). This does not, however, account for the very rich, and in this context it is important to emphasize that there is an enormous gap between the moderately well off and the very rich. The top people are indeed millionaires, and in some cases many times over. Sir John Ellerman of the shipping family left £36.5 million at his death in 1973. The fortune of the Grosvenor family, headed by the Duke of Westminster, was reputed to be some £300 million in the mid-1970s. These amounts are very hard to put in perspective; one way of looking at it is that £300 million would in 1975 have paid British Rail's wage bill for some four months. How people get to be so rich is a question discussed in Chapter 8.

2.3 Changes over time

A much longer-term view has been taken by Soltow (1968) in a study of the distribution of income before tax in Britain from 1688 to 1962-3. The evidence for the first of these years is based on the estimates prepared by Gregory King at that time, giving the number and average incomes of 26 classes of persons, ranging from temporal lords with £3200 per annum, through gentlemen with £280, to common soldiers with £14 and 'vagrants, beggars, gipsies, thieves and prostitutes' with £2 a year. (The reliability of these estimates is not discussed here!) From this information we can plot a Lorenz curve in the same way as if we had data on incomes by ranges, and this is shown in Fig. 2.5, together with the curves corresponding to the income distributions available for 1801-3, 1867 and 1978/9 (this being the *Blue Book* distribution described in Section 2.1). (For a recent critique of this evidence, see Lindert and Williamson, (1983).)

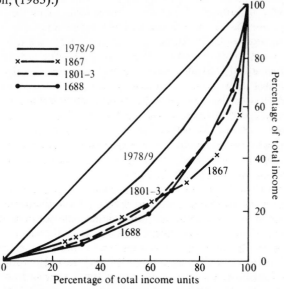

Fig. 2.5 Distribution of income in Britain, 1688–1978/9. The data relate to England and Wales for 1688 and 1801-3, to Great Britain and Ireland for 1867, and to the United Kingdom for 1978/9. (*Source:* Soltow, 1968, p. 20, and data in Table 2.1)

From the evidence set out in Fig. 2.5, Soltow concluded that there was little change in the distribution of income between 1688 and the beginning of the nineteenth century; that the movement between 1801 and 1867 was rather unclear; and that there has been a clear reduction in inequality since 1867. These conclusions can be related to the position of the Lorenz curves. In the case of 1867, the Lorenz curve lies completely outside that for 1978/9, and, as with the diagram for height, IQ and income, we can conclude that the distribution was more dispersed in 1867. Comparing 1801-3 and 1867, however, the Lorenz curves intersect. While the bottom 30 per cent of the population had a larger share of total income in 1867 than at the beginning of the century, the share of the bottom 90 per cent fell, so that the top 10 per cent were better off in 1867.

On balance, there appears from these estimates to have been a long-run trend towards less dispersion of incomes. This decline is attributed by Soltow to the reduced importance of income from land, and he comments that 'the onslaught of the Industrial Revolution, with growth in profits from trade and professional income, could not have introduced an element of greater inequality than that existing with property income' (1968, p. 28). Soltow goes on to suggest that the trend towards less dispersion has accelerated in the twentieth century. This view has been widely expressed. At the beginning of the 1960s, Lord Boyle stated in the House of Commons that 'we have a better and fairer distribution of incomes today than we had ten or eleven years ago'; and a member of the opposition front bench wrote that 'the distribution of personal income has become significantly more equal' (Crosland, 1964, p. 31). On the other hand, the examination by Titmuss of the official statistics on which these conclusions were based led him to conclude that 'there are other forces, deeply rooted in the social structure and fed by many complex institutional factors inherent in large-scale economies, operating in reverse directions' (1962, p. 198). In Chapter 4 we examine what can be said about the trends over time.

Trends in the dispersion of incomes must reflect changes in the distribution of the two main components of income (earnings and income from wealth) or a change in the relative importance of these sources. If we consider first the distribution of earnings, there has undoubtedly been a decline in the position of upper income earners as a group over the past sixty years. The estimates of Routh (1980) show that the average earnings of higher professional workers fell from four times the average for all men in 1913-14 to twice the average in 1978. An extreme example was that of bishops of the Church of England, whose average income did not rise in money terms for over forty years, despite a more than fourfold rise in prices. At the same time, there has been surprisingly little apparent change in the distribution of earnings in recent years. In Table 2.3 we show the results of the *New Earnings Survey* from 1968,

TABLE 2.3
Changes in earnings distribution in Great Britain, 1968-1980

Percentage of median	Gross weekly earnings of full-time male workers (pay not affected by absence)						
	1968	1970	1972	1974	1976	1978	1981
Lowest decile	65.7	65.4	65.5	66.8	67.6	66.8	65.6
Lower quartile	80.0	79.7	79.7	80.7	81.3	80.6	79.8
Upper quartile	126.7	126.7	126.4	124.6	125.6	125.1	129.5
Highest decile	161.4	160.6	160.9	157.0	159.5	157.9	167.7

Sources: Department of Employment, *New Earnings Survey 1970*, p. 21; *New Earnings Survey 1981*, Table 15.

when it started (although it should be noted that the results are not fully comparable as a result of changes in the survey). Despite the fact that the median earnings rose by more than five times, the shape of the distribution appears to have altered relatively little. This does not mean that the earnings in all occupations have increased by the same percentage, but that the gains in one occupation have been offset by the relative losses in another (or by changes in dispersion within occupations) in such a way that the overall shape remains much the same.

The trend in unearned incomes depends on the underlying changes in the concentration of wealth and in the yield on wealth. The evidence about the distribution of wealth shows a clear decline in the share of the top 1 per cent over the past fifty years. This is likely to have led to a reduction in the dispersion of investment income, although it must be borne in mind that much of the increased wealth of the bottom 99 per cent consists of owner-occupied houses, consumer durables and other personal assets, which do not yield an income that appears in the official figures under consideration. The trend in the distribution of wealth raises wider issues. It has been argued that there is a spontaneous process of equalization which may be projected into the future, and the conclusion is drawn that there is no need for government intervention through measures such as a wealth tax. However, before we can project the trends of the past fifty years into the future, we must examine the forces underlying changes in the distribution of wealth. How far is it due to factors such as the use of gifts to spread property, the increased holding of wealth by women, the avoidance of capital taxes, or temporary movements in asset prices? These questions are discussed in Chapters 7 and 8.

Finally, there is the division between earned and unearned incomes, or the distribution by *factor shares*. For a long time it was widely believed that the factor distribution was highly stable in the long run, the most celebrated statement of this view being that of Keynes, that 'the stability of the proportion of the national dividend accruing to labour, irrespective apparently of the level of output as a whole and of the phase of the trade cycle . . . was one of the most surprising, yet best-established, facts in the whole range of economic statistics' (1939, p. 48). This view was based on the estimates by Bowley and Stamp of the share of wages, which showed that it remained essentially constant between 1911 and 1924, despite the disruption of the First World War and the subsequent boom and depression. However, these figures were misleading in that they related only to wage-earners, defined broadly as 'operatives', and excluded salaried workers (clerical, technical, professional, managerial, etc.). If salary earners are included in an estimate of the share of *total pay*, then the stability vanishes: the share, expressed as a percentage of gross national product, has risen substantially over this century. 'Total pay' may not be the ideal definition, since it excludes the earned income component of self-employment income, but even if the whole of income from self-employment is included, there would still have been a sizeable increase in the share.

In broad terms, therefore, it appears that there has been a rise in the share of earned incomes and a fall in the shares of profits and rents. If it is assumed that unearned incomes accrue largely to upper-income groups, then these movements would be consistent with a reduction in overall income dispersion. The relationship between factor shares in total national income and the distribution among persons is, however, less straightforward than this. Profits accrue not only to the wealthy with private means but also to the old age pensioner with a small holding in a unit trust. Rents go not only to property magnates but also to the widow leasing out the shop her husband used to run. In Chapter 9 we examine the link between factors and persons in more detail, as well as describing some of the theories put forward to explain the observed change in factor shares.

2.4 International comparisons and the distribution of world incomes

International comparisons are often used to score debating points, and it is frequently suggested that Britain has a greater or smaller dispersion of incomes than other advanced countries. Such international comparisons are difficult to make with any confidence, however, since, in addition to the deficiencies of each set of national figures, there are enormous problems of comparability.

To underscore this point, we begin with a comparison of two sources for the United Kingdom − the *Blue Book* figures (in this case for 1977/8) and those derived from the *Family Expenditure Survey* (*FES*) for 1977. The two sources are not totally independent, since the *Blue Book* estimates make use of some *FES* findings, but they illustrate the differences that may arise. The *FES* is an annual survey of households, which has certain advantages (for example, it is not related to the administration of the tax system) and certain disadvantages (such as the fact that response is voluntary and typically averages around 70 per cent) compared with the income tax data. It also differs in the definition of the income unit, which is the household, in the definition of income (it includes an imputed rent for owner-occupiers), and in the time period, which is a 'normal' week. For these reasons, we would expect the estimates of the distribution to differ. As may be seen from a comparison of the figures in the upper and lower parts of Table 2.4, the shares of both the top and the bottom 20 per cent are somewhat lower in the *FES*. (If we drew the Lorenz curves, they would intersect.)

TABLE 2.4
Income distribution in eight countries

		Shares in total income before tax (%)				
		Top 20	20–40	40–60	60–80	Bottom 20
Nuclear families						
United Kingdom	1977/8	42.5	24.4	16.4	10.5	6.1
(*Blue Book*)						
United States	1972	48.4	24.5	15.9	8.8	2.4
West Germany	1971	39.4	25.1	19.0	12.9	3.6
Sweden	1970	42.7	24.0	16.9	10.7	5.7
France	1970	44.4	20.8	15.1	11.7	8.0
Republic of Ireland	1974/5	43.5	23.5	16.7	11.5	4.8
Households						
United Kingdom	1977	39.4	24.8	18.3	11.8	5.7
(*FES*)						
United States	1974	46.4	23.7	16.1	10.0	3.8
Australia	1966/7	38.9	23.3	17.9	13.6	6.3
France	1970	47.0	23.0	15.8	9.9	4.3
Japan	1971	46.2	22.8	16.3	10.9	3.8
Republic of Ireland	1973	44.5	23.8	16.6	11.1	4.1

Sources: Stark (1977), Tables 135 and 142; *National Income and Expenditure, 1980*, p. 113, and Royal Commission on the Distribution of Income and Wealth (1977), Table A9.

International comparisons

In Table 2.4 we also show the estimates for eight countries assembled by Stark (1977) for the Royal Commission on the Distribution of Income and Wealth. They are grouped into those based on the nuclear family, or tax unit, in the upper part and those based on the household in the lower part. There are of course other important differences between the estimates, and listing them together in this way does not imply that they are comparable. Moreover, the individual estimates have been the subject of criticism. For instance, the announcement by *Le Monde* that France, on the basis of the figures shown in Table 2.4, had won a gold medal for inequality (it was the time of the Montreal Olympics) led to an official rebuttal (see Bégué, 1976). Finally, the estimates relate to different years and may be influenced by changing macroeconomic conditions or other factors.

Bearing these qualifications in mind, we may consider the position of Britain, compared with the other countries, in terms of the shares of income received by different groups. The most obvious comparison to make is that between Britain and the United States. It might well be expected that the latter country, with its more capitalist *laissez-faire* ethic, less government intervention, and greater regional and ethnic disparities, would have much greater income differences than Britain. From Table 2.4 we can see that, in both cases, the share of the top 20 per cent is indeed larger in the United States and the share of the bottom 20 per cent is smaller. Interestingly, the evidence for the 1970s in Table 2.4 differs from that given earlier by Lydall and Lansing, who concluded that in 1953-4 'pre-tax income per spending unit is, in general, very similarly distributed in the two countries' (1959, p. 66). In Chapter 4 we examine in more detail the factors lying behind the trends over time in the two countries.

Turning to the other countries, the picture is more mixed. The West German figures, for example, suggest that the share of the bottom 20 per cent is lower than in Britain, but so is that of the top 20 per cent. The figures from Sweden are close to those for Britain. Those for Australia suggest that the shares of lower income groups are higher than in Britain. In general, the differences are not sufficiently marked that, taking account of the problems of comparability, we can reach firm conclusions about Britain's relative position.

Comparisons have also been made of the dispersion of *earnings*. The study by Saunders and Marsden, (1979), for example, produced the results shown in Table 2.5 for the hourly earnings of adult male manual workers in industry in 1972 in the EEC. On this basis, Britain, France

TABLE 2.5

Hourly earnings of adult male manual workers in industry in the EEC, 1972

	Ratio of upper quartile to lower quartile
Great Britain	1.50
Belgium	1.30
France	1.42
West Germany	1.26
Italy	1.40
Netherlands	1.26

Source: Saunders and Marsden (1979), Table 2

and Italy appear to exhibit greater dispersion than the other countries (see the original source for an account of the problem of comparability). Reference should also be made to the estimates of the distribution of earnings presented by Lydall (1968), who discusses in detail the differences in definition. His data cover a wider range of countries, including Eastern Europe and a selection of developing countries. The Eastern European countries appeared in the early 1960s to have rather less dispersion of earnings, this being particularly marked in the cases of

Czechoslovakia and Hungary. Finally, in the developing countries earnings differentials appeared to be considerably greater, although given the unreliability of the data it would be very dangerous to draw any definite conclusions about the relationship between the distribution of earnings and the level of development.

The world distribution of income

The reference to developing countries brings us to the last subject of this section: the world distribution of income. There can be little doubt

TABLE 2.6
National average incomes, 1980

	(US dollars)*
Switzerland	16 440
West Germany	13 590
Sweden	13 520
France	11 730
United States	11 360
Saudi Arabia	11 260
Canada	10 130
Japan	9 890
Australia	9 820
Libya	8 640
United Kingdom	7 920
Italy	6 480
Spain	5 400
Israel	4 500
Greece	4 380
Venezuela	3 630
Chile	2 150
Mexico	2 090
Turkey	1 470
Nigeria	1 010
Thailand	670
Egypt	580
Indonesia	430
Sudan	410
Pak.stan	300
China	290
India	240
Burma	170
Ethiopia	140
Bangladesh	130

*The figures relate to gross national product per capita calculated at market prices and converted at an average exchange rate. They are rounded to the nearest $10.

Source: World Bank (1982), Table 1.

that income differences on a world scale are of a quite different order of importance from those within a single country.

If we begin with the differences between countries in terms of average per capita incomes, which we may call the *international* distribution of income, then this is usually represented in terms of per capita incomes expressed in a common currency, here taken as the US dollar, using international exchange rates as a basis for the conversion. Although there are a number of drawbacks to such a measure, and these are discussed further below, it provides a first indication of the distribution between countries. Table 2.6 shows the per capita incomes of selected countries in 1980. It brings out the magnitude of the gap, measured in this way, between Switzerland at the top (we have left out the United Arab Emirates) and the African and Asian countries at the bottom. In 1980 the ratio of per capita income in the United States to that in Bangladesh was nearly 90:1, a difference that is many times larger than that between the earnings of the prime minister and the average worker in Britain.

The second feature illustrated by the table is the continuous gradation in incomes between countries. One tends to think of advanced and developing countries in polar terms, but, even leaving aside the differences between oil exporters and oil importers, no such sharp distinction can be drawn. If the ratio between the United States and Bangladesh is some 90:1, it would also be (in round terms):

Zaire	50:1
China	40:1
Senegal	25:1
Bolivia	20:1
Ivory Coast	10:1
Chile	5:1
Venezuela	3:1

Nor can a straightforward geographical criterion be used to classify developing countries; there is no simply hierarchy (in ascending order) of Africa, Asia, Middle East, Latin America, and southern Europe. Within Africa, per capita income was $120 in Chad, but nearly ten times that amount in Nigeria; within Latin America, it ranged from $270 in Haiti to $3630 in Venezuela. There is clearly a great heterogeneity of income levels, reflecting differences in history and social structure, as well as differences in natural endowments.

The method of comparing living standards in different countries on the basis of per capita incomes, as in Table 2.6, is open to a number of serious objections. Indeed, some people have gone so far as to argue that such international comparisons are meaningless. The first objection is that the quality of the underlying data is too poor to allow any comparison to be made. There can be little doubt that the national accounts estimates are subject to substantial error, particularly in the case of the less developed countries. There may also be considerable inaccuracies in the population figures. Bauer (1971), for example, refers to the official estimate of the population of Nigeria in 1963, which was 56 million, compared with an independent estimate of 37 million. (The reason for the difference may have been that representation in the federal parliament depended on population, so that each region appeared to have 'padded' its population figure.) This is probably an extreme case, and it is important to examine the likely magnitude of the errors and whether they are apt to lead to a systematic bias in the measurement of the gap between rich and poor countries. The second objection is that the limited scope of national income accounts leads to a relative understatement of incomes in less developed countries, particularly through the exclusion of production for own consumption. The main example is the output of subsistence agriculture, which tends to be undervalued in national income statistics; since this sector is more extensive in poor countries, the size of the gap tends to be exaggerated.

The third objection concerns the use of exchange rates to convert all figures to a common standard, and it is widely recognized that exchange rates may be a poor guide to purchasing power. Even if they reflect the relative prices of goods entering foreign trade, they do not adequately represent goods and services that are not exchanged internationally (e.g., haircuts). This is important because there tends to be a systematic relationship between the level of development and the extent to which the exchange rate differs from a rate of conversion reflecting purchasing power. The relative prices of goods not entering international trade tend to be lower in less developed countries, so that a given income will buy relatively more than the exchange rate would suggest. The World Bank (1982, p. 162) made use of the alternative estimates, based on equivalent purchasing power, constructed by Kravis *et al.* (1982). These adjustments raise per capita average incomes relative to the United States by the following factors (only a selection is given):

India	3.22
Thailand	2.61
Kenya	1.95
Mexico	1.70
Spain	1.36
United Kingdom	1.11
Japan	1.10
West Germany	0.88

So the adjusted gap between the United States and India becomes

11 360:(240 × 3.22) = 14.7:1, rather than 47.3:1. Even with this kind of adjustment, the gap between rich and poor countries remains very great. The problem cannot be made to disappear by statistical sleight of hand: 'the main effect of better statistics is not to make us change our views about the extent of poverty in the underdeveloped countries, but rather to make us attach different numbers to the scale of poverty and wealth' (Usher, 1966, p. 40).

So far we have treated each country as a unit, but this masks the inequality *within* countries, which makes a substantial contribution to inequality in the *world distribution* of incomes. This is illustrated in Fig. 2.6, which takes the average per capita incomes in nominal terms in

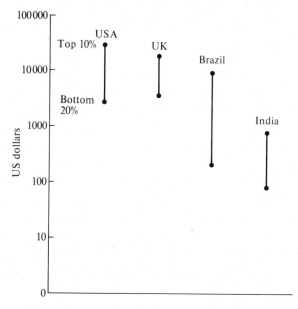

Fig. 2.6 The effect of income differences within countries on world distribution. The income distribution data relate to the 1970s, various years; the level of incomes relates to 1980. (*Source:* World Bank, 1982, Tables 1 and 25)

1980 for four countries, together with data for the distribution of income within those countries. The data show the average position of the top 10 per cent and the bottom 20 per cent. It brings out the overlap between the poor in one country and the rich in another. The bottom 20 per cent in the United States come quite a long way down the income scale: they have an average income considerably less than that of the top 10 per cent in Brazil. The bottom 20 per cent in the United Kingdom have, on average, an income only three and a half times that of the top 10 per cent in India. On the other hand, the gap between the top and the bottom is clearly greater. If we take the top 10 per cent in the United States and the bottom 20 per cent in India, we find the gap widening to a ratio of 360 : 1. (Applying the adjustment factor described in the previous paragraphs reduces the ratio to around 100:1.) This is a sobering thought to bear in mind throughout the book — which concentrates on income differences within advanced countries.

Notes on sources and further reading

The major sources of official evidence on the distribution of income and wealth are the reports of the Royal Commission on the Distribution of Income and Wealth ('The Commission' for short). For ease of reference, a complete list of the Commission's reports is given here. A convenient starting point is provided by the glossy *An A to Z of Income and Wealth*, published by the Commission in 1980, although this brief summary provides neither details nor necessary qualifications. The Commission published five reports on its 'standing reference' to inquire into the distribution of income and wealth:

No.1 *Initial report on the standing reference* (Cmnd 6171, July 1975a)

No.4 *Second report on the standing reference* (Cmnd 6626, October 1976b)

No.5 *Third report on the standing reference* (Cmnd 6999, November 1977)

No.7 *Fourth report on the standing reference* (Cmnd 7595, July 1979a)

No.8 *Fifth report on the standing reference* (Cmnd 7679, October 1979b)

Extracts from reports no.5 and 7 are reprinted in Atkinson (1980b). The Commission published three reports on special references:

No.2 *Income from companies and its distribution* (Cmnd 6172, July 1975b)

No.3 *Higher incomes from employment* (Cmnd 5383, January 1976a)

No.6 *Lower incomes* (Cmnd 7175, May 1978)

In addition, the Commission published eight background papers and four volumes of evidence. The background papers of particular interest here are (with reference to bibliography):

No.2 *Analysis of managerial remuneration in the United Kingdom and overseas* (Hay–MSL, 1976)

No.3 *The effect of certain social and demographic changes on income distribution* (Dinwiddy and Reed, 1977)

No.4 *The distribution of income in eight countries* (Stark, 1977)

No.5 *The causes of poverty* (Layard *et al.*, 1978)

No.6 *Low incomes in Sweden* (Greve, 1978)

No.7 *The distribution of wealth in ten countries* (Harrison, 1979)

No.8 *A six-country comparison of the distribution of industrial earnings in the 1970s* (Saunders and Marsden, 1979)

After the abolition of the Royal Commission in 1979, some of the statistical material was provided in government publications. The *Blue Book* income series has been published in *Economic Trends* and *National Income and Expenditure*; the distribution of wealth statistics have been published in *Inland Revenue Statistics*. The *New Earnings Survey* results appear in annual publications (in several parts) with that title, and a summary is given in the *Employment Gazette*.

Among the books providing a general overview of the distribution of income in Britain are Field (1981), Halsey (1981), Marshall (1980) and the Open University units by Batten *et al.* (1976) and F. Johnson (1975). The long-run trends in the income distribution in Britain are discussed by Soltow (1968), which is reprinted in Atkinson (1980b). *What people earn* is the title of the book of wages and salaries by Cappelli (1981), which contains a lot of information on individual jobs, including the fact that a university teacher receives the same rate per pupil as a free-lance embalmer does per body. Routh (1980) analyses the trend in occupational differentials over this century; Williamson (1980, 1981) examines the longer-term movements; and Phelps Brown and Hopkins (1981) contains a series of essays on earnings back to the thirteenth century. The distribution of wealth in Britain is investigated in Atkinson and Harrison (1978a); the trends over time are the subject of Atkinson and Harrison (1979), which is reprinted in Atkinson (1980b). Wider issues of inequality and deprivation are discussed by Brown and Madge (1982), which contains an extensive bibliography. Inequalities in health and education, not specifically discussed here, are treated by Townsend and Davidson (1982) and Mortimore and Blackstone (1982), respectively.

In this chapter we have made use of the compilations of international data by Stark (1977) and Saunders and Marsden (1979) for the Royal Commission. These studies contain references to the sources of income distribution data for the countries of the European Community, the United States, Australia, Canada, Japan and Sweden. The article by Sawyer (1976) analyses income distribution data for the OECD countries. Estimates for a wider range of countries were given by Paukert (1973), and the World Bank has recently been devoting considerable resources to the collection of income distribution data (an early compilation is that of Jain, 1975).

The comparison of per capita income across countries is discussed by Kravis, Heston and Summers (1978, 1982) and Summers, Kravis and Heston (1980). Earlier treatments include Kuznets (1966), Usher (1966), Beckerman and Bacon (1970), several papers in Ranis (1972), and the Open University unit by Drago (1975). For references to inequality within developing countries, see Chenery *et al.* (1974), Fei, Ranis and Kuo (1979), Fields (1980), Paukert, Skolka and Maton (1981). The world distribution of income, taking account of differences within and between countries, is studied by Berry, Bourguignon and Morrisson (1983), Summers, Kravis and Heston (1981), and Whalley (1979).

The general subject of social measurement and indicators is discussed by Carley (1981). For a critical approach to the use of statistics in the social sciences, see Hindess (1973), Irvine, Miles and Evans (1979), and Radical Statistics Education Group (1982).

3
CONCEPTUAL PROBLEMS

The setting up of reasonably clear, and yet difficult specifications is not merely an exercise in perfectionism. For if these specifications do approximate . . . the real core of our interest when we talk about the shares of economic classes or long-term changes in these shares, then proper disclosure of our meaning and intentions is vitally useful. It forces us to examine and evaluate critically the data that are available; it prevents us jumping to conclusions based on these inadequate data . . . and most important of all, it propels us toward a deliberate construction of testable bridges between the available data and the income structure that is the real focus of our interest.

(Simon Kuznets)

The features of the distribution of income and wealth described in the previous chapter raise a number of questions of a conceptual nature. The aim of this chapter is to clarify these before proceeding to the main part of the analysis. We discussed, for example, the distribution of income among tax units in a particular year, but this left a number of issues unresolved. Is it with income that we should really be concerned? Should we consider the distribution among individuals, families or households? Is it sufficient to look at annual incomes or should we take incomes over the life-cycle?

The conceptual framework set out in this chapter is intended to apply throughout the book, but it is important to remember that the approach adopted may depend on the subject under discussion. When considering the incidence of poverty, we may be more concerned with week-to-week variations in income than if we are trying to form an overall assessment of the distribution of life-chances. More generally, many issues depend on judgements that have to be made by society, and the focus here is on bringing out the implications of different social decisions.

3.1 Access to economic resources and the definition of income

Access to economic resources has several different dimensions and it may be helpful first to distinguish between income, expenditure and wealth. For this purpose, let us consider the hypothetical life history of a single man, Mr A, reserving for later discussion the problems that arise if he marries and has children. In any year he is in receipt of resources from a number of different sources: earnings, investment income from the assets he owns, transfers from the government (student grant when young, pension when old) and capital receipts (legacies and gifts). After allowing for tax, he can dispose of the resources in three ways: he can use them for personal expenditure; he can pass them on to others as a capital transfer; or he can add them to his stock of wealth (saving). In the last case, his investment income in the next year will be correspondingly greater. Schematically, we may set out the process as follows:

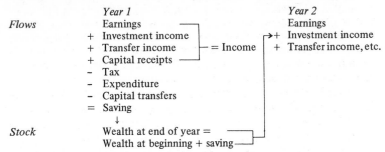

(The definition of income is discussed more fully in the next section.)

From the diagram we can see how annual decisions about flows of resources affect the stock of assets that the person possesses. The stock provides a link in money terms between different periods of his life. (There are obviously other links: for example, his earnings in year 2 may depend on decisions about training in year 1.) The process goes on year after year from his reaching the age of economic independence to the day he dies. At his death, his wealth is by definition zero, since his estate is transferred to his heirs (and the government in estate tax, if he is wealthy). Over his life as a whole, just as he proceeds from dust to dust, so his wealth goes from zero to zero, and all the resources received during his life are disposed of, through either expenditure or capital transfers (including the final transfer at his death).

In assessing the economic position of Mr A in year 1 (we take up later the question of whether it is right to consider his position in a single period), there are, therefore, a number of indicators that we could take:

Income before tax
Income after tax
Expenditure
Wealth

Of these, income, before or after tax, is the most commonly employed, and it is the main aspect considered here. It is important, however, to consider its relationship to the other measures.

The most natural measure may in fact appear to be not income but expenditure, since this represents the purchasable benefits that a person enjoys. To echo the question posed by Hobbes in *The Leviathan*, should we regard a person who 'laboureth much, and sparing the fruits of his labour, consumeth little' as being of higher economic status than a person who 'living idly getteth little, and spendeth all he gets'? Expenditure has, however, been used as a measure of economic status much less frequently than income. The reason for this may lie in the relative availability of evidence, but it also reflects the fact that income represents *potential* spending power. As expressed in the famous definition by Simons (1938), income is the value of rights that a person *might have* exercised in consumption without altering the value of his wealth.

What difference does it make if we take income as a measure of potential spending power, rather than actual expenditure? In any one period of Mr A's life, the difference between his income (after tax) and his expenditure consists of capital transfers and saving. In the latter case, it can be argued that, if he decides to save and thereby postpone consumption, this will be taken into account at a later date, so that over his lifetime as a whole net saving is zero. The difference in this respect is therefore one of timing. The case of capital transfers is rather different, since these would not usually be counted when measuring expenditure, even if we consider the whole lifetime of Mr A. An important difference between the use of income for measurement or expenditure is, therefore, whether or not one considers that the control exercised through gifts or bequests should be taken into account. A miserly millionaire who lived on virtually nothing would from one point of view appear rich, and from the other, poor.

This brings us to the question of control over economic resources, related not to flows but to the stock of wealth that a person owns. The possession of wealth may generate income but is that all wealth means? A person may save 'for the sake of increasing his control *per se* of the economic institutions of a capitalistic society, and for the sake of the various satisfactions . . . which such control brings over and above [that] derived from the expenditure of the income from this capital' (Vickrey, 1947, p. 340).

This is most obvious in the case of owner-controlled firms, such as the Sainsbury food chain, and in trusts and charitable foundations, such as the Rockefeller Foundation. At the same time, the links between personal wealth and control are far from straightforward, and we need also to take account of the other aspects of control, vested in executives, civil servants and politicians. For this reason no systematic treatment of the relationship between resources and control is attempted in this book. Moreover, the links depend crucially on the form in which wealth is held: whether Mr A's wealth is in the bank, in physical assets such as his house and furniture, or in shares in the A Manufacturing Company Ltd. Money invested in a building society does not provide the owner with any control over industry, whereas the same amount invested in shares in a private company may be associated with considerable influence over its activity.

This last point draws attention to the fact that, although we shall be concerned primarily with aggregate variables, there are cases in which certain components may be more significant than others. This may be illustrated by expenditure, where particular items may be regarded as being of special importance. We may be more interested in the equality of access to medical care than of access to theatre tickets. We may want to single out food consumption, because we are concerned with the distribution of nutritional intake in relation to recommended standards. Such 'specific egalitarianism', or the view 'that certain specific scarce commodities should be distributed less unequally than the ability to pay for them' (Tobin, 1970, p. 264), is not examined here, but may be an important explanation as to why governments pursue certain redistributive policies.

Finally, the impact of the tax system on the distribution of resources, while not a primary concern of this book, is of major importance. In the schematic history of Mr A, he was shown as paying tax on his income, but he clearly comes into contact with the fiscal system at many different junctures. He may be taxed, under a value-added or sales tax, on his expenditure, and he may be subsidized. He may pay taxes on his house to local authorities. The capital transfers he makes may render him liable for duty. In the discussion above, attention was focused on the resources available to the individual after tax, and it appears from the point of view of spending power, either actual or potential, and of control over economic decisions, that this is the relevant indicator. Two qualifications should, however, be mentioned. First, income before tax may be more relevant as a measure of status or of social respect. It is gross earnings 'which tell people how they stand compared to others, how they are valued by their employers compared to colleagues and how they are progressing compared to similar reference groups outside work' (Daniel, 1968, p. 236). Second, the benefit side of government activity has to be taken into account, and consumption clearly depends not only on personal expenditure but also on publicly provided goods such as hospitals, parks and schools.

The definition of income

In the schematic representation of a year in the life of Mr A, we defined his income as being equal to the sum of his earnings, investment income, transfers and capital receipts. This definition does, however, raise a number of issues (many of which also apply if we are concerned with expenditure).

At first sight, 'income' may appear to be a straightforward, everyday concept. There have, however, been years of controversy about its correct definition, and there is a wide divergence between income as defined for the purposes of income tax and the definition that would now be accepted by most economists. The latter definition is that described earlier: *income in a given period is the amount a person could have spent while maintaining the value of his wealth intact*. Or, as it was described in the classic treatment by Simons, 'Personal income may be defined as the sum of (1) the market value of rights exercised in consumption and (2) the change in the value of the store of property rights between the beginning and end of the period' (1938, p. 50).

The first significant feature of this definition is that it is comprehensive. As was pointed out by the Minority Report of the Royal Commission on the Taxation of Profits and Income, in a much quoted passage, 'No concept of income can be really equitable that stops short of the comprehensive definition which embraces all receipts which increase an individual's command over the use of society's scarce resources – in other words, his "net accretion of economic power between two points in time"' (1955, p. 355).

It is in its comprehensive nature that the definition departs from the practice of the tax authorities, and hence from much of the statistical data on the distribution of income, and this will prove of great importance when we examine the evidence about incomes in the next chapter. For the present, attention is drawn to the kind of items that would be included under the comprehensive definition but are often excluded from the statistics on income distribution (the list is far from exhaustive).

Capital gains According to the Simons definition, capital gains and losses clearly form part of income. As is noted by the Minority Report, income 'includes the whole of the change in the value of a man's store of property rights . . . irrespective of whether the change has been brought about by the current addition of property [or] by accretions to the value of property' (p. 356). If Mr A had invested £500 in shares that increased in value over the year by £50, he could have spent £50 more without reducing the value of his wealth, leaving one one side for the moment the effects of inflation. This capital gain, even if not realized by the sale of the shares, should be regarded as part of his income in just the same way as if he received £50 in dividends. Conversely, if his shares had fallen in value, the capital loss should be deducted from his income.

Fringe benefits In many jobs there is payment not only in cash but also in kind in the form of fringe benefits, ranging from free canteen meals and concessionary coal at the bottom end of the income scale to the company car and penthouse for the top executive. Moreover, the use of the term 'fringe' may give the misleading impression that they are of subsidiary importance. At the same time, there are serious problems of valuation. The benefits may not be marketable, in which case the value to the individual is hard to assess. One example is foreign travel by a businessman: 'is he giving himself a holiday under the bogus guise of a commercial purpose, or is he spending all day and half the night trying to sell a product in which he has no interest to people he dislikes in a place from which he is longing to get away?' (Runciman, 1974, p. 94): Yet it would clearly be wrong to assume that no fringe benefits provide any addition to economic resources, and an attempt should be made to include estimates of the amount involved.

Production for home consumption Although the Simons definition refers to 'market value', this does not mean that the consumption must arise through a market transaction. The consumption of home-produced output, for example by farmers, clearly represents the exercise of command over resources and should be taken into account. That is likely to be important when making comparisons between countries, particularly those at very different stages of development.

Imputed rent Another example of income in kind that does not arise through a market transaction is the rent that should be imputed to physical capital that is owned by persons and yields them services. The most important instance is the benefit received by home-owners. Owning a house does not provide a cash income, but it has much the same effect, in that it saves the owner from paying rent. If Mr A lived in his own house, we should therefore want to add to his income an amount equal to the market rent he could have obtained (similarly an addition would be made to his expenditure). The same consideration applies to other assets, such as cars, pictures, yachts, clothes, and consumer durables, but their quantitative significance is likely to be considerably less.

A second feature of the ideal definition is that it is concerned with *real* income, or its purchasing power, and that allowance should be made as far as possible for differing price levels. This is relevant, for example, where prices vary within a country, so that a given money income represents different spending power for people living in different places. In the United States, an index of the comparative cost of living in autumn 1974 (US urban average = 100) ranged from 88 in Austin, Texas, through 96 in St Louis and 104 in Chicago, to 108 in Boston and

San Francisco and 149 in Anchorage, Alaska (US Department of Health, Education and Welfare, 1976, Table 12). The most obvious source of such variation is housing costs, and when we come to consider poverty we shall see that the criterion employed in Britain takes into account differences in rents. The variation in prices is not only geographical. It has been argued in the United States that in certain cities the rents paid by blacks are higher than those paid by whites for comparable housing (Kain and Quigley, 1972). Similarly, the poor may pay less than the rich for the same goods because they have more time to shop around, or they may pay more because they cannot purchase in bulk.

The definition of income in terms of purchasing power means that in any comparison of distributions at different dates the changes in the relative prices of goods must be taken into account. If all prices have risen by 15 per cent, then all money incomes have been reduced by the same amount, and relative purchasing power is unaffected. However, if prices have risen more for the goods that are bought by low-income households than for those bought by the rich, then the movement in money incomes overstates any trend towards reduced concentration, and vice versa. In the next chapter, we examine how far this has been the case in the recent inflationary years.

The interpretation in real terms applies not just to the flow of income but also to the value of wealth: it means that the value of wealth has to be maintained in terms of purchasing power. As a result, allowance has to be made for inflation when calculating the return to wealth-holding. Earlier we referred to Mr A's making a capital gain of £50 on his share-holding of £500, but part or all of this gain may simply reflect a general rise in prices. If prices had increased generally by 8 per cent over this period, then £40 of his capital gain is simply keeping up with inflation. The real gain is only £10. However, it is not simply those who hold shares who are affected. Anyone holding assets is subject to a capital loss on account of inflation. A person with money in the bank is equally suffering a real capital loss of 8 per cent, and this should be deducted from the interest received to give the *real* return. The adoption of a definition based on real income implies, therefore, that an allowance should be made in the case of all assets for the effect of inflation.

3.2 Definition of the time period

Earlier we referred to the income of Mr A accruing over a year. In this section, we consider whether the period of assessment should be a week, a year, a decade or a whole lifetime.

The shortest period of measurement that could realistically be taken is the week, but for many people weekly income is subject to considerable variation: in any particular week a person may have worked a short shift or received a special bonus. The weekly income may vary with the weather, as for a window-cleaner, or with the season, as for a shopkeeper. Income may be received monthly or annually (in the case of investment income). As a result of these short-run fluctuations, the distribution of weekly income appears more unequal than when income is measured over a longer period such as a year. This is illustrated by the numerical example in Table 3.1, where Mr A is joined by Messrs B–J. The first two columns show their earnings in two pay-weeks, where in each case the distribution of weekly earnings is the same. In each week, there is a uniform frequency (of two men) at each of the earning levels. The third

TABLE 3.1

Hypothetical example of earnings distribution and averaging over time

Mr	Earnings week 1	Earnings week 2	Average for two weeks
A	32	32	32
B	32	36	34
C	34	38	36
D	34	38	36
E	36	32	34
F	36	40	38
G	38	34	36
H	38	34	36
I	40	36	38
J	40	40	40

column shows the total earnings averaged over the two weeks and the distribution is clearly less dispersed. There is only one person whose average earnings for the two weeks are at the lowest value of 32 a week, and four people now have earnings equal to the average (36). The example is obviously based on rather large changes in earnings from week to week, but it illustrates the basic effect of averaging income over a longer period.

From this analysis it appears that taking a longer period of assessment tends to reduce the observed degree of dispersion. How far we want to proceed in this direction is likely to depend on the extent to which short-term fluctuations in income have an important effect on the individual, i.e., how far he can even out such fluctuations by spreading his income over good and bad periods. This in turn is influenced by the terms on which he can lend and borrow, or the effectiveness of the capital market. It may well be that there is considerable scope for averaging incomes over time at the upper end of the scale, but not at the lower end. The millionaire whose shares have fallen in value may not be too worried if he feels confident that they will rise again later, but the manual worker whose plant is put on short-time may be quite unable to borrow in anticipation of better times ahead. The family whose social security payment is delayed in the post may have no reserves on which they can draw: the only way in which they can borrow to finance living expenses may be by not paying the rent or the electricity bill. The important factor is clearly possession of assets that can be used to meet any temporary drop in income, or the ability to borrow on the capital market, and in both cases the low-income groups are likely to fare least well. Moreover, on the lending side, they typically obtain a lower rate of interest on short-term savings, and in times of inflation the value of such savings is more likely to be eroded than for wealthier people holding real assets (such as houses).

The varying scope for averaging incomes over time means that we may want to apply different periods of assessment for different income groups, but this would be very difficult to put into effect. We can, however, use different periods for different purposes. If we are measuring the number of people in poverty, and if it is correct to assume that averaging is difficult for low-income groups, then we may be concerned with weekly income. We would want to know how many people have incomes in a particular week that are below the prescribed minimum, independently of the fact that in two months' time they may be much better off. On the other hand, if we are concerned with the distribution of income among the population as a whole, we may feel that income averaged over a year is more appropriate. Such a judgement would be based on a view that for the majority of the population some averaging of income was possible, and that at the upper end of the scale it would be quite misleading to take any shorter period.

So far we have been concerned with measuring income in a *current* period, but we should consider the arguments for moving to a concept of *lifetime* income. This would clearly give quite different results. At any moment there are people who currently have low incomes, but will have higher incomes later (e.g., students or apprentices), or have had higher incomes in the past (e.g., pensioners). Lifetime incomes will, by the same argument as that used earlier, in generally be less unequally distributed than current incomes.

The significance of this factor may be brought out by a very simple example of a society in which everyone has the same lifetime income, in that a person's income at forty is the same as that of everyone else of the same age and as that of his father when he was forty. This would be regarded as a completely egalitarian society from the standpoint of lifetime income, but there could still be considerable dispersion in the distribution of current incomes. Again, let us suppose that all those at work receive the same wage, but that pensioners receive only one-third of the wage. There are the same number of people (1 million) in each age group, and people work from twenty-five to sixty and are retired from sixty-one to when they die at the age of seventy-five. The retired population therefore number 15 million and constitute 30 per cent of the population, ignoring those below the age of twenty-five. The pensioners' share of total income may be calculated to be:

$$\frac{15 \text{ million} \times \frac{1}{3} \times \text{wage}}{35 \text{ million} \times \text{wage} + 15 \text{ million} \times \frac{1}{3} \times \text{wage}} = \frac{5}{40} \text{ or } 12\frac{1}{2} \text{ per cent}$$

In this society we should find therefore that the bottom 30 per cent received decidedly less than 30 per cent of total income. This serves to demonstrate that life-cycle differences can lead to a marked divergence between the distributions of lifetime and current income. (It should be emphasized that this does not imply that the actual distribution can be explained in this way.)

Whether we should adopt a lifetime assessment period depends again on the question being asked. If our concern is with measuring poverty, then the lifetime approach may not be regarded as very relevant; the fact that an old person had a high income thirty years ago does not make up for his having a pension that is below his needs today. On the other hand, we may be concerned with the distribution of life-chances, as represented by a person's work career, by the capital he inherits, by his investment opportunities, by his pension and other access to state benefits. In that case, it can certainly be argued that these are better measured by his lifetime income than by his income in any single period. The use of lifetime income takes account of factors such as investment in education (human capital): the earnings forgone while training are offset by higher earnings later in life. It deals with the fact that 'the short working life of a baseball player means that the annual income during his active years must be much higher than in alternative pursuits open to him to make it equally attractive financially (Friedman, 1962, p. 170). The lifetime approach allows for people with differing preferences about consumption at different ages.

Lifetime income is defined here to mean the total value of all receipts in the form of wages, capital transfers and state benefits, discounted to a common date. (We take the *discounted* value rather than a simple sum in order to allow for the fact that income accruing later is worth less to a person than if he received it today, since he loses the interest.) In other words, for Mr A, who had a bequest in the second period of his life, his lifetime income discounted to the beginning would be of the form:

$$\text{Earnings in period 1} + \frac{\text{Earnings in period 2} + \text{bequest}}{(1 + \text{rate of interest})} + \ldots$$

(Here only the first two elements in the sum are shown. The value of £1 received in the second period is given by $1/(1+r)$ where r is the rate of interest; the value of £1 received in the ith period is similarly $1/(1+r)^{i-1}$.) The difficulties in applying this definition arise from the choice of the rate of interest and of the base date to which the value is discounted (here, period 1). The problems with the rate of interest have been brought out by our discussion of imperfections in the capital market. The rich may be able to lend or borrow on much better terms than the poor. Moreover, any one person may face different rates for borrowing and lending, paying rates of 20 per cent and higher on instalment credit but only being able to obtain 4 per cent from the savings bank. (An example of the high interest rates at which people effectively borrow is embodied in the rates for car licences in Britain: a person choosing to license his car for six monthly periods rather than a year at a time is in effect borrowing at a rate of some 40 per cent per annum.)

A more immediate problem with the lifetime approach is that of obtaining the required data. If we were to start collecting information now about individual cohorts, we should not have any complete cohorts for fifty years or more. Obtaining figures retrospectively involves serious problems. Information supplied from memory would be unreliable, and piecing together figures from tax returns on a national scale would be an immense undertaking even if access were granted to them. There have, however, been some interesting steps in this direction. For example, Bourguignon and Morrisson (1982) have assembled data for a particular group of workers from the records of French pension schemes covering some thirty years of earnings; they have found that inequality of lifetime total (discounted) earnings is some 80–90 per cent of the average annual figures. Similarly, Schmähl (1982) has collected lifetime earnings data from the West German social security records, for workers born in the early part of the century and retiring in the first half of the 1970s.

If this kind of information is not available we may be able to make some deductions about the lifetime distribution from the degree of dispersion within age groups. In the simple example given earlier, of a society where incomes were the same for everyone in an age group but varied with age, the distribution over all age groups showed inequality; however, the absence of lifetime inequality would have been revealed by looking at individual age groups. This is not fully adequate, since the life-cycle pattern of incomes differs between social groups, the earnings of manual workers reaching a peak earlier than for professional workers. None the less, an examination of the extent to which inequality is attributable to differences between age groups allows us to eliminate those life-cycle differences that are common to all individuals.

Up to this point we have concentrated on income, but it could be argued that in the case of expenditure the divergence between current and lifetime measures would be less, since current expenditure is determined more by lifetime income than by current income. Explanations of consumption such as the permanent income hypothesis advanced by Friedman (1957) suggest that individuals implicitly make calculations of the kind described above and that these are reflected in consumption decisions. There may therefore be an argument for using consumption as an indicator of lifetime income, although consumption would in this case have to be defined to include capital transfers.

Finally, we should consider the relationship between lifetime income and the concept of inter-generational mobility. Suppose that Mr A has a higher lifetime income than his school friend Mr B. If there is no inter-generational mobility, the children of Mr A will similarly be better off than the children of Mr B; on the other hand, if there is significant inter-generational mobility, the positions may be reversed in the next generation. Just looking at the lifetime distribution for one generation will not reveal the extent of mobility, and for this reason we may want to take a *dynastic* view, taking the incomes of different generations of the same family together. In our follow-up of the families interviewed by Seebohm Rowntree in 1950, Atkinson, Maynard and Trinder (1983) collected information on the incomes of fathers and sons. In the case of earnings, the evidence suggests that − for this rather special group of people − there is a significant correlation across generations, not far short of that observed for heights.

3.3 Families, households and differing needs

We have so far discussed the case of a single individual, but Mr A is likely to marry and have children, and we need to consider the treatment of the family or household. The *Blue Book* income data presented in Chapter 2 were effectively based on the nuclear family (man, wife, and dependent children), but this is not the only possible unit for analysis. We could use a household unit, which would include other non-dependents who lived with the nuclear family, such as a grandmother or a grown-up son, as was the case with the *Family Expenditure Survey* data discussed in Section 2.5. (The definition of a household used in the *FES* is 'a group of people living together at the same address with common housekeeping'.) Alternatively, we could use the smallest possible unit, which is the individual. Income distributions are not typically presented in this form, and where they are the share of the bottom income group is typically very small; for example, in Sweden in 1966 the share in total gross income of the bottom 20 per cent of individuals was 0.0 per cent (Stark, 1977, Table 101).

The implications of these different units of analysis can be seen in terms of the degree to which a group of people share their resources. Suppose that we take the individual as the basic unit of analysis. We would then find, as in the Swedish case, a substantial number of individuals with virtually no recorded income, notably children and wives who do not go out to work. These people may well, however, be enjoying a high standard of living as a result of sharing the income of their parents or their husbands. In our society most married women do share their husbands' income (perhaps not equally), and most children are supported by their parents, so that there is a very important degree of income-sharing. If the extent of these intra-family transfers was known with reasonable accuracy, it would be possible to add them to the income of the wife and children, and we could then retain the individual unit.

Such calculations of intra-family transfers are not likely to be possible, and we may therefore decide to take a wider unit of analysis than the single individual. A natural candidate, in view of the extent of income-sharing, is the nuclear family. Adopting this unit would be equivalent to assuming that all income received by members of the family is shared, and for any given distribution of individual incomes the amalgamation into family incomes tends to reduce the overall degree of dispersion. It means in effect replacing the individual incomes of husband and wife by the average of their incomes, and unless all marriages are between people with the same income, the relative differences in income decrease. If we were to go beyond the nuclear family, and take the household as the basic unit, then the degree of dispersion would be still further reduced. We would be assuming in effect that not only the family but also other household members pooled their incomes equally.

The choice between the different units depends in part on the empirical question of how far in practice incomes are shared, and on this there is very little evidence. Earlier it was suggested that within the nuclear family there is an important degree of income-sharing, but we know little about just how *equally* income is divided among different members. As is noted by Pahl, 'the control and allocation of financial resources within the family has not so far received very much attention, even though a taken-for-granted cornerstone of family social policy has been the idea that the money that goes into a household will be pooled' (1980, p. 315). The same applies when we consider people who are not members of the nuclear family but who live in the same household. It seems likely in practice that income is shared to a considerable extent, but it may still be true that working teenage children enjoy a higher, and grandparents a lower, standard of living than the basic family unit.

From the above discussion it appears that the choice of the unit of analysis lies between the family and the household. Both of these involve units which vary in size; for example, in the United Kingdom *Family Expenditure Survey* for 1979 there is the following range of households (from Department of Employment, 1980, Table 1):

	Percentage of total
	%
Single person	22
Married couples with no children	28
Couples and 1, 2 or 3 children	30
Other	20
	100

These households clearly have differing needs, which arise simply from their differences in size. These in turn raise two important questions. First, how should we adjust measured income to obtain a comparable, or 'equivalent', indicator of welfare? Second, how should we weight income units of different sizes when making judgements about overall dispersion?

Equivalent scales and equivalent incomes

Allowance for household or family composition can be made in a number of different ways. The simplest is to treat all members as having the same needs and to calculate the income per head. This does not however recognize the variation of need with age, and the possible economies of scale (the 'two can live as cheaply as one' hypothesis). In order to allow for these factors, attempts have been made to construct *adult equivalent scales* to allow comparison between different types of unit.

The first main approach used to construct equivalence scales is based on *a priori* consideration of the needs of children and adults, and effectively consists of listing what are considered the minimum requirements. The equivalence scales derived in this way are clearly subjective, being based in large part on the judgement of the investigator. An early example is the study by Rowntree of poverty in York in 1899, for which he obtained an equivalence scale based on dietary needs plus estimated 'minimum necessary expenditure' on rent, clothing and household sundries. The relativities are shown in column 1 of Table 3.2., and it can be seen that the amount allowed for children is between a third and a half of that for a single adult. For comparison, we show the scale implicit in the current supplementary benefits programme in Britain. The main difference is in the provision for children. In Table 3.2, it has been assumed that the children are all under 11; if, for example, the four-child family included two teenagers, the ratio would rise to 205.

TABLE 3.2
Equivalence scales for different households (married couple = 100)

	(1) Rowntree (UK)	(2) Supplementary benefits* (UK)	(3) US poverty scale	(4) McClements (UK)	(5) Lazear and Michael
Single person	60	62	80	61	94
Couple	100	100	100	100	100
and 1 child	124	121	119	121	122
and 2 children	161	142	152	142	139
and 4 children	222	184	201	184	–

Sources: col. (1), Rowntree (1901), p. 143; col. (2), Department of Health and Social Security, *Social Security Statistics 1981*, Table 34.01. The scales relate to November 1981, and exclude housing costs; col. (3), Plotnick and Skidmore (1975), Table 2.1. The scales relate to non-farm families with a male head under 65 years; col. (4), Van Slooten and Coverdale (1977), Table 3.1. The scales include housing costs and assume children aged 5–7; col. (5), Lazear and Michael (1980), Table 4.

The approach adopted in the United States in deriving the official poverty standard, shown in column (3) of Table 3.2, is similar in that it makes use of calculated 'requirements' but differs in employing information only on food. The origin of the US poverty threshold is described by Plotnick and Skidmore:

it first estimated the annual food costs for families of varying size and composition, assuming they ate the 'economy' diet developed by the Department of Agriculture. A nonfarm family of three or more was judged to be 'poor' if its purchase of the 'economy' food budget would absorb more than 33 percent of its cash income, a figure suggested as reasonable by studies of household budgets. (1975, p. 32)

In its use of actual budget information, the US poverty line is intermediate between the first approach to equivalent scales, based on subjective judgement, and the second approach, which relies solely on observed differences in consumption patterns for households of different sizes. This technique has been the subject of considerable recent research, but has a long history, dating back more than a century to the work of Ernst Engel. Deaton and Muellbauer describe how

it goes back to Engel's famous observation that, for poorer households, a higher share of total expenditure goes on food than is the case for richer households. He also observed that the same was true for large households at the same level of total expenditure. This suggested to him that the share of food could be used as an indirect indication of welfare. . . . two households with the same food share must have the same level of real income, irrespective of differences in size. Hence, comparison of their *money* incomes at the same foodshare will yield an index of the cost of maintaining the larger relative to the smaller family and this is the equivalence scale. (1980, p. 193)

The Engel approach is illustrated in the upper part of Fig. 3.1. This shows the (hypothetical) budget shares for households without children and households with children. If we start with an income Y for those without children, then the foodshare is W per cent, and the 'equivalent'

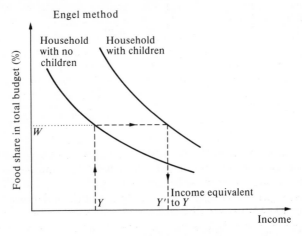

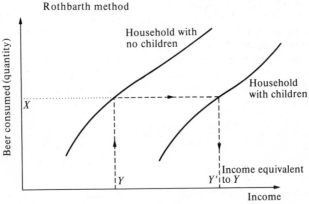

Fig. 3.1 Derivation of equivalent incomes.

income for households with children is Y', at which the budget share is also W per cent.

An alternative approach is that proposed by Rothbarth (1943) and developed by Nicholson (1949). This supposes that we can find a commodity, such as beer or adult clothing, which is consumed only by adults and can be taken as an index of the adult standard of living. If we then compare households with and without children, we shall expect that at any given income level, the consumption will be higher for the household with no children, since the adult standard of living is higher. This is illustrated in the lower part of Fig. 3.1, where we take beer for the purposes of illustration and it is assumed that beer is not an inferior good (i.e., that adults do not switch to whisky as their standard of living rises). Again we can locate the equivalent income Y' corresponding to Y by following the arrows. There is of course no reason to expect the two methods to yield similar answers. Indeed, Deaton (1981), in his application to data for Sri Lanka, finds large differences in the scale for children.

The Engel method and the Rothbarth method both depend on strong assumptions. The former assumes that the share of the budget spent on food can be treated as an indicator of welfare, and it is not clear that this is plausible. The Rothbarth method rests on the identification of an 'adult' good, or class of goods, and is open to the objection that parenthood may be accompanied by a change in tastes. Parents may consume the same amount of beer not because they have the same standard of living, but because the children drive them to it!

The techniques can be elaborated — see Deaton and Muellbauer (1980, Ch. 8). In columns (4) and (5) of Table 3.2, we show the results of two studies, one from the UK and one from the United States. (In the latter case, the authors note the big difference from the US poverty scale for single-person households.) But even these do not avoid the need for strong assumptions or the use of additional information, such as nutritional scales (Muellbauer, 1979).

In this brief review of a highly technical subject, it has not been possible to deal with all the issues that arise. But it should be clear that the different methods are all subject to reservations. Moreover, it should be stressed that the existence of differences in standards of living between families of different sizes does not mean that allowance *should* be made for differing composition. This is a matter for social judgement. Indeed, it might be argued that the benefits of having children are such that in a country where birth control is widespread no allowance should be made for the cost of children.

Finally, we should note that children are not the only group for whom special adjustments might be made. It could be, for example, that the needs of the retired are less than those of the working population. The fact that the food requirements of old people are usually estimated to be less may, however, be offset by greater needs for fuel, lighting, and domestic help. A wide range of other needs may also be taken into account: for example, those of the blind and the disabled.

Weighting different income units

In discussions of family size, it is typically the calculation of equivalent income that has received most attention; however, the second question raised earlier — the weighting of different income units — is also of considerable importance. There are, in fact, several possible procedures. Suppose that the income of a family (or household) is Y and that the family has n members. Then we could treat the family as 1 unit with income Y, as in the statistics quoted in Chapter 2, or as 1 unit with income (Y/n), or with income (Y/n^*), where n^* is the 'equivalent' number of adults. On the other hand, we could treat the family as n units, each with income Y, or each with income (Y/n), or each with income (Y/n^*). Finally, we could treat the family as n^* units, with again three possible measures of income.

One will find in the literature a variety of different approaches, and, indeed, in some cases the different concepts appear to be confused. Discussing the distribution of wealth, Polanyi and Wood (1974) argue first that 'married women should be excluded from the total of "potential" owners' (p. 35), but subsequently suggest that 'if every person included in the top 10 per cent had only one recorded dependant, the formula would be reduced to 20 per cent (rather than 10 per cent) of the people owning 40 per cent of the wealth' (p. 40). The first of these statements adopts the definition with a family as 1 unit; the second treats the family as having n units, with an income of (Y/n) each.

The choice of weights may make a significant difference. Some of the effects may be seen from the simple example of a hypothetical, male-dominated, society where there are 20 men each with wealth of £20 000, 80 men with £7500, and 100 women with no wealth. All the 20 rich men are married, as are 40 of the 80 men with £7500, leaving 40 single men and 40 single women. On an individual basis (commonly employed in wealth statistics, since they are often based on records of estates at death), the top 10 per cent (20 out of 200) own 40 per cent of the wealth (£400 000 out of £1 million). Suppose now that we consider the total wealth of the family (Y), and first treat all families, or single individuals, as one unit, as in the first of the Polanyi–Wood definitions. There are 140 such families, so that 40 per cent of wealth is owned by 14.3 per cent (20 out of 140) of families. On the other hand, suppose that we treat a married couple as two units, each with the benefit of Y wealth. This means, of course, that the total 'equivalent' wealth is now greater than £1 million (it rises in fact to £1.7 million), which may upset the accountants but is logically quite correct. The 20 rich couples account for 20 per cent of the effective population, and benefit from 47.1 per cent (£800 000 out of £1.7 million) of the total equivalent wealth. However, if we treat a couple as two units, but only allocate each a benefit of $Y/2$, as in the second of the Polanyi-Wood definitions, then the top 20 per cent has 40 per cent of total wealth (which in this case remains at £1 million). The reader should consider other possible variations, including the cases where some of the wealthy are not married and where women possess wealth.

3.4 The measurement of inequality

In discussions of the distribution of income and wealth, reference is frequently made to summary measures of concentration. These summary statistics, which include the Gini coefficient, the variance, the variance of logarithms, and the relative mean deviation, are widely used for two purposes:

(i) to compare distributions: e.g., the distribution in 1950 and that in 1980, or that in Britain and that in the United States;
(ii) to attach some absolute measure to the degree of inequality, or to give some idea whether the inequality is 'large' or 'small'.

The most popular of these summary measures is the Gini coefficient, named after the Italian statistician. This coefficient may be interpreted in two ways. First, it may be seen geometrically in terms of the Lorenz curve defined in Chapter 2 (see Fig. 2.2):

$$\text{Gini coefficient} = \frac{\text{Area between Lorenz curve and diagonal}}{\text{Total area under diagonal}}$$

The coefficient may be seen to range from 0 when incomes are equal (the Lorenz curve follows the diagonal) to 1 at the other extreme (the Lorenz curve has an ⌐ shape). For those who do not like geometry, its meaning may be presented in another way. Suppose we choose two people at random from the income distribution, and express the difference between their incomes as a proportion of the average income, then this difference turns out to be on average twice the Gini coefficient: a coefficient of 0.4 means that the expected difference between two people chosen at random is 80 per cent of the average income. Other measures that are commonly used include the coefficient of variation, which is the standard deviation divided by the mean, and the variance of the *logarithm* of income. These measures, like the Gini coefficient, are not affected if all incomes are multiplied by the same number, so that it does not, for example, matter if we measure incomes in pounds sterling or pence.

The Gini coefficient is used in official publications in Britain to summarize the distribution of income and wealth. The government statistics show, for example, that the Gini value for the distribution of marketable wealth has fallen from 0.81 in 1966 to 0.74 in 1980 (*Inland Revenue Statistics 1982*, Table 4.8). The likely effect of a value-added tax on the distribution of income was summarized in terms of increasing the Gini coefficient by 0.002 (National Economic Development Office, 1969, Ch. 5). It is far from clear, however, what these statements mean. Is there any reason to doubt that the direction of movement is in fact as shown? Would all summary measures give the same answer? Does the use of such an apparently neutral statistic conceal judgements about the desirability of different forms of redistribution?

Summary measures of inequality

To show how questions such as these may be answered, let us take for purposes of illustration the data for three different countries referred to in Chapter 2: the United Kingdom, West Germany, and the United States. From the information given about the distribution among families in the upper part of Table 2.4, we can construct the Lorenz curves. If we consider first the United Kingdom and the United States, the Lorenz curves have the form shown in Fig. 3.2(a), and in particular we can see that the curve for the United Kingdom lies everywhere inside that for the United States. (In terms of Table 2.4 this is equivalent to the share of the bottom x per cent being larger in each case for the United Kingdom.)

Now, *if the Lorenz curves for two distributions do not intersect, then we can say unambiguously that, for a wide class of inequality measures, the distribution closer to the diagonal is less unequal than the other*, subject to the condition that we are ranking the distribution independently of the average levels of income. (In making this statement, it is assumed that people are otherwise identical.) The class of inequality measures for which this is true is described in Atkinson (1970) and includes most of those commonly employed. Any of these summary statistics would indicate a higher degree of income inequality in the United States.

On the other hand, if the Lorenz curves intersect, it is quite possible to reach different conclusions using different summary measures. This is shown by the comparison of the United Kingdom and West Germany. The Lorenz curves intersect (see Fig. 3.2(b)): the share of the bottom 20 per cent is lower in West Germany, but above that point the distribution becomes more unequal in the United Kingdom. We can see by

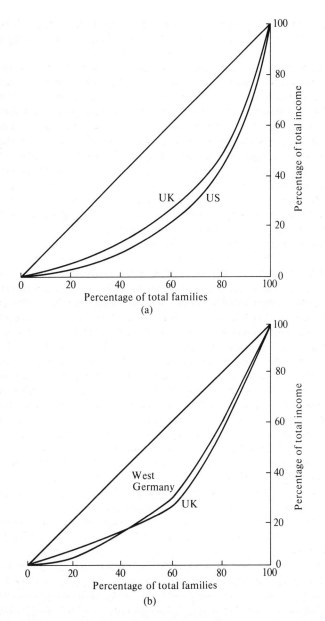

Fig. 3.2 Comparison of Lorenz curves: (a) UK and USA: curves do not intersect; (b) UK and Germany: curves intersect. (*Source:* Table 2.4)

eye from Fig. 3.2 that the Gini coefficient, which ranks according to the area between the Lorenz curve and the diagonal, will give a higher value for the United Kingdom (it is in fact 0.372 as opposed to 0.357 for West Germany). However, a measure that attaches greater weight to the bottom income groups may indicate greater dispersion in West Germany; for example, in the extreme case we might be concerned only with the share of the bottom 20 per cent, and this group fares worse in West Germany. The possibility of different rankings is illustrated by the league table drawn up for OECD countries by Sawyer, where in terms of the distribution of post-tax income, Sweden comes 'top' according to the Gini coefficient but Japan comes top according to the variance of logarithms (Sawyer, 1976, Table 6).

This analysis is not intended to yield firm conclusions about the distribution of income in the three countries. (Indeed, the earlier data for the 1960s, used in the first edition of this book, showed an almost complete reversal of the position of the Lorenz curves for the United Kingdom and West Germany.) Rather, the aim is to bring out a number of important points about the use of summary measures. First, *the degree of inequality cannot, in general, be measured without introducing social judgements*. Measures such as the Gini coefficient are not purely 'statistical' and they embody implicit judgements about the weight to be attached to the inequality at different points on the income scale. The fact that the Gini coefficient shows a decrease does not necessarily mean that everyone would agree that there has been a decline in inequality. Second, the Lorenz curves play a key role in determining in which cases summary measures will agree and in which cases there is likely to be ambiguity. If we are concerned solely with comparing two distributions of income and wealth (and the ranking is being made independently of the average levels), then the first step should be to draw the Lorenz curves.

An alternative approach

Given that the conventional summary measures inevitably introduce distributional values, it may well be preferable to consider such values explicitly. Only then can it be clear just what distributional objectives are being incorporated as a result of adopting a certain measure. One method by which this can be achieved has been suggested in Atkinson (1970). The measure proposed there introduces distributional objectives through an explicit parameter ϵ. This parameter represents the weight attached by society to inequality in the distribution. It ranges from zero, which means that society is indifferent about the distribution, to infinity, which means that society is concerned only with the position of the lowest income group. This latter position may be seen as corresponding to that developed by Rawls (1972) in his contractual theory of justice, where inequality is assessed in terms of the position of the least advantaged members of society. Where ϵ lies between these extremes depends on the importance attached to redistribution towards the bottom.

The precise formula for this alternative measure is given in the notes to Table 3.3. It may look intimidating, but the measure has a very natural interpretation as the proportion of the present total income that would be required to achieve the same level of social welfare as at present if incomes were equally distributed: a value of 0.12 means that we could reach the same level of social welfare with only $(1.00 - 0.12) = 88$ per cent of the present total income. Alternatively, the gain from redistribution to bring about equality would be equivalent to raising total

TABLE 3.3
An alternative measure of inequality

| Value of ϵ | Values of index (I) | |
	United Kingdom	West Germany
0.1	0.021	0.020
0.5	0.100	0.107
1.0	0.194	0.229
2.0	0.350	0.472

Note: the formula for the index I (where $\epsilon \neq 1$) is:

$$I = 1 - \left[\sum_{i=1}^{n} (Y_i/\bar{Y})^{1-\epsilon} f_i \right]^{1/(1-\epsilon)}$$

where Y_i denotes the income of those in the ith income range (n ranges altogether); f_i denotes the proportion of the population with incomes in the ith range; and $\bar{Y}$ denotes the mean income.
In the case above where $\epsilon = 1$,

$$I = 1 - \exp\left[\sum_{i=1}^{n} f_i \log_e (Y_i/\bar{Y}) \right]$$

Source: calculated from the data in Table 2.4.

income by 12 per cent. In this way the measure is an index of the potential gains from redistribution, and provides a tool that can be used for the second of the two purposes outlined at the beginning of this section.

A key role is played in this alternative approach by the distributional parameter ϵ. How can people make up their minds about what value it should take (between zero and infinity)? One way of interpreting ϵ may be seen from the following 'mental experiment'.

Suppose that there are two people, one with twice the income of the other (they are otherwise identical), and that we are considering taking 1 unit of income from the richer man and giving a proportion x to the poorer (the remainder being lost in the process, for example in administering the transfer). At what level of x do we cease to regard the redistribution as desirable? If the person is at all concerned about inequality, then $x = 1$ is considered desirable. What is crucial is how far he is prepared to let x fall below 1 before calling for a stop. The answer determines the implied value of ϵ from the formula $1/x = 2\epsilon$. For example, if the person stops at $x = \frac{1}{2}$, this corresponds to $\epsilon = 1$, but if he is willing to go on until only a quarter is transferred, then the implied ϵ equals 2.

This calculation is similar to the 'leaky bucket' experiment of Okun (1975). He considers a transfer of $4000 per head from the top 5 per cent, giving, in principle $1000 to each of the bottom 20 per cent. However, some leaks from the bucket on the way, and Okun asks how much leakage people would be willing to accept if necessary to make the transfer. He himself would accept up to a 60 per cent leakage. What value of ϵ is implied? (The average income of the top 5 per cent is nine times the average for the bottom 20 per cent.)

Returning to the comparison of the United Kingdom and West Germany, we can calculate the value of the alternative measure (I) for different values of ϵ (see Table 3.3), where a higher value denotes a greater degree of inequality. The value of the index is higher in the United Kingdom for $\epsilon = 0.1$, but for $\epsilon = 0.5$ and above the index is higher in West Germany. This reflects the fact that, as ϵ rises, more weight is attached to the lower-income deciles, which have a smaller share in West Germany.

Finally, it should be emphasized that the alternative approach described above is concerned with the implications for social welfare – it goes beyond the description of differences. Sen has found it 'worrying' (1978, p. 84) that a person with the view that $\epsilon = 0$ would be indifferent between the two-person distribution in which A gets £10 000 and B nothing and that in which both get £5000. But this is the difference between description and social judgements referred to in Chapter 1. What the person is saying is that the income dispersion has no welfare cost. At the same time, the alternative approach is only one of a number possible. We may, for instance, want to allow for social judgements being concerned with notions of 'distance'. Plato recommended that the ratio of the top income to the bottom should not exceed 4:1 (quoted by Cowell, 1977, p. 26). Such concern could lead to the use of other indices of inequality. Wiles (1974, p. x) has suggested taking 'the *average* of the top centile (which gives explicit weight to millionaires) – the *average* of the bottom decile (which includes all the old, unemployed and sick we need to worry about)'.

Notes on sources and further reading

The general issues covered in this chapter are discussed by Beach, Card and Flatters (1981), Dinwiddy (1980), Fiegehen, Lansley and Smith (1977), Health and Welfare Canada (1977), and Taussig (1976).

The *definition of income* is treated in the classic references on taxation: Simons (1938), Kaldor (1955a), Vickrey (1947), and the Royal Commission on the Taxation of Profits and Income (1955). Extracts from this literature are conveniently reprinted in Houghton (1970). More recent references are Kay and King (1980, p. 6) and Pechman (1977). The definition of income in the context of national accounts is considered in Beckerman (1980), Kendrick (1979), and Usher (1980), among others. The development of broader measures of economic welfare is illustrated by Morgan and Smith (1969), Taussig (1973), and the work of the Institute of Research on Poverty (see Moon and Smolensky, 1977).

The effect of income variability and the choice of *different assessment periods* was brought out in Friedman's celebrated study of the consumption function (1957). The application to income distribution data, and the relationship to the individual life-cycle, have been discussed by Lydall (1955) and Morgan (1962, 1965), Creedy (1975), and Paglin (1975) – but see comments on this article, including Danziger, Haveman and Smolensky, 1977). The use of panel income data with different assessment periods is examined by, among others, Benus and Morgan (1975), Kohen, Parnes and Shea (1975), and Shorrocks (1981). The concept of lifetime income or earnings is discussed by Creedy (1977), Layard (1977), Lillard (1977a, b), von Weizsäcker (1978), Cowell (1979), Irvine (1980), and Jorgenson and Pachon (1980).

The choice of *unit* for analysis is treated by Morgan *et al.* (1962, Ch. 20), and by Morgan (1965). See also Atkinson (1974). The distribution of income within the family is discussed by Land (1977) and Pahl (1980), who give further references.

There is a large literature on *equivalence scales*. For reviews of this subject, see Brown and Deaton (1972), Nicholson (1976), McClements (1978), Pollak and Wales (1979), and Deaton and Muellbauer (1980). A recent discussion of the 'needs' of children is Piachaud (1981). Recent studies of equivalence scales using household budgets include McClements (1977 – see comment by Muellbauer, 1979) and Muellbauer (1977a, 1980) in the UK and Lazear and Michael (1980) in the United States.

The *weighting of units* of different sizes is discussed by Atkinson and Harrison (1978a, pp. 244-6), Danziger and Taussig (1979), and Cowell (1980).

The classic article on the *measurement of inequality* is that by Dalton (1920b). A bibliography of the recent extensive literature following Kolm (1969) and Atkinson (1970) is given at the end of Chapter 1 of Atkinson (1983). The subject is well covered in Sen (1973), Cowell (1977), and Nygård and Sandström (1981). The 'leaky bucket' experiment is described by Okun (1975) and Blinder (1982).

4

INCOME DISTRIBUTION: EVIDENCE

Greeting!
We have deemed it expedient that a Commission should issue to inquire
into, and report on, such matters concerning the distribution of personal
incomes, both earned and unearned, and wealth, as may be referred to
it by the Government.

Royal Warrant establishing the Royal Commission on the Distribution
of Income and Wealth.

This chapter examines the evidence about the distribution of incomes,
before and after tax, in Britain and the United States, paying particular
attention to the changes that have taken place since the end of the Second
World War. It draws heavily on the framework described in the previous
chapter, and tries to show how the concepts developed there may be
applied to actual income distribution data.

4.1 Popular beliefs and official statistics

The extent of inequality in the distribution of income, and how it is
changing over time, is a subject about which people hold very definite
views. In Britain, it was widely believed in the 1950s and 1960s that the
distribution of income had been moving in the direction of equality:

Much has been written in recent years about the strongly egalitarian
effects of the social and economic policies pursued by British Governments since the end of the Second World War . . . Full employment . . .
was leading to a steady reduction in wage and salary differentials . . .
Above all, it was considered that the wealthy were a disappearing class
in Britain. (Titmuss, 1962, p. 15)

This led Titmuss to write *Income distribution and social change* (1962),
an influential critique of the official evidence.

More recently, the official position has become more cautious. The
Royal Commission on the Distribution of Income and Wealth, referred
to below as the Royal Commission, concluded in 1979 that:

The overall impression from the figures is of a reduction in inequality
but, if the decline in the share of the top 1 per cent is ignored, the shape
of the distribution is not greatly different in 1976–77 from what it was
in 1949 . . . The income distribution shows a remarkable stability from
year to year. (Royal Commission, 1979a, p. 17)

On the other hand, there are still those who believe that:

Since the war, income differences before tax have diminished and in-income differences after tax have diminished very sharply.

and

When more is known about the economic history of our own decade [the 1970s], it is likely that the gradual equalisation of Britain will be shown to have accelerated sharply. (Joseph and Sumption, 1979, p. 118.)

In the United States, Miller (1966) referred to the view 'shared by influential writers and editors' that incomes are becoming more evenly distributed, and quoted the announcement by *Fortune* in 1953 that 'though not a head has been raised aloft on a pikestaff, nor a railway station seized, the US has been for some time now in revolution.' The same magazine returned to the subject twenty years later and concluded that 'we seem to be making progress towards greater equality'. The views of academic observers have been more diverse, as is illustrated by the following quotations collected by Taussig (1976):

there has also been a marked trend towards equality over the 20-year [1952–72] period. This is particularly apparent for the lowest quintile (Browning, 1976, p. 93)

Whereas Budd argues:

from the immediate postwar years to the 1960s the evidence points to a gain by the middle and upper part of the distribution, relative to the lower groups and the upper tail (Budd, 1970, p. 260)

and according to Schultz:

income inequality . . . has apparently increased substantially among both men and women since World War II [1947–70]. (Schultz, 1975, p. 155)

Official estimates

In assessing the validity of these different views, our starting point is the official evidence on the distribution of income. In Britain, the main source covering the postwar period is the *Blue Book* series described in Chapter 2. In Table 4.1 we show the percentage share of total income received by different groups over the period 1949–1978/9. If we consider first the share of the top 10 per cent, we find an apparent move towards less dispersion, this top group having suffered a fall of some 7 percentage points in terms of before-tax income and a similarly marked reduction in the case of income after tax. This loss by the top group has not, however, been reflected in a corresponding gain by those at the bottom: the share of the bottom 60 per cent rose by only 1.8 percentage

TABLE 4.1

*Blue Book estimates of the distribution of income before and after tax,
United Kingdom 1949–1978/9*

	Before tax*				After tax*			
	Top 10%	Next 30%	Middle 30%	Bottom 30%	Top 10%	Next 30%	Middle 30%	Bottom 30%
1949	33.2	34.9	21.6	{31.9}	27.1	36.9	{36.0}	
1954	30.1	38.0	21.6	10.3	25.3	39.3	23.8	11.6
1959	29.4	38.4	22.5	9.7	25.2	39.8	23.7	11.2
1964	29.1	39.0	22.4	9.5	25.9	40.1	22.4	11.6
1967	28.0	38.9	22.8	10.4	24.3	39.2	24.5	12.0
1970/1	27.5	40.0	22.3	10.2	23.9	40.4	23.8	11.8
1973/4	26.8	39.7	22.6	10.9	23.6	39.9	23.7	12.8
1976/7	25.8	40.5	22.7	11.0	22.4	40.6	24.1	12.9
1976/7**	26.2	40.6	22.4	10.8	23.2	40.6	23.6	12.6
1977/8**	26.2	40.7	22.3	10.7	23.3	40.9	23.3	12.6
1978/9**	26.1	41.2	22.3	10.4	23.4	41.1	23.4	12.1

Percentage shares of total income

* The shares may not add up to 100 per cent because of rounding.
** These estimates differ from those given above in that they are before the deduction of mortgage interest.

Sources: Royal Commission (1979a), Table 2.3 and *National Income and Expenditure* (1980), p. 113; (1981), p. 116.

points in before-tax terms, and 1 percentage point in after-tax terms, between 1949 and 1976/7. As Nicholson (1967), and earlier Paish (1957), pointed out, the redistribution has been from the extreme ends to the middle ranges, a feature brought out clearly by the middle column ('next 30 per cent'). Finally, attention should be drawn to the break in the series in 1976/7, when the definition of income was changed; in the estimates above the line in Table 4.1 mortgage interest and certain other items have been deducted from gross income.

The official source most commonly employed in the United States is the annual *Current Population Survey* carried out by the Bureau of the Census. The resulting estimates for 1947-77 are summarized in Table 4.2. The share of the top 20 per cent appears to have first fallen, as in

TABLE 4.2
Estimates of distribution of income before tax
United States 1947-1977

Year	Top 20%	Next 20%	Middle 20%	Fourth 20%	Bottom 20%
			Percentage share of total income*		
1947	45.5	23.6	16.8	10.6	3.5
1952	44.3	24.1	17.3	10.9	3.5
1957	42.9	24.7	18.0	10.9	3.4
1962	43.9	24.8	17.5	10.4	3.4
1967	43.4	24.8	17.5	10.6	3.6
1972	44.8	24.7	16.9	10.0	3.7
1977	45.2	24.9	16.5	9.7	3.8

*Income distribution data for the United States are commonly presented in separate tables for families and unrelated individuals. These are combined in the estimates given above.

Source: Blinder (1980), Table 6.9.

Britain, and then risen, so that it was virtually the same in 1977 as it was thirty years earlier. From this table, Blinder concludes that 'the central stylized fact about income inequality has been its *constancy*' (1980, p. 433; his italics).

The fact that the figures shown in Tables 4.1 and 4.2 are based on official estimates does not imply that they are adequate to measure changes in the income distribution, as indeed the government statisticians would be the first to admit. There are many obvious deficiencies. The estimates make no allowance for the needs of families of different sizes. The concept of income falls a long way short of the theoretical definition described in the preceding chapter. No account is taken of inflation. Annual incomes may bear no relation to lifetime incomes. The only taxes considered are those on income, and other aspects of government activity may have a significant effect on the distribution.

These deficiencies have led many people to reject the official statistics and any conclusions based on them. Titmuss's case against the popular belief in declining inequality was based on a lengthy catalogue of the shortcomings of the Inland Revenue statistics. In many cases these criticisms were, and remain, valid, but he did not go on to try and correct them or to assess their quantitative importance. He did not demonstrate that the observed trend in Britain over the 1950s would be reversed in more accurate statistics. Similarly, Johnson (1973) refers to the extremely naïve statistics used to validate the demonstration of inequality, but does not give any indication of the likely quantitative importance of the objections he raises; nor does he attempt to produce any alternative.

There are in fact two choices open. One can either point to the deficiencies and conclude that nothing can be said, or one can try to allow for them, possibly making use of alternative sources, and see what (qualified) statements can be made. The first of these choices is very tempting, particularly when one considers in greater detail the difficulties that arise. Such a nihilistic position is, however, extremely limiting. There is no presumption that the distribution is equal unless proved otherwise; we can say literally nothing, either about the current state of the distribution or about proposals for change. In this chapter we take the second route, examining how far the deficiencies of the official statistics can be overcome and the likely effect of correcting for their shortcomings.

It may be helpful to distinguish several different types of criticism:

— that, given the basic data on incomes, the method of analysis is inappropriate;
— that conclusions about inequality cannot be drawn by simply considering the distribution of income at a particular date;
— that the data do not provide an adequate measure of income;
— that we need to allow for the impact of the government budget;
— that the evidence needs to be interpreted in the light of changing economic and social circumstances.

In other words, a person who felt that the figures in Tables 4.1 and 4.2 exaggerated the dispersion of incomes might argue under the first heading that the distribution should be computed on a per capita basis rather than per income unit (and that units with higher incomes were simply larger) or, under the second, that *lifetime* income should be considered. Under the third heading, it could be suggested that substantial amounts of income had been left out of account. The fourth criticism would lead him to point to the redistributive effect of taxes and government spending, not fully taken into account in Tables 4.1 and 4.2. Finally, he might argue, for example, that the more rapid inflation of the 1970s must be considered with interpreting the evidence for that period and the changes over time.

In what follows, we present examples of all five types of criticism, although space does not permit an exhaustive treatment.

4.2 Methods of analysis

In this section we consider two objections to methods commonly employed in presenting official statistics: the fact that summary measures of inequality may conceal divergent movements in the distribution, and the neglect of differences in needs associated with family size.

Measurement of inequality

The evidence shown in Tables 4.1 and 4.2 was presented in terms of the shares of different groups in total income, but this information is often summarized by a measure such as the Gini coefficient. Such a procedure is, however, potentially misleading. In cases where there have been divergent movements at different points on the income scale (i.e., where the Lorenz curves intersect), then, as shown in the previous chapter, different summary measures may give different answers.

The dangers are well illustrated by comparison of the *Blue Book* figures for before tax income in the United Kingdom for 1954 and 1964. According to the Gini coefficient, there has been a (slight) reduction in inequality: the coefficient fell from 0.403 in 1954 to 0.399 in 1964. We have seen, however, that there has been, according to the estimates in Table 4.1, redistribution away from the extremes towards the middle ranges. The share of the top 10 per cent fell from 30.1 to 29.1 per cent, but the share of the bottom 30 per cent fell also (from 10.3 to 9.5 per cent). Given that is what happened, any judgement about inequality must depend on the weight attached to gains and losses by different groups. A person who attached more weight to the fall in the share of the bottom 30 per cent than to the redistribution away from the top 10 per cent might well conclude that inequality had increased rather than decreased as indicated by the Gini coefficient. Certainly, a person concerned with 'distance' as measured by the ratio of average incomes in the top 10 per cent and in the bottom 30 per cent would regard inequality as higher in 1964 (ratio 9.2) than in 1954 (ratio 8.8).

One of the advantages of the alternative approach suggested at the end of the last chapter is that it allows a range of different social judgements to be embodied as the parameter ϵ varies between zero and infinity. Its use may be illustrated with the data given in Table 4.1 for before-tax incomes in 1954 and 1964, when we know that the possibility of ambiguity arises. If we consider the range $0 < \epsilon < 1$, then the inequality index can be calculated from the formula:

$$(1 - I)^{1-\epsilon} = \sum_i f_i (Y_i/\overline{Y})^{1-\epsilon}$$

where the income relative to the mean, $Y_i/\overline{Y}$, is obtained by dividing the share of the total income by the share of total population (i.e., 9.5/30.0 for the bottom 30 per cent in 1964). So that, where $\epsilon = \frac{1}{2}$, we have:

1954 $\sqrt{(1-I)} = 0.1 \times \sqrt{3.01} + 0.3 \sqrt{1.267} + 0.3 \sqrt{0.720} + 0.3 \sqrt{0.343}$

1964 $\sqrt{(1-I)} = 0.1 \times \sqrt{2.910} + 0.3 \sqrt{1.300} + 0.3 \sqrt{0.747} + 0.3 \sqrt{0.317}.$

From this we conclude that $I = 11.35$ in 1954 and 11.5 in 1964, so that a person regarding this value of ϵ as appropriate would feel that inequality had increased. On the other hand, if we were to take $\epsilon = 0.1$, then the ranking would be reversed. Such a value of ϵ corresponds to a much reduced willingness to make transfers: in terms of the leaky bucket experiment, the person would call a halt if the leak exceeded 7p in the pound.

As we have seen in Chapter 3, the difficulties arise where the Lorenz curves cross; and in the analysis of the income data an important step is the construction of the Lorenz curves. In Fig. 4.1 we show the pair-wise comparisons for the years 1954-76/7 in the UK (all those years for which the data are complete and directly comparable). In 16 of the 21 possible comparisons the Lorenz curves do not intersect, and the ranking

	1959	1964	1967	1970/1	1973/4	1976/7
1954	×	×	○	×	○	○
1959		×	○	○	○	○
1964			○	○	○	○
1967				×	○	○
1970/1					○	○
1973/4						○

× Lorenz curves intersect

○ Lorenz curves do not intersect

Fig. 4.1 Intersections of Lorenz curves, United Kingdom, 1954–1976/7 (income before tax). (*Source:* data in Table 4.1)

is the same for all values of ϵ. But for 5 of the 21 cases the Lorenz curves intersect and we have to be on our guard in using any summary statistic.

(In using the data for four broad groups shown in Table 4.1, we are effectively *interpolating* over a wide range, using the assumption that incomes are equal within the group. The Lorenz curves are in effect being approximated by straight lines. In any actual application, we should make use of the individual income data, or − if the individual data are not available − of more sophisticated techniques of interpolation.)

Needs and family size

The estimates in Tables 4.1 and 4.2 make no allowance for differences in needs. A person living alone is treated the same as a family of six. Allowing for differences in needs may affect our assessment of both the level of dispersion at a point in time and the trends over time. If young people have tended to leave home sooner, and old people to continue living on their own longer, as they undoubtedly have, there are likely to be more small-sized income units than in the past.

As shown in Chapter 3, we need both to adjust the measure of income and to consider the weighting of units of different size. The possible quantitative significance of these factors is illustrated by the study of Danziger and Taussig (1979) using data for the United States similar to those shown in Table 4.2. From the Bureau of the Census data, it is clear that the size of units tends to vary across the income ranges. In 1976 the mean size of all income units in the United States, including both families and unrelated individuals, was 2.73 persons. When ranked by the total income of the unit, as in Table 4.2, the mean size of the top 10 per cent was 3.71, whereas that for the bottom 10 per cent was only 1.54. So that the top tenth of *units* included more than twice the number of persons as the bottom tenth.

The consequences of adjusting the measure of income, while still treating each unit as having a weight of one, are indicated in the upper part of Table 4.3. Danziger and Taussig use the Gini coefficient, although they recognize the limitations of this measure (noting that some of the Lorenz curves intersect). Two types of adjustment are shown. The first uses a simple per capita correction; the second uses the equivalence scale implicit in the official poverty line (similar to that shown in column (3) of Table 3.2). As the authors observe, there is no consistent pattern to the results. The move to a per capita basis raises the Gini coefficient in 1967 but reduces it in 1976. Possibly the major conclusion is that the differences appear relatively small, certainly less than might have been expected in the light of the substantial differences in the mean size of units. The largest absolute difference is 0.0275, or some 7 per cent of the Gini value. But such a difference may be larger when viewed

TABLE 4.3

Alternative adjustments to income and weighting of income units, United States, 1967 and 1976

	Gini coefficient	
	1967	1976
Weight = 1 per unit		
Total income	0.3992	0.4061
Per capita income	0.4122	0.4027
Equivalent income*	0.3850	0.3786
Weight = number of persons		
Total income	0.3536	0.3658
Per capita income	0.3963	0.3906
Equivalent income†	0.3623	0.3592

* As in official estimates.
† Using US poverty line.

Source: Danziger and Taussig (1979), Table 2

in relation to the changes observed over time; and different conclusions would indeed have been drawn about the direction of the trend over the period. Using total income of the unit, the Gini coefficient appears to have increased between 1967 and 1976, whereas using the per capita or equivalent income measures, the Gini coefficient appears to have declined.

The weighting of income units by the number of members, introduced in the lower part of Table 4.3, seems to have a more marked impact on the estimates. With the total income measure, the Gini coefficient is reduced by some 4 percentage points. However, the effect is less when combined with the adjustment to the income measure. Suppose that we weight by the number of persons, and take per capita income, as in the fifth line of Table 4.3. (This means that total income is unchanged, which will keep the accountants happy.) Then the fall in the Gini coefficient in 1976 is only from 40.61 to 39.06 per cent. But even this is enough to reverse the apparent direction of change over time: the fifth line shows a fall in inequality, compared with the rise indicated by the first line.

The findings of Danziger and Taussig, like those of other studies (see notes at the end of the chapter), show how the conclusions drawn may depend on the methods of analysis adopted. In particular, they underline the need to be cautious in attaching significance to small changes in the distribution over time.

4.3 Income, the life-cycle, and demographic factors

The use of annual incomes in the official estimates of the distribution is unlikely to be supplanted in the near future by the use of *lifetime* incomes, since the limited data available for the latter typically cover only sub-groups of the population and relate only to earnings. We need nevertheless to consider (a) how far the effect of the life-cycle can be separated by using information for age groups, and (b) to what extent the observed changes over time are the result of changing demographic composition.

Age and income distribution

As noted in Chapter 3, we may be able to make some deductions about the distribution of lifetime incomes by considering the dispersion within age groups. If life-cycle factors are significant, we may find less dispersion among people in the same age range. In the UK, the *Blue Book* data cannot be classified by age, but Mookherjee and Shorrocks (1982) have used the *Family Expenditure Survey* information for this purpose. (The main features of the survey were described in Chapter 2.)

In Table 4.4, we show the results of Mookherjee and Shorrocks for the distribution by age groups in the UK for years spanning the period 1965–80. The concept of income is total household income, not adjusted for family size. The age is that of the head of the household. The first point to be seen is that there is a very definite hump-shape. The average income increases up to the age range 40–49 and then declines, falling below the overall average for those aged 60 or more. Over the period, there appears to have been a substantial increase in the relative income of the age groups 30–39 and 40–49. This may have come about, for example, because of more married women going out to work. There has been a decline in the relative position of households headed by someone aged 65 or over. Taken together, these mean that the hump-shape has become more accentuated. The data for the United States assembled by Blinder (1980) show a similar pattern, both with regard to the hump and with regard to the changes over time – see Fig. 4.2. on page 76.

Two measures of dispersion are used in Table 4.4. The first is the alternative measure described in Chapter 3, with $\epsilon = 1$; the second is the coefficient of variation. Both suggest that there is rather less dispersion within age groups up to the age of 60, but that above this age incomes are, if anything, more dispersed than in the population as a whole. Standardizing for age reduces the spread of incomes where the household head is of working age, but it still remains quite substantial. The evidence of Taussig for the United States shows a similar pattern. The Gini coefficients, for incomes in 1967, are around 0.27–0.33 for age groups up

TABLE 4.4
Income by age groups, United Kingdom

	Age group (age of household head)						Whole population
	0–29	30–39	40–49	50–59	60–64	65–	
Relative mean incomes							
1965	0.95	1.03	1.27	1.22	0.89	0.60	1.00
1970	0.96	1.10	1.32	1.22	0.90	0.55	1.00
1975	1.01	1.17	1.36	1.23	0.90	0.51	1.00
1980	0.97	1.17	1.42	1.25	0.87	0.50	1.00
Inequality measure $\epsilon = 1$*							
1965	0.084	0.080	0.105	0.150	0.182	0.238	0.178
1970	0.104	0.084	0.118	0.162	0.219	0.235	0.194
1975	0.110	0.100	0.114	0.162	0.202	0.205	0.201
1980	0.132	0.115	0.123	0.164	0.201	0.192	0.211
Coefficient of variation†							
1965	0.454	0.447	0.531	0.621	0.688	0.907	0.656
1970	0.500	0.463	0.546	0.632	0.767	0.908	0.677
1975	0.496	0.486	0.506	0.597	0.691	0.859	0.665
1980	0.512	0.522	0.531	0.618	0.704	0.801	0.693
Population share (%)							
1965	10.5	16.6	20.0	20.9	9.2	22.8	100.0
1970	14.0	17.3	19.0	17.6	9.8	22.4	100.0
1975	14.7	18.0	16.3	16.9	9.4	24.6	100.0
1980	13.4	20.4	16.0	16.8	7.5	25.9	100.0

* Calculated from I_0 in the original source.
† Calculated from I_2 in the original source.
Source: Mookerjee and Shorrocks (1982), Tables 1 and 3.

to the age of 54, compared with 0.38 for all families; above the age of 55 the coefficients are higher. The limited impact of the age standardization is brought out by the fact that, if we were to take two people at random from the age group 25–34, the average difference in their incomes would be $4300, compared with $5950 for any two persons drawn from the population as a whole.

Age is one variable that can be used to indicate the stage of the life-cycle; an alternative is household composition. The position of a single man aged 30 may be different from that of a four-person family headed by a man of that age, and different again from one headed by a woman of 30. In Table 4.5 we show the findings of Danziger and Plotnick in the United States using a classification that takes account of both age and certain aspects of household composition. Once more they use the Gini coefficient. For pre-transfer income, the overall value in 1974 was 47.7 per cent. Exactly half of the groups shown had values above this. These were the families headed by a person over 65 or a woman with a family. For post-transfer income, the number above the overall population figure is reduced to 3 out of 12, but the Gini coefficient is above 36 per cent for all except families headed by a man aged under 65. Once more, therefore, we find that consideration of relatively homogeneous groups, with respect to the life-cycle, leaves a substantial element of dispersion. It cannot all be explained away by age or family type.

Demographic trends

Demographic changes over the postwar period have been quite substantial. In Table 4.4 we show the variation between 1965 and 1978 in the UK age composition (measured by the age of the household head). The proportion of young households (under the age of 40) has increased, from 27.1 per cent in 1965 to 32.9 per cent in 1978, as has the proportion aged 65 and over. There has therefore been a shift towards the groups that on average have lower incomes – those on either side of the peak.

In the United States the demographic changes have been even more pronounced. The proportion of income units consisting only of single individuals has risen from 17.9 per cent in 1947 to 28.8 per cent in 1977 (Blinder, 1980, Table 6.12). Table 4.5 shows the position in more detail for the shorter period 1965–74. (Although it should be noted that the data are drawn from different sources and may not therefore be fully comparable.) Kuznets (1974) has drawn attention to the shift away from the 'standard' family headed by a prime-age (25–64) man. This is demonstrated by the fall from 57.8 per cent in 1965 to 51.0 per cent in 1974. The move has been towards people living on their own (+ 5.3 percentage points) and towards families headed by a woman (+ 1.5 percentage

TABLE 4.5

Income by age and household type, United States

	Population share (%)		Gini coefficient*			
			Pre-transfer income		Post-transfer income	
	1965	1974	1965	1974	1965	1974
	%	%	%	%	%	%
Single individuals						
Young men (less than 25)	0.7	2.2	45.7	41.7	44.5	40.3
Prime-age men (25–64)	4.9	6.4	43.8	45.4	40.3	40.7
Men aged 65–	2.0	2.0	71.1	75.6	37.8	44.2
Young women (less than 25)	1.4	1.8	52.0	45.1	51.8	42.8
Prime-age women (25–64)	5.4	6.2	47.4	47.2	42.3	40.1
Women aged 65–	5.7	6.8	74.3	76.2	41.6	37.2
Families headed by:						
Young men (less than 25)	4.4	4.7	28.5	28.8	27.9	26.6
Prime-age men (25–64)	57.8	51.0	31.0	32.5	30.0	30.4
Men aged 65–	9.6	9.3	64.8	64.2	43.7	39.6
Young women (less than 25)	0.5	1.0	58.6	64.5	43.8	42.6
Prime-age women (25–64)	6.0	7.2	48.3	53.6	37.5	40.6
Women aged 65–	1.7	1.5	53.6	56.7	40.5	36.2
Whole population	100.0	100.0	44.1	47.7	39.2	40.8

*The 1965 data are derived from the *Survey of Economic Opportunity* and the 1974 data from the *Current Population Survey*.

Source: Danziger and Plotnick (1977), Tables 1–3

points). These are again groups that tend to have below-average incomes. For example, the average post-transfer income of families headed by a woman aged 25–64 was 48 per cent of that for families headed by a man of the same age (Danziger and Plotnick, 1977, Table 1).

These demographic shifts could well have affected the overall distribution of income. Trends in the age composition may lead to a change in the annual distribution even when there has been no change in individual life histories of income. This aspect has been stressed by a number of writers, including Paglin, who claims that 'The widely accepted estimates of current inequality, and of historical changes in Gini ratios, . . . have misrepresented an important characteristic of the US economy' (1975, p. 598).

There are a number of methods that can be employed to assess the quantitative impact of demographic shifts. Paglin suggests adjusting the observed overall inequality measure (in his case the Gini coefficient) by subtracting the contribution due to differences in average incomes by age. However, subsequent comments (see notes on sources) have shown that such an adjustment is difficult to interpret, especially in the case of the Gini coefficient. Moreover, it is useful to consider how the effect is built up from the different factors at work (and their interaction): the demographic shifts, the change in the average income profile, and changes in within-group dispersion.

The first of these may be illustrated for the United States by the data in Table 4.5 (although we must bear in mind that the data are drawn from different sources). In the case of pre-transfer incomes, the overall Gini coefficient rose by 3.6 percentage points. If the results are standardized by weighting the 1974 income units to give the same demographic composition as in 1965, then the calculated hypothetical increase is 1.7 percentage points (Danziger and Plotnick, 1977, Table 4). The increase is halved by the standardization; and for post-transfer income, the standardization accounts for almost all the observed increase. These findings may appear to conflict with the conclusion of Blinder that 'the effect of the shifting age distribution on quintile shares, while disequalising, was very modest' (1980, p. 451). But it must be remembered that, certainly in the case of post-transfer incomes, one is talking about relatively small changes in the overall distribution. The age effect may be small in absolute terms but large in relation to the trends.

In the UK, the impact of changing household composition is illustrated by the study of Semple (1975), using *Family Expenditure Survey* data for thirteen household groups. Standardization on the 1961 household composition yields the results shown in Table 4.6 for the Gini coefficient. Once again, the standardization makes quite a difference to the conclusions drawn about the trends over time.

TABLE 4.6
Gini coefficient: standardization on the 1961 Family Expenditure Survey household composition

	Original income (before taxes and benefits)		Final income (after taxes and benefits)	
	Actual	Standardized	Actual	Standardized
1961	38.4	38.4	33.5	33.5
1973	42.2	39.7	32.8	31.7

Source: Semple (1975), Table 2

The *Family Expenditure Survey* data have been used by Mookherjee and Shorrocks in a more extensive exercise, which considers in addition the changing age profile and within-group dispersion. As shown in Table 4.4, the overall distribution showed a moderate rise in the dispersion of income. (The concept used here differs from 'original' income in that transfers are included.) The authors concluded that the within-group changes in dispersion (in five out of six cases in the same direction as the overall change) did not contribute much to the overall effect, the main factor being the age effect, which included both the age structure and the age profile.

The decomposition of the trend in this way is helpful not only in understanding the sources of dispersion, but also in assessing the implications for social welfare. As is emphasized by Mookherjee and Shorrocks, while we may wish to standardize for changes in the age composition, there is no justification for discounting the changes in the profile of average incomes by age. If the evolution of pay structures (for example in the pay of young workers), or of pension schemes, has led to a change in the distribution between age groups, then this may well be a factor that we wish to take into account when judging distributional equity.

Inter-cohort equity

More generally, this introduces the issue of inter-cohort equity. Consider, for example, a hypothetical Mr Smith a US citizen aged 35 in 1947, who both then and in 1977 had the average income for his age group. From Fig. 4.2, we can see that in 1977 his income was broadly the same as that of the average 35-year-old, but of course in real terms he was considerably better off than he himself had been at the age of 35 in 1947 – real incomes having approximately doubled. It would therefore be quite wrong to suggest that, in terms of lifetime real income, his position was identical to that of a 35-year-old in 1977. Put another way, we cannot simply ignore the difference in average incomes between age

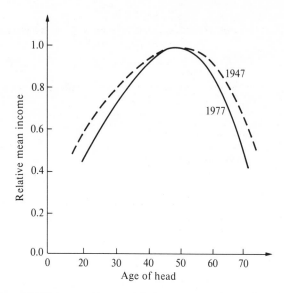

Fig. 4.2 Age–income profiles for US families. (*Source:* Blinder, 1980, Fig. 6.3)

groups and concentrate only on the inequality within groups: that would be to ignore the cohort effects.

The example just given suggests that things are getting better over time, but different cohorts have lived through quite different economic circumstances. Today's octogenarians spent much of their working lives in the relatively depressed conditions of the 1920s and 1930s and then in the Second World War. Their lifetime incomes are likely to be well below those of subsequent cohorts. In contrast, the cohort born in 1930, entering the labour force in the relatively prosperous postwar period, may fare better than the cohort born thirty years later, faced with the world recession of the 1980s. Moreover, the size of one's birth cohort may be a significant factor. Gordon, for example, has described the position of a person born during a temporary trough in the birth rate:

When he opens his eyes for the first time it is in a spacious hospital, well-appointed to serve the wave that has preceded him . . . When he comes to school age, the magnificent buildings are already there to receive him. . . Then he hits the job market. The supply of new entrants is low, and the demand is high, because there is a new large wave coming behind him providing a strong demand for the goods and services of his potential employers. . . He is truly demographically lucky. (cited by Easterlin, 1980, pp. 31–2)

4.4 Towards a comprehensive measure of income

Objections may be raised to a measure of income on two different grounds. First, it may be argued that it does not record accurately what it sets out to measure. Second, what it sets out to measure may not coincide with the definition desired on theoretical grounds.

Accuracy

The US figures shown in Table 4.2 were obtained from the Current Population Survey, in which participation is voluntary. One's immediate reaction is to ask why anyone should take part and why people should tell the truth. The experience on the first point, however, is that the response rate is surprisingly high: in 1972 only 12 per cent of those who were asked the income questions failed to provide complete information. On the second aspect – the accuracy of the answers given – there is evidence of understatement, particularly of investment income. Comparison with independent estimates of total income from different sources indicated that one-half of property income was missing in 1972, compared with only 2 per cent of wage and salary income (US Bureau of Census, 1973, p. 15). In Canada, a comparison of the Survey of Consumer Finances with the national accounts shows that both investment income and self-employment income were under-reported by about a third and that there was substantial under-statement of government transfers (Health and Welfare Canada, 1977, p. 51).

Differential reporting of income in this way may lead to a biased estimate of the degree of dispersion. Property income is likely to be more important at the top and the bottom (among pensioners). The attempt by Budd (1970) to adjust for the unreported income in the United States suggests in fact that the share of the bottom 40 per cent would be raised by approximately 0.7 per cent, while that of the top 5 per cent would increase from 11.5 to 11.9 per cent. In the Canadian case, in 1973 the share of the bottom 40 per cent was raised from 14.4 to 15.5 per cent by the adjustment for under-reporting, and the share of the top 20 per cent reduced by 0.5 percentage points (Health and Welfare Canada, 1977, Table 6.2).

The UK *Blue Book* series in Table 4.1, based as it is in large part on tax returns, raises the question of tax evasion – a subject that is much discussed but about which little is known. The Inland Revenue is continually expressing disquiet. Its first report stated that (in 1806) 'it is notorious that persons living in easy circumstances, nay, even in apparent affluence, have returned their Income under £60, although their annual expenditure has been treble that sum' (quoted in Inland Revenue's *Annual Report for the Year Ended 31st March 1980*, p. 24).

In 1949 a government committee reported the serious and widespread
nature of evasion, and counteracting steps were taken; thirty years later,
the Chairman of the Inland Revenue was telling the Expenditure Committee of the House of Commons that it was 'not implausible' that the
'black economy' amounted to some 7½ per cent of national income.
Estimates of the extent of such 'missing' income are much disputed;
and it is harder still to predict its distributional implications. If the
typical tax evader is the small shopkeeper failing to ring everything up
on the till, or the labour-only subcontractor, then the true distribution
may show less dispersion than the official figures suggest; if it is the rich
who evade tax then the opposite is true. The same obviously applies to
illegal income.

Definition of income

In the previous chapter we described the comprehensive definition of
income that has been widely accepted by economists as the basis for
assessing the equality of its distribution. This definition is very different
from that employed in constructing the official estimates. In the case of
Britain, Titmuss (1962) lists at the end of his chapter on 'Statutory
income and real income' nineteen kinds of income that were tax-free at
the end of 1960 and did not appear in the Inland Revenue figures. In
some cases these are of doubtful quantitative importance: for example,
the expense allowances for members of the House of Lords. In what
follows, attention is focused only on some of the most important items
of 'missing' income.

Capital gains

Capital gains and losses have effectively been omitted from the official
estimates, and there can be little doubt that these are important. In the
long run, assets such as real property (land and buildings) and company
shares have generated substantial capital gains, at least in money terms
(the adjustment for inflation is discussed later); certain other assets,
such as undated government bonds, have led to long-run capital losses.
The impact of capital gains on the distribution of income depends,
therefore, on the holdings of these assets by different income groups.
With the exception of owner-occupied homes, it seems reasonable to
assume that assets generating capital gains are held disproportionately
by upper income groups. Personal holdings of ordinary shares, for
example, are heavily concentrated in Britain in the hands of the top 10
per cent. Owner-occupied houses are an exception, because many
pensioners own their own houses and among the working population
home ownership extends some way down the income scale. Rising house
prices may, therefore, lead to less of an increase in dispersion than

capital gains on other assets, and may add to incomes at the bottom as well as the top.

Direct estimates of the effect of capital gains on the distribution of income are hard to obtain. In the United States, the tax returns provide information on realized gains (i.e. assets actually sold in that tax year), but not on the accrued gains which are relevant to the Simons income concept described in Chapter 3. In view of this, two indirect methods have been employed. The first, used in the United States by Goldsmith *et al.* (1954) and in Britain by Lydall (1959), is to take the value of retained company profits as a measure of capital gains accruing to shareholders. This assumes that the profits ploughed back into companies generate future profits, and that the expectation of these future profits leads to a rise in share prices. As Lydall himself stresses, this relationship may very well not hold, and retained profits may not in fact be reflected on a one-for-one basis in capital gains to the shareholders. A dramatic fall in share prices, such as occurred in Britain in 1974, means that shareholders have made capital losses, even though retained profits may be positive. The retained earnings method is probably best regarded as a measure of the 'permanent' income accrued. A further objection is that this method takes no account of capital gains on other assets. The second approach is to calculate the increase in the value of different classes of asset during the period in question, using stock exchange price indices for shares, average house prices for land and buildings, etc. In this way all capital gains and losses are taken into account, not just those on company shares, and the estimates relate to actual gains accruing, rather than assumed gains, as in the case of undistributed profits.

The results obtained by Prest and Stark (1967), applying the second method of estimating capital gains to the data for the UK in 1959, show that the share of the top 10 per cent is increased, as expected, and that the effect on the top 1 per cent's share is quite marked, rising from 8.3 to 14.1 per cent. The bottom 30 per cent also benefited from capital gains, and it was the middle-income groups whose share fell. The large gains accruing in 1959 were far from typical, reflecting in part the outcome of that year's general election, and for other years the estimated effect is less: in 1963 the Gini coefficient rose from 0.35 to 0.37 (Stark, 1972, p. 77). In the United States, a rather similar approach by Bhatia (1974) exhibits the year-to-year variation: in 1962 capital losses reduced the Gini coefficient from 0.41 to 0.35, but the average gains over the period 1960–4 would have increased it by 0.02. It should be stressed that these estimates depend on a number of assumptions. For example, all holders of a particular type of asset are assumed to have enjoyed the same rate of capital gain, whereas some will have beaten the market and others will have backed losers. The allocation of gains by income range has been disputed. In the United States the estimates of Browning (1976) for 1972 allocate 53 per cent of capital gains to the top 20 per cent of families and 9 per cent to the bottom 20 per cent of families, whereas Smeeding (1979) allocates 68 and 3 per cent respectively.

Imputed rent on owner-occupied houses

In Britain the position with regard to the imputed rent on owner-occupied houses is rather complicated. Until 1963 this imputed rent was taxable under Schedule A of the income tax and appeared in the income survey, but the valuation was based on prewar assessments and the imputed rent recorded in the survey had been falling steadily behind its true value. Since 1963–4, no imputed rent at all has appeared in the survey. In the United States estimates it is missing altogether.

The inclusion of imputed rent could make a substantial difference, since the aggregate amount is large. In the UK in 1977 the estimated total imputed rent was nearly £5 billion, or some 4 per cent of total personal income (*National Income and Expenditure 1981*, Table 4.1); and there are some reasons to suspect that this is on the low side (it represents about 4 per cent of the value of owner-occupied housing). In Canada an estimate based on the value of housing for 1973 came out at around $6 billion, or around 7 per cent of total money income (Health and Welfare Canada, 1977, p. 52). The Canadian study showed that the inclusion of imputed rent raised the share of the bottom 40 per cent and reduced that of the top 20 per cent (by 1 percentage point). In the UK the estimates of the distribution including imputed rent, based on the *Family Expenditure Survey*, for 1972/3 show virtually no change (Royal Commission, 1975a, Table 13). This may be because the total allocated is too low, but almost certainly it reflects the number of retired owner-occupiers in the lower income ranges, for whom imputed rent constitutes a relatively large part of their income.

Fringe benefits

The *Blue Book* figures in Britain include estimates of income in kind accruing to domestic and agricultural workers but make no other allowances for fringe benefits; the United States census concept of income excludes all employer-paid fringe benefits. However, despite their misleading title, there are good reasons to expect that fringe benefits are of substantial importance and that their extent has grown over time. Sinfield refers to

the much greater growth of these, which Titmuss described as the 'concealed multipliers of occupational success' . . . Today employers are much readier and staff more willing to use fringe benefits to maintain or even increase inequalities for executives and other salaried workers

when pay differentials are too conspicuous or are being narrowed ...
These developments have become increasingly important during wage
or income freezes and have gained further significance as inflation has
eroded wages faster than some provisions in kind. (1978, p. 137)

In the US, Taussig notes that, 'during the postwar period, large employers
in both the public and private sectors have provided their employees,
especially their top employees, with a wide variety of nonmoney benefits
... These developments amount to the growth of a welfare state for the
individuals concerned' (1976, p. 21).

There is very limited information about the distribution of fringe
benefits. In the United States 'there exists no consistent time series on
the distribution of fringe benefits ... that can be linked to size distributions of money income over time' (Taussig, 1976, p. 21). The same
applies in the UK. There is of course evidence from surveys of earnings.
For example, the Royal Commission shows how in 1978 the cost to the
employer of superannuation and fringe benefits for managers rose from
18 per cent of cash salary for 'superintendents' to 37 per cent for 'general
managers' (1979a, Table 2.22). Such fragments of evidence indicate
that allowance for fringe benefits would tend to accentuate the degree
of dispersion of incomes.

Home production and leisure

The potential importance of non-market production (for example,
housework and do-it-yourself) will be obvious to the reader, and the
attempts that have been made to estimate its quantitative significance
bear out that it is in aggregate very large. Nordhaus and Tobin (1972),
in one of the best-known estimates for the United States, conclude that
the value of 'non-market work' would in 1965 have added some 65 per
cent to national income.

The impact on the distribution of allowance for home production is
a matter for speculation. It is often suggested that the value of home
production is likely to be inversely related to income, not only because
of the food grown for home consumption in rural areas, but also because
'people in the higher income groups spend less time doing work around
the house' (Scitovsky, 1973, p. 115). Scitovsky goes on to quote an
estimate that in 1964 allowance for such non-market services would have
reduced the share of the top 25 per cent of families and raised that of the
bottom 25 per cent. An earlier study (Morgan et al., 1962) suggested,
however, that the time spent on home improvements rose with income,
there being more owner-occupiers at higher income levels, and that,
overall, the money saved through home production was proportional to
money income, although the range of items taken into account was
more limited than in the Scitovsky estimate.

The incorporation of the value of leisure may be even more important. The estimate of the aggregate value in 1965 in the United States by Nordhaus and Tobin is some one and a third times recorded national income. However, it is apparent that it poses severe problems of valuation, and experiments have shown that the results regarding the distribution are highly sensitive to the assumptions made. The estimates by Taussig, for example, show that, when hours are valued at a common wage rate (the then minimum wage), there is substantial fall in the Gini coefficient. But a valuation based on the net market wage faced by the individual leads to a distribution virtually the same as that for money income. Moreover, at a time of high unemployment the reader will not need reminding that leisure may well be involuntary, being valued at zero or negatively.

4.5 Impact of the government budget

To this point, taxes and government expenditure have been in the background of our picture of the distribution of income, and we should now consider more systematically the effect of the government budget. As indicated in the previous chapter, we may be concerned with income as potential spending power, in which case the relevant definition is income after taxation, allowing for the benefits from government expenditure; alternatively, we may be concerned with income before government intervention, as a measure of status. The concept of income employed in the official statistics falls between these two stools. In neither Britain nor the United States are taxes and government expenditure fully taken into account, even in the 'after tax' figures in Table 4.1; but in both cases certain elements of government activity, notably transfer payments, have been included, so that the statistics cannot be taken as representing purely the outcome of the market process. As noted by Blinder in the United States, 'census income is an awkward halfway house which includes transfers but fails to deduct taxes' (1980, p. 443). In this section, we examine some of the ways in which a fuller accounting may be made for government activity in order to reach a distribution of disposable income which allows for government expenditure.

   In considering the role of the government budget, it may be useful to consider in turn the different stages in going from 'original' income (wages, property income, occupational pensions, etc.) to 'final' income:

(1) Original income
(2) + cash transfers from the government
(3) − direct taxes
(4) + benefits in kind from the government

(5) – Indirect taxes
= final income.

The list is not, of course, exhaustive, and certain items are not readily classified (for example, pensions paid by the government to former employees).

Cash transfers

Cash transfers (such as sickness and unemployment benefits, child benefits, state old age pensions, etc.) are in general included in the pre-tax income figures in Tables 4.1 and 4.2. If they were not, then many people would have had incomes recorded as close to zero or zero. The *Economic Trends* study of taxes and benefits in the UK, using data from the *Family Expenditure Survey*, shows that in 1980 the bottom 10 per cent had original income averaging £10 per year.

The main features of the *Economic Trends* study are summarized in Table 4.7. The bottom 20 per cent receive considerably more in cash

TABLE 4.7
Effects of taxes and benefits in the United Kingdom, 1980

	Average per household (£ per year) (households ranked by original income)					
	Bottom 20%	Next 20%	Middle 20%	Next 20%	Top 20%	All households*
Original income	170	2705	5905	8540	14 445	6350
+ cash transfers	+ 1970	+ 1320	+ 600	+ 450	+ 390	+ 950
– direct taxes	– 5	– 420	– 1165	– 1790	– 3280	– 1330
+ benefits in kind	+ 960	+ 990	+ 1170	+ 1220	+ 1270	+ 1120
– indirect taxes	– 545	– 1020	– 1415	– 1780	– 2530	– 1460
Final income	2550	3580	5090	6640	10 295	5630

* The figures may not add up exactly because of rounding.
Source: Economic Trends, January 1982, Table B

transfers than other groups – more than twice the average amount. In large part these transfers are age-related or income-related (e.g., the means-tested supplementary benefits). This is not to say that cash transfers are confined to the lowest income groups. The top 20 per cent received some £400 a year, of which a half consisted of child benefit (which goes to all children, unrelated to parental income). It is clear that cash transfers make a major difference to the distribution. At the same time, we should emphasize that the government cannot necessarily take credit for this as positive redistribution. If its actions elsewhere, say in the field of monetary policy, lead to higher unemployment, then it would seem perverse to regard the consequent increase in the payment of unemployment benefit as evidence of greater redistribution.

The extent of government cash transfers has been investigated in the United States by Danziger and Plotnick, with particular reference to the trend over the period 1965–74. The results may be seen by referring back to Table 4.5. As we would expect, the difference between 'pre-transfer' and 'post-transfer' income is much more marked for some demographic groups than for others. There is, for example, a slight reduction in the Gini coefficient for families headed by a prime-age man, but the coefficient is virtually halved for single men aged 65 and over. Danziger and Plotnick conclude that the impact of government transfers increased over the period. The overall Gini coefficient was reduced by 4.9 percentage points in 1965 but by 6.9 percentage points in 1974. Blinder comments that 'it is surprising that the explosive growth of transfers did not push inequality down even faster' (1980, p. 446), but, as he notes, there are several possible explanations. One is that increased transfers may have allowed more people to live on their own, rather than with relatives, giving rise to the demographic changes discussed earlier. Another is that the growth in expenditure has been in benefits less concentrated on low-income families.

Direct taxes

A starting point in considering the impact of direct taxation in Britain is provided by the comparison of the before-tax and after-tax figures in Table 4.1, although it should be noted that the only tax deducted is income tax (national insurance contributions are not allowed for). A feature of these estimates is the closeness of the income shares before and after tax. The share of the top 10 per cent is reduced, as we would expect, but only from 26.1 to 23.4 per cent, and the share of the bottom 30 per cent rises only from 10.4 to 12.1 per cent. The same picture is given by the *Economic Trends* estimates in Table 4.7, which also include national insurance contributions paid by employees. The bottom 20 per cent pay little in the way of direct tax, but for the next 20 per cent the tax is already a tenth of gross income, and overall the tax structure is not particularly progressive. The top fifth, for example, pay 22 per cent of gross income, which is not a great deal more than the average of 18 per cent.

The effect of federal personal tax, in the United States is shown by

Blinder (1980, Table 6.17) to be rather similar. The share of the top 20 per cent of families is reduced in 1972 from 42.7 to 41.0 per cent. The calculations of Reynolds and Smolensky for 1970 show the Gini coefficient being reduced by 0.8 per cent by the income tax, but with this largely being offset by the social security taxes (1977a, Table 6.3). Moreover, these authors suggest that the progressive impact of the direct tax system had been eroded over the period 1950–70, chiefly because the tax exemption level had not kept up with the average rise in incomes. As they note (Reynolds and Smolensky, 1978), the situation has changed dramatically since the 1913 Act that initiated the modern income tax, when fewer than 1 per cent of the population were liable; even prior to the Second World War income taxation was largely confined to the top 10 per cent.

Benefits in kind from the government

The *Economic Trends* studies in the UK make an allowance for certain benefits in kind and subsidies, including education, school meals and welfare foods, the national health service, housing and transport subsidies. The method of calculation is open to question. Each person of school age in the household, for example, is allocated an amount equal to the average expenditure on that type of education; in the case of the health service, estimates are made of the average use according to age and sex, and the total state expenditure allocated accordingly. The estimates shown in Table 4.7 must therefore be regarded with due caution. As may be seen, the average amount tends to rise with income, but nothing like in proportion to gross or original income, so that benefits in kind tend to be progressive. For the bottom 20 per cent, the most important element (over a half) is the health service; for the top 20 per cent, the largest is education.

The redistributive role of government spending has been the subject of controversy in the UK. Le Grand, for example, has recently argued that 'almost all public expenditure on the social services in Britain benefits the better off to a greater extent than the poor' (1982, p. 3). In the United States there has similarly been controversy, although here the disagreement has been not about the direction, in-kind transfers being regarded as equalizing, but about the quantitative significance. Thus, the estimates of Browning (1976) raised the share of the bottom 20 per cent in 1972 from 5.4 to 7.7 per cent, whereas those of Smeeding (1979) raised it only to 7.2 per cent. The difference may appear small, but once again it may be significant when it comes to assessing the trends over time.

Indirect taxes

The *Economic Trends* study in the UK takes account of indirect taxes, assuming that these result in higher prices to consumers, reducing real incomes. (The study also includes employers' national insurance contributions and local rates.) The figures in Table 4.7 show that the estimated indirect tax payments rise with income but less than proportionately: for the bottom 20 per cent, indirect taxes are 25.5 per cent of original income plus cash transfers, and the proportion falls steadily: 25.3 per cent, 21.8 per cent, 19.8 per cent and 17.1 per cent for the top 20 per cent of income units. In the United States where indirect taxes are of less aggregate importance, the estimates of Reynolds and Smolensky (1977a, Table 6.3) show the Gini coefficient as being increased.

The rationale of the adjustment for indirect taxes in the present context may be questioned. Hicks argues that disposable incomes 'are the incomes which people can spend in the shops. The fact that some of the things they buy are taxed . . . does not prevent the incomes which are spendable in this way being a fair measure of relative wealth or poverty' (1971, p. 250). But he goes on to recognize that, in considering trends over time, the fact that the tax has gone up more on some goods than others may be relevant — a point to which we return in the next section when examining differential rates of inflation in general. We should however note that it does not necessarily follow that the method adopted above is the appropriate one: for example, it ignores the effect on income that is saved.

An assessment

The introduction of the government budget in the kind of way described above takes account of a major element of modern society. The fairness, or otherwise, of the distribution of income cannot be considered without regard to the activities of the government. At the same time, the methods used to measure its redistributive pattern are open to a number of objections.

The first concerns the incomplete coverage. Thus, in the UK studies taxes on company profits are not included. Omissions are particularly important for the expenditure side, where the *Economic Trends* studies leave out items that are not of individual benefit (e.g., defence) or that go to other sectors of the economy (e.g., industrial research) or that although directly benefiting individuals, cannot readily be allocated (e.g., parks). Calculations can be made allocating these on different assumptions (see Nicholson, 1974), but the assumptions are to a considerable extent arbitrary. It may seem reasonable to divide the benefit equally, or to allocate it proportionately to income, but it could well be argued that the benefit rises more than proportionately with income — for example, that the rich gain more from police protection.

The second objection is that the analysis has taken insufficient account of the mobility induced by government activity. A family may have been in the bottom 20 per cent when ranked according to original income, but they receive sufficiently large social security benefits to be raised to the next 20 per cent in terms of gross income. Such changes in ranking have implications for the statistical methods employed. In Table 4.7, for example, the households have not been re-ranked. In order to do this, access is necessary to the individual household data. The significance of this has been demonstrated in the United States by Smeeding, who shows that, maintaining the original money income ranking, there is a rise in the share of the bottom fifth from 5.4 to 7.4 per cent, while re-ranking families by adjusted income increases the share to only 7.0 per cent. Moreover, the extent of re-ranking may be of interest in its own right — it may be an aspect of the government's activity that we wish to monitor and that has implications for horizontal equity.

Finally, it should be emphasized that our objective has been to calculate the distribution of final income after allowing for the effect of the government. We have *not* attempted to isolate in itself the impact of the government budget. This would involve estimating what incomes would have been in the absence of taxes and benefits (or, equivalently, the incidence of taxes and benefits) — a difficult undertaking. Our exercise should be seen as one in accountancy rather than accountability.

4.6 Interpretation of the evidence

The evidence about trends over time in the distribution of income has to be seen against a background of major economic and social change. In his criticism of comparisons of Britain before and after the Second World War, Titmuss drew attention to the large-scale changes in the social and economic framework that may have profoundly affected the distribution of income, and argued that 'we should be much more hesitant in suggesting that any equalizing forces at work in Britain since 1938 can be promoted to the status of a "natural law" and projected into the future' (1962, p. 198).

In this section, we discuss three examples of the kind of factor that need to be considered: the increased employment of married women, the level of unemployment, and the rate of inflation.

Working wives

At the end of the 1950s, Lydall argued that in Britain the increased employment of married women, coupled with the trend towards earlier marriage, had contributed to the reduction in dispersion of income since the 1930s:

since a greater proportion of young married women – and especially of working- and middle-class women – go out to work, [the effect] has been mainly to increase the incomes of the lower and middle income families . . . At the same time the people who are already in the top 1 per cent of income units cannot usually benefit proportionately very much from their wives' earnings, since the earnings of wives are more equally distributed than incomes in general. (1959, p. 23)

More recently, Dinwiddy and Reed (1977) have examined the consequences of the rise in the participation rate of married women from 24 per cent in 1951 to 49 per cent in 1971. Standardizing the *Family Expenditure Survey* data for the change in female employment status, distinguishing full-time and part-time workers, they show that the share of the bottom 20 per cent in 1972/3 would have been 5.4 per cent, rather than 5.2 per cent, if the 1951 employment levels has pertained. The share of the top 10 per cent would have been 26.9 per cent rather than 26.2 per cent (1977, Tables D17 and D19). The effect of increased participation over this period appears to have been to reduce the shares of both top and bottom groups.

The changing impact of married women's participation has been noted in the United States by Danziger, who comments that:

During the early post World War II period, married women were more likely to work if family income from other sources were low. In such cases, the earnings of wives raised the incomes of families located at the bottom of the income distribution and reduced family income inequality. In recent years, due in part to the women's movement and to efforts to equalize opportunity, the negative relationship between wives' work experience and family income has weakened. The most rapid increases in work experience have been among women in families with higher incomes. (1978, p. 1)

At the same time, he finds that the correlation between the earnings of husbands and wives is not particularly high; and, altogether, he finds that the effect of working wives remained relatively stable between 1967 and 1974, having a small equalizing impact.

The results described above refer to the distribution of money income, and we should point out the interaction between this factor and the adjustment for non-market production discussed in Section 4.4. If every housewife went out to work for her neighbour, then participation would increase and money incomes change, but the real picture might be little altered.

Unemployment

Studies comparing the distribution of income before and after the Second World War concluded that an important factor had been the reduction of unemployment. In the United States, Solow suggested that in the early part of the period 'the main cause of the equalization was the approach to full employment from the relatively depressed conditions before the war' (1960, p. 104). In Britain, Lydall concluded that the single most important cause of the egalitarian trend shown by his estimates was the achievement and maintenance of full employment, which entails 'the elimination of a large group of very low incomes, not only of the unemployed themselves but also of workers on the margin of unemployment whose wages are particularly depressed' (1959, p. 33). More recently, concern has been expressed about the distributional consequences of the rise in unemployment in the late 1970s and early 1980s.

The distributional impact of increased unemployment is governed by several considerations. First, it depends on *who* becomes unemployed. As is well known, unemployment is not shared equally. If it were, then everyone in Britain in 1982 would have been out of work for some six weeks during the year. In fact, unemployment is concentrated, and many people face recurrent spells. Moreover, the unemployed are drawn disproportionately from the lowest earnings ranges. The Department of Health and Social Security cohort study showed that half the men entering unemployment in the autumn of 1978 came from the bottom 20 per cent of the earnings distribution. Although some were redundant managers, it was much more likely that their jobs had been semi-skilled or unskilled manual ones (Moylan and Davies, 1980).

Second, the distributional impact depends on the extent to which earnings are replaced by social security benefits. The magnitude of the 'replacement ratio' has been much debated. In Britain, a lot has been made of the hypothetical calculations regularly produced by the Department of Health and Social Security, which indicate that incomes out of work are a substantial fraction of incomes in work (at least up to the abolition of the earnings-related supplement in 1982). However, examination of the incomes actually received by the unemployed demonstrate that these hypothetical calculations can be highly misleading (for example, where benefit is not in fact being received). The evidence from the 1978 cohort study, for men unemployed for at least three months, shows that nearly 50 per cent received unemployment benefits that replaced less than half of their lost net earnings, and that for a third total family incomes out of work were less than half their incomes in work (*Employment Gazette*, June 1982, p. 243).

The finding just quoted introduces the third important element — the income of other family members and the position of the unemployed in the distribution by family income. It may be the case that the unemployed are drawn from lower paid workers, but that their position is better than that of the pensioners who make up a large proportion of the bottom income range.

The impact of unemployment on the distribution, therefore, reflects several ingredients. There are two main ways of assessing their overall quantitative significance. The first is via the construction of a counterfactual 'no unemployment' situation; the second seeks to relate the trends in the distribution over time to the aggregate unemployment rate.

The first of these approaches is illustrated in Table 4.8, which shows the calculations for Britain as part of the *Economic Trends* study cited earlier. This shows the effect of identifying households where a person

TABLE 4.8

Unemployment and the distribution of incomes in Britain 1980

| | Gini Coefficients (per cent) | | | |
| | Original income[a] | | Disposable income[b] | |
Household type	Actual	Hypothetical no unemployment situation	Actual	Hypothetical no unemployment situation
1 adult[c]	39.7	36.6	27.9	27.0
2 adults[c]	31.2	29.9	24.5	23.9
2 adults and 1 child	29.1	26.7	23.2	22.1
2 adults and 2 children	25.1	23.8	21.4	20.8
2 adults and 3 or more children	33.7	29.8	23.4	22.1
3 or more adults	29.4	28.0	22.2	21.5
3 or more adults with children	27.9	25.3	21.1	20.2

Note: [a] Annual income before the deduction of taxes or the addition of state benefits
[b] Original income plus cash benefits minus direct taxes
[c] Non-retired
Source: Economic Trends, January 1982, Table V, p. 107

was unemployed and replacing their income by the estimated amount that they would have received in work, using for this purpose the *Family Expenditure Survey* for 1980. It may be noted that the level of unemployment was only some 60 per cent of that reached by the time the results were published in January 1982. An important feature of the calculations is that they relate to *annual* incomes, so that the actual figures represent in most cases an average of employment and unemployment incomes; for example, where a person is off work for two months, his actual income is one-sixth unemployment benefit plus five-sixths work income, which is compared with a hypothetical figure that is all work income. As can be seen, original income exhibits noticeably less dispersion in the hypothetical no-unemployment situation, the Gini coefficient being reduced by more than 3 percentage points in some cases. On the other hand, the effect on disposable income, which allows for the benefits paid and the reduced direct taxes, is quite a lot less marked. None the less, the effect is not trivial, ranging from 0.6 to 1.3 percentage points.

The model just described allows for the effect of unemployment on earnings, and for the consequential changes in social security and taxes, but does not incorporate the impact of a recession on investment income. The more ambitious study in the United States by Mirer (1973a) investigated how different types of income varied with macroeconomic conditions and simulated the distributional effect of a recession. He finds a 'reclining S-shape', with the bottom groups suffering less than the 'working poor' immediately above them, who in turn lose more than upper middle-income ranges, and with the wealthiest families losing through the fall in business incomes.

The second approach, based on the observed changes in the distribution, has received quite a lot of attention in the United States. To take one example, Blinder and Esaki (1978) estimate econometric relations between the share of total income accruing to different groups and the level of aggregate unemployment (and other variables). They estimate that a 1 percentage point increase in unemployment is associated with a rise of some 0.3 percentage points in the share of the top fifth. This is not necessarily inconsistent with the results of Mirer, in that the top fifth includes higher earners as well as those with business income. Blinder and Esaki also estimate that the share of the bottom fifth is reduced by about 0.15 percentage points. Their findings indicate a straightforward transfer from the bottom to the top – at least with the broad income groups. At the same time, we must recognize the difficulty of separating the effect of one macroeconomic variable from others – and in particular the rate of inflation, to which we now turn.

Inflation

Inflation affects our interpretation of the income distribution statistics in a number of ways. First, there is the question – parallel to that discussed for unemployment – as to how the distribution of money income is affected by increases in the rate of inflation. How much of the changes in the 1970s could be attributed to accelerating inflation? There is an

expectation that different types of income would be differently affected.
For example, Robinson and Eatwell argue that:

[inflation] favours property at the expense of earnings, for when an
expectation of rising prices in the future has become normal, the money
value today of an income-yielding asset is raised by the belief that its
money value will be higher in the future. Purchasing power is continually
falling into the lap of owners of shares in successful businesses, land,
houses and old masters . . . Secondly, among earnings, pensions and
payments to relieve poverty, inflation is continually redistributing real
income in favour of groups in the strongest bargaining position. (1973,
p. 307)

The consequences for the distribution of income depend on the
relation between *type* of income and the size distribution (a subject
discussed in Chapter 9). Empirically, the same two approaches have
been adopted as with unemployment. There have been studies seeking
to simulate the impact, using information on household asset ownership.
For example, Budd and Seiders (1971) in the United States find that
the top 5 per cent and the bottom 40 per cent tend to lose in relative
terms, although the authors comment that 'perhaps the most striking
result for the income models is the relatively small effect our simulated
inflations . . . have on the relative distributions' (p. 134). The econometric approach may be illustrated by reference to Blinder and Esaki
(1978). They find a slightly different pattern, with the poor and middle
classes tending to lose relatively less than the rich, but the most salient
conclusion is that 'the effects of inflation on the income distribution
. . . are much less important than those of unemployment' (p. 608).

The second important aspect of inflation concerns the adjustment
from *money* to *real* income. As explained in Chapter 3, allowance needs
to be made for the real capital loss that inflation imposes on all those
holding wealth, and the real capital gain by those in debt. In principle,
such an adjustment is straightforward, the decline in the purchasing
power of assets being subtracted from money income, to give potential
spending power *holding real wealth intact*. This reduces the net property
income and is likely to lead to a fall in the share of top income groups.
In practice, such an estimate would clearly have to be made in conjunction with adjustments for capital gains. For a person holding a real asset,
the money value of which rose with the general price level, the net effect
would then be zero. Blinder has indeed argued, in the US context, that
the two adjustments (for inflation and for capital gains) would more or
less cancel (1980, pp. 447–8).

The third aspect is that of changes in *relative* prices over time (we
have earlier referred to the possibility that this may arise because of
indirect tax changes). If all goods went up in price at the same rate, the

cost of living would rise by the same amount for everyone, and we could take money incomes in two different years as an indicator of purchasing power. It would be true that an income of £1000 meant less than it did ten years ago, but its purchasing power would be reduced by the same percentage as an income of twice that size. However, in fact not all prices do go up at the same rate, as should be clear from everyday shopping. Taking a long view, from 1914 to 1968, shows that in Britain the price index for food rose by less than four times, whereas the index for clothing rose by over five times. Within the food group itself there was considerable diversity, with milk going up from 1¼d to 10d a pint, but margarine only going up from 7d to 1s 10d a pound. In the more recent past, food prices have risen faster than the general price index. The most marked movement has of course been in energy prices. Between 1971 and 1981, the retail price index in Britain rose by a factor of 3.7, whereas the fuel and light component increased by a factor of 4.7. Differential price changes of this kind can, of course, occur even without there being any overall inflation; the question is one of *relative* price changes. The introduction of the value-added tax in place of purchase tax in Britain, for example, caused some goods to become cheaper and some more expensive.

The fact that prices go up at different rates would not be a matter for concern in the proportion of income spent on each class of goods were the same for all families. If food represented the same percentage of the budget of a millionaire as of a low-wage family, then inflation would still reduce the purchasing power of all incomes by the same proportion. But household budgets do not in fact take the same form at different income levels. The proportion of income spent on food ranges from 20 per cent for a high-income family to over a third for a pensioner household. It is therefore wrong to apply a single retail price index to all income groups. In estimating the changes that have taken place in the distribution of purchasing power, allowance has to be made for differences in the rates of price increase and for differences in family budgets.

The way in which such an adjustment would work may be illustrated by the special price indices compiled for pensioner households in Britain. The weights show (*Employment Gazette*, April 1982) that pensioners spend a larger fraction of their budget on food, fuel and light and less on alcoholic drink, clothing, footwear, transport and on durables, than do the households who make up the 'index'. To give an impression of the possible effect, let us take the case of fuel and light, which makes up 20 per cent of the budget of a single pensioner, compared with 7 per cent overall (in both cases, housing is excluded). Between 1971 and 1981, fuel and light rose in price by 27 per cent more than the overall index.

Taken together, these mean that the cost of living rose by (20 - 7) per cent × 27 per cent more for the single pensioner, or a difference of some 3.5 per cent. This is of course only one element — and that most likely to generate a large difference — and the calculation needs to be refined. What is shown by the official indices is that, between 1971 and 1981, the price index for a single pensioner rose by 303 per cent, compared with 294 per cent for the overall index. The difference may appear small, but for a person living on an old age pension it may be a serious matter.

There is no necessary reason why prices should rise more rapidly for the goods that form a larger part of the budget of low-income groups; and we may expect the pattern to change over time. This point has been made in the United States by Williamson (1977). For example, Hollister and Palmer (1972) calculated for the period 1947–67 special price indices for those below the poverty line and for the aged poor. Although the differences in budget patterns follow the same kind of pattern as in Britain, relative price movements were such as to cause the price indices to rise by a very similar extent. But from 1967 the position changed, and Williamson finds that over the period 1967–75 relative price movements contributed significantly towards increasing inequality.

4.7 Concluding comment

Ideally, we would end this chapter by drawing together the different elements and reaching a clear-cut conclusion about the path of income inequality in Britain and the United States. After all, the research described in the preceding sections has provided many of the necessary building blocks. At the same time, it will be apparent that this goal is some way off. There remain substantial problems in adjusting and interpreting the evidence. Moreover, while the implications of the different factors discussed here may be fairly readily established for the *level* of inequality, the uncertainty surrounding their effect on the *trends* over time may remain quite difficult to resolve.

Note on sources and further reading

The *official statistics* on the distribution of income in the UK are described in the reports of the Royal Commission (see the notes to Chapter 2) and in Stark (1978). The official statistics in the United States are outlined in Miller (1966), Taussig (1976), and Blinder (1980).

In Britain there have been a number of academic studies of the distribution of income, including Paish (1957), Allen (1957), Lydall (1959), Brittain (1960), R. J. Nicholson (1967), Prest and Stark (1967), Stewart

(1972), Stark (1972), Townsend (1979), and Lansley (1980). In the United States, the principal references include Goldsmith *et al.* (1954), Solow (1960), Kravis (1962), Kuznets (1953), Schultz (1964), Miller (1966), Haley (1968), Budd (1970), Taussig (1973), Schultz (1975), Browning (1976), Williamson (1976), and Blinder (1980).

Methods of *interpolation* are treated in Gastwirth (1972), Atkinson and Harrison (1978a, Appendix V), Kakwani (1980, Ch. 6) and Cowell and Mehta (1982).

Studies that adjust for *differences in family size* in the UK include Prest and Stark (1967) and Stark (1972), using the *Blue Book* data, and van Slooten and Coverdale (1977), McClements (1978) and Lansley (1980), using the *Family Expenditure Survey*. Other US studies include Kuznets (1974) and Cowell (1980).

The *age pattern and the role of demographic factors* is discussed in the UK by Semple (1975), Dinwiddy and Reed (1977), and Mookherjee and Shorrocks (1982). In the United States an early reference is Morgan (1962). The article by Paglin (1975) sparked off considerable controversy – see Danziger, Haveman and Smolensky (1977), Kurien (1977), Nelson (1977), and Paglin's reply in the same issue of the *American Economic Review*. There is a useful summary in Blinder (1980). The view of *cohort* differences in incomes is discussed extensively in Easterlin (1980). The effect of demographic trends in the United States is examined by Kuznets (1974).

The *definition* of income is discussed in the UK by Titmuss (1962) and Stark (1972); in the United States by Browning (1976), Smeeding (1979), and others. The size of the 'black economy' is examined by MacAfee (1980) and Dilnot and Morris (1981) in the UK, and by Feige (1979) in the US. This is the subject of considerable controversy. The accuracy of income data recorded in the *Family Expenditure Survey*, and their relation to the national accounts figures, are examined by Atkinson and Micklewright (1983). The calculation of imputed rent on owner-occupied housing is discussed by Atkinson and King (1980). The value of household services in relation to national income is discussed by Hawrylyshyn (1976) and Ferber and Birnbaum (1980). The basic literature on the effect of the government budget on the distribution of income is represented by J. L. Nicholson (1965) in Britain and Gillespie (1965) in the United States. For more recent results, see Nicholson (1974) and Stephenson (1980) in the UK, and Musgrave *et al.* (1974), Reynolds and Smolensky (1977a, b) in the United States. For criticism of the methods employed, see, among others, Aaron and McGuire (1970), Thurow (1971, Ch. 4), Michelson (1970), Webb and Sieve (1971), Peacock (1974), Levitt (1976), O'Higgins (1980), and Ruggles and O'Higgins (1981).

The relation between *macroeconomic* conditions and the distribution of income in the US is examined by Metcalf (1969, 1972), Mirer (1973a, b), Beach (1977), and Blinder and Esaki (1978). On the effect of unemployment, see Gramlich (1974).

The analysis of the distributional consequences of *relative price* changes in Britain is discussed by Tipping (1970), Muellbauer (1974 – but see Irvine and McCarthy, 1980), J. L. Nicholson (1975), Leser (1976), Muellbauer (1977a, b), and Piachaud (1978). The US literature includes Hollister and Palmer (1972), Palmer and Barth (1977), and Williamson (1977).

5

THE DISTRIBUTION OF EARNINGS
AND PERSONAL CHARACTERISTICS

The market for economists is perhaps the only job market that seems to improve during a recession.

(P. Cappelli, *The Book of Wages and Salaries*)

One of the principal sources of income inequality is the dispersion of earned incomes; indeed, earnings are for most people the major source of income. This chapter and the following one are concerned with some of the main factors that lead to such earnings differentials.

5.1 The evidence to be explained

The landmarks of the earnings distribution were described in Chapter 2, which demonstrated the existence of marked differences in earnings according to occupation. The earnings tree showed that a teacher is likely to earn twice as much as a farm labourer, that a hospital consultant is likely to earn six times as much, and top executives many times more. More complete information about the average earnings of men in different occupational groups in Britain and the changes over time is shown in Table 5.1. Unskilled manual workers received some 80 per cent of

TABLE 5.1

Average earnings of men in different occupational groups, Great Britain, 1913–1978

	Percentage of average for all groups (men and women)						
	1913/14	1922/4	1935/6	1955/6	1960	1970	1978
Higher professional	405	372	392	290	289	211	209
Lower professional	191	204	190	115	120	136	137
Managers and administrators	247	307	272	279	263	245	203
Clerks	122	116	119	98	97	97	93
Foremen	152	171	169	148	144	121	118
Skilled manual	131	115	121	117	113	104	110
Semi skilled manual	85	80	83	88	83	93	97
Unskilled manual	78	82	80	82	76	83	86

Source: Routh (1980), Table 2.29

average earnings, skilled manual workers about a third more; higher professional and managerial workers earned about twice the average. The trends over the course of the century need to be interpreted with care, in view of changes in classification and other problems of comparability. They show a substantial decline in the relative earnings of professional workers and clerks. Within the manual occupations, there has been greater stability.

The occupational groups set out in Table 5.1 are broad, and the figures conceal considerable variation. (The definition of an 'occupation' is clearly to some extent arbitrary, and some groups are wider than others: in the US census, for example, painters are separated from paperhangers, whereas all accountants come in a single category.) Within the group of higher professional workers, actuaries earn on average nearly half as much again as accountants, and architects earn only two-thirds the amount received by the average doctor. Even within narrowly defined occupational groups, the degree of dispersion remains very considerable. This may be illustrated by Table 5.2 showing figures for the distribution

TABLE 5.2

Distribution of earnings within selected occupations in Britain, 1981

	Weekly earnings (% of average)	
	Lowest decile	Top decile
All full-time adult men	59	151
Train drivers	78	128
Primary schoolteachers	71	130
Finance clerks	67	139
Scaffolders	56	155
Doctors	53	157

Source: New Earnings Survey 1981, Table 8

in Britain in 1981. In each case the earnings of the decile are expressed as a percentage of the average *for that group*, so that 10 per cent of train drivers earn less than 78 per cent of the average for train drivers. This gives a rough indication of the amount of dispersion within groups relative to that in the distribution as a whole. For some groups, such as train drivers, the degree of dispersion is less than for all men taken together, the top decile being only 28 per cent away from the average, coupled with 51 per cent overall. Schoolteachers are similar. But for other groups, including doctors and scaffolders, the dispersion *within* occupations is no less than for men as a whole. This means, for example, that, although doctors earn an average nearly two and a half times the average for finance clerks, the top decile of the latter comes *above* the bottom decile for doctors.

The variation of earnings within occupations is in fact such that knowing what a man's job is tells us relatively little about his likely earnings. This may be rather surprising, since we are accustomed to thinking that it does. The proportion of the variation in earnings that can be explained by occupational differentials is fairly small, as was found by the Royal Commission on the Distribution of Income and Wealth:

It can be seen therefore that much less than half of the dispersion of men's earnings, measured in terms of the variance, can be accounted for by occupation, and just about half in the case of women . . . the expected difference between the earnings of two men, if they were taken at random from the distribution, [is £36]. If we know they have the same occupation, the expected difference is reduced to £33. (1976b, p. 64)

Similarly, Saunders and Marsden conclude, from their comparison of the distribution of industrial earnings in Britain, Belgium, France, Italy, Netherlands and West Germany, that 'an important characteristic of the British pay distribution, accounting for much of the relatively high degree of overall inequality in industrial pay, is the exceptionally wide variance of pay levels, among both men and women, within the same occupational groups' (1979, p. 33).

The observed differences within occupations may have a number of explanations. They may reflect differences in the number of hours worked per week or may compensate for other differences in the conditions of work. They may be associated with differences in age. Fig. 5.1 shows the variation of weekly gross earnings by age for men, considering manual and non-manual workers separately, in April 1981. The figures are expressed as a proportion of the overall average for men, and bring out a number of interesting features. The earnings of teenagers, both manual and non-manual, appear to be around 40 per cent of the overall average and to exhibit relatively little dispersion (the dotted line shows the top decile for the age group and the dashed line shows the bottom decile). For manual workers, earnings rise with age through the twenties, reaching a peak in the range 30-39, and then decline. The top and bottom deciles for manual workers show a similar pattern, and they retain broadly the same ratio throughout the age range, indicating that the degree of dispersion remains the same through the life-cycle. For non-manual workers, the profiles are close to those for manual workers at the outset, and then begin to pull away in the late twenties. (There are of course changes in the composition, as those with higher education join the labour force.) For non-manual workers the peak is in the range of 40-49, when they earn about a third more than the overall average. The profile then declines, but it should be observed that the degree of

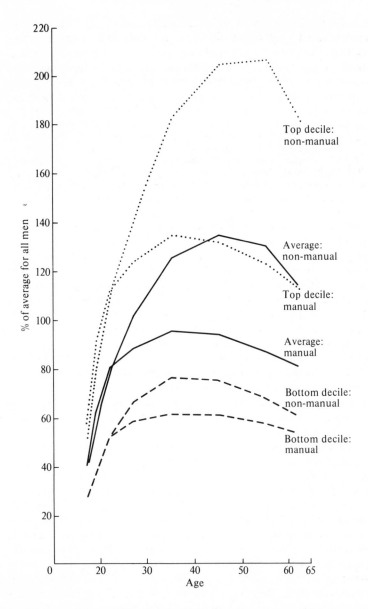

Fig. 5.1 Age–earnings profiles, Britain, 1981. The figures cover all full-time male workers, of all ages, whose pay was not affected by absence. (*Source: New Earnings Survey 1981*, Table 10)

dispersion tends to widen over the lifetime. The ratio of the top to the bottom decile is initially 2:1 but reaches 3:1 by the end of the age range.

The shape of the earnings distribution in Britain is illustrated more fully in Fig. 5.2, which gives the frequency distribution for weekly earnings in 1981. (In Chapter 2 we presented a frequency distribution

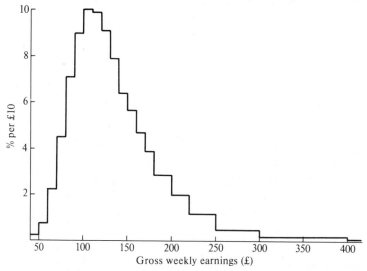

Fig. 5.2 Frequency distribution for earnings in Britain, 1981. The figures relate to all men aged 21 and over in full-time work whose pay was not affected by absence. (*Source: New Earnings Survey 1981*, Table 19)

for *incomes*.) As with incomes, there is a bunching around the middle, with nearly 40 per cent of the men in the range £90–£130. On either side of this range the frequencies fall away, but the right-hand tail is clearly much longer. (It should be noted that it is truncated at £400 a week, which is less than a fifth of the earnings of a top company chairman.) In other words, the distribution is not symmetric, but positively skewed. This skewness is also demonstrated by the decile figures for Britain. If the distribution were symmetric, then the distance between the lowest decile and the median would be the same as the distance between the median and the highest decile, but that is not the case (see Table 5.3). At the same time, it is interesting to note that the *ratio* is more nearly the same in each case, so that if we were to plot not earnings but the *logarithm* of earnings, this would be closer to symmetry.

This lack of symmetry in the earnings distribution may be contrasted with the distribution of such characteristics as height: the lower quartile

TABLE 5.3

Distribution of all adult male employees whose pay is not affected by absence

			Percentage of median		
Lowest decile	66				
		Distance = 34	Ratio $\dfrac{\text{Median}}{\text{Lowest decile}} = 152\%$		
Median	100				
		Distance = 68	Ratio $\dfrac{\text{Highest decile}}{\text{Median}} = 168\%$		
Highest decile	168				

Source: New Earnings Survey 1981, Table 19

of heights in Britain is 1.9 inches below the median and the upper quartile is 1.9 inches above. The frequency of heights does, in fact, follow broadly the *normal* curve, which is bell-shaped and symmetric. Such a normal curve would clearly provide a poor description of the earnings distribution; however, the observation about the ratios suggests that the logarithm of earnings may follow the normal distribution. In such a case, the distribution is said to be *lognormal* in form. From an examination of earnings data for a large number of countries, Lydall concluded that in general 'the central part of the distribution from perhaps the tenth to the eightieth percentile from the top, is close to lognormal' (1968, p.67).

As Lydall points out, the lognormal does not provide a good description of the upper tail of the distribution, because there are more people with high earnings than the lognormal would predict. He argues that the upper tail, in fact, follows more closely the *Pareto* distribution. On the basis of an examination of the distribution of income for an unlikely collection of places — Prussia, Saxony, eighteenth-century Peru and the cities of Florence, Perugia, Basle, and Augsburg (in 1471) — Pareto concluded in 1897 that the distribution followed a particularly simple 'law': if Y denotes income, the number of people with incomes greater than or equal to Y is given by AY^{-a} where A and a are constants, the a being the Pareto index. One interesting feature of the distribution is that the average income of those in the range Y and above is always $a/(a-1) \times Y$. If, for example $a = 1.5$ (as Pareto supposed), then the average income of those above £1000 is £3000 and the average income of those above £10 000 is £30 000. Since that time, empirical work has cast doubt on the general validity of Pareto's law, and it is clear that it cannot provide an adequate description of the whole range of incomes or earnings, since it does not lead to the hump-shape characteristic of such distributions.

The frequency falls with earnings throughout the range of the Pareto distribution, so that the highest frequency is at the left-hand tail, which is clearly inconsistent with the pattern shown in Fig. 5.2. Whether it can provide a satisfactory fit to the upper tail is the subject of debate.

Earnings in the United States

The earnings distribution in the United States has a number of similarities to that in Britain. The frequency distribution has a broadly similar shape to that shown in Fig. 5.2, being hump-like and skewed to the right. There is considerable variation within occupational groups: Lydall (1968, Ch. 4) concludes that not more than a quarter of the total variation in earnings could be attributed to differences in median earnings between occupations. The age profile is similar to that in Fig. 5.1. But there are also significant differences, and here we pick out two aspects for particular attention.

The first is the historical trend in occupational differentials. Historians have drawn attention to the divergent movements in the skilled/unskilled pay ratios in the United States and Western Europe. Whereas, at the outset of the nineteenth century, skilled labour had been relatively abundant, by the early 1900s the premium on skilled labour 'was extraordinarily high in America. Skills were very expensive even by West European standards' (Williamson and Lindert, 1980, p. 67). This may be seen from Table 5.4, where the skilled/unskilled ratio of pay was around double, which is significantly higher than the figures shown for the pre-First World War period in Britain in Table 5.1. Since that time, the differential in the United States has narrowed, with a particularly noticeable fall between the interwar and the post-Second World War periods.

The decline in differentials has also applied to certain professional groups. The time has passed since university professors earned four times the average wage. The series in Table 5.4 for professors shows the fall after the Second World War, although there is little apparent trend in recent years. The table also demonstrates the ability of one professional group — physicians — to achieve an improvement in its relative standing over the postwar period.

The second aspect concerns the age-earnings profile. As noted, such a hump-shaped pattern is found in the United States, but the shape appears to have 'twisted', as is illustrated by Table 5.5. According to Freeman,

The remarkable increase in the income advantage of older over younger male workers . . . appears to be primarily due to the changed age composition of the work force . . . because younger and older male workers are imperfect substitutes in production. (1980, p. 382)

TABLE 5.4

Earnings ratios in the

Ratio to earnings of

	1907–8*	1918–19*
Physicians	–	–
Associate university professors	4.5	2.2
Schoolteachers	1.5	0.9
Skilled workers	2.1	1.8
Skilled workers in building trades	1.9	1.8

* Where both years are given, the figures are averaged.
† Annual earnings of unskilled industrial workers, except for
  'skilled workers' where hourly wage rate for certain unskilled
  jobs are used, and 'skilled workers in building trades', where

TABLE 5.5

Average usual weekly earnings, full-time white workers

	1967	1975	1977
Ratio of the earnings of men aged 45–9 to those of men aged 20–4	1.27	1.57	1.60
Ratio of the earnings of men aged 45–9 to those of men aged 25–9	1.06	1.19	1.21

Source: Freeman (1979), Table 2

This introduces the issue of explaining the observed earnings distribution, to which we now turn.

The range of explanations

A wide range of theories has been put forward to explain the evidence described above. In many cases the theories are based on very different assumptions about the labour market, and as a result they are difficult to present within a common framework. It may none the less be useful to classify the different explanations according to the assumptions made about three main factors: the working of the labour market, the extent of differences between people, and the differences between jobs.

Given a perfectly functioning, competitive labour market, and all people and jobs being alike, there would be no differences in earnings. If there were any differentials, then everyone would flock into the

United States, 1907-1972

unskilled labourers†

1931-2*	1947-8*	1955-6*	1961-2*	1972-3*
4.3	4.7	5.4	6.4	7.7
				(1969)
3.9	2.2	2.0	2.0	1.9
1.9	1.1	1.2	1.3	1.3
1.8	1.6	1.4	1.4	1.5
1.8	1.4	1.3	1.2	1.2

average hourly wages of journeymen, helpers and labourers in the building trades are used.

Source: Calculated from Williamson and Lindert (1980), Appendix D

higher-paying positions and equality would be restored through the competitive process. If all people were alike, and if the labour market were perfectly competitive but jobs differed, then there would be earnings differentials such that everyone was indifferent about which job he did, i.e., there would be an equalization of 'net advantages'. As it was described by Adam Smith,

the whole of the advantages and disadvantages of the different employments of labour [must] be either perfectly equal or continually tending towards equality. [If] there was any employment evidently either more or less advantageous than the rest, so many people would crowd into it in the one case, and so many desert it in the other, that its advantages would soon return to the level of other employment. (1776, pp. 76-7)

Such equalization could apply to aspects such as the degree of responsibility, the pleasantness or otherwise of the work, the danger or health hazards, and the social prestige. The dimension that has probably received most attention, however, is the training required for a particular job, and it is this that provides the basis for the human capital theory discussed in the next section.

This picture of the equalization of net advantages is clearly unrealistic. A person might prefer to be a policeman than a porter but fail to pass the physical examination; he might prefer to be a surgeon than a butcher, but lack the money required to support himself through medical school. Theories that emphasize differences between people — differences in abilities and differences in opportunities — are discussed in Sections 5.3 and 5.4.

Finally, the assumption of a perfect competition may well seem out of place in a world where wages appear to be determined largely by negotiations between trade unions and employers' federations and an increasing degree of government intervention, and where the working of the market is impeded by frictions of all kinds. In the next chapter we examine in greater detail the institutions of the labour market and the role played by factors such as status and custom.

5.2 Human capital theory

The human capital theory is of old vintage, Adam Smith having recognized that one major application of the principle of equal net advantages was that 'a man educated at the expense of much labour or time . . . must be expected to earn over and above the usual wages . . . the whole expenses of his education, with at least the ordinary profits of an equally valuable capital'. It is only relatively recently, however, that the implications of this approach have been spelled out, as in the work of Mincer (1958) and Becker (1964). These authors have tried in particular to see how far human capital (education and training) on its own can explain earnings differentials. In order to focus on this aspect, the human capital theory in its simplest form makes strong assumptions about other aspects. The labour market is assumed to be competitive and perfectly functioning, so that a person can have a free choice of his occupation: if he wishes to train for a particular job, then there are no barriers to his doing so. Second, everyone has the same opportunities. There are no environmental inequalities, such as differences in intelligence, physical skills, or in home background. Everyone has access to the capital market on the same terms.

If these assumptions are satisfied, then, as Adam Smith argued, the occupations requiring a longer period of training have to provide a correspondingly higher level of earnings if they are to attract people. In order to bring this out more clearly, let us make a number of simplifying assumptions.

(1) Training involves postponement of entry into the labour force (i.e., there is no on-the-job training), where the number of years of training beyond the minimum school-leaving age is denoted by S.

(2) Everyone works for the same number (N) years after completing his training, so that those with longer training retire at an older age, and no one dies before reaching retirement.

(3) There are no costs of education apart from forgone earnings, and there are no student grants.

(4) The earnings of a person who has S years of education, denoted by

E_S, are assumed constant over his working life, and there is assumed to be no unemployment.

(5) All jobs are alike in every feature except the length of training required, and there is no intrinsic benefit from education.

These assumptions may be summarized in terms of the stylized lifetime for a person with S years of training:

Income =   zero E_S

├─────────────────┼──────────────────────┤
0 Training S Work $N+S$
↑   ↑
Minimum school-leaving   Retire
    age

The decision to undergo training involves the person's borrowing to finance his living expenses for that period, and it is assumed that he can borrow (from parents, from the bank, etc.) as much as he requires at a constant interest rate, r per cent, per annum. Given this, and the fact that all jobs are otherwise alike, he chooses the length of his education according to the stream of earnings desired over his lifetime, discounted at this interest rate. (The stream has to be discounted since earnings at a later date are worth less than those at an earlier date.) This means that, for a person to be indifferent between leaving school at the minimum legal age and training for a job requiring S years of education, the present discounted value of earnings must be equal. In the highly simplified case we are considering, this condition reduces to the formula (Mincer, 1970, p. 7):

Earnings with S years of training = Earnings with no training

$$\times (1 + r)^S$$

Postponing entry into the labour force means that earnings are delayed, and if the person has to borrow at an annual cost of r per cent, then E_S has to be higher to allow for this. The differential has to be larger, the longer the training period and the higher the interest rate. Writing E_S for earnings with S years of training, and E_0 for earnings with no training, the condition is

$$E_s = E_0 (1 + r)^s. \qquad (1)$$

Or , if we take logarithms of both sides and use the approximation that $\log (1 + r) = r$ (where r is small):

$$\log E_s = \log E_0 + rS. \qquad (2)$$

Coupled with the assumption that everyone faces the same opportunities, this condition determines the distribution of earnings. If the condition did not hold, then everyone would flock into, or out of, jobs requiring training. On the basis of these strong assumptions, we have therefore a theory of the explanation of earnings differentials: earnings are directly related to the training required. There are different jobs, with associated differences in training requirements, and this means that we observe dispersion in the distribution of earnings. But everyone is equally well off in terms of the lifetime present value of earnings.

The human capital theory is not however confined to the treatment of education, and a principal concern has been the analysis of on-the-job training (relaxation of the first simplifying assumption). As it is put by Mincer,

An important source of earnings differentials among people who have completed the same level of education is age or the amount of time already spent in employment. . . The profiles do not automatically follow a particular level of schooling. Their shapes differ among people even at the same level of schooling and they are subject to explanation by the same human capital framework in which investments continue in the labour market after completion of schooling (in Atkinson (1980b), p. 106).

In seeking to implement this approach to on-the-job training, we face the difficulty that such post-school investments are typically unobservable. This may be seen in terms of equation (2), where the years of education are in effect the investment, and we are concerned with the rate of return, r, to this investment. To this right-hand side, we now want to add the investment in on-the-job training and its associated rate of return, which may well be different. But the extent of this investment is not readily measured. Mincer and others have typically therefore made assumptions about the time path of investment. For example, the assumption that it declines at a steady rate as more time is spent in the labour force means that we obtain a quadratic expression in work experience (denoted by EXP) on the right-hand side of the earnings equation:

$$\log E_s = \log E_0 + rS + a\,EXP - b\,EXP^2. \tag{3}$$

On this account, earnings are likely first to rise and then to decline as the training becomes obsolete and investment is reduced. In this way, it may capture the hump-shape pattern of earnings that we have observed, although it should be noted that age and experience are not identical. At the age of thirty, Roger Smith, who left school at sixteen, has fourteen years of work experience, compared with only nine years' experience for Christopher Brown who completed a degree before starting work. We examine below the empirical evidence and its relation to equation (3).

The other simplifying assumptions may also be relaxed. The second assumption, about the expected working career, can be modified to allow for different retirement dates and for the possibility of death in service (in which case the person is assumed to base his decision on the actuarial value of future earnings). Where people retire at broadly the same age, so that the working life for the highly trained is shorter, then the differential will have to be correspondingly greater.

The third assumption — that there are neither costs associated with training nor student grants — can be relaxed by taking account of fees, books, travel, and other costs specifically associated with the course of education. To the extent that there are such additional costs, the required differential is increased. (It should be noted that ordinary living costs should not be taken into account, since these are incurred whether or not the person is in education.) Student grants work in the opposite direction, since they reduce the cost of education and provide some limited compensation for forgone earnings.

The assumption about the pattern of earnings over a person's lifetime is clearly unrealistic, but it can be modified. In the same way, an expected rate of unemployment can be introduced, where this rate is likely to vary with the level of training. A person with low education is more likely to suffer unemployment, and this factor narrows the differential required to make people indifferent between two occupations. It is also possible to incorporate uncertainty about the level of earnings. Adam Smith suggested that this uncertainty was greater for occupations requiring more training: 'Put your son apprentice to a shoemaker, there is little doubt of his learning to make a pair of shoes, but send him to study the law, it is at least twenty to one if ever he makes such a proficiency as will enable him to live by the business' (1776, p. 82). However, it is not clear that today earnings are more uncertain in jobs requiring more training. Finally, account can be taken of non-pecuniary features of different occupations. Casual observation would suggest that the more highly trained occupations are *on average* more attractive in terms of aspects such as safety, prestige, control over working environment, etc. This is further reinforced when one takes into consideration the fact that people may enjoy education to some extent as a consumption good.

To sum up, the human capital theory leads to the prediction that earnings differentials depend on the degree of training required, in terms both of formal education and of on-the-job training, and are just sufficient to compensate for the costs of this training, taking into account length of working life, uncertainty of earnings, unemployment, and non-pecuniary benefits.

Empirical evidence: cross-section studies

The human capital model, in its simplest form, leads to a predicted relation between earnings, education and years of work experience (as represented by equation (3)). It appears natural therefore to begin testing its empirical validity by fitting this equation to observed data of the kind described above. (Unfortunately, we cannot use the *New Earnings Survey* in Britain, since it contains no information on education.)

Suppose, for example, that the distribution of schooling were independent of age. Then, if we were to plot the logarithm of earnings against the number of years of education, we should expect to find a straight-line relationship' for every further year of schooling, the logarithm of earnings should increase by r. The evidence for the United States for the earnings of white men in non-farm employment in 1959 shows a clear positive relationship of this kind (Mincer, 1974, p. 46).

The test just described, while straightforward, is open to many objections. Even leaving on one side the effects of differential ability and other factors discussed in the next section, there is no reason to expect the age composition of the population to be the same at all educational levels. With the spread of education the lower educational groups contain disproportionately large numbers of older people. To the extent that the pattern of earnings varies systematically with age, this will introduce a bias into the results. These issues have been discussed at length by Mincer (1974), using the data for the United States in 1959, standardized at a comparable level of experience. On the basis of the earnings of men eight to ten years after they left school, Mincer estimated that differences in education explain about one-third of the variation in the logarithm of annual earnings for that group. Extrapolating to the distribution as a whole, he concluded that schooling accounts for a quarter of the variation for all age groups, and that this may be higher if allowance is made for the quality of education.

Mincer draws attention to the superior explanatory power of the human capital equation when compared with statistical studies, which employ a large number of explanatory variables on a largely *ad hoc* basis. At the same time, it should be noted that the direct contribution of education is small, and that a major role is played by the experience variable, which could be given a number of interpretations. Also, the explanation of 25 per cent of the variation is still consistent with considerable dispersion of earnings among those with the same education and experience: the mean difference would in fact be 87 per cent of that for the population as a whole. A striking, if rather exceptional, illustration of this is given by Rees (1973, p. 196): the distribution of earnings in 1967 of the Princeton class of 1942. These people had spent four years at the same college, and were about the same age, yet the spread was such that the upper quartile earned over one and a half times the median.

Cross-section evidence for Britain has been analysed by Psacharopoulos and Layard (1979), using information on men interviewed in the General Household Survey in 1972. They present a variety of results, but the following equation may provide some insight (Psacharopoulos and Layard, 1979, Table IV, equation 4.2):

$$\log E_S = 1.692 + 0.085\,S + 0.070\,EXP - 0.012\,(EXP)^2. \qquad (4)$$

To interpret what this means, let us consider the position of the (hypothetical) Roger Smith, aged 30 with eleven years of education (he left school at 16), and Christopher Brown, of the same age, with sixteen years of education. The coefficient on S means that Christopher has an advantage of

$$0.085 \times S = 0.425.$$

Taking anti-logarithms (since this relates to the logarithm of earnings), we find that he is predicted, other things being equal, to earn 53 per cent more than Roger. This represents the return to staying on at school and going to university. But other things are not equal, since Roger has five years more experience of work (all this assumes that neither has been unemployed), and at the beginning of the work career this gives him an advantage. The experience effect for Roger is

$$0.070 \times 14 - 0.0012 \times 14^2 = 0.7448$$

whereas that for Christopher is

$$0.070 \times 9 - 0.0012 \times 9^2 = 0.5328.$$

Taking all these elements together, the net advantage to Christopher is 24 per cent (again we have to take the anti-logarithm). As time goes on, the work experience effect begins to decline. The maximum point can in fact be calculated from equation (3) as $a/2b$, and using the values from the empirically estimated equation (4) this can be seen to be

$$\frac{0.070}{2 \times 0.0012} = 29.2 \text{ years}$$

i.e., for Roger Smith it is at age 45.

The implications for the distribution of earnings

The estimated earnings relationships have been used to assess the contribution of different elements to the observed earnings differences. From equation (3), for example, we can calculate the variance of the logarithms of earnings (one of the inequality measures that has been employed — see Chapter 3). Thus, with the assumption that r is the same for everyone, and ignoring the square term in experience, we can see from (3) that the variance depends on the variance of years of education, the variance of years of experience, the covariance between them, and the variance of individual effects ($\log E_0$). This approach has been followed by Chiswick and Mincer (1972), who allow r to vary across the population, although they assume that it is uncorrelated with years of education (see Marin and Psacharopoulos, 1976). Since they are using data on annual incomes, they include weeks worked, in this case allowing for its possible correlation with S and EXP. They then seek to relate the observed changes in income inequality in the United States, 1949–69, to changes in these elements. For example, the average level of schooling had risen by two years over the period, and the variance had fallen. They conclude that, 'although greatly oversimplified, the model achieves high explanatory power in the analysis of annual-income inequality' (Chiswick and Mincer, 1972, p. S56).

It should be noted that the variable considered by Chiswick and Mincer (1972) is annual *income*, and that the population includes not just employees but also the self-employed. It is therefore rather different from the distributions of earnings discussed in the first section of this chapter. This choice was forced on the authors because an annual time series of the distribution of earnings was not available, but it is important to bear in mind that the human capital theory cannot be expected to apply without modification to self-employment income or to income from capital. The same criticism applies to the widely-quoted study *Inequality* by Jencks (1972).

The estimated earnings relationship has also been used to predict the effect of changes in educational policy. A good example is provided by the study of Blaug, Dougherty and Psacharopoulos (1982) of the effect of raising the school-leaving age in Britain from 15 to 16 in 1972. Using data from the General Household Survey in the way described above, they calculated the effect of increasing S by one year for those affected (and of reducing experience accordingly). They showed that the predicted reduction in the variance of the logarithm of earnings is quite substantial within age groups, but that the overall degree of dispersion may be increased, since the differences *between* age groups are intensified.

Such exercises are however open to a number of objections. First, there is the question as to how equations such as (3) should be interpreted. We have derived this equation as an equilibrium property that has to hold for people to be indifferent between the choice of different earnings streams. It does not follow that this is a structural relationship, such that the variables on the right-hand side can be varied at will (as with the simulation of the raising of the school-leaving age). Indeed, the interpretation given earlier was that there is a structure of jobs, each requiring a specified education level, and on this view it is the *structure of jobs* that determines the distribution of earnings. To use an athletic analogy, there is a fixed structure of prizes, and changing the qualifications of the competitors does not lead to any change in the outcome. This is of course an extreme view, and in Chapter 6 we explore further the demand side of the market.

It would be possible to give another interpretation. It could be that education makes workers more efficient, and that the resulting 'efficiency units' of labour are perfectly substitutable in production; for example, doubling the educational experience of the population may double their productive efficiency. In terms of the athletic analogy, we have a situation like the award of swimming certificates, where it depends not on the number of qualified swimmers but simply on how far one person has swum. However, in this case, as has been noted by Rosen,

if all workers were exactly alike, everyone would rationally stop school at the same age. Both the variance of observed schooling and of earnings among members of the labour force would be zero. [In this case] observed earnings and schooling inequality fundamentally are due to inequality in the distributions of 'abilities' and school financial constraints ('opportunity'). Inequality in earnings cannot be attributed to inequality in the distribution of schooling *per se*. (1977, p. 12)

We have therefore to consider the implications of differential abilities and opportunities, and this is the subject of Sections 5.3 and 5.4.

A second major objection concerns the use of cross-section data on earnings rather than evidence on the lifetime experience of individual cohorts. Since the major contribution of the human capital approach is described by Mincer as 'the shift from analysis of current earnings of groups to complete lifetime earnings profiles' (1979), this is an aspect we need to consider further.

Empirical evidence: career earnings and cohort effects

The calculation of lifetime present discounted values of earnings in different occupations has a long history, pre-dating the human capital literature. Particular reference must be made to the pioneering study by Friedman and Kuznets (1945) of earnings in the professions in the United States. They began by observing that in the 1930s there was a difference of some 85 to 180 per cent between the average incomes of professional and non-professional workers in the same community who had been in the labour force for the same number of years. They then proceeded to calculate the differential that would have been required to compensate the professional workers for the longer training required, which was on average seven years. After allowing for the specific costs of training (tuition fees, books, special equipment, etc.), for the longer life expectancy of professional workers, and for an annual cost of borrowing of 4 per cent they estimated that the required differential would be in the range 55-70 per cent, or considerably less than that observed. They concluded that 'the actual difference between the incomes of professional and non-professional workers seems decidedly larger than the difference that would compensate for the extra capital investment required' (1945, p. 84), and went on to say that:

there is nothing surprising about this finding. It is clear that young men are, in fact, not equally free to choose a professional or non-professional career . . . First, the professions require a different level of ability than other pursuits; second, the economic and social stratification of the population leaves only limited segments really free to enter the professions. (p. 88)

In the comparison of the present values of earnings in different occupations, the choice of the interest rate to apply could make a substantial difference, and the Friedman-Kuznets study has been criticized on the grounds that the rate of 4 per cent was unreasonably low. (One important question is whether the interest rate is specified in money or real terms. If we assume that earnings are fixed in real terms, then it is the real cost of borrowing that is relevant, so that 4 per cent means a money rate of interest of 4 per cent plus the rate of price increase.) The more recent study by Mennemeyer (1978) compared the net present value of a medical education against other professional alternatives in the United States. Compared, for example, with a first degree in engineering, medical education offered an advantage of 38 per cent at a discount rate of 4 per cent and of 22 per cent at a discount rate of 10 per cent. When account was taken of differences in the hours worked, 'physicians' earnings become roughly equal to those of dentists and lawyers, but remain clearly superior to those of the other professions considered' (Mennemeyer, 1978, p. 87).

These calculations have a lifetime perspective, but are typically based on cross-section data. As such they are open to the criticism that they do not allow for differences between cohorts or for the actual time path of individual earnings.

The need to adjust for cohort differences arising from the growth of real earnings is clearly recognized by Becker: 'the cohort of college graduates aged 25 in 1939 received a higher real income at age 35 than did the cohort aged 35 in 1939' (1964, p. 139). He illustrates the point with data drawn from the decennial censuses (although he warns about problems of comparibility), which show the income of cohorts in the case of college graduates (see Table 5.6). The cross-section picture is seen by reading down a column. This suggests a less steep age profile

TABLE 5.6
Income of cohort, college graduates

Age of cohort in 1939	1939	1949	1958
25–34	$5 155	$ 8 960	$12 269
35–44	$8 386	$11 543	$10 966
45–54	$9 430	$10 732	retired
55–60	$8 338	retired	retired

Source: Becker (1964) Table 19

than is actually experienced (reading across): those aged 25 in 1939 earned $8960 when they reached the age of 35 in 1949, compared with $8386 earned by those aged 35 in 1939. For the cohort aged 45–54 in 1939 the earnings profile carried on rising, rather than declining, as indicated by the cross-section snapshot picture.

For Becker, writing in the early 1960s it was natural to stress the secular growth of earnings. More recently, attention has been paid to the effects of different cohort size, associated with the entry into the labour force of the children of the postwar baby boom. In an article subtitled 'The baby boom babies' financial bust', Welch examines the changes in earnings over the period 1967–75 and finds that the increase in the size of the cohort had a depressing effect on wages, being typically greatest at the point of entry. (This of course is related to the 'twist' in the age–earnings profile referred to earlier.) The predicted reduction in weekly earnings for new entrants was 8 per cent for high school graduates and 13 per cent for college graduates (Welch, 1979, p. S91).

The study of the average earnings by cohorts does not allow for the variability of individual earnings around that average. To the extent that educational decisions are based on the expectation of earnings, this may be a reasonable procedure (although one would expect the degree of variation to be a factor). But we still need to allow for movement in and out of the relevant group. This is most obvious in the case of individual occupations. A person may train as a doctor but not practise, or he may practise only for part of his working career. To the extent that 'survival' is related to success, a calculation based only on those who continue may overstate the returns to training. For this purpose we need individual life histories, and evidence of this kind is described in Section 5.3.

Assessment

Education and training are only part of the human capital theory, and it is clear that they can explain only part of the observed dispersion in earnings. It is not simply a question of equalizing net advantages; indeed, if it were then, as Cannan pointed out in 1914, 'we should find well-to-do parents in doubt whether to make their sons civil engineers or naval stokers, doctors or road-sweepers' (1914, p. 207). Today, education explains only part of the dispersion of individual earnings, and people with the same schooling and experience may well be paid very different amounts. One reason for this, as Friedman and Kuznets observed, is that the simple human capital approach leaves out important elements: differences in individual abilities and background, and the fact that the labour market does not necessarily operate in the smooth, perfectly competitive way posited.

5.3 Unequal opportunities and abilities

Imperfect capital markets and family background

In the exposition given above, it was assumed that everyone could borrow as much as he wished at a given interest rate, a situation that no student is likely to regard as realistic. It is, in fact, highly unlikely that the capital market will operate in this perfect manner; especially in the case of education, the terms of borrowing depend on how much is involved and on who the borrower is. Difficulties in borrowing arise particularly because human capital cannot be held as a collateral, since that would be equivalent to a person's selling himself into slavery, so that the lender has no security, as he would have if he held the title to a house or a claim against other physical assets.

The effects of such imperfections are likely to work in two ways. First, any one individual probably faces a rising cost of borrowing the larger the amount required. This means that to finance a further year of schooling he has to pay more than before and hence that the earnings differential must be enough to give a higher rate of return − see the cost of borrowing curve in Fig. 5.3. Initially, a person is likely to borrow from parents or relatives, and the cost is relatively low; he may then begin to borrow from the bank by running up an overdraft, which would involve a higher interest rate; and finally, he may be unable to borrow any more at all, as shown in the diagram by the line's becoming vertical. The second aspect of imperfect capital markets is that different people are likely to face different conditions of borrowing. A person coming from a wealthy family is probably able to borrow more from his parents and is regarded as more credit-worthy by banks and other lending institutions. Children from poor families may get little help from their parents (they may be under pressure to leave school as soon as possible) and are much less able to borrow on the market (although in the United States there are tuition programmes designed to help students from

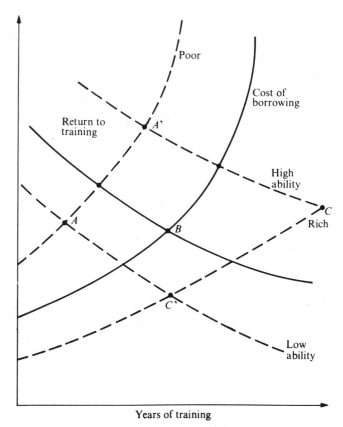

Fig. 5.3 Inequality of ability and opportunity

low-income families.) As a result, there is a range of cost of borrowing for different people, such as that illustrated in Fig. 5.3.

Inequality in access to borrowing, and hence in access to education, may lead to earnings differentials in excess of those predicted by the simple human capital theory. Suppose that the annual cost of borrowing to go on from university to three years at medical school is 15 per cent for a person from a poor family, compared with 5 per cent for a person with a wealthy father. The earnings differential required to make this attractive to the person from a wealthy background, leaving on one side any government grant received or other income, is (from equation (1)) $(1 + 0.05)^3 = 1.16$, or 16 per cent more than the earnings of an ordinary university graduate. The person from a poor background, however, would require a differential of $(1 + 0.15)^3 = 1.52$, so that the actual differential could lie anywhere between 16 per cent and 52 per cent without it being the case that poor people would flock into medical schools. The existence of high rates of return to training for many occupations is consistent with barriers to entry of this form, although it may also be explained by other factors, such as differences in ability.

The advantages stemming from family background may operate more generally. First of all, parents may influence the educational performance of their children by routes other than the cost of borrowing. Parents may play an important role in motivating their children to succeed at school and in informing them about educational opportunities. Where entry to higher education is limited, parents may be instrumental in securing access. It is widely reported that this is the case with the medical profession and with apprenticeships to certain trades, such as printing.

Second, children from a favoured family background may have an advantage when it comes to entering better paid jobs. This would be a *direct* effect of family background, in contrast to the *indirect* effect via education. It may be that parents actively seek to obtain jobs for their children, or that, as Bowles has argued, the recruitment policies of firms are such that:

children of parents occupying a given position in the occupational hierarchy grow up in homes where child-rearing methods and perhaps even the physical surroundings tend to develop personality characteristics appropriate to adequate job performance. (1972, p. S225)

Other writers have argued that such effects should be brought within the rubric of human capital:

it would be hard to argue that employers [are willing to] pay workers for having had richer families. The families' income must have been used to provide an attribute – such as higher quality schooling, or health – which increases productivity. (Leibowitz, 1977, p. 29)

It is of course possible to say that the fact that one's father played golf with the boss represented human capital formation, but there is an attendant risk that the concept is reduced to vacuity.

Unequal abilities

It has long been believed that earnings are related to differential abilities, where these include physical characteristics (such as strength, energy, and dexterity), intellectual capacity, and personal qualities. Many authors were indeed puzzled by the fact that earnings did not follow the normal curve according to which abilities were thought to be distributed among the human population. Pigou, for example, argued that 'there is clear evidence that the physical characters of human beings – and considerable evidence that their mental characters' are distributed according to the normal curve (which he described as being shaped like a cocked hat), and that as a result 'we should expect that, if, as there is reason to think, people's capacities are distributed on a plan of this kind, their incomes will be distributed in the same way. Why is not this expectation realized?' (1952, p. 650).

The first explanation of Pigou's paradox is that abilities may not, in fact, be distributed according to the normal curve. While physical measurements such as height satisfy this relationship, there is no necessary reason why the abilities relevant to determining productive capacity should follow the same pattern: 'there is at present really no such thing as *the* distribution of ability: the distribution depends upon the measuring rod used and cannot be defined independently of it' (Mayer, 1960, p. 194). The arbitrary nature of the distribution of scores in the case of intelligence tests is brought out by a hypothetical example given by Mayer. Suppose that the test consists of ten questions, each involving the addition of two numbers. Most people are likely to score close to 100 per cent on such a test. On the other hand if the ten questions involved solving differential equations, most of the population would score zero. By varying the ratio of easy and difficult questions, we can get almost any distribution that we like. The fact that most actual IQ tests lead to a distribution of scores that follows the normal distribution does not necessarily tell us anything, therefore, about the distribution of abilities; it may simply reflect the way in which the tests have been constructed.

A second explanation of the Pigou paradox is that the relationship between abilities and earnings is more complex than he supposed. The productivity of a worker may be related to a number of different dimensions of ability. If these operate multiplicatively, it may then be that output has an approximately lognormal distribution, even if the individual attributes are themselves distributed normally. Roy (1950) gives a number of examples, although these are rather specialized (for example thirty-five girls packing boxes of chocolates). The role of different types of ability in securing occupational success is discussed by Hartog (1976), who refers to the study by Thorndike and Hagen (1959), following up more than 10 000 men tested by the US Air Force. They found certain systematic connections between occupations and types of ability. For example, lawyers scored high on the 'verbal' dimension and engineers high on the 'quantitative' dimension. To the extent that people allocate themselves to the job for which they are best suited, the resulting distribution of earnings – even though proportional to that particular dimension of ability – may be quite different from the distribution of

① ridiculous argument!
Test scores for floating ability = 0% = 100% standard

abilities. Houthakker (1974) illustrates how, with only two dimensions, an L-shaped distribution for abilities can lead to a hump-shape pattern like that in Fig. 5.2.

Finally, the abilities relevant to the determination of earning power may take different forms from those usually measured in tests, certainly from those that concentrate on cognitive and related skills. As Jencks (1972) has noted, it may be the ability to 'persuade a customer that he wants a larger car' that is significant. It may be a question of personality and character. Lydall has stressed the importance of the 'D-factor (where D stands for drive, dynamism, doggedness, or determination)' (1976, p. 27). Moreover, as has been suggested earlier, these characteristics may be related to family background.

Abilities and education

The possession of abilities interacts with the acquisition of training. This may be seen to affect the operation of the model discussed earlier in two respects. First, the educational decision involves not simply a choice by the individual but also his or her acceptance by the educational institution. Entry into higher education is usually contingent on successful completion of secondary or high school, and graduation from college or university depends on the student's passing examinations and other hurdles. A person with higher intellectual abilities is more likely to be successful in this process, and hence we should expect the return to further training to be higher, other things being equal, for him than for someone with a lower level of intellectual ability who is less likely to pass examinations.

The second way in which differential ability affects the human capital theory is through a direct link between ability and earnings. Irrespective of its contribution to educational success, higher ability may raise the earnings of a person once he has qualified, more able lawyers earning more than less able, and so on. This does not, however, necessarily make education more attractive to the person with higher ability, since it may also mean that he would earn more if he did not train. The opportunity cost is also higher. If ability enters multiplicatively, so that one person would earn twice as much as another whether they were carpenters or accountants, then it would not affect the decision about the length of schooling (both sides of equation (1) would be double for the first person). It has, none the less, usually been assumed (e.g., by Becker, 1967) that ability and education are complementary: i.e., that the effect of ability on earnings increases with the level of education, taking account of both the factors mentioned, is higher for a person with higher ability. In Fig. 5.3 this is shown by the position of the dashed lines, the one for a person with high ability being above that for a person with low ability. (The downward slope of all the 'return to training' curves is based by Becker (1967) on the limited length of human life and the increasing cost of time.)

The combined effect of unequal opportunity (cost of borrowing) and unequal abilities is shown in Fig. 5.3. The nature of the observed relationship depends on the relationship between ability and access to borrowing. If there is a positive correlation (ease of borrowing and high ability go together), then the observed pattern would be that marked ABC in the diagram, with the wealthy/high-ability group being concentrated in occupations requiring considerably more education. In contrast to this, if there were a negative correlation, and the children of poor families were on average more able than children from rich families, then the pattern would be $A'B'C'$, with much less marked differences in the years of education, but large differences in the rate of return.

It has been argued by Chiswick that the correlation is probably positive (i.e., the same person is likely to have high ability and to be able to borrow easily):

First, if ability is related to genetic factors it is reasonable to expect a positive correlation between the parents' and a child's 'genetic ability'. Since parental ability tends to be positively related to parental wealth, there would be a negative correlation between a child's ability and the marginal cost of funds. Second, wealthier parents presumably invest more in the non-schooling characteristics of their children [who may thus] appear to have a higher level of ability when they approach school-leaving age. Third, it is easier for youths of high ability to obtain . . . scholarships from schools. (1969, p. 499)

There are a number of points here with which issue can be taken, particularly the statements about the hereditary component. It is not clear, for example, that parental ability tends to be positively related to parental wealth, especially where the latter has been inherited. However, on balance Chiswick's conclusion may well be correct, and the positive relationship observed between ability and years of education provides some indirect support for this position (Mincer, 1974).

A more complete framework

There remain a number of important elements to be incorporated, but the discussion of this section has led to a more complete framework for the analysis of individual earnings. This is summarized schematically in Fig. 5.4. The theory considered in Section 5.2 was concerned with the link between education and earnings, as indicated by the heavy line. In this section we have introduced the influence of family background, which may act indirectly via the length of education or directly on earnings. Similarly, ability may enhance earnings prospects directly, or

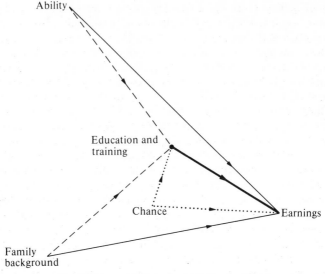

Fig. 5.4 Factors influencing individual earnings.

or it may do so indirectly through the interaction with education. (The indirect links are shown by dashed lines.) Finally, we have to remember that at all stages of the process the outcome may be influenced by chance events. A person in the top 1 per cent of the earnings distribution may have no superior abilities, may have left school at the earliest possible age, and may have no family advantages – he (or she) just may have happened to be in the right place at the right time.

5.4 Empirical studies of earnings, ability and family background

There have been a large number of studies of different aspects of the earnings process summarized in Fig. 5.4, mostly using data from the United States. The form of these studies has varied, depending on the primary concerns of the investigator and on the data available, the latter being an important consideration since the requirements are demanding and measurement and other errors are potentially serious.

Earnings and ability

A major strand has been concern with the relation between ability and earnings, and the way in which this may confound the conclusions drawn about the effect of education. Seen in terms of the triangle relating these variables in the diagram, it may be that we are observing a relationship between education and earnings in part because both are related to ability.

In the previous section, we stressed the multi-dimensioned nature of 'ability', and it is unfortunate that much of the empirical work has concentrated on performance in intelligence tests, referred to as 'measured IQ'. Not only are the tests themselves open to question as measures of intellectual skills, but also they capture only one dimension. However, researchers typically have to rely on data collected by others, not least because they are often seeking to relate *current* earnings to abilities measured earlier in the person's life.

The evidence about measured IQ and earnings suggests in fact that the direct influence of measured IQ is relatively unimportant. At first sight this is not the case, since there appears to be an association between intelligence and earnings. This is illustrated in the top part of Table 5.7, which is taken from a study by Bowles and Gintis (1973) of the earnings of non-black males aged 25–34 from a non-farm background in the United States in 1962, where 'economic success' is based on an individual's income and an index of occupational prestige. The association between IQ and economic success is portrayed in Table 5.7 in terms of the differing chances of people in different IQ classes entering different deciles of economic success: for example, a person in the top decile of IQ is three times as likely as the average person to appear in the top decile of success.

However, the immediate impression is misleading. If we were to draw up similar tables relating economic success to education or family background, they would show an even stronger association. The relationship between IQ and economic success may derive simply from the common association of both these variables with family background and the level of schooling. On the basis of a statistical analysis of the data, Bowles and Gintis argue that this is in fact so, and that the *independent* influence of IQ is very small. The magnitude of the effect, as estimated by them, is represented in the lower part of Table 5.7. Where education and social class background are held constant, a person in the top decile of IQ stands only a slightly higher chance than the average person of being in in the top decile of economic success. The results in Table 5.7 relate to the direct link between measured IQ and economic success. In order to measure the genetic contribution in full we need to allow for the indirect effect via years of schooling. The related work of Bowles and Nelson suggests, however, that this too is small. They conclude that 'the genetic inheritance of IQ is a relatively minor mechanism for the intergenerational transmission of economic and social status' (1974, p. 47).

The methods applied in arriving at the results described above are recognized by these authors to be subject to error and to a variety of interpretations. None the less, the same conclusion about the relative

TABLE 5.7

IQ and economic success, United States, 1962

	Economic success by deciles									
	1	2	3	4	5	6	7	8	9	10
Probability of attainment of different levels of economic success by individuals of differing levels of adult IQ										
Adult IQ by deciles:										
Top decile	30.9	19.2	13.8	10.3	7.7	5.7	4.1	2.8	1.7	0.6
Third decile from top	14.4	14.5	13.7	12.6	11.4	10.1	8.7	7.1	5.4	3.0
Third decile from bottom	4.4	8.0	8.7	10.0	11.0	11.7	12.3	12.6	12.4	10.9
Bottom decile	0.6	1.7	2.8	4.1	5.7	7.7	10.3	13.8	19.2	30.9
Probability of attainment of different levels of economic success by individuals of equal levels of education and social class background but differing levels of adult IQ										
Adult IQ by deciles:										
Top decile	14.1	12.4	11.4	10.7	10.1	9.5	9.0	8.4	7.7	6.6
Third decile from top	11.4	10.9	10.6	10.4	10.2	9.9	9.7	9.4	9.1	8.5
Third decile from bottom	8.5	9.1	9.4	9.7	9.9	10.2	10.4	10.6	10.9	11.4
Bottom decile	6.6	7.7	8.4	9.0	9.5	10.1	10.7	11.4	12.4	14.1

Example of use: Suppose two individuals have the same levels of education and social class background, but one is in the third decile from top in adult IQ, while the other is in the third decile from bottom in adult IQ. Then the first individual is 11.4/8.5 = 1.3 times as likely as the second to attain the top decile in economic success (lower part of the table, row 2, column 1, divided by row 3, column 1).

Note: It should be emphasized that this table has *not* been constructed by directly observing the decile position of different individuals. What the table brings out are the implications of the observed correlation between the variables in question. Rows do not necessarily add up to 100 per cent because of rounding.

Source: Bowles and Gintis (1973), Tables 1 and 4.

unimportance of the link between IQ and earnings has been reached in other studies: Griliches and Mason (1972), for example, found a low independent contribution of ability measured according to the rather different Armed Forces Qualification Test. This is particularly interesting in view of the rather different sample under study — post-Second World War veterans of the US armed forces — and because the test related to mature ability rather than childhood attributes. Another sample that has been intensively studied is that of Thorndike and Hagen (1959), referred to above, where the men had taken the Aviation Cadet Qualifying Examination. This group were traced at age 33 and again at age 47, and, interestingly, the estimated effects of test scores were similar at both ages. The advantage to a person in the top fifth of ability, relative to someone in the bottom fifth, was 14 per cent at age 33 and 19 per cent at age 47 (Taubman, 1975, p. 37).

In considering this evidence, several points need to be borne in mind. The first is that the data often relate to small and unrepresentative samples, and it may be dangerous to seek to extrapolate to the population as a whole. Second, key variables such as IQ and years of education may be measured with error. After all, respondents to surveys may misunderstand the question, or mis-remember the year in which they left school; they may write down the answer wrongly; or the interviewer may make a mistake. The answer may be incorrectly transcribed; there may be a key-punching error; the data-handling program may contain a bug. (A classic instance is the discovery by Coale and Stephan (1962) of a surprising number of widowed 14-year-old boys in the United States Census of Population for 1950, where they concluded that 'the number of white males under 17 reported in marital status categories other than "single" was determined more by cards punched in wrong columns than by actual marriages, divorces, or deaths of spouse' (p. 346).) Third, the IQ and other tests capture only limited dimensions of ability. This means that it may be better to recognize explicitly the 'unobservable' nature of ability, and to seek techniques of controlling for its impact. We return to this approach later, but before that we need to consider the role of family background.

Earnings and family background

To this point we have considered only part of the earnings process; and again it is possible that the omission of crucial variables — in this case family background — is causing us to draw misleading conclusions. The apparent relationship between education and earnings could be explained by their joint association with home advantage. Moreover, it is possible, although not shown in Fig. 5.4, that measured ability is affected by family background, and that part of the (weak) association with earnings may arise for this reason.

The effect of family background is not always taken into account (there is no treatment of it, for example, in Mincer, 1974), and the indicators that are employed are often little better than proxies. The reasons for this again lie in the paucity of suitable data. Where information has been collected on parental income, it is not always possible to acquire data on other aspects: for example, the follow-up study of families in York by Atkinson, Maynard and Trinder (1983) contains information on incomes of the parents in 1950 but nothing on ability.

The need to recognize the limitations of the available data is illustrated by the study of Bowles (1972). He uses fathers' education and occupation *as recalled by the respondent* as indicators of family background, which cannot be regarded as ideal, but he pays particular attention to the problems that arise from such imperfect measures and makes corrections for measurement error. From the results, he concludes that socio-economic background has a significant effect on earnings. This works through the higher educational level achieved: 'a high status individual's origins − at the eighty-ninth percentile of the composite social class distribution − are translated into an advantage of 4–6 years of schooling over the respondent whose low status origins place him at the eleventh percentile'; as well as through a direct effect on earnings: 'even in the evidently unlikely event that both individuals attained the same years of schooling, the individual of high status origins could expect to earn $1630 more annually' (1972, p. S240).

In Britain, a similar kind of indicator has been employed by Psacharopoulos (1977) in a study using the General Household Survey data described earlier. He finds a relatively modest effect of family background, but the indicator of background has severe shortcomings. It is based on recall, and no adjustment is made for the likely measurement error. The variable used is father's occupation, coded according to the Hope-Goldthorpe scale, but it is not evident that this is closely related to family economic status. As is shown by Phelps Brown (1977, Fig. 4.3) there is considerable variation in the earnings of occupations with the same value on this scale. Moreover, the 'ability' variable is the number of 'O' level or equivalent passes, which seems more likely to be related to educational achievement (or the date at which one was at school).

There seems little doubt that progress in this field is going to require the patient collection of data on a large scale. It is also going to involve refinement of the theoretical apparatus we bring to bear. Both of these aspects are illustrated by the recent studies of siblings.

The earnings of brothers and twins

The fact that we may not be able to observe key attributes of ability or family background suggests that we should seek to 'control' for their effect by considering people from the same family. This has led to the study of the earnings of brothers and − an even better control − of twins. That is, we cannot necessarily measure the benefit derived by Christopher Brown from his parents, but it may be reasonable to assume, as a first approximation, that it is close to the (also unobserved) benefit derived by his brother James.

The use of evidence on brothers is surveyed by Griliches (1979). In essence, the procedure involves taking the *difference* between the earnings of brothers and relating this to the difference of characteristics such as years of education. In the majority of studies reviewed by Griliches, including his own work, the coefficient on education obtained in this way is similar to that in the uncontrolled case. At the same time, he notes a number of problems that may arise with this more sophisticated use of data. In particular, the fact that one is considering a group of people more similar than the general population means that errors of measurement may acquire greater significance. Given that Christopher and James Brown come from the same family, we should not expect to find a large difference in years of education, and if 16 gets reported as 19 this may make a large difference to the findings.

If Christopher and James were twins, we should expect their background to be even more similar. What is more, we should expect that we could learn about the contribution of genetic relative to environmental factors by knowing whether they were identical or fraternal twins. These facts have been exploited in an extremely ingenious study by Behrman *et al.* (1980), which serves to illuminate the possibilities and the difficulties of this type of research.

First, there is the acquisition of the data. The starting point was the panel of white male twins born in the United States in 1917–27 maintained by the National Research Council (NRC) for medical and other research. This body worked back from the birth certificates for all recorded twins (in most but not all states, since some failed to co-operate) to the master file of the Veterans' Administration to obtain current addresses. This latter stage limited the sample to those cases where both served in the armed forces, reducing its size from 54 000 pairs to some 16 000. The authors, who recognized the potential of this source for economic research, mailed a questionnaire to some 12 500 sets of twins for whom addresses were available in 1974. Replies were received from 2468 matched pairs, and useable earnings data were available for 1926 pairs (of which 1019 were identical). This procedure, of which our description is necessarily abbreviated, demonstrates the skill and patience required to assemble a data set of this kind. It also warns us of the risks that the resulting sample may be unrepresentative − even of the population of twins. Out of the original cohort of twins of 54 000, only 3.6 per cent appear in the final analysis; and there are good reasons to expect the attrition to be non-random. Those who did not qualify for the forces, those who died before 1974, those who failed to respond to questionnaire, and those out of work are not likely to be drawn at random.

Second, there is the use of the data. The investigators have been particularly concerned with the separation of the effects of genetic inheritance of abilities from other aspects of family background. Taubman (1978b) concludes in one study that genetic endowment accounts for about 45 per cent, and family environment for about 12 per cent, of the variance in the logarithm of earnings. What is at stake may be seen from Fig. 5.4, if we interpret ability as genetic ability and solve out for the effects via education, so that we are left with genetic ability and family background (and chance) as determinants of earnings. Suppose that we begin with identical twins, who by definition have identical genetic endowments, and that we decompose the correlation between their earnings into G and B, where G denotes the genetic component and B the remainder (including the covariance). In Taubman's sample, the correlation between the earnings of identical twins is 0.54. If we now assume that the genetic component for non-identical (fraternal) twins is $\frac{1}{2}G$, as would be predicted by a simple genetic model, and that B is the same as for identical twins, then the correlation of their earnings is $\frac{1}{2}G + B$. Since the observed value for fraternal twins in Taubman's sample is 0.30, this implies that $G = 2 \times (0.54 - 0.30) = 0.48$ and that $B = 0.06$. The impact of the genetic factor appears to be large, and that of environment appears to be small.

This account of the twins' method is over-simplified, and Taubman bases his conclusions on a more sophisticated treatment; but it serves to bring out the key role played by the assumptions. In particular, the calculation is made possible by the assumption that both types of twin have the same degree of correlation of benefit from the family environment. There are some grounds for believing that the correlation may be higher for identical twins, if only because parents are reputed to treat them alike (for example, with respect to dress), and because they share more common experience. On the other hand, the extent of the difference is not easily measured, and we have in effect a further unobservable. That is, the use of twins' data allows us to control for the unobserved genetic component, but only at the expense of assumptions about other latent factors. The crucial nature of these assumptions for the conclusions is brought out by Goldberger, who concludes that, as far as the size of the genetic contribution is concerned, 'there is little hope for narrowing the range between 0 and 48 [per cent]' (1979, p. 341).

The second difficulty with the use of twins is that they represent a small, and rather special, group of the population. In the studies of genetic heritability of intelligence, the observations on twins have been found to be out of line with those of the kinship correlations (Goldberger, 1978a). The findings should therefore be seen in conjunction with those for other groups. We have referred to brothers. Another example is provided by data on fathers and sons, such as that collected by Atkinson, Maynard and Trinder (1983). Using a simple model similar to that described above, Atkinson (1980c) shows how a father–son correlation of 0.47 (around that observed in Britain), together with a correlation of 0.30 for brothers, would imply a genetic contribution of 26 per cent, compared with 48 per cent obtained for twins. This again brings out the range of possible findings.

The study of family data has enriched our knowledge about the processes at work, but it has also two important lessons for the analysis of earnings. The first is that we have little knowledge as to how the family behaves as an institution with regard to the determination of earnings potential. This aspect has been emphasized by Becker (1981), who discusses the allocations by parents of resources to their children. Do they spread them equally? Or do they seek to compensate for genetic disadvantage? Or do they accentuate differences in the inherited abilities by giving the more able children better education and opportunities? The second lesson is that we have been attributing the common background component of brothers to the family, but it is also the case that they share the same race, the same culture, the same neighbourhood, and (often) the same school and the same friends. It could be that what we are capturing is the advantage, or disadvantage, of growing up in a particular neighbourhood or of entering a particular local labour market. This raises questions of the wider structure of the labour market, which are discussed in the next chapter.

Notes on sources and further reading

This and the next chapter draw heavily on the work of labour economics. There are a number of textbooks on this subject, including Fisher (1971), Fleisher (1970), Phelps Brown (1962), Rees (1973), Freeman (1979) and Hunter and Mulvey (1981). Books specifically focusing on the distribution of earnings are Lydall (1968) and Phelps Brown (1977), both of which are strongly recommended. A useful collection of readings is contained in King (1980).

The evidence about the distribution of earnings in a number of countries is summarized by Lydall (1968). For Britain, see Thatcher (1968) and Routh (1980). For the United States, see Henle and Ryscavage (1980) and Freeman (1980). The lognormal and Pareto distributions are described by Lydall (1968) and Cowell (1977). For an application to data for Britain, see Harrison (1981). Information about the earnings of different cohorts and panel data is surveyed by Hart (1981).

The human capital theory is clearly set out in Mincer's original article (1958), and in his subsequent contributions (1970, 1974, 1979), the latter being reprinted in Atkinson (1980b). The work of Becker is contained in (1964) and (1967). A 'slightly jaundiced' survey (his sub-title) of the human capital literature is provided by Blaug (1976). Other useful critiques include Lydall (1976), Rosen (1977) (which is reprinted in part in Atkinson, 1980b), and Sattinger (1980, Ch. 2). The role of ability and family background are discussed by Bowles (1972, 1973), Bowles and Gintis (1973) and Bowles and Nelson (1974), for one perspective, and by Liebowitz (1977), Hill and Stafford (1974, 1977), and Becker (1981) for a rather different one. In Britain, see Psacharopoulos (1977) and Papanicolaou and Psacharopoulos (1979). The study by Atkinson, Maynard and Trinder (1983) uses British data on the earnings of fathers and sons to investigate a number of different aspects of inter-generational mobility. General treatments of the determinants of earnings, making reference to the empirical evidence, include Jencks (1972), Jencks *et al.*, (1979), Phelps Brown (1977) and Taubman (1975).

The use of data on brothers and twins is surveyed by Griliches (1979). The volume edited by Taubman (1977) on 'kinometrics' contains a number of valuable papers, including a description of the twins data by Behrman *et al.* and sceptical assessments of the value of evidence on twins by Chamberlain and Goldberger. Further accounts of the twins data and results are given in Taubman (1976, 1978a) and Behrman *et al.* (1980). These should be read in conjunction with the critique by Goldberger (1978b, 1979), the latter being reprinted in Atkinson (1980b). For an interesting discussion of the 'F-connection' (families, friends and firms), see Ben-Porath (1980).

6

THE DISTRIBUTION OF EARNINGS
AND THE LABOUR MARKET

It would appear that no commodity in this country presents so great a variation in price, at one time, as agricultural labour.

(Frederick Purdy to the Royal Statistical Society, 1861)

The analysis in the previous chapter was concerned largely with the individual and his personal characteristics; in this chapter we examine in greater detail certain aspects of the labour market — the structural features that may have an important influence on the distribution of earnings. These include (Section 6.1) the bargaining power of unions and employers, (Section 6.2) the structure of jobs and the demand for labour, and (Section 6.3) the role of custom and the segmentation of the market. In the last part of the chapter (Section 6.4) we consider the application of these theories, together with those discussed in Chapter 5, to the causes of low pay, and the effectiveness of policy measures, particularly minimum wage laws.

6.1 Institutions of the labour market — trade unions and employers

The assumption of perfect competition in the labour market precludes consideration of an aspect of wage determination that must appear to the average newspaper reader to be of considerable importance: the role of trade unions and collective bargaining with employers. In this section we examine their impact on the structure of earnings differentials.

Unions and bargaining power

Trade unions have grown in importance over the past hundred or more years and now occupy a position of considerable influence in many industries. In Britain, membership has increased from 1½ million in the 1890s to 13½ million in 1979 (over half the labour force), with particularly rapid increases in 1910–13, in the late 1930s, and in the 1970s. In the United States, union members comprised less than 2 per cent of the labour force in 1897, but this proportion rose, notably between 1935 and 1945, to about one-third of the non-agricultural labour force in the mid-1980s. Since then it has declined to around a quarter, so that the degree of unionization is less than in Britain.

The impact of trade unions on the structure of earnings depends on the objectives pursued, and these involve a complex variety of motives. Union leaders are concerned with many factors besides wages: employment, redundancy, control over working conditions and practices, fringe benefits, etc. It would be wrong, therefore, to regard unions as simply concerned with wage maximization; at the same time, it seems reasonable to suppose that raising wages is one of their main objectives:

we can probably assume with some conviction that *one* of the principal aims of a trade union will be to maintain and if possible improve the wage position of its members, though the degree to which it will pursue this aim will be governed by the union's need to take account of the consequences of that policy for employment, membership and other objectives. (Hunter and Robertson, 1969, p. 275)

The power of the union to raise wages arises from the control that it can exercise over the supply of labour. In the older craft unions there is the natural restriction that all craftsmen have to serve a period of apprenticeship, typically five years, and the number of apprentices is often limited: for example, there may be no more than one apprentice per time-served craftsman. A second form of restriction is the closed shop, limiting recruitment to union members, or the union shop, where the employer may recruit non-union workers on the understanding that they will join within a certain period after starting work. A third form of regulation is where the union not only restricts total employment but also insists on the right to nominate workers to fill vacancies. In addition to controls over the supply of workers, there are those related to the supply of effort (restrictions on output or on the allocation of labour) and the sanction of the withdrawal of labour through strikes, overtime bans, etc.

To the extent that unions can make use of such bargaining power, wages in the unionized sector are higher, but there may also be a 'spill-over' effect on non-unionized workers. This effect could go in either direction. If employment in the unionized sector is reduced, this tends to increase the supply of labour to the sector that is not covered, and hence to depress wages. On the other hand, employees may be attracted to the unionized sector by the prospect of the union premium on wages, so that the effective supply to the non-unionized sector is reduced (and there is unemployment as jobs in the union sector are rationed). Moreover, the threat of possible unionization may lead employers in unorganized sectors to raise wages, as a pre-emptive move.

The last paragraph has begun to introduce the employer's bargaining position, and this is the other side that needs to be considered. The strength of the employers depends on the labour market position of individual firms, and on the degree of collusion. The latter may be informal, or it may be formalized in the existence of employers' associations: for example, employers' federations in engineering. Like unions, such bodies have manifold objectives, although they are likely to be less cohesive in nature than the union side. However, it seems reasonable to suppose that employers, collectively and individually, are anxious to use their bargaining power to limit the wages paid. Where labour is unorganized, this may lead to labour receiving less than it would under perfect competition, as is shown in the textbook analysis of a firm with monopoly power in labour and product markets. The existence of such a gap was referred to by Pigou as 'exploitation' (for discussion of this concept in relation to Marxian analysis, see Chapter 9). Where labour is unionized, the level of wages depends on the relative bargaining strength of the two sides.

Empirical evidence on union/non-union wage differentials

Ideally, empirical studies of the influence of bargaining power would include indices of the strength of both unions and employers. Although the extent of unionization provides an indicator for the former, the power of employers is less readily measured, and most studies have concentrated on the relationship of wages to the degree of unionization, and in particular the union/non-union wage differential.

There are several types of data that have been used to assess the union differential in Britain and the United States. The first is information on average earnings for industrial/occupational groups, the use of which was pioneered by Lewis (1963), who investigated the impact of unionization on relative earnings of different industries in the United States over the period 1920-58. These results were based on an analysis of the average earnings of the group of heavily unionized industries, containing more than 80 per cent of union labour, relative to the average earnings of the rest of the economy. Lewis hypothesized that relative earnings would be determined by:

A × degree of unionization + other demand and supply factors.

The coefficient A has the following interpretation: if 100 per cent of the labour force in the first sector were unionized and none of the second sector, then wages would be higher in the fully unionized sector by an amount A.

Lewis found that the effect varied considerably, both across industries and over time. The estimated proportionate differential increased from 17 per cent in 1920-4 to 46 per cent in 1930-4, fell to 2 per cent in 1945-9, and then rose to 16 per cent in 1955-8. He argued that unions had been successful in preventing cuts in money wages in the 1930s, but that non-union labour had caught up during the tight labour market of the Second World War. For the most recent period covered by this study, he concluded that 'the average union/non-union differential was of the order of 10 to 15 per cent' (1963, p. 5).

In Britain, a variety of estimates have been made based on data for industrial groups collected in the *New Earnings Survey* and other sources. In the context of the British structure of collective bargaining, it is important to distinguish between union membership and the wider group of workers who are *covered* by collective agreements. According to Mulvey and Foster (1976), in manufacturing about 55 per cent of adult full-time manual workers were union members but around 80 per cent were covered by agreements. This has to be borne in mind when comparing the findings of Pencavel (1974), using union membership, who found for 1964 a differential for manual workers of between zero and 10 per cent, and those of Mulvey (1976), using coverage, who found an effect in 1973 of 26–35 per cent, with the main impact being associated with plant bargaining. One must also be careful to distinguish between hourly earnings (used in these studies) and weekly earnings, since unions may negotiate reduced hours and part of the differential may be missed if weekly earnings are used.

The approach described above rests on a number of assumptions: for example, that the differential increases are in proportion to the extent of unionization, whereas the effect of going from 80 to 90 per cent may be different from that of increasing from 20 to 30 per cent. It is assumed that the determinants of the non-union wage have been adequately captured by the other variables. Mulvey and Abowd (1980) produce evidence on the pay both of workers who are covered and of those not covered, by industry, for Britain in 1974, and estimate with these more complete data that the differential was only some 6 per cent. It is assumed that factors such as the extent of shift work and region are controlled for in the analysis. Wabe and Leech (1978) find union coverage to be insignificant for basic average hourly earnings in UK manufacturing, when a range of other variables is introduced.

All of the studies using industrial/occupational data described above are open to the objection that they make inadequate allowance for the differences in personal characteristics of the workers (the data do not typically allow this to be investigated). An alternative source is the survey evidence on individual earnings of the type discussed in Chapter 5. In some cases, this has not included information on the person's union status or coverage, and recourse has been made to the average for the industry or occupational group. Thus Weiss (1966) used data on individual earnings from the 1960 census in the United States to estimate the relationship between earnings, personal characteristics, and measure of union strength and the monopoly position of the employer (represented by the degree of concentration in the industry). He found that the effect of unionization was slightly smaller than that indicated by Lewis — around 6-8 per cent — although it was still significant. In the case of industrial concentration, Weiss found that wages tend to be higher in highly concentrated industries, but he argued that this is explained by differences in personal characteristics; in other words, it reflects the fact that monopolistic industries get a higher 'quality' of labour, rather than the ability of workers to extract part of the monopoly profits.

Information on individual trade union status from the US Current Population Survey has been used by Ashenfelter (1978) to estimate the differential for several groups — see Table 6.1. These results show an overall differential of 12-17 per cent, with an apparent increase over the period, which Ashenfelter associates with the rise in unemployment (as in Lewis's earlier study). In 1975 the differential was similar for white males and both black and white females, although the proportion of women workers unionized was lower. Black males tend to enjoy a significantly larger differential.

TABLE 6.1

Union/non-union wage differentials in the United States, 1967-1975

	Estimated effect (estimated standard error in brackets)				
		Male workers		Female workers	
	All workers	White	Black	White	Black
	%	%	%	%	%
1967	11.6	9.6	21.5	14.4	5.6
	(0.1)	(1.3)	(1.3)	(2.4)	(2.1)
1973	14.8	15.5	22.5	12.7	13.2
	(0.6)	(0.7)	(1.9)	(1.1)	(2.3)
1975	16.8	16.3	22.5	16.6	17.1
	(0.6)	(0.7)	(1.9)	(1.1)	(2.2)

Source: Ashenfelter (1978), Table 2.1

Evidence on individual earnings in Britain from the General Household Survey 1973 has been used by Layard, Metcalf and Nickell (1978), although they lacked data on individual union status. They found a coverage effect of 27 per cent for male manual workers in manufacturing. In contrast, Stewart (1981), with information on individual union status but less adequate earnings data, finds a differential of only some 8 per cent (although it should be noted that this relates to union membership rather than coverage).

We have therefore a range of results, from 6 to 25 per cent or more. It is also clear that they need careful interpretation. We have, for instance, been treating union status as fixed, whereas it may be simultaneously determined: for example, high wages may be associated with low turn-over and this may facilitate union organization. In this case the estimates may be biased (G. E. Johnson, 1975), although this may be less serious when the variable is coverage rather than membership.

Finally, it must be remembered that trade unions are not the only bodies that use bargaining power to raise their relative earnings; many professional associations perform much the same function, although some members would no doubt be horrified by the thought. In certain cases professional bodies have a legal or effective monopoly over the supply of particular services. In Britain, solicitors have a legal monopoly of the drawing of documents under seal 'for gain' and of originating proceedings in court; and qualified accountants have a monopoly over auditing for public companies.

Unionization and the distribution of earnings

The reference to professional bodies raises the question of how the gains from unionization are likely to affect the distribution of earnings. If the main gainers are doctors and airline pilots (Lewis estimated for the latter group a relative wage effect in the United States of 21-34 per cent), then overall dispersion may be increased. Lewis did indeed con-clude that unionization *increased* differences in average earnings between industries. Some writers, such as Friedman (1954) suggest that the better paid skilled workers would be more likely to gain, on the grounds that they represent a smaller part of the wage bill and hence face a less elastic demand. (This is Marshall's Third Rule of Derived Demand – 'the importance of being unimportant' – and is valid only where there is limited scope for substitution. Airline pilots would be a clear example.)

There is, however, a second effect of unions on the distribution of earnings via the reduction of dispersion *within* industries. The impor-tance of the standardization of wages has long been recognized: 'among trade union regulations there is one which stands out as practically universal, namely, the insistence on payment according to the same definite standard, uniform in its application' (Webb and Webb, 1902, p. 279). In Britain, it has been argued by Turner (1957) that the equal cash increases demanded by mass trade unions were responsible for the narrowing of differentials between the 1920s and the 1950s, and that where the unions were dominated by skilled workers and presented per-centage wage demands, no such narrowing took place. In the United States, Freeman (1980) has investigated the impact, finding that dis-persion among unionized workers is considerably lower than among non-unionized workers, and that the production worker/non-production worker differential within establishments is narrowed by unionization.

He argues that these effects dominate the industry differences and that overall trade unions reduce earnings dispersion in the United States.

Lastly, we must remember that the distributional consequences of unionization depend also on whether the relative gain of union members is achieved at the expense of non-union labour or at the expense of profits. This involves the general equilibrium of the economy as a whole, a subject that is taken up in Chapter 9, which considers the effect on the total share of wages in national income.

6.2 Earnings dispersion and the structure of jobs

In the discussion of the effects of trade unions, we referred to the possibility that jobs in the union sector might be rationed. This would mean that people with identical characteristics would be paid different amounts. The 'lucky' ones would secure union jobs, with the associated premium, and the 'unlucky' ones would be either lower paid in the non-union sector or unemployed.

Everyday observation of the labour market does indeed suggest that there may be considerable dispersion in the pay of seemingly identically qualified people. This is of course difficult to demonstrate. The fact that statistical investigations of the relation of earnings to personal characteristics typically explain only part of the variation does not necessarily mean that identical people are being paid different amounts. The observed differences may be due to measurement error in the data used; they may be temporary departures from normal earnings; they may reflect differences between people that we have failed to identify or to measure. One piece of evidence, although this too needs to be interpreted with care, is provided by studies that introduce demand side variables into the earnings relationship, in addition to the personal characteristics examined in the previous chapter. Wachtel and Betsy (1972) use data on individual earnings in the United States for full-time workers in 1967. They first examine the influence of personal characteristics (education, years in present job, race, sex, age, and marital status), and then investigate how far the remaining variation was related to demand characteristics (occupation/industry, region, city size, and union status). They find that all these demand factors had independent significance, and indicate that a person with the same supply characteristics would have earnings that differed systematically across industries. Individuals employed as labourers, with the same personal characteristics, earned from $4708 to $6136 depending upon the industry in which they are employed. Similarly, Rees and Schultz (1970), in a study of the Chicago labour market, find that 'establishment' variables (location, industry, unionization and size) contribute to the explanation of earnings over and above personal characteristics, particularly for blue-collar workers.

These findings suggest that we need to look more closely at the demand side. Differences in earnings may be associated with the kind of industry. Or we may find that within industries there are systematic factors leading to certain firms or plants paying more than others. In an examination of the earnings of ten occupations in thirteen urban labour markets in the United States, Douty found that the major component in occupational wage dispersion within labour markets was differences in wage levels between plants. He concluded that 'the findings confirm the widespread impression of the existence within labour markets of a hierarchy of wage levels among firms' (1961, p. 72). None the less, dispersion *within* plants was also important. Studies of local labour markets have shown considerable variation in the pay for similar jobs within a plant. Fig. 6.1 shows the range of earnings for one of the towns covered by the study of Mayhew (1977) of engineering workers in 1972.

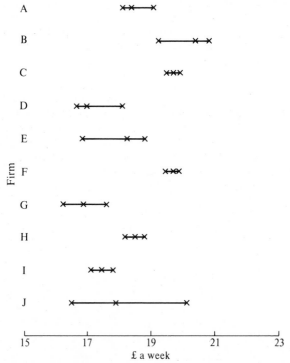

Fig. 6.1 Example of earnings dispersion: unskilled manual workers in ten firms in Leicester, 1972. (*Source:* Mayhew, 1977, Fig. 2)

Each line corresponds to one of ten firms, and the crosses indicate the bottom decile, the median and the top decile of weekly earnings of unskilled male manual workers. (The people are not identical with regard to age and certain other relevant characteristics, and this may account for part of the variation.) Certain firms appear to pay systematically higher wages, but there is also substantial overlap.

The structure of jobs, hierarchies and internal labour markets

The need to introduce the demand side was recognized in the previous chapter, where it was argued that the most reasonable interpretation of the human capital theory was as an equilibrium condition ensuring that (identical) people are indifferent between jobs that require different amounts of education. It is then the structure of available jobs that determines the pattern of earnings. The role of job opportunities has been emphasized by a number of recent writers, and the following passage from Thurow and Lucas is perhaps representative:

One set of factors determines an individual's relative position in the labor queue; another set of factors, not mutually exclusive of the first, determines the actual distribution of job opportunities in the economy. Wages are paid based on the characteristics of the job in question and workers are distributed across job opportunities based on their relative position in the labor queue. (1972, p. 2)

This means that we have to look at the features of jobs, and this in turn is likely to lead to a consideration of the structure of industry and of organizations. This may be illustrated by the rather special, but none the less suggestive, theory of managerial salaries that has been developed by Simon (1957) and Lydall (1968), based on the hierarchical structure which is typical of many (but not all) organizations. They suppose that the hierarchical organization is broadly pyramid-shaped, so that each person has a certain number of subordinates below him, typically between three and ten. The salary of an executive is then assumed to be a constant multiple of that of his subordinates, or his salary span of control, which Simon describes as a widely accepted principle of executive remuneration. The resulting distribution of salaries turns out to be of the Pareto form described in the previous chapter. Lydall goes further, and suggests that the hierarchical principle may explain why the overall earnings distribution follows the Pareto formula at the upper tail. This, however, involves a jump from the earnings distribution of an individual enterprise to that for the whole economy, which may not be warranted. Many highly paid employees do not work for hierarchical organizations, and even if they all did, the pattern of earnings would depend on the size of such organizations. Indeed, this brings out the dependence of the structure of jobs and earnings on the organization of production. The role of such status differentials is related to the extent of corporate and similar institutions and to the size distribution of firms. We should expect differentials to be smaller where production was typically in the hands of small enterprises and to be larger in a world of big business.

The hierarchical theory illustrates how consideration of the job structure may lead to a rather different set of considerations being introduced. It may mean, for instance, that, in seeking an explanation of trends over time in the distribution of earnings, we should look to the changes in industrial structure as well as to changes in personal characteristics. This may be illustrated by the example of Tinbergen (1975), who characterizes the changes in the relative earnings of graduates in terms of a 'race' between the expansion of higher education and the growth in demand arising from technological development.

The theory cannot, however, as described so far, account for people with identical qualifications receiving different amounts of pay. It is still being assumed that the labour market is in equilibrium, and that all workers identical in training, ability, and other respects relevant to their productivity receive the same earnings. If they do not, then, as Adam Smith described, so many would crowd into the higher-paying job and so many desert the other, that wages would be brought into line. At the same time, the example of managerial salaries brings to the fore the fact that the employment contract is typically one of some considerable duration, and that we have to consider earnings in terms of a person's career, not just for a particular pay period. Hall (1982), for example, has recently estimated that the typical worker in the United States is holding a job that has lasted, or will last, eight years, and that over a quarter are holding jobs that will last twenty years or more.

The extended duration of the typical employment contract has an evident rationale in the importance of on-the-job training. In the previous chapter, this was treated in terms of an individual's total work experience, but it may well be that the skills that are acquired are specific to a particular firm, in contrast to general skills, such as being able to drive, which can be applied more widely. The significance of such specific skills has been emphasized by Doeringer and Piore:

Almost every job involves some specific skills. Even the simplest custodial tasks are facilitated by familiarity with the physical environment specific to the workplace ... Even mass-produced machines have individual operating characteristics which can markedly affect work performance ... performance in some production and in most managerial jobs involves a team element, and a critical skill is the ability to operate effectively with the given members of the team. (1971, pp. 15–16)

The importance of specific on-the-job training has led Doeringer and Piore to develop the concept of an *internal labour market* — or the idea that employment within a firm or plant is largely insulated from the outside labour market. It is characterized by a pattern of jobs, arranged in a line of progression, with entry into the labour force being limited to a number of points towards the bottom of the ladder and the remainder of the jobs within the internal labour market being filled by the promotion or transfer of workers who have already gained entry — see the hypothetical example in Fig. 6.2. As a result, these jobs are protected

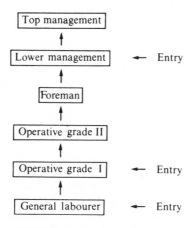

Fig. 6.2 A hypothetical internal labour market.

from direct competition by outside workers. An early illustration of this is provided by the 1907 inquiry into railway earnings in Britain: 'engine drivers are in the main recruited from the firemen, who in turn are recruited from the engine cleaners. Goods guards and brakesmen are largely taken from the ranks of shunters.'

The specific nature of skills and the importance of on-the-job training provide a strong incentive for the employer to develop internal labour markets with a low degree of turnover and internal promotion. Similarly, the workers gain from a structured long-run career within the enterprise with job security and chances of advancement; and trade unions have a clear preference for the resulting stability, often reinforcing it through rules such as seniority governing promotion. It is for these reasons, Doeringer and Piore suggest, that the internal labour market characterizes a substantial fraction of the US economy. In industries such as steel, petroleum, and chemicals, for example, workers are hired almost exclusively into low-skill jobs and most blue-collar skills are developed internally. At the same time, they recognize that there is an important sector of the economy where the internal market is weak, where turnover is high, and jobs offer little prospect of a lifetime career. The implications of such a 'secondary' sector are discussed when we come to the question of the segmentation of the labour market.

The implications of the internal labour market for the determination of earnings are seen by Doeringer and Piore to be that, while textbook competitive forces place constraints upon wage differentials, they do not in general establish a unique wage rate. Rather, they provide upper and lower bounds on the range of possible variation. This reflects, first of all, the fact that both employers and employees take a longer view: 'When the [employment] relationship is permanent, neither employers nor workers necessarily concern themselves with the connection between wages and marginal productivity at any point in time' (1971, p. 76). There is therefore scope for flexibility in determining the wage for any particular job. At the same time, we should still expect to find equality of *career* earnings for people with the same characteristics. (In this respect it would run parallel to the human capital theory of occupational choice.)

This brings us to the question of *recruitment* into the internal labour market. Where specific skills are important, then general training received through formal education may be of little value to the employer, and he will select workers on the basis not of skills already acquired but of potential training costs. Doeringer and Piore argue that 'by far the largest proportion of blue-collar job skills is acquired on the job' and that even in managerial positions on-the-job training may be a prerequisite for the successful application of formal education. It may, however, be the case that potential training costs are seen by employees to be related to educational achievements. Thurow and Lucas suggest that the employer is not able to judge the suitability of any one worker with great accuracy, and obtaining further information involves substantial screening costs, so he bases his decision on certain easily observed personal characteristics, such as age and education. Where there is imperfect information about the true characteristics of workers in the labour queue, identical individuals may receive different earnings; on the other hand, it is possible that the rate of pay for a job will be in line with the *average* characteristics of the workers employed. We should then observe an equilibrium in a 'statistical' sense. Differentials are related to the personal characteristics of workers, but do not account for the whole variation in earnings, because of the limited information available to employers. Individuals with identical potential productivity as workers may end up with different earnings, depending on which characteristics employers use as a basis for hiring and on the luck of the draw.

The use of different 'screening' devices for potential employees has been analysed with particular reference to education. If employers use educational qualifications as a filtering mechanism, then this affects the incentives for individuals to acquire these qualifications; and it also means that an expansion of education may have no impact on the productivity of the labour force:

the contribution of education to economic growth (on this view) is simply that of providing a selection device for employers, and the way is now open to consider the question of whether formal schooling is indeed the most efficient selection mechanism. (Blaug, 1976, p. 847)

This 'signalling' or 'credentials' view of education has rather different implications from the human capital theory. It leaves open, however, the question of the role of education after entry to the firm. What governs the matching of workers to jobs? How are promotions decided?

In the empirical analysis of the internal labour market, longitudinal data on employment histories are likely to be particularly valuable. This is well illustrated by the study of Wise (1975) of the information collected by a large US corporation on some 1300 college graduates in their employment who were aged not more than 30 when they joined the firm. From the observed grade level in the organization, Wise estimates the relationship between promotion probabilities and individual characteristics. He finds, in contrast to the views of Doeringer and Piore described earlier, that educational attainment is a significant determinant, particularly the ranking of the college attended and the standard of college performance. At the same time, he emphasizes that it is in the nature of such a model that 'we could not expect to explain all of the variation in salary between individuals by personal characteristics, even if they were all known and precisely measured' (1975, p. 919). To bring out this point, he gives an illustrative calculation in which the upper limit on the proportion of the variation which can be explained is some 40 per cent.

The theory just described, of a statistical equilibrium, has certain affinities with the possibility of a persistent trade union differential mentioned at the start of this section. In that case, identical people received different pay, but equilibrium was maintained by the fact that there was a probability that a union job would come along. On the other hand, there is a big difference between a situation where a person has many opportunities, so that on average earnings are equal, and that where there is a single chance (on career entry). In the former case, life-time earnings may be equalized, but in the latter the equilibrium is quite consistent with large differences in lifetime earnings. Two Yale graduates may have stood the same chance of getting a management traineeship with IBM, but the one who was successful may, over his lifetime, earn thousands of dollars more than his unlucky classmate.

6.3 Custom, segmentation, and discrimination

The previous section set out a variety of theories that sought to explain the emergence of earnings differences while retaining the assumption that there are forces equilibrating the labour market. It is possible however that these forces are weak and slow-working. There are, indeed, reasons to expect that there will not be immediate adjustment if wages move out of line with those obtained elsewhere by workers with the same characteristics. In the worker's case, his scope for mobility is limited in an internal labour market by the restrictions on entry to other markets. Workers who have reached higher-level jobs may be earning well above the wages on entry jobs elsewhere, and will not leave their present employment even though the level of pay has fallen behind. Conversely, if earnings elsewhere are pulling ahead, the worker may not be able to 'bargain' his way in. If, as has been argued by Thurow and Lucas (1972), people compete not on the basis of wages, but for the available jobs ('job competition'), then he cannot undercut those enjoying advantageous salaries. Thurow gives the example from the early 1970s of 'unemployed aerospace engineers in New England who were not allowed to bid against those engineers who remained employed. Technically, the individuals had the necessary job skills but they were frozen out of the market' (1976, p. 85).

The role of custom and history

To the extent that wage differentials are not constrained by market forces, they are, according to Doeringer and Piore, influenced by considerations of custom and status. The former is particularly relevant in the case of short-run changes in the labour market. Any wage relationship, they argue, 'which prevails over a period of time tends to become customary; changes are then viewed as unjust or inequitable, and the work group will exert economic pressure in opposition to them' (1971, p. 85). This kind of customary wage differential applies not simply within a firm or an industry, but also across occupations. A well-known example is the tradition in both the United States and Britain that policemen and firemen get paid the same. Despite the shortage of policemen and the relative over-supply of firemen, this convention has been sustained over long periods. The role of custom over a long period is brought out by Phelps Brown:

Between 1912 and 1914 the rate for the mason . . . rose fourteenfold, but at one end of the five centuries as the other . . . it was half as much again as the labourer's . . . the simple ratio of three to two appears far too widely and too long for us to suppose that it was reached each time by an equilibrium of market forces: it must have been what it was primarily because men were following custom. (1962, p. 132)

The force of custom does not prevent wage differentials from changing, the very differentials described by Phelps Brown having changed in Britain over this century; but within a given range of conditions, differentials are unresponsive to changes in the labour market situation.

The effect of custom is to reduce the sensitivity of differentials to economic conditions, but it does not in itself determine what these differentials will be (within the constraints imposed by competitive forces). Within the internal labour market, Doeringer and Piore stress the role played by the social status of the job in question and particularly its position in the hierarchy of production. They refer to the fact that workers whose jobs involve the direction of others must typically be paid more than their subordinates in order to perform this function effectively. Workers responsible for providing on-the-job training for new entrants may feel threatened by the trainee, and may give adequate training only if their seniority is reflected in higher pay. More generally, pay is seen as an indicator of status in society at large. A number of examples in the British context are given by Wootton: for example, the instruction to a government committee making recommendations for the pay of doctors to give 'due regard to . . . the desirability of maintaining the proper social and economic status' of the profession, and the argument by *The Times* that 'it is of first-rate public importance that [judges] should continue to be men of substance and security. The vast moral authority of the law in this country is bound up in the public mind with the visible dignity of the men who dispense the Queen's justice' (1962, pp. 128-9).

An alternative − and more explicitly historical − approach to the explanation of customary differentials is that described by Dunlop (1957). He emphasizes the historical sequence of growth, with new and expanding industries having to offer a differential to attract labour and this wage 'contour' becoming established as a matter of custom. This 'geological' theory is explained by Lutz as follows:

The oldest manufacturing industries (e.g. textiles, footwear, etc.) had to offer a wage premium in order to secure the necessary transfer of manpower from agriculture. Subsequently, non-economic forces of custom and tradition have successfully maintained the transitory pay differential. Each subsequent new industry had to attract employees by offering increasingly attractive wages. The newest industries (e.g. computers, aircraft) now pay the highest wage premiums. (1976, p. 473)

Segmentation

The contours described by Dunlop have evident similarity to the 'noncompeting groups' of John Stuart Mill. In his criticism of Adam Smith's view of the equilibrating forces in the labour market, Mill argues that the market is in fact divided: 'so complete, indeed, has hitherto been the separation, so strongly marked the line of demarcation, between the different grades of labourers, as to be almost equivalent to an hereditary distinction of caste' (1891, p. 270). Such segmentation means that wage differentials can persist, either between firms or between industries, and that, again, the source of earnings dispersion has to be sought in the structure of jobs. It is this idea that has been taken up in the segmented labour market theories of the 1970s.

The notion of segmentation is a complex one, and the term is used in many different ways. One widely quoted is the concept of a 'dual labour market' developed by Doeringer and Piore. They suggest that there are two broad sectors. The *primary* sector is characterized by the structured internal labour market we have described earlier, by employment stability and promotion from within, with the stability of the market often being reinforced by strong trade unions. Workers in this sector are typically well paid, in contrast to the *secondary* sector, where most low-paid workers are concentrated. This sector involves little on-the-job training, unstable employment, poor promotion opportunities and often a low level of union organization. The sectors can also be distinguished according to the conditions of demand, the secondary sector typically facing greater competition, and this is one of the features that contributes to the instability of employment. An example in the United States is that cigarette manufacture is capital-intensive, unionized, and faces a steady demand; whereas in the cigar industry the conditions are reversed. The latter has a high proportion of low-paid workers, the former very few.

The interpretation of segmentation just outlined depends on the differences in technology and on the skills that are required. A rather different emphasis is given in the radical theories (for example, Gordon, 1972, and Edwards, Reich and Gordon, 1975), which see the internal labour market as related less to the development of skill and more to the need by employers to control the labour force: 'monopoly capitalist firms established internal labour markets to thwart the development of class consciousness and maintain their control over production' (Edwards, 1975, p. 11). This interpretation is in line with the thesis of Braverman (1974) that increased mechanism has led to a reduction in skill requirements. If for most manual jobs the level of skill required is less than that needed to drive a car (Blackburn and Mann, 1979), then the segmentation of the labour market cannot be explained in terms of job content. Instead, the radical theories have tended to stress the historical development of labour markets, and the degree of organization of employers and workers.

The segmented labour market theories have been criticized on a number of grounds. It has been suggested that 'it does not begin to offer a theory of the labour market that can replace neoclassical theory' (Cain, 1976, p. 124). The assumptions have indeed been less fully spelled out and the analysis has been less explicit than in the case of other theories. At the same time, such a rigorous treatment may well be possible. Starrett presents a series of formal models, which show that 'a man's marginal product will depend on the job he winds up in, and this . . . may bear no relationship to his "true" marginal product due to distortions in the job allocation process' (1976, p. 282). Ishikawa (1981) has provided a dynamic model of the dual labour market, showing how the long-run development of the distribution of income depends on the entry conditions into the primary sector, the costs of education (a prerequisite for entry), and the bargaining power of unions.

A second line of criticism concerns the empirical relevance of the segmentation theories. The difficulty of devising an adequate test of the theories means that this criticism is hard to evaluate. For example, Cain (1976) suggests that a test of the dual theory is whether the frequency distribution of jobs, ranked according to desirability, has two distinct peaks, but this seems to take a too simplistic view of the relation between the theory and the observed data. None the less, the problems that arise in seeking to construct a test are themselves an indication that the theories are not yet fully developed. There is, for instance, the important question of the unit of segmentation. The dual labour market theory is conceived in terms of the internal labour market of the firm, and this suggests that we should examine differences between firms (or plants). But primary sector employment conditions may apply only to part of a firm's labour force. Craig *et al.* draw attention to the example of canteen workers, 'most of whom were employed in large establishments, [which] showed that a minority of workers still had unregulated wages even employed in primary type firms operating systems of collective bargaining for their main labour force' (1982, p. 74).

Discrimination

Where segmentation leads to wage differentials, we have to explain why it is that one person enjoys advantage over others. To the extent that it is not simply a matter of luck, this rationing of entry to 'good jobs' brings us back to personal characteristics. The theories highlighting on-the-job training attach particular weight to the cost of training, as discussed earlier; the radical theories tend to regard stable behaviour and attitudes towards authority as the main prerequisite of employers. But one major feature, not yet discussed, is discrimination according to race and sex.

The failure of the 'orthodox' approach to explain persistent earnings differentials between black and white workers or between men and women has been one of the major reasons for the development of the alternative segmentation theories. A theory of discrimination, based on discriminating attitudes on the part of the employers, or customers, or of the privileged employees, has been advanced by Becker (1957), but Arrow (1972) has shown that there are good reasons to expect such differentials to be eliminated in the long run through the operation of competitive forces. He concludes that 'if there were any firms that did not discriminate at all, these would be the only ones to survive the competitive struggle. Since in fact racial discrimination has survived for a long time, we must assume that the model . . . must have some limitation' (1973, p. 10).

The segmentation approach sees race and sex as principal characteristics by which entry into desirable primary sector jobs is regulated, placing considerable emphasis on the dynamics of the process. A brief account of black employment in the United States is provided by Edwards, Reich and Gordon:

During the period of transition to monopoly capitalism, blacks still remained largely in the rural South. As late as World War I the only industries to which blacks had gained access were those which had imported black workers for strikebreaking purposes. . . The more recent pattern of economic life for blacks developed during and after World War II. Many blacks came North during the labor shortages of the war . . . and found themselves in segregated or isolated urban ghettoes. In that context, black employment began to be dominated increasingly by three kinds of jobs: (1) low-wage jobs in the secondary market, mainly in peripheral industries; (2) some jobs in the primary labour market, largely in the core industries into which blacks had already gained access . . . ; (3) jobs in the rapidly expanding service sectors, most of them in the secondary labour market. (1975, p. xvi)

Similarly, their account of the evolution of women's employment stresses

the continuing influence of segmentation within the labour process and labour markets. First, the continued dramatic expansion of clerical work and the channeling of women in the lower-level clerical occupations were a major development. . . Second, the equally dramatic increase in the number of service jobs in the economy, particularly in health and education; [although] the top of the occupational hierarchies in both schools and hospitals was dominated by men. Finally, employers in the secondary labour market . . . turned increasingly to female employees. These three categories . . . dominate female employment today. (1975, p. xvii)

This is in effect the 'crowding' explanation advanced for the lower pay of women by Edgeworth (1922) and developed for racial discrimination by Bergmann (1971).

According to this approach, discrimination operates *indirectly* via recruitment and promotion practices rather than *directly* via unequal pay for similar jobs. The latter may be illustrated by the example given in the *Economic Journal* for 1918:

John Jones earned good wages from a firm of outfitters . . . he fell ill and was allowed by the firm to continue his work in his own home. He taught his wife his trade, and . . . she did more and more of the work . . . as long as he lived it was taken to the firm as his work and paid for accordingly. When, however, it became quite clear, John Jones being dead and buried, that it could not be his work . . . the price paid for it by the firm was immediately reduced to two-thirds. (Fawcett, 1918, p. 1)

There are a number of reasons why this may happen. In particular, employers may take advantage of the weaker supply position of women, particularly those with family responsibilities:

the fact that women seek part-time jobs, or are unwilling to work overtime, or to be geographically mobile, and are expected to take time off to care for sick children, provides a means of differentiating the wage structure despite trade union and legislative efforts to establish a unisex payment system. (Craig *et al.*, 1982, p. 91)

The existence of differentials in pay could be given other explanations. The human capital approach has been utilized by Mincer and Polachek (1974) to explain the male–female earnings gap in terms of the differential work experience of married women and associated decisions about education. On this basis, the differentiation of roles within the family leads to women earning less than men who are otherwise doing identical work, because they are able to acquire less human capital. It is a matter of some importance to establish the relative importance of the different mechanisms, since they lead to people's making quite different policy recommendations. The human capital view indicates that attention should be focused on the intra-family allocation of time and the sex-linking of roles. The explanation based on employer exploitation has led to support for equal pay legislation; and the discrimination in recruitment view has given rise to proposals for employment quotas: 'if women constitute 35 per cent of those who by objective criteria qualify for a given rung of occupation, they should have approximately 35 per cent of those jobs' (Bergmann and Adelman, 1973, p. 513)

6.4 Low pay

We have considered a variety of explanations for the distribution of earnings, and in this section we show them 'in action', as applied to the problem of low pay. How far can low pay be explained by the different factors discussed, and what are the implications for policy measures, particularly the effectiveness of minimum wage legislation?

The first question is what one means by 'low pay', since a variety of definitions could be adopted. In the United States two natural standards suggest themselves. The first is the level of the minimum wage set by the federal government for certain industries, or $2.65 an hour in 1978 ($3.35 in 1981). This minimum wage is around 50 per cent of the average hourly wage in manufacturing and covers some four workers out of five (Welch, 1978, Table 1). The second possible definition is the official poverty standard (see Chapter 10), set at around $6200 per annum for a family of four in 1978, which gives a rather higher figure on an hourly basis ($3.10 an hour, assuming that a person works fifty weeks at forty hours per week). Both definitions are employed by Kniesner (1981) in his study based on the US Current Population Survey of 1978. We should expect the minimum wage provisions to mean that there is considerable bunching at the ruling minimum, and this was in fact the case: of the workers for whom hourly earnings are reported, 16 per cent earned $2.65. There were however 4 per cent *below* the minimum. The higher, poverty-line, cut-off gave a figure of 35 per cent low paid.

In Britain there has also been a variety of approaches to the definition of low pay. The Low Pay Unit (1981) shows how several approaches lead to similar cash standards. The use of the supplementary benefit standard for a family with two children, analogous to the American poverty line calculation, led to a standard in November 1980 of £74 a week. This may be seen as implementing the injunction in the 1924 Act to regulate agricultural wages so that they should be adequate 'to enable a man in an ordinary case to maintain himself and his family', but raises the question, just as does use of the American poverty line, as to what is meant by an 'ordinary case'. The Low Pay Unit prefer an alternative definition based on earnings relative to the median, as adopted by the Trades Union Congress, which they take to be two-thirds of median earnings. In April 1980 this gave a figure of £75 a week, or £1.88 an hour. (They note that this was the rate offered by a large London store for temporary part-time staff, and comment that this suggests that the definition of hour pay adopted here is not unrealistic in commercial terms' (1981, p. 4)). Applying this standard to the *New Earnings Survey* data for 1980, they found that 13 per cent of adult men and 55 per cent of adult women were low paid.

The implications of low pay depend on the circumstances of those concerned. In Britain, the *New Earnings Survey* shows that the incidence of low pay is greatest for young workers (aged under 25) and for older workers (50 and over). This may suggest that low pay is unlikely to be associated with family responsibilities, but Atkinson, Micklewright and

Sutherland (1982), using the *Family Expenditure Survey* for 1977, find that a quarter of low paid men either have dependent children or are married with a wife who is not in paid work. Similarly, one in six of low paid women are household heads, have dependent children, or are married with a husband not at work.

The causes of low pay

The different theories of earnings described in this, and the preceding, chapter provide a range of possible explanations for low pay.

The personal characteristics analysed in Chapter 5 suggest that the low paid are those with poor educational qualifications and limited on-the-job experience. The low paid lack productive skills. They may have failed to acquire such skills because they are without the necessary ability to complete formal education or to benefit from training. They may have missed educational opportunities on account of their family background: for example, because they had to leave school early to add to the family income. Family background may be important in that employers are seeking recruits with appropriate personality traits and attitudes. In these cases, we may expect low pay to be associated across generations.

The role of personal characteristics may be represented by the supply curves shown in Fig. 6.3(a). The curves correspond to people with 'high',

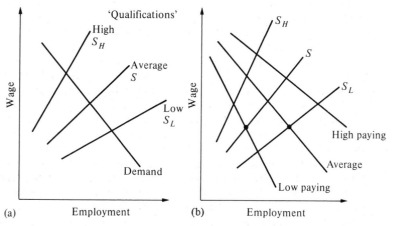

Fig. 6.3 Low pay – a schematic representation

'average', or 'low' qualifications, where these may be education, skill, or other attributes (such as attitude to authority); the more able or better educated or more easily 'bossed' person obtains a higher wage at any given level of employment on account of his greater productivity.

In contrast to the explanation of earnings in terms of supply factors, the theories discussed in this chapter have emphasized the institutions of the labour market. If earnings are influenced by bargaining power, we should expect to find the relatively low paid in industries where unions were weak and employers strong. This is represented in Fig. 6.3(b) by the different demand curves, one corresponding to a highly unionized, high-paying industry, one to an average industry, and the third to a less organized, low-paying industry. (It should be noted that the term 'demand curve' is being used in a slightly unconventional way, in that it incorporates the effects of unionization.) A relatively unskilled worker in the average industry may earn as much as a worker with average skill in the low-paying industries because of union pressures and barriers to mobility. These different demand curves may also be seen as corresponding to the segmented labour market theories. For example, the high-paying industry could correspond to the primary sector in a dual labour market, and the low-paying industry to the secondary sector.

Low pay and minimum wage legislation

The view taken of the causes of low pay has major implications for the design of policy. In the 1960s the influence of the human capital theory led to a great deal of the discussion about public policy being directed towards the supply side of the labour market. Much of the War on Poverty in the United States was concerned with increasing the human capital of the low paid, through training programmes and the expansion of education. As described by an assistant director of the Office of Economic Opportunity, 'many of the poor have essentially zero productivity now. They lack skills, education, motivation, and sometimes even literacy. This is why there is so much emphasis on training and education in OEO programmes' (Kershaw, 1965, p. 57). At the same time, the setting of minimum wages was condemned by many economists: a survey of academic economists in the United States in 1966 showed that 88 per cent supported the War on Poverty but that 61 per cent opposed extension of the minimum wage law.

The enthusiasm for measures based on human capital formation has tended to wane. The alternative view of the labour market taken by Thurow and Lucas was seen by them as raising 'substantial doubts about the feasibility of altering the structure of American incomes with government programmes that are exclusively focused on the supply side of the labour market' (1972, p. 39). Similarly, the Secretary of Labor recognized that the human capital formation approach is constrained by the structure of available jobs: 'our economy has a lot of jobs that pay low wages . . . we can only put people in the jobs that exist' (quoted in Wachtel and Betsy, 1972, pp. 127–8). One consequence has been a renewed interest in government intervention to influence the demand for labour and in minimum wage legislation. If human capital formation cannot be relied on to eliminate low pay, then other measures of this kind may be necessary.

In both Britain and the United States there has been minimum wage legislation for a long time. In the United States the federal minimum was established by the Fair Labour Standards Act of 1938, and in Britain there have been Wages Councils since 1909, dating back to the investigations of sweated labour by Charles Booth and Beatrice Webb. The coverage of this legislation is, however, far from complete, and the minimum rates established by Wages Councils have typically been well below the definition of low pay used earlier. Moreover, we saw that in the United States the minimum rate is below that derived from the poverty line.

What would be the consequences of a higher minimum wage and extended coverage? The standard textbook view is that minimum wage laws 'often hurt those they are designed to help. What good does it do a Negro youth to know that an employer must pay him $1.60 per hour, if the fact that he must be paid that amount is what keeps him from getting a job?' (Samuelson, 1967, p. 377). If the labour market is competitive and perfectly functioning, and differences in earnings reflect productivity, then a universal minimum wage – without any accompanying measures – clearly reduces employment opportunities. The higher wage that has to be paid causes employers either to replace low paid workers with more skilled workers or capital, or else to raise prices, in which case there will be substitution away from the product in question. The extent of the fall in employment depends on the ease with which the low paid workers can be replaced and on the elasticity of demand for the product.

Even within the compass of its assumptions about the labour market, the textbook view leaves out important considerations. We must distinguish between numbers employed and hours of work, as is illustrated by the example of the employee of a fast-food chain cited by Welch:

"Cheryl Anders . . . won't be losing her job after all". Instead, as her hourly wage was increased from $2.30 to $2.65, her hours would be reduced from twenty-three to eighteen per week and her pay from $53 to $48. (Welch, 1978, p. 25)

We must allow for the incomplete coverage of the typical minimum wage, and for the fact that compliance is less than 100 per cent. Where there is scope for movement between the covered and not-covered (or non-compliant) sectors, then we have to consider the effect on employment and wages in these sectors.

What happens if the assumptions of competition and a perfectly equilibrating labour market are not satisfied? Even in the standard text-book treatments it is recognized that, where the employer possesses greater bargaining power, the introduction of minimum wage legislation may have no adverse effect on employment. To this extent, the impact depends on the degree of competition:

If one thinks of labour markets as fairly competitive, then minimum wage legislation results in unemployment of low-skilled workers . . . If one thinks of all capitalists conspiring together to exploit workers of low skills (many of whom may belong to particular groups in the population), then minimum wage legislation is an important element in the reduction of that exploitation. (Stiglitz, 1973, pp. 294–5)

Although Stigler (1946) pointed out that industries with a high proportion of low paid workers are typically more competitive, so that this argument may not be relevant, the lower monopoly power of the employer may be more than offset by the lower level of union organization on the workers' side. To the extent that there is disequilibrium in the labour market, the link between wages and employment may be looser than assumed in the conventional theory. The pattern of jobs may not respond, at least not at all quickly, to the introduction of a minimum wage. Lester (1964), for example, draws attention to the possibility that minimum wages may stimulate a search for improvements in the productivity of a given labour force.

Where the labour market is viewed as segmented, as in the dual hypothesis, into primary and secondary sectors, then the implications of minimum wages have to be assessed in terms of the criteria for employment in the two sectors. If the rationale for an internal labour market is the provision of on-the-job training, then the minimum wage may reduce the incentive for employers to provide such training:

jobs needing training must be financed, at least in part, by the worker or apprentice, usually in the form of a reduced initial wage. This means that, even if current productivity of some of the employed youngsters warrants paying the minimum wage, job training is precluded for them because its provision would require paying initially a sub-minimum. (Leighton and Mincer, 1981, p. 158)

On the other hand, the minimum wage may provide an *incentive* for the acquisition of formal education, since it raises the projected future return and reduces the present employment probability for young people.

There has been a great deal of empirical research in the United States, particularly on the effects on the employment of teenagers. The impact on adult workers has been less studied. In general, the findings appear to show a definite reduction in employment but one that is relatively modest. Eccles and Freeman summarized two major studies, by the Congressional Minimum Wage Study Commission and by the American Enterprise Institute, as indicating 'modest/moderate impacts' (1982, p. 227). The survey by Brown, Gilroy and Kohen (1982) concluded that, in the case of teenagers, a 10 per cent increase in the minimum wage reduced employment by around 1 per cent, and that for adults the direction of the effect was uncertain (since they benefited from reduced competition from teenagers).

Whatever interpretations are placed on the evidence from the United States, it is not possible to reject decisively the hypothesis that minimum wages may reduce employment. Most advocates of a higher minimum have therefore proposed complementary measures to influence the demand of labour. One common suggestion in the 1970s was for the government to guarantee employment: 'the preferred method would be minimum wage legislation coupled with public employer-of-the-last-resort programmes to guarantee that everyone who wanted full-time work at the minimum wage could have it' (Thurow, 1973, p. 80). On the other hand, those who feel that public employment would be 'unproductive' argued for a wage subsidy to private employers (Feldstein, 1973); this would clearly need to be integrated with the system of income maintenance discussed in Chapter 11. In the early 1980s, with unemployment very much higher, such proposals may appear quite unrealistic. Indeed, there have been calls for *reductions* in minimum wage protection in order to stimulate employment. This takes us into the arena of macroeconomic policy — where views differ as much, or more, as in labour economics. One can only say that it is hard to believe that a solution of macroeconomic difficulties can be found only by worsening the relative position of the low paid, or that the macroeconomic measures could not be found to allow minimum wage policy to be used if it is felt desirable on distributional grounds.

Notes on sources and further reading

The issues discussed in this chapter are very much at the centre of the 'institutionalist' tradition of labour economics, and reference should be made to texts such as Reynolds (1982), which give some emphasis to the industrial relations and institutional aspects.

The classic reference on the impact of *unionization* in the United States is Lewis (1963). For a succinct survey of a number of the issues, see G. E. Johnson (1975). A more extensive survey relating to both the United States and Britain is given by Parsley (1980). The British evidence is reviewed by Metcalf (1977). See also Burkitt (1975). The 'spill-over' to non-union members is examined by Rosen (1969). A number of aspects of union impact are not discussed in the text, including job satisfaction (Borjas, 1979) and labour turnover (Freeman, 1980).

The *job structure* theory is particularly associated with Thurow and Lucas (1972) and Thurow (1976).

The concept of an *internal labour market* is described by Doeringer and Piore (1971), who refer to earlier writers such as Kerr (1950). The idea is developed by Alexander (1974), Starrett (1976), Althauser and Kalleberg (1981), and Ishikawa (1981). The 'statistical equilibrium' is related to the models of signalling developed by Arrow (1973b), Spence (1974, 1976), Stiglitz (1975) and others — see Spence (1981) for a recent review.

There has been a large literature on *segmented labour markets*, and reference should be made to Gordon (1972), Edwards, Reich and Gordon (1975), Loveridge and Mok (1979), Berg (1981), Wilkinson (1981), and Gordon, Edwards, Reich (1982). A critical assessment is given by Cain (1975, 1976). Wachter (1974) examines the applicability of the dual labour market hypothesis to the United States. A less extensive treatment for Britain is given by Bosanquet and Doeringer (1973) and Psacharopoulos (1978).

The theory of discrimination has in large part been stimulated by Becker (1957), although there had been earlier analyses — for example, Edgeworth (1922) on sex discrimination. Important recent contributions to the theory of racial discrimination include Arrow (1972, 1973a), Krueger (1963), Thurow (1969), Stiglitz (1973, 1975), and Reich (1981). For the literature on sex discrimination see Amsden (1980), Blau and Jusenius (1976), Chiplin and Sloane (1976), Lloyd (1975), and Sloane (1980).

The evidence on low pay in Britain is surveyed by the Low Pay Unit (1978), an extract from which is reprinted in Atkinson (1980b), and Metcalf (1981), and Craig *et al.* (1982). The publications of the Low Pay Unit provide an up-to-date source of evidence. For analysis of the cases of low pay, see Field (1973), Fisher and Dix (1974), Craig *et al.* (1982), Duncan (1981), and Rubery (1978). The impact of incomes policy on the low paid is examined by Steele (1981) and Thomas (1981). On low pay in the United States, see Bluestone (1968, 1970), Bell (1981), and Kniesner (1981).

There is a great deal written on minimum wage legislation in the United States. A valuable recent survey is given by Brown, Gilroy and Kohen (1982). Reference should also be made to the papers of the Minimum Wage Study Commission (1981) and those collected by the American Enterprise Institute (Rottenberg, 1981).

7

THE CONCENTRATION OF WEALTH: EVIDENCE

I detest a man who conceals the extent of his wealth — it is as bad as leaving out the date of one's birth in *Who's Who*.

(Lord Beaverbrook)

In this chapter we examine the distribution of the ownership of capital, with particular reference to Britain and the United States. How much of total wealth is really in the hands of the top 1 per cent or the top 0.1 per cent? What are the likely future trends in the distribution? How does Britain compare with the United States? What are the implications of the concentration of wealth-holding?

7.1 Sources and methods

There are three main methods by which information can be derived about the distribution of personal wealth.

A sample census of wealth

The ideal source of information about the distribution would be a regular census, possibly on a sample basis, giving the details of the wealth of all families or individuals. Everyone would be required to complete a form giving details of all assets and liabilities. The assets would include personal possessions, such as cars, houses, or consumer durables, and financial assets, such as money in the bank, cash, government bonds, shares, and so on. Liabilities would include items such as a mortgage on a house, overdrafts at the bank, and money owed. The value of assets minus the value of liabilities would then constitute one's net worth, or wealth, and from such a census we could derive the distribution of wealth among all families.

Such a census would run into a number of difficulties. The first would be that of securing an adequate response. In theory it would be possible to make compliance compulsory: for example, by including questions covering wealth in the population census. If this information were provided accurately, which would be hard to guarantee, then we would have a clear picture of wealth-holding at ten-year intervals. It seems unlikely that the census would in fact be extended in this way, since the introduction of questions about wealth would no doubt arouse considerable hostility and censuses are unpopular enough as it is. The alternative is to have a voluntary survey. The experience in Britain with the national savings surveys carried out by the Oxford Institute of Statistics in the early 1950s, and the feasibility studies conducted by the Office of Population Censuses and Surveys (OPCS) in 1976 and 1977, strongly suggest that it is difficult to secure a reasonable response rate and that there are good grounds for believing that the wealthy would be under-represented. The OPCS report concludes that the response rate to a wealth survey 'would be unlikely to rise much above 50 per cent' and that 'there was obviously a severe danger of non-response bias' (Knight, 1980, p. 36). Moreover, there may be under-statement of assets even among those who are 'successfully' interviewed.

A second major difficulty concerns the definition of wealth and the method of valuation. In parallel with the earlier discussion of income, we may want to adopt a comprehensive definition of wealth, including all assets and liabilities, but the significance of this turns on the method of valuation. A range of methods is possible, and two are considered here. The first corresponds to that adopted by the Inland Revenue in Britain and may be seen as a 'realization' value, that is the amount obtained if assets were sold on the open market. The person completing the census would therefore value his furniture at what he would get from a second-hand dealer. In contrast to this, we can consider a 'going concern' value, or what the assets are worth if they remain in his hands. On this basis, the furniture would be valued at what it would cost to replace. The difference between the two approaches is that the value as a going concern is likely in many cases to be higher than the realization value: for example, shares in a family business may be worth much more than the price obtainable on the market. In certain cases, for example, pension rights and interests in discretionary trusts, an asset may have no realization value but be worth something on a going concern basis.

There would be problems in obtaining accurate responses whichever method of valuation were adopted. With the going concern basis, these would be particularly acute, since for certain assets this would involve complex calculations concerning life expectancies, etc. Even with the market valuation, there are assets with no ready market price: e.g. houses, jewellery, unquoted shares. To give a reliable answer might therefore involve the respondent in work that is time-consuming, and expensive if he employs a professional valuer. This is all likely to lead to inaccurate valuations.

The experience with sample surveys in Britain suggests that they are unlikely to provide by themselves an adequate source of estimates of the size distribution of wealth — although they may be a useful supplement to the other sources described below. In the United States sample surveys have played a more important role, reflecting the more limited information from other sources (see below). Two of the most widely used surveys are the Survey of Financial Characteristics of Consumers of 1963–4 (SFCC) and the 1967 Survey of Economic Opportunity (SEO). The former is described by Taussig as 'the single best source of data on the distribution of wealth in the United States' (1982, p. 501), but he recognizes that it suffers from serious shortcomings, including the fact that its coverage of assets is less than comprehensive (omitted are the value of life insurance, annuities and pensions, durables other than cars, works of art, etc.), and that there is a substantial under-reporting of asset values.

Estate data

Under the present systems of taxation in Britain and the United States, the only occasion when a person's total assets and liabilities have to be revealed is at death, when a return is required for the purposes of estate taxation (Capital Transfer Tax in Britain). The estate returns are therefore an important source of information about wealth-holding and they have provided the basis for nearly all estimates of the distribution of wealth in Britain and the United States.

In effect, this method uses the estates of those dying in a particular year as a sample of the wealth of the living population. If we assume that those dying are a random sample of the living population of the same age and sex – clearly a strong assumption – then we can estimate the wealth of the living. To do this, we multiply their wealth by what is known as the 'mortality multiplier'. The mortality multiplier is the reciprocal of the mortality rate, so that if the death rate is 1 in 100, the estates are multiplied by 100 to reach an estimate of the wealth of the living. In other words, if, in a given year, 15 men aged 45–54 died leaving over £200 000 each, and the mortality rate is 1 in 100, then we assume that there are 1500 such people in the population as a whole. Since there are systematic factors influencing the rates of mortality, the multipliers are in practice adjusted in certain respects, most importantly to allow for the fact that the wealthy tend to live longer. The mortality rate applied is that for the upper social classes rather than for the general population. The multipliers are also distinguished according to marital status.

Despite such refinements, the estate method is liable to error on a number of accounts. The social class mortality rates may not in fact be appropriate for the wealthy. Mortality may be influenced by factors not taken into consideration. In the classification of estates by age and size, some of the cells contain very few estates, and there may be chance factors that cause the estimates to vary from year to year. The very nature of the estate source brings with it certain problems. The tax authorities are directly concerned with estates that are likely to be liable for duty, and the coverage below the tax exemption level is far from complete. The tax law does not necessarily embody the definition of wealth we should like to employ, and certain classes of assets may be excluded or given special treatment. The taxpayer has an incentive to reduce the value of his estate, and tax avoidance or evasion may lead to bias in the estimates. The problems are discussed further in the next section.

The investment income method

Although the estate method has been that most commonly employed in recent years, a rather different approach was much used by early writers. This takes as its starting point the statistics for investment income collected by the tax authorities, and works back from these to the capital from which the income must have been derived. The estimates are obtained not from the recorded wealth of the dead but from the recorded investment income of the living.

The main feature of this approach is the use of a 'yield multiplier' to convert the distribution of investment income to an underlying distribution of capital. The yield multiplier is the reciprocal of the yield on the wealth: if, for example, the yield is 5 per cent, then the multiplier would be $1/0.05 = 20$. In other words, with such a multiplier, an investment income of £25 000 would be converted into wealth of £500 000. The yield multiplier clearly depends on the form in which wealth is held, and the normal procedure has been to calculate a weighted average yield, based on the composition of wealth indicated by the estate statistics. In this calculation, allowance has to be made for the fact that the composition of wealth varies with the size of the holding – that cash and bank deposits (with no yield) tend to be held more by those at the lower end of the distribution and company shares (with a relatively high yield) more by the rich.

In Chapter 4, we saw that the income statistics were not necessarily accurate. To some extent, these shortcomings can be taken into account in the construction of the yield multipliers. For example, the fact that capital gains and imputed rent on owner-occupied houses are missing from the statistics does not lead to any necessary bias in the use of the investment income method, since the yield multiplier is adjusted for these omissions, only the taxable yield being taken into account. There are, however, a number of problems that cannot readily be resolved, such as the limited coverage of the investment income returns, which relate only to the top 1 per cent or so. In view of this, the investment income method is unlikely to replace the estate data as the principal source of evidence about wealth-holding; it does, none the less, provide a valuable cross-check on their accuracy.

7.2 Wealth in Britain – evidence

The 'official' Inland Revenue estimates of the distribution of wealth in Britain in 1979 are shown in Table 7.1. The estimates are derived from the estate returns but cover the marketable wealth of the entire adult population (in this respect, the figures represent a significant improvement over earlier official estimates). The results show the numbers in the adult population (those aged 18 and over) with net wealth in different

TABLE 7.1
Inland Revenue estimate of the distribution of wealth in Britain, 1979

Range of net wealth	Number of people (thousands)*	Percentage of adult population
Not over £5000	26000	63.0
Over £5000, not over £15 000	9000	22.0
Over £15 000, not over £50 000	4900	12.0
Over £50 000, not over £100 000	575	1.4
Over £100 000	250	0.6

Total wealth (£ billion) owned by		Percentage of total personal marketable wealth
Top 1 per cent of adult population	110	24.0
Top 2 per cent of adult population	147	32.0
Top 5 per cent of adult population	207	45.0
Top 10 per cent of adult population	271	59.0
Gini coefficient		0.74

*The figures have been rounded.
Source: Inland Revenue Statistics 1981, Table 4.8

ranges. The table does not, unfortunately, give the number of million-aires, but it may be seen that there were some quarter of a million people with net wealth over £100 000. It should be noted that we are concerned here with *individuals*, not families or households (this is discussed below), so that a couple could be worth £200 000. If we go down to £50 000, then about three-quarters of a million were worth this or more, and they made up some 2 per cent of the adult population.

Some indication of the degree of concentration is provided by the lower part of Table 7.1, which shows the shares in total wealth of different groups. The 2 per cent above £50 000 own 32 per cent of the total wealth. The top 1 per cent own just short of a quarter of the total wealth, which gives them an average of £¼ million each. The Inland Revenue also calculates the Gini coefficient, and the value of 0.74 is around double that found for pre-tax income (although it must be noted that the wealth figures relate to individuals, whereas the income data relate to tax units).

While the conventional picture takes the share of these top percentage groups as relating to the really rich, it is important to remember that there are great differences within the top 5 per cent, and even within the top 1 per cent. The gap between Mr X who just qualifies for the top 1 per cent and the millionaire with a household name is much larger than that between Mr X and the average wealth-holder. It may there- fore be more useful for the purposes of analysis to take a higher dividing line, closer to the level where people can begin to think about living a life of leisure (although not many, of course, choose so to do). One crude, but readily understood, criterion would be an amount equal to the total earnings of an average worker over a working lifetime: that is, the undiscounted sum of what the average person could expect to earn, allowing for the fact that real earnings are likely to rise. This would have given a figure of some £400 000 in 1979, which corresponds in broad terms to the beginning of the top 0.1 per cent of the adult popu- lation, and this is the group that will receive particular attention in the analysis of the next chapter.

The results described above are based on the estate data, and, as we have seen earlier, the mortality multiplier technique is not ideal. It is interesting, therefore, to see whether the estimates are broadly con- sistent with those obtained by the investment income method. This alternative approach does not permit estimates to be made covering the whole distribution, and in comparing the results, it has to be remembered that the basic estate estimates relate to individuals, whereas the invest- ment income data relate to income tax units in which the wealth of husband and wife is aggregated. As a result, we should expect the invest- ment income method to give higher estimates of the numbers above a given wealth level: a man worth £125 000 married to a woman worth £75 000 would appear as a single unit worth £200 000 in the invest- ment estimates. This qualification needs to be borne in mind when con- sidering the results of Atkinson and Harrison (1978a, Ch. 7), which show, for example, that in 1972/3 there were in the UK some 60 000 income units with wealth in excess of £200 000, which may be com- pared with an estate-based figure (adjusted to be comparable) of some 32 000. This suggests that the estate estimates do not exaggerate the number of large wealth-holdings.

The techniques used to obtain the official estimates were considerably improved in the course of the latter half of the 1970s (and quite a number of the deficiencies noted in the first edition of this book no longer apply). The estimates now incorporate adjustment for property held in surviving spouse settlements, discretionary trusts, and other forms that were previously missing. Consumer durables have been revalued, so that the valuation is now based on written down replacement cost rather than second-hand market prices (which certainly understated their value to a family as a 'going concern'). In the opposite direction, the value of life policies was overstated in the estate figures, since the value to living persons is significantly below the maturity value at death, and a downward adjustment has been made. These refinements are not unimportant, as is illustrated by the effect on the estimated share of the top 1 per cent in 1975 (from Dunn and Hoffman, 1978, Table 8):

Life assurance revaluation   + 1.4 percentage points
Consumer durables revaluation   - 0.6 percentage points
Discretionary and other Trusts
   adjustment   + 1.5 percentage points

There remain however a number of issues that need further investigation. Here reference is made to two of these: the incorporation of pension wealth, and family as opposed to individual wealth.

Value of pension rights

The wealth estimates in Table 7.1 did not include the contingent rights of people to occupational or state pensions. That is, when considering the wealth of Mr X when about to retire, we included the value of his house and money in the bank, but took no account of the fact that he was about to retire on a pension equal to two-thirds of his final salary. There can be little doubt that the rights to a pension have a value to the person. If he were not covered by the scheme, then he would have had to accumulate assets such as shares or bonds to generate the equivalent income stream. Put another way, why should we treat Mr X differently from Mr Y, who was self-employed and acquired financial assets in order to finance his retirement? But the problem is one of valuation.

The value of Mr X's pension rights can in principle be calculated as the expected present discounted value of the stream of pension payments. It is 'expected' since he cannot be certain what he will receive. This uncertainty is in part related to mortality, and to this extent the calculation is a matter for the actuaries. But in part it concerns the future prospects of his pension scheme. Will it continue to be able to deliver the goods? How much indexation will be provided? These are matters for the economic and political forecasters. It is 'discounted' because the payments accrue in the future, and in order to calculate the value to Mr X, we need to know what rate of discount is applicable. As we have seen in Chapter 3, there may be considerable difficulties arising from imperfections in the capital market. If the estimation of the value of his pension rights is difficult for Mr X on the point of retirement, it is a great deal more so for Mr Z aged 40, who has contributed to the scheme for nearly a quarter of a century but will have to wait the same length of time until he draws any benefit. In that time there could well be five or more governments, each with quite different views of the desirability of state pensions.

These factors need to be borne in mind when considering the estimates produced by the Inland Revenue for the distribution of wealth with allowance for occupational and state pension rights, shown in Table 7.2.

TABLE 7.2

Distribution of wealth in Britain, including the value of pension rights, 1979

Owned by most wealthy:	Percentage of total wealth		
	No allowance for pension wealth (as Table 7.1)	Occupational pension included	Occupational and state pension included
1 per cent of adult population	24	20	13
5 per cent of adult population	45	38	27
10 per cent of adult population	59	51	37
Gini coefficient	0.74	0.66–0.72	0.48–0.53
Total wealth (£ billion)	460	550	816

Source: Inland Revenue Statistics 1981, Tables 4.8, 4.9, and 4.10

The total sums involved are very substantial: £90 billion in the case of occupational pensions and £266 billion (more than half total personal marketable wealth) in the case of state pensions. Not surprisingly, the addition of these amounts makes quite a difference to the distribution. A simple 'back of the envelope' calculation brings this out. Suppose that the pension worth were owned equally by all adults, which gives some £8500 each: then the share of the top 1 per cent would become

(24% × £460 billion + 1% × £356 billion) ÷ £816 billion = 14%

The degree of concentration would fall markedly.

The method employed by Inland Revenue in constructing the estimates shown in Table 7.2 is more sophisticated in that it makes allowance for the differences in the value of rights between people, although it has no direct information on individual pension entitlement. The figures for 1975 show that the value of rights to state pensions was estimated by the government actuary to rise from £540 for men aged 20–24, and £961 for women of that age, to £6656 for men aged 65–69 and £8577 for women aged 55–59 (Royal Commission, 1977, Table 42). The state pension wealth is assumed to be allocated equally to all those of a particular age and sex. In the case of occupational pensions, two alternative assumptions are made: that rights are allocated equally, and that there is a positive correlation between the value of pension rights and other wealth. These two assumptions lead to the range for the Gini coefficient (the effect on the shares of the top 1, 5, and 10 per cent is small). As may be seen from Table 7.2, the resulting estimates of the size distribution show the major shift towards less concentration that was suggested by our 'back-of-the-envelope' calculation.

This attempt by the official statisticians to extend the scope of the wealth estimates is to be commended, and one can only wish that equal enterprise had been shown in the case of the income statistics (for example, by including the imputed rent of owner-occupiers or fringe benefits). At the same time, there are serious objections to the calculations shown in Table 7.2. It is assumed that the appropriate rate of discount is equal to the rate of earnings growth plus 1 per cent, but it is noted that 'the results depend heavily on the assumptions made as to the relationship between, on the one hand, future interest rates, and, on the other, future rates of increase in earnings' (Royal Commission, 1977, p. 88). At the very least, estimates should be presented on a variety of assumptions. After all, the value to Mr Z, aged 40, of a pension equal to 20 per cent of earnings at age 65 is some 15.5 per cent with the Inland Revenue assumption, but only 9.5 per cent if the rate of discount is 3 per cent higher than the rate of earnings growth. If the value of total pension wealth were reduced by the same proportion (i.e., to some 60 per cent of the Inland Revenue figure), then the share of the top 1 per cent would become, on our 'back-of-the-envelope' basis,

$$24\% \times £460 \text{ billion} + 1\% \times £215 \text{ billion} \div £675 \text{ billion} = 17\%.$$

The estimated size distribution may therefore be quite sensitive to the method of calculation.

Perhaps most importantly, the official treatment of the value of pension rights makes insufficient allowance for the diversity of individual rights depends on a whole range of factors, including work history, marriage and divorce, the preservation or otherwise of rights on job change, the expectations regarding the solvency of occupational schemes, etc. Individuals are likely to have quite different rates of discount. Individual life expectancies vary a great deal, depending on current health, occupation, etc. The value of state pension rights to Mr Z is considerably less if he is chain-smoking barman than if he is abstaining Free Church minister.

In short, the incorporation of the value of pension rights is a significant step, but it is important that those making use of the estimates should be fully aware of all that lies behind them.

Individuals and families

The estate-based estimates of the distribution of wealth relate to individuals — for a quite understandable reason. But, just as in the case of incomes, we may wish to take the family as the unit of analysis. As was pointed out by Daniels and Campion, 'it would be obviously misleading to place the wives and children of persons with £50 000 in the same category as paupers' (1936, p. 55). They go on to say that the 'inequality of the distribution of capital will be exaggerated in our estimates in so far as it is general practice for the whole or main part of the capital of a family to be legally vested in one of the parents' (p. 55).

Before investigating the quantitative significance of this factor, we must clarify what is meant by 'family wealth' and the weighting for family size. The interpretation, which is parallel to that used in the income distribution statistics, is that the family is the 'nuclear' family of husband, wife and dependant children. In the present context, since we are concerned only with the adult population, this means marrying up husbands and wives. On the other hand, popular usage often seems to have in mind a concept closer to 'dynastic' wealth, which would mean combining the wealth of parents, children, grandchildren, etc. Thus in the case of Sir George Wills of the Wills tobacco family, who left £9 million in 1931, we are concerned not only with the wealth of his wife, who left £73 000 in 1961, but with the fact that his sisters Hilda, Alice, Mary, and Margaret left over £3 million between them when they died in the 1940s (the source of the figures, which have been rounded, is Harbury and Hitchens, 1979). Such a concept is difficult to implement, not least because there is no natural boundary to the family (do we include Sir George's cousin, who left £200 000?), and in what follows we concentrate on the nuclear family. But the dynastic evolution of wealth-holdings will be considered in the next chapter.

The weighting by family size was discussed in principle in Chapter 3, where we saw that there were several possibilities — something that is often overlooked in empirical work. Thus the Royal Commission, in its calculations of the effect of adjusting for marriage (1975a, p. 96), treats a married couple as one unit and makes no adjustment for family size. There are a number of other assumptions that could be made, and we show below the effect of treating a couple as two units, each with half the total wealth.

The impact of 'marrying up' is governed by the degree of correlation between the wealth of husbands and wives. This depends not just on who marries whom but on the pattern of wealth-holding within marriage. Rich men may marry Eliza Doolittles but subsequently transfer wealth to them; they may marry heiresses who make over their wealth to their husbands. There is very limited evidence on this question, and the esti-mate is based on two extreme assumptions: that wealth is perfectly correlated (rich married to rich) and that the correlation is inverse (rich married to poor).

The results obtained for the share of the top 1 per cent in Great Britain in 1970 by Atkinson and Harrison (1978, Table 9.3) are shown below.

	Rich married to rich	Rich married to poor
couple = 1 unit	31.4	25.6
couple = 2 units	30.5	25.1

These figures may be compared with a corresponding figure for the dis-tribution among individuals of 30.8 per cent. The findings are similar to those for 1972 of the Royal Commission, who observe that 'the limited range of the quantile shares . . . is noteworthy' (1975a, p. 96) and con-clude that 'the distribution of wealth among single persons and husband and wife units is not greatly different from that among individuals' (1975a, p. 126).

7.3 Trends over time in the distribution of wealth in Britain

Over the course of this century, there has undoubtedly been a decline in the share of personal wealth owned by the top people. In this section we examine in greater detail the significance of this and some of the factors underlying the reduced concentration. The need for such an examination is clear from the importance attached in some quarters to the continuation of this trend. Polanyi and Wood, for example, have referred to 'The spontaneous process of "levelling-up" as the incomes and savings of the majority rise. As this process is still in its early stages by comparison with the USA, further spreading of wealth may reasonably be expected to take place without deliberate government action' (1974, p. 76). If it is true, this statement has important implications for the way in which we think about the distribution of wealth; it means that the present concentration may be only a passing phase. In what follows, we investigate whether the trends of the past may in fact be projected into the future.

In making comparisons of the distribution of wealth at different dates, or between different countries, it must be ensured that the estimates are made as far as possible on a consistent basis and that any inconsistencies are taken into account when interpreting the findings. In the present case, this poses a number of problems. The figures usually referred to go back as far as 1911-13, and while estate data do exist in a form that can be used for this purpose, they need to be treated with caution. Estimates for that year, and for the interwar period, were given in the pioneering studies of Daniels and Campion (1936) and Langley (1950); estimates for the 1950s are given in the study of Lydall and Tipping (1961). Although the basic data used by these authors were of the same form, their estimates differed with respect to coverage and to the assumptions made. The early estate data were published only for England and Wales, and the earliest estimates for Great Britain as a whole are for 1938. The multipliers applied by different investigators were in general adjusted for differences in mortality between social classes, but the early estimates were based on less accurate multipliers than those employed

TABLE 7.3
Trends in the distribution of wealth in Britain

| | Percentage of total personal wealth | | | |
| | England and Wales | | Great Britain | |
	Top 1 per cent %	Top 5 per cent %	Top 1 per cent* %	Top 5 per cent* %
1923	61	82	–	–
1925	61	82	–	–
1927	60	81	–	–
1929	56	79	–	–
1930	58	79	–	–
1936	54	77	–	–
1938	55	77	–	–
1950	47	74	47	74
1952	43	70	43	70
1954	45	72	45	72
1956	45	71	44	71
1959	41	68	42	68
1960	34	59	34	60
1962	31	55	32	55
1964	35	59	35	59
1966	31	56	31	56
1968	34	58	34	59
1970	30	54	30	54
1972	32	56	32	57

* – , data not available
Source: Atkinson and Harrison (1978), Table 6.5

by the Inland Revenue. The extent of 'missing' wealth has varied with the tax threshold and with the form of the tax law, and a variety of adjustments have been made for those below the exemption level, for settled property, etc.

Table 7.3 shows the results of an attempt to prepare consistent estimates going back to the 1920s (1938 in the case of Great Britain). The main aim is to ensure consistency, and for this reason the figures for the more recent years do not include the refinements described earlier. No allowance has been made, for example, for exempt settled property and no adjustment made to the valuation of consumer durables or life assurance policies. In view of this, we also show in Fig. 7.1 the shorter time series formed by linking the more refined estimates of Atkinson and Harrison for the period 1966–72 with the Inland Revenue estimates for 1971–9. (The former relate to Great Britain, and the latter to the United Kingdom.)

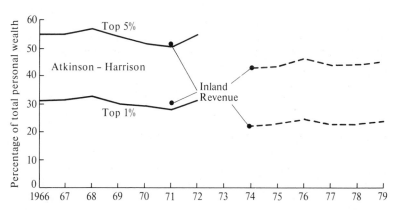

Fig. 7.1 Trend in distribution of wealth in Britain, 1966–1979. *Source*: Atkinson and Harrison (1978a), Table 5.4 and *Inland Revenue Statistics*, 1978, Table 4.22, and 1981, Table 4.8

In considering the trend shown in Table 7.3, it has to be remembered that there are still respects in which the estimates for different years are not fully comparable, particularly because of changes in the form and coverage of the estate statistics. The most serious breaks are indicated by spaces between the relevant rows in the table. It can be seen that there is a discrete downward shift in the shares between 1959 and 1960: the share of the top 1 per cent falls by 7–8 percentage points and that of the top 5 per cent falls by 8–9 percentage points. This must in part reflect a lack of comparability in the statistics.

When allowance is made for the breaks in the series, the figures suggest that there has been a downward trend over the period of approximately 0.4 percentage points in the share of the top 1 per cent (Atkinson and Harrison, 1978, Ch. 6). The trend appears to have been quite steady. Despite the claim of the *Sunday Times* that 'the erosion of the share of personal wealth held by the richest [has been] gathering momentum since the Second World War' (3 August 1975), there is no evidence of an acceleration. It may also be noted that the downward trend for the top 5 per cent is similar in absolute magnitude, suggesting that those in the range immediately below the top have not suffered a reduction in their share.

The trend over this century is often extrapolated into the future, with the suggestion that before long the present high degree of concentration will disappear. Whether it is legitimate to make such predictions on the basis of past experience depends crucially, however, on the causes of the decline. That the interpretation of the evidence is of central importance is illustrated below, with reference to four possible forces underlying the changes in the distribution.

Tax avoidance Over the course of this century, the nominal rates of tax have risen very considerably: in 1911 an estate of £1 million paid duty of 14 per cent. There can be little doubt, therefore, that the incentive to avoid taxation has increased. This need not affect the interpretation of the evidence in Table 7.3. Avoidance does not necessarily lead to property being missing. One important avenue of avoidance, however, for much of the period (up to the introduction of Capital Transfer Tax) was through gifts. The wealth given away still appears in the statistics, but it belongs to someone else, and an increase of gifts may well affect the *distribution* of wealth. Revell (1965) argued that wealthy persons had increasingly relinquished part of their capital to their heirs before death. This may be expected to have reduced the share of wealth held by the top 1 per cent and to have raised that of the heirs, who were probably in the top 5 per cent. For example, if a person worth £100 000 gave half of it to his two sons, divided equally, then the share of the top 1 per cent fell and the wealth put his sons in the top 2½ per cent. From the table it would appear that Revell's view could explain part of the change over the period 1923–59, when the top 1 per cent in England and Wales lost 20 per cent and the next 4 per cent of wealth-owners *gained* 6 per cent, although since 1960 the share of the next 4 per cent has remained broadly unchanged.

Women and wealth Over the course of the century there has been an increase in wealth-holding among women. There have always been women of means, but in recent years two factors have increased the share of property owned by women: the tendency for married couples to hold property jointly, and the increased longevity of women (the estimates of Revell show that the increase in wealth-holding is particularly marked among widows). The effect of married couples sharing ownership is rather like that of gifts. If husbands born in a post-Victorian era shared their wealth equally with their wives, then a single wealth holding of £50 000 might be replaced by two of £25 000 which again would have the effect of lowering the share of the top 1 per cent of individual wealth-holders while raising that of the next 4 per cent. The trends may in part, therefore, reflect a move towards sexual equality and not a redistribution between rich and poor *families.*

Owner-occupation One of the most striking social changes since the beginning of this century has been the increase in owner-occupation. Between 1900 and 1970, the proportion of owner-occupied dwellings rose from around 10 per cent to 50 per cent. Coupled with the rise in house prices, this must have had a profound effect on the distribution: 'when one individual owned several houses which he let out as an investment, he had a good chance of appearing in the top 1 per cent, whereas the houses now appear in a number of smaller estates' (Revell, 1965, p. 381). The fact that a person owns a house does not, of course, imply that he has significant *net* worth, and if the increase in owner-occupation was largely made up of young couples with 90 per cent mortgages, then the quantitative effect would be small. However, the increase of house prices over the past decades has meant that most owner-occupiers now own a substantial part of the value of their house. It is reasonable to suppose that the increase in owner-occupation has led to a definite reduction in the degree of concentration.

Share prices Given that assets take different forms at different levels of wealth-holding, changes in their relative prices may well affect the distribution. This is particularly important in the case of shares, quoted and unquoted, which are held disproportionately by the very rich, and which vary considerably in price. According to the estimate of the Royal Commission (1979a, Table 6.11), well over three-quarters of personally held company shares are in the hands of the top 5 per cent of wealth-holders. Personally held shares are now in a minority, but the indirect effect of asset prices via the holdings of institutions such as banks and insurance companies is likely to operate slowly. The main impact of short-term movements in stock exchange prices is likely therefore to be on top wealth-owners. In a statistical analysis of the changes between 1923 and 1972, Atkinson and Harrison (1978, Ch. 9) found a significant relationship between the share of the top 1 per cent and the share price index. A collapse of the stock market such as that in 1973-4, when the index fell by some 40 per cent, would on this basis be associated with a decline of some 3 percentage points in the share of the top 1 per cent.

The analysis of the four factors just described is not intended to cast doubt on the changes in the distribution; the spread of home ownership, for example, is clearly a genuine reduction in concentration. The main point is to bring out the need to understand the forces at work before one can make confident predictions *about the future*. To the extent that the trend is due to increased owner-occupation, the spreading of this effect through the whole population depends on a further growth in home ownership or a rise in house prices relative to other assets. To the extent that it is attributable to falls on the stock exchange, it must be borne in mind that these may be reversed in different economic and social conditions. The evidence for the 1970s shown in Fig. 7.1 is instructive. From the Inland Revenue figures, there appears to have been a fall in the shares of the top groups in the early part of the decade; and the fall in the stock market is likely to have been part of the explanation. After that, the series shows little sign of a downward trend, which may reflect factors such as the slower growth of owner-occupation. This provides a warning that one cannot simply extrapolate a process of 'spontaneous levelling-up' into the future.

7.4 Wealth in the United States

In the United States, *Fortune* magazine reported in 1968 a study of 'America's centi-millionaires', which identified 153 individuals whose wealth exceeded $100 million, including that owned by spouses, minor children and trusts. The list, which contained a lot of familiar names (five Rockefellers, three Fords, three Du Ponts, the founders of Hewlett-Packard, Chester Carlson who invented Xerox, and so on), was built up by considering each person's assets. As such, it undoubtedly involved a substantial element of guesswork, but it may give a better impression of the very top of the wealth scale — at that date — than the sources to which we now turn.

The first source is the sample survey described earlier: the Survey of Financial Characteristics of Consumers in 1962. According to the presentation of the results by Taussig (1982), the degree of concentration indicated by that survey was not dissimilar from that found in Britain.

The Gini coefficient is reported as 0.76 (Taussig, 1982, Table 1), with the top 1 per cent of family units owning some 30 per cent of total wealth. At the same time, Taussig emphasizes the shortcomings of the survey, including its limited coverage of assets. Moreover, it is now considerably dated.

More recent evidence, and evidence that can be compared more directly with the statistics for Britain, is provided by studies based on the estate records. This approach was particularly developed by Lampman (1962), who applied mortality multipliers to the basic estate returns, and the multipliers were adjusted to apply to higher wealth classes. He distinguished between 'prime' wealth ('to which a person has full title and over which he has the power of disposal') and 'total' wealth, which is a broader concept, including private pension rights and property held in trust. These two definitions correspond in broad terms to 'realization' and 'going concern' valuations. As in Britain, the estate returns cover only the larger wealth-holders, with the shortfall being even more serious in view of the relatively high exemption level ($60 000). Lampman concentrated on the group owning $60 000 or more, whom he referred to as 'top wealth-holders', although since the lower limit is less than one-thousandth of the amount required to appear in the *Fortune* list, the term 'top' may be rather misleading. In order to allow for the wealth of those not covered by the estate data, Lampman made use of independent estimates of the total holdings of different assets (the total personal holding of government bonds, for example, can be estimated from the issuing source). He also made adjustments for wealth missing from the estate returns.

Lampman found that in 1953 the top wealth-holders made up 1.6 per cent of the adult population and owned 30 per cent of prime wealth (it is interesting that the alternative definition, total wealth, gave the very similar figure of 32 per cent). For purposes of comparison, it is easier to take the share of the top 1 per cent of the adult population, which was 24 per cent in 1953. This may be compared with the estimates for Britain for the early 1950s, of over 40 per cent belonging to the top 1 per cent. Lampman himself concluded that there was much greater concentration in England and Wales than in the United States.

The long-term trends were examined by Lampman, who presented estimates going back to 1922. These showed that the share of the top 1 per cent of the adult population rose during the 1920s from 32 per cent to a peak of 36 per cent in 1929; that it fell with the great crash in 1929, and reached 28 per cent in 1933. It fell still further to 21 per cent in 1949, but after that date the trend appeared to have ceased.' Lampman also drew attention to the effect of taking the distribution among *families* rather than individuals. The share of the top 2 per cent of families was estimated very approximately to have fallen only from 33 per cent in 1922 to 29 per cent in 1953. Lampman concluded that 'a considerably greater amount of splitting of estates between spouses was being practised in 1953 than in 1922' and that 'the decline in inequality shown on the basis of individuals tends to be an overstatement of the decline which would be found on a family basis' (1959, p. 388).

The estate method has been used in more recent years by Natrella (1975) and Smith and Franklin (1974). Natrella calculates that in 1972 the share of the top 1 per cent in total wealth in the United States was some 26 per cent and that the share of the top 5 per cent was 45 per cent. These figures are close in definition to the Inland Revenue estimates described earlier, and provide the basis for the conclusion of Harrison that 'the shares of top wealth-holders in the USA at the turn of the 1970s were appreciably lower than those in the UK' (1979, p. 69). On the other hand, the difference may be narrowing. Smith and Franklin investigate the trends over time, using the estate approach, and suggest that there had been little change in the United States over the postwar period. Their estimates, designed to be consistent with those of Lampman, indicate that the share of the top ½ per cent of the total population was no lower in 1969 than in 1949. The conclusion reached by Smith and Franklin is that:

Wealth in the United States has become less concentrated in the last half century. The diminution has not been great, however, and it all occurred during periods when the market system was functioning under duress or was in administrative abeyance, specifically, the Great Depression and World War II. (1974, p. 163)

This conclusion may need to be modified in the light of further refinements, but it has important implications for those who believe that the US experience is relevant to that in Britain: there may be no certainty of a trend towards reduced concentration.

7.5 Distribution of wealth and the individual life-cycle

Up to this point we have been concerned with the concentration of wealth-holding in the entire adult population at a particular date (the 'current distribution'), and this clearly needs careful interpretation before we can draw conclusions about the existence of inequality. In this section we examine one important consideration: the relationship between wealth-holding and the individual life-cycle. In the analysis of the distribution of income, it was recognized that annual income data may overstate the degree of lifetime inequality as a result of the systematic variation of income with age. In the same way, the current distribution of wealth may overstate the degree of inequality in a lifetime sense, as a result of age differences. Great importance has been attached to age differences, for example, by Polanyi and Wood (1974), who suggest that the observed distribution of wealth is not very different from 'the "10 per cent owns 30 per cent" which would reflect differences in wealth from savings accumulated through a lifetime, even if incomes and inheritance were equal'.

The extent of concentration of wealth in a hypothetical egalitarian society of this kind may be seen as follows. Suppose everyone is identical in every respect apart from age (having the same market opportunities and the same tastes), and inheritance and gifts are prohibited. Let us assume that, after reaching the age of 25, all individuals live for a fixed period (50 years). They spend the first 40 years of this period working for a wage which is the same for everyone, and during this period they save for their retirement. They can borrow or lend freely at a constant interest rate (again the same for everyone). They are assumed to know for certain that they will live for 50 years and to plan for a constant stream of consumption. They leave no bequests and make no gifts. If we take a zero rate of interest and assume a constant population, the pattern of wealth-holding has the particularly straightforward form shown in Fig. 7.2. From this it can readily be calculated that the wealthiest 10 per cent of the adult population (those aged 62–66) account for 19 per cent of the total wealth.

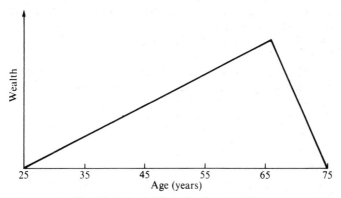

Fig. 7.2 A simple life-cycle of asset-holding

This model is highly simplified and does not take account of factors such as a positive rate of interest, a growing population, propertyless married women, and the existence of (equal) inheritance. If allowance is made for these factors, the results suggest that the share of the top 10 per cent could in this hypothetical egalitarian society reach 30 per cent of the total wealth (Atkinson, 1971), but the share of the top 1 per cent in the hypothetical society would be some 3 per cent, which *is* very different from that observed in Britain.

What relevance have these hypothetical calculations to the distribution of wealth in Britain? In order to assess this, we may look at the actual pattern of wealth-holding by age. From the estate statistics it is possible to make estimates of the distribution of wealth within age (and sex) groups. By standardizing for age in this way, we should be able to eliminate the major life-cycle differences, and hence throw light on the importance of life-cycle factors in giving rise to 'apparent' inequality in the current distribution.

TABLE 7.4

Distribution by age and sex groups, Great Britain, 1975

Age	Male			Female		
	Proportion of wealth in that class owned by top					
	1%	5%	10%	1%	5%	10%
25–34	20	36	50	29	55	73
35–44	16	35	48	39	63	78
45–54	21	41	54	24	49	66
55–64	26	48	61	23	49	68
65–74	30	55	70	21	45	63
75–84	24	47	63	17	39	57
85–	23	45	59	17	40	57
Whole population aged 25 and over (male and female combined)	22	44	59	22	44	59

Note: these figures are not comparable with those in Tables 7.1–7.3; for example, they relate to the population aged 25 and over, and make no allowance for missing wealth.

Source: Royal Commission (1977), Table 32.

In Table 7.4, we show the estimates given by the Royal Commission for 1975. These allow us to compare the degree of concentration within age groups with that in the population as a whole. If there were significantly less concentration among people of the same age, then this would indicate that life-cycle factors were important. In fact, this does not seem to be the case. For the whole population, the share of the top 1 per cent was 22 per cent. Considering men first, in only three age groups is the share less than 22 per cent, and in no case is the difference very large: the lowest figure is 16 per cent for the age group 35–44. In the case of women, the share of the top 1 per cent is again lower in only three age groups, and in no case does it fall below 17 per cent. These figures suggest that the degree of concentration within age groups is not markedly less than in the population as a whole. It should however be noted that the figures in Table 7.4 are not adjusted for the valuation of life assurance (which tends to vary with age), nor do they include the value of pension rights.

In the United States, the age pattern has been investigated using the data collected in the 1962 survey. Whereas the Gini coefficient for all consumer units was 0.76, it was 0.70 or 0.71 for the three age groups 35–44, 45–54, and 55–64, and rises to 0.76 for those 65 and over and 0.83 for those aged under 35. Taussig concludes that the 'Survey results suggest that the overall wealth inequality cannot be explained simply as the result of the expected life-cycle variation in wealth holdings between individuals and families at different stages' (1982, p. 503). Similarly, Brittain reaches the view that 'neither the US nor the British evidence proves the wealth–age relationship . . . to be a major factor in generating inequality' (1978, p. 71).

If the observed concentration of wealth cannot be attributed largely to life-cycle differences, then we have to seek the explanation elsewhere. It may result from differences in earnings and savings; it may reflect differing luck in investment; it may be due to inheritance. In the next chapter we examine these possible mechanisms.

Notes on sources and further reading

The methods used to estimate the size distribution of wealth in Britain are described in Atkinson and Harrison (1978a, b) and in the reports of the Royal Commission on the Distribution of Income and Wealth. The developments to the official statistics in the late 1970s are discussed in Dunn and Hoffman (1978, 1981).

The trends over time in the distribution of wealth in Britain are discussed at length in Atkinson and Harrison (1978a). Reference should be made to the classic studies of Clay (1925), Daniels and Campion (1936), Campion (1939), Langley (1951), and Lydall and Tipping (1961). The statistical analysis of share prices, and other factors, (including owner-occupation), is reported in Atkinson and Harrison (1978a, Ch. 9; 1978b), the latter being reprinted in Atkinson (1980b, 1983).

The evidence on the distribution of wealth in ten countries (the United States, Canada, Australia, New Zealand, Denmark, Sweden, Belgium, France, West Germany, and Ireland) is summarized by Harrison (1979), who discusses the problems of securing comparable estimates. The recent evidence in the United States is described in Smith and Franklin (1974), Wolff (1980), Smith (1982), Taussig (1982), and Greenwood (1981). The Canadian evidence is described by Davies (1979) and Wolfson (1979); the Australian evidence is covered by Podder and Kakwani (1976). Extensive research on the distribution of wealth in France has been undertaken by the Centre de Recherche Economique sur l'Epargne (see Kessler, Masson and Strauss-Kahn, 1982). The evidence on the Irish Republic has been developed by Lyons (1974), who has also provided evidence for Northern Ireland (Lyons, 1972).

The life-cycle aspects of wealth-holding are discussed by Lydall (1955), Atkinson (1971; reprinted in Atkinson, 1983), Astin (1975), Shorrocks (1975), Atkinson and Harrison (1978a, Ch. 9), Dunn and Hoffman (1981), Wolff (1981), and, using Canadian data, King and Dicks-Mireaux (1982). The calculation of the possible contribution of the life-cycle factor to wealth concentration is the subject of Atkinson (1971), Royal Commission (1975a; 1977, Ch. 9), Flemming (1979), Oulton (1976), Jones (1978), and Davies and Shorrocks (1978).

8

WEALTH AND THE CAUSES OF CONCENTRATION

The ownership of personal or material productive capacity is based upon a complex mixture of inheritance, luck and effort, probably in that order of relative importance.

(Frank H. Knight)

The last chapter described the degree of concentration of wealth-holding in Britain and the United States. We saw that the distribution, particularly the holdings at the very top, could not be explained entirely by age. We now examine some of the main forces at work, focusing especially on how people get to be very rich (the top 0.1 per cent).

8.1 The steady saver

Suppose first we consider a simple process of accumulation, where a person saves out of his earnings and ploughs back the income on his capital, including the capital gains. He is a portfolio investor, putting his money into quoted company shares or government securities — or even into the savings bank. Now this can generate differences in the wealth owned by people of the same age. These differences may arise because of differences in earnings, which allow the higher-paid to save more; or people may get different returns on their saving; or some people may be more thrifty than others.

In order to see the force of thrift, let us take a concrete example. Suppose that Mr A has average earnings, which rise in real terms at an annual rate of 3 per cent, and that he saves 5 per cent of his earnings each year. He receives interest of 4½ per cent in real terms and all of this is reinvested. If he begins at age 25, he will have amassed capital of something like nine times his initial annual earnings (in real terms) by the time he retires at 65. This will not put him in the top 1 per cent, let alone anywhere near the top 0.1 per cent. If the proportion of earnings saved were a quarter rather than 5 per cent, he would accumulate an amount equal to some forty-five times annual average earnings, and would be about halfway to joining the top 0.1 per cent. Even to get this far would require a high degree of abstinence, and it is interesting to note in this context the example cited by Runciman (1974, p. 104) of Mr Rowse, a London bus driver who died in 1972 leaving £62 388; he was reported to have had no children, to have never taken a holiday and to have had just the bare necessities.

The force of the numerical example given in the previous paragraph depends on the rate of return that the person was assumed to get on his capital, as can be seen from the following variations on the calculation:

Return on wealth %	Amount accumulated at age 65 as multiple of initial earnings (in real terms)*
10	33
8	20
6	12
3	7

* (Saving 5 per cent of earnings from age 25.) These figures may be compared with the amount required to enter the top 0.1 per cent, which is some 100 times average earnings.

Whether a small saver stands any chance of catching up with the top 0.1 per cent in his lifetime depends, therefore, on the yield he can expect on his wealth. If we base the predicted yield on the return to ordinary shares over the past fifty years, it is at first sight encouraging, if we look at the combined dividend income and capital appreciation. However, we need to allow for inflation and for the effect of taxation. When the rise in prices is taken into account, and the income tax and capital gains tax subtracted, then the real return on ordinary shares has been some 5 per cent or less: for the period 1950–77, Hemming and Kay (1981) indicate that the real return *before tax* was 4.8 per cent. For the 1970s alone, the real return has been negative. Forecasting future rates of return is dangerous, and it may be that the next half-century will see higher rates of yield, but at least historically the ordinary investor's return is likely to have been towards the lower end of the range shown above.

It is of course possible to beat the market, and Hemming and Kay draw attention to the fact that the real return to Bordeaux First Growths from 1970 to 1977 was 7.8 per cent. Differences in rates of return is undoubtedly an element that needs to be taken into account. Russell (1982) has shown how random investments on the New York Stock Exchange can generate after forty years a distribution with a Gini co-efficient close to that observed for wealth. At the same time, this entails investors being willing to accept large risks: 'if one is willing to take enormous risks, the New York stock exchange lottery can confer enormous rewards albeit with low probability' (Russell, 1982, p. 390). Although it may be possible to explain part of the concentration in this way, taking into consideration differences in attitudes towards risk, in effect it involves an activity more akin to the entrepreneurship discussed in the next section than 'steady' accumulation. Moreover, to the extent that the effect would be compounded over time, we would expect the concentration of wealth to increase with age, but the evidence of the previous chapter did not suggest that this happens.

So far we have considered Mr A with average earnings. The combination of high earnings and exceptional thrift could well allow a person to save enough to join the top 0.1 per cent. However, at a return of 5 per cent he would not do so until late in life. A person with three times the average earnings, saving a quarter of his earnings, would not reach wealth of one hundred times national average earnings until nearly the age of 60. This cannot account for the substantial proportion of the top 0.1 per cent under this age – in 1968 nearly one-third were aged under 45.

The limited ability of those with high earned incomes to accumulate may come as a surprise, as is well brought out by Kay and King's hypothetical senior manager retiring from a senior positon on the board of a large British corporation, earning £50 000:

Few people are as successful as this: the number of company directors who matched his peak salary . . . was around a hundred, and there are perhaps twenty people starting work this year who can aspire to these heights.

Our hypothetical manager has fairly frugal tastes and throughout his lifetime has reckoned to save around a quarter of his after-tax income . . . Feeling, with some justice, that he has been unusually fortunate in his career and unusually thrifty in his actions, he may be somewhat surprised to discover that there are in Britain at least 100 000 people richer than he is. (Kay and King, 1980, p. 59)

It appears that the distribution of wealth cannot be attributed simply to age differences coupled with earnings differentials: while life-cycle considerations together with earnings inequality may well account for a lot of inequality of wealth, they cannot account for its peak, or for the distribution of estates, or for the fact that wealth in each age group is distributed more like that of wealth in the population as a whole than like the distribution of earnings (Flemming and Little, 1974, p. 4).

8.2 Self-made fortunes

If differences in thrift and earnings cannot provide the answer, then it is the rate of return that must be the key factor in explaining the origin of new fortunes. We have already seen that the 'lucky' investor, who obtains a return considerably above the market average, may be able to accumulate enough to join the top 0.1 per cent, but the main way in which it can be done is by becoming an active and successful entrepreneur. As described by *Fortune*, 'it is necessary to enter a business at or near the ground floor, to hold a major interest, and to resist selling during hard times' (May 1968). Not only is the return to the successful likely to be much higher than from armchair investment, but the process of accumulation is favoured by the tax system. A businessman can set the costs of expansion against taxable profits, and when he floats his company on the stock exchange, the resulting capital gains are taxed at a lower rate than investment income. It is as the result of this, according to Copeman and Rumble, that 'one can see really successful new business owners become millionaires or even multi-millionaires in 10 to 20 years, even in very highly taxed countries where top salaried men are very tightly pinched' (1972, p. 25).

The process may be illustrated by one British 'success' story described in the *Guardian* (19 May 1979). Mr Richard Tompkins left school at 14 and worked as a delivery boy in a laundry, but he went on to found Green Shield trading stamps and the Argos catalogue showrooms. According to the newspaper report, he was the highest-paid executive in Britain at £350 000 a year, but this was dwarfed by the amount received for the sale of the Argos business to B.A.T. Industries, expected to be some £30 million. This capital sum is nearly a hundred times his salary as the highest-paid executive – and puts him in a totally different league from Kay and King's hypothetical manager.

The sources of self-made fortunes are very varied, as is illustrated by the *Fortune* list of American centi-millionaires, who range from the Rockefellers to Bob Hope. Some important routes to such wealth can be distinguished. The first is the invention or development of a new technique or product. The wealth of such men as Mr Chester Carlson (Xerox) and Dr Land (Polaroid Camera) represents, in part, the monopoly rent that can be extracted by inventors or innovators. Invention, by itself, is not enough, there being many instances where the originator was not the person who obtained the monopoly rent, and the commercial exploitation of the idea is clearly of great importance. Commercial success depends to a large extent on an ability to forecast future consumer needs, and indeed this responsiveness to market trends is in itself a second major source of self-made fortunes. The success of many entrepreneurs derives not so much from inventing a new product or mode of production, as from being in a rapidly growing industry. This was probably true of the motor industry millionaires, of those who developed airline travel, of those who saw the prospects for electronics and computing after the Second World War, and those who developed supermarket and chain trading.

A third, rather different, element is the ownership of natural resources. The discovery of oil or other minerals has led to many self-made fortunes, often unrelated to any active entrepreneurial effort. The substantial increase in the value of building land has, on a smaller scale, had a rather similar effect. The ability to exploit natural resources depends in some cases on decisions by government bodies, particularly planning and zoning. This introduces a fourth element: the impact of government restrictions and the gains that can be made by those able to circumvent the restrictions. This has been apparent in the case of property development in Britain. On top of an acute shortage of office accommodation in London after the Second World War were imposed planning controls, which generated very substantial gains to those with the knowledge to exploit restrictions such as those on permitted floor-space. In the same way, the ban on office building in 1964 led to large capital gains on complete buildings. The fifth, and final, element is that of pure luck, of being in the right place at the right time, or of a gamble coming off. In this context it must be remembered that the generation of self-made fortunes very often involves a substantial element of risk-taking. Whether it arises from uncertainty concerning the outcome of an invention (Land worked for years perfecting the Polaroid camera) or of exploration for natural resources, whether it arises from uncertainty concerning the decisions of competitors or the government, there is an ever-present risk of loss or outright failure. The successful entrepreneurs discussed here are only a small fraction of those who set out to make money this way. To quote Josiah Wedgewood (1929), himself the descendant of an archetypal self-made entrepreneur, they must 'take great risks and [have] exceptional luck or exceptional talent'.

The relative importance of these different elements can be determined only by taking a representative sample of self-made millionaires and examining in detail the role played in the origin of their fortunes by the five factors described above. An illustration is provided in the study by Rubinstein (1971) of the industrial origins of British fortunes (both self-made and inherited), which are classified as 'old' (agriculture, textiles, foreign trade, etc.). 'intermediate' (brewing, engineering, etc.) and 'new' (retail, newspapers, property development, etc.). Of the millionaires dying in the latter part of the last century, 81 per cent were classified as having wealth originating from old industries; by 1920–39 this proportion had gone down to 48 per cent and that of new industries had risen to 25 per cent; finally, by 1960–9, old and new industries were equally represented. This shows, as expected, a steady shift in the direction of industries that were growing more rapidly.

8.3 Inheritance and the transmission of wealth

What happens to the wealth of self-made entrepreneurs when they die? As Rubinstein (1980) has noted, the 'science-fiction fantasy of a single estate snowballing over the decades' has not materialized:

Had Vanderbilt's $100 million of 1877 been kept intact and reinvested in the leading growth sectors of the American economy, its size a century later would be simply beyond reckoning. On the contrary, the Vanderbilt dynasty itself is now largely vanished from the rollcall of the very rich. (1980, p. 27)

On the other hand, inheritance is an important element in many cases. Sir George Wills, for example, referred to in the previous chapter, had been preceded by his father, of the same name, who left £24 million in 1928 and his grandfather, Henry Overton Wills III, who died in 1911 leaving £21 million. In this section we examine the role of 'inheritance', a term used here to denote all wealth receipts, including both bequests and transfers from living people.

A stylized pattern of wealth transmission between generations is shown in Fig. 8.1. It begins with a self-made man, who through the processes described in the previous section has accumulated a substantial

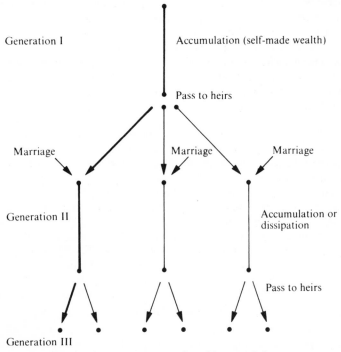

Fig. 8.1 A stylized pattern of wealth transmission

fortune. This fortune is passed on to his heirs, who belong to Generation II. The heirs may also inherit from other members of Generation I (e.g. an uncle or aunt), and they may marry into money. The total received through inheritance and marriage provides the 'start' in life of the second generation. This wealth may be augmented through further saving, and indeed the heirs may become active entrepreneurs; alternatively, it may be dissipated. The resulting wealth then passes to their heirs in Generation III and the process continues.

The pattern set out in Fig. 8.1 was described as 'stylized' because it leaves out a number of elements. Transfers of wealth do not necessarily pass from one generation to the next; they may pass from brother to brother; they may pass from employer to chauffeur; they may skip a generation (grandfather to grandchild). Wealth may be transferred to charitable or other bodies. In Britain there is little evidence that charitable bequests exercise an important equalizing influence, although they are clearly much more common in the United States, as is exemplified by the Ford, Rockefeller, Carnegie and other foundations. Finally, transfers need not necessarily take place at death, and estate taxation may provide a strong incentive for gifts before death.

The pattern of wealth transmission shown in Fig. 8.1 does, nevertheless, serve to bring out some of the important influences at work in determining whether the wealth of this dynasty grows or dies away over time. If Generation I made a million through his enterprise, how likely is it that Generation III will still be millionaires? Will we have a situation like that of the Vanderbilt family, or will it be more like the Rockefellers?

The pattern of inheritance

Laws and customs regarding the division of wealth among heirs vary greatly between societies. In some cases there are legal restrictions placed on the disposal of estates at death. The law of *legitim* (or reserved portion) found in some European countries entitles the heirs to a certain proportion of the estate, depending on the degree of relationship. Similar provisions apply in other countries when a person dies without making a will. An example of such intestacy succession is shown below (taken from the Ohio State Law). When there is no surviving spouse, the estate

Decedent with surviving spouse

No children	1 child	2 or more children
Spouse $\frac{3}{4}$	Spouse $\frac{1}{2}$	Spouse $\frac{1}{3}$
Parents $\frac{1}{4}$	Child $\frac{1}{2}$	Children share $\frac{2}{3}$

is divided equally among all children, and if there are no surviving children, it goes to more distant relations.

The broad effects of laws of *legitim* or intestacy for the transfer of wealth to the next generation are to divide estates equally among all children. This pattern of inheritance gives the greatest force for the equalization of wealth. If the average self-made millionaire (and spouse) has 2.4 children, and they in turn have 2.4 children, the amount inherited by Generation III under equal division would be £175 000 and by Generation V it would be down to £30 000 (assuming no new accumulation took place). This strong equalizing tendency may be modified by marriage, but it is clear that equal division could lead to a relatively rapid departure from the top 0.1 per cent.

Equal division is not, however, the only possible pattern of inheritance. At the other extreme is the custom of primogeniture, by which all wealth is passed on to the eldest child or eldest son. In terms of Fig. 8.1 this would mean that wealth followed the route marked with a heavy line; it would remain intact, leaving aside savings or dissaving, from generation to generation. This custom was associated in the past with landed estates, but appears to have been practised also in the case of other forms of wealth. Between the extreme cases of primogeniture and equal division are various other patterns of division. Estates may be equally divided among male children; estates may be divided between sons and daughters in an unequal proportion. A pattern that is not uncommon is that all children receive a 'comfortable' amount and the remainder goes to the eldest child (a modified form of primogeniture).

Evidence about the division of estates can be obtained from the probate records and the wills of the deceased, although it should be stressed that this information is often difficult to interpret (for example, where it is a question of valuing the interest in a settlement). This approach was used in the pioneering study in Britain by Wedgwood, who found that:

There is little doubt that, among the very wealthy, equal division of the spoils among the family, irrespective of place and sex, is not the general rule. It appeared to be usual, among wealthier predecessors in my sample, for the sons to receive a larger share than the daughters. In the case of the smaller estates, equal division is much more common. (1928, p. 48)

He also found that 'frequently the lion's share of the estate went to one particular son — usually, but not always, the eldest' (1929, p. 164).

In the United States, evidence has been collected by Menchik from a sample of estates in Connecticut leaving more than $40 000 in the 1930s and 1940s. His findings are quite different from those of Wedgwood for Britain:

wealth bequeathed to children is shared equally between children of opposite sex . . . the bequest proportion received by males does not significantly increase with the size of the estate bequeathed . . . First- or earlier-born children do not receive larger bequests than their later born siblings . . . In most cases the children received equal, or within one percentage point of equal, shares. (1980, p. 314)

That his findings should be different is in no way surprising. Customs with regard to inheritance patterns may be expected to vary across countries; and it is of course quite possible that the position has changed in Britain since Wedgwood's study.

Family size

Where wealth is shared among all children, the question of family size becomes important. If the wealthy tend to have larger-than-average families, then the tendency towards equality will be stronger. If wealthy families had three children, rather than 2.4, £1 million would be reduced to £12 500 each by Generation V. However, from the very limited evidence regarding the family size of the top 0.1 per cent, it seems unlikely that this is a major equalizing factor.

One aspect that is often overlooked is the relationship between family size, the sex of the children, and the pattern of division. There are reasons to expect primogeniture, in its pure or modified form, to be preferred in a large family. This is especially the case where primogeniture is linked with the control of a business enterprise or of an estate, and for this purpose the next generation must contain a son willing and able to take over. As Dr Johnson said of the Thrale brewing family, 'the desire of male heirs is not appendant only to feudal tenures. A son is almost necessary to the continuance of Thrale's fortune; for what can Misses do with a brewhouse?' Although these remarks may not apply with equal force in a more liberated age, the reasons for maintaining wealth intact via primogeniture are still likely to be less pressing where there is no heir to play an active role in management.

Marriage

In the examination of the effect of primogeniture and equal division, we referred to the influence of the patterns of intermarriage between families on the development of wealth-holding. If no property were vested in women, marriage as such would have little effect on the distribution: wealth would pass from father to son(s) in the way described above. However, there have always been wealthy heiresses, and it has become increasingly common over this century for women to hold wealth in their own right. As a result, an heir may receive a substantial part of his fortune through his mother's side of the family.

The influence of marriage patterns where there is equal division and women inherit on equal terms with men can be seen in terms of the following example. Suppose that all families have two children (a boy and a girl) and that the whole of the wealth of the country is initially in the hands of the top 5 per cent. If people choose their marriage partners at random, most of the children of the top 5 per cent marry people with no wealth and the degree of concentration tends to fall over time. In practice, however, it seems unlikely that the pattern of marriage will take this form. The rich tend to marry the rich because they have the same social background and are quite simply more likely to meet each other. From an analysis of the estates of the fathers and fathers-in-law of top wealth-holders in Britain, Harbury and Hitchens concluded that 'approximately 60 per cent of rich sons (daughters) of rich fathers marry daughters (sons) from wealthy families' (1979, p. 96). In the extreme case, where the rich intermarry completely, the degree of concentration will not be reduced, even though estates are equally divided. Class marriage, where husband and wife come from families with the same level of wealth, leads to effectively the same situation as where all property is inherited by sons; it is equivalent, in this sense at least, to everyone marrying his sister.

We have described three important elements determining the outcome of the transmission process: the division of estates, family size, and the pattern of marriage. It is evident that a large fortune is more likely to be dissipated if it is equally divided at death, if there are several children, and if they marry outside the wealthy class. What is less evident is the interaction between the different elements. This is illustrated in Table 8.1, where for simplicity we assume that there is no new accumulation, and that each family has an equal number of boys and girls.

Where the eldest son inherits (the second column in Table 8.1), and each family has two children, the distribution remains unchanged over time. In this case, the marriage pattern makes no difference. Where the family size is greater than two, then the distribution becomes more concentrated over time, in the sense that the wealth-owning families become a smaller proportion of the total. The degree of concentration also increases where the wealth is left to the eldest child, whether boy or girl, and this applies even where there are only two children (see column 1 in Table 8.1). The family size does however affect the *speed* with which the distribution becomes more concentrated, as does the pattern of marriage (with random marriage it is less likely that heirs will marry heiresses). Where wealth is equally divided among male children, the distribution again remains stable, in the sense that the share of the top groups is unchanged. In the case of no population growth this is, of course, the same as primogeniture. Equal division among *all* children, on the other hand, brings marriage into importance; and where marriage is random, there is a tendency to equalization. Unless there is purely class marriage, the share of the top groups will be falling over time.

TABLE 8.1
*Wealth transmission under different assumptions**

	Primogeniture (eldest child)	Primogeniture (eldest son)	Equal division among sons	Equal division among all children
Each family has two children:				
Marriage random	Tendency towards increased concentration – slower	Stable distribution	Stable distribution (same as primogeniture	Tendency to equalization
Class marriage	Tendency towards increased concentration – faster			Same as equal division among sons
Each family has more than two children				
Marriage random	As above, but more rapid divergence	Tendency towards increased concentration	Stable distribution	Tendency to equalization
Class marriage				Same as equal division among sons

*It is assumed that each family has an equal number of boys and girls, and that there is no new saving.

8.4 The distribution of wealth — inheritance and self-made fortunes

Earlier in this chapter, we saw that the average person starting from nothing is likely to join the top 0.1 per cent of wealth-holders only if he engages in active entrepreneurship or enjoys considerable good fortune. In each generation a small number of self-made men, owing their success (in varying proportions) to ability, willingness to take risks, and luck, emerge from this process to join the propertied class — see Fig. 8.2. This

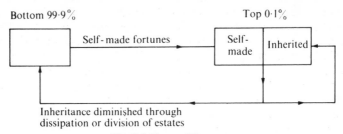

Fig. 8.2 The wealth process

wealth is then passed on to their heirs, and as a result may be consolidated or depleted, depending on the factors described in the previous section, and on the heirs' propensity to save.

In this section, we examine the balance between 'self-made' and inherited wealth in the top 0.1 per cent. This is a question of considerable importance, and one that has major implications for the conclusions we draw about inequality. We can imagine two polar situations. In the first, the top group consists entirely of self-made men, who have started from nothing, and whose wealth disappears at their death. This society would be very fluid. The top 0.1 per cent might own 10 per cent of total wealth, but they would be quite different families from those who made up this group in the previous generation, as in Schumpeter's description of the capitalist 'hotel', always full but with the guests always changing. At the other pole is the case where there is no 'new' wealth, and the top 0.1 per cent have all inherited. In this society the top group would belong to the same families as had constituted the top 0.1 per cent in the previous generation, and indeed for time immemorial. The difference between these two societies would not be apparent from examining the share of the top 0.1 per cent, but there is clearly a major difference from a 'dynastic' view of equity. In the first society, it could then be the case that everyone stood the same chance that he, or one of his descendants, entered to top 0.1 per cent, but this would not be true of the second case, where there would be clear dynastic inequality.

Some of the factors influencing the balance between self-made and inherited wealth have already been discussed. The analysis of the previous sections suggested that the persistence of inherited wealth depends on the patterns of inheritance and marriage, and on the savings behaviour of the children. If estates are divided equally among all children, if marriage is random, and if heirs are given to riotous living, then the departure of a dynasty from the top 0.1 per cent will be relatively rapid. In such a situation we should observe self-made men at the top of the *Fortune* list, with inherited wealth taking up the lower ranks and disappearing after a number of generations. On the other hand, where there is primogeniture and the heirs add to their inheritance, then the descendants of the self-made man may remain in the top 0.1 per cent. Indeed, it will be the oldest fortunes that come at the top of the list, since they have been accumulating for the longest period. The addition of self-made wealth to the top 0.1 per cent then serves to dilute the inherited wealth and prevent its share in the total from growing over time, but the self-made will make up only a proportion of the total.

In order to go further, we need to look at the empirical evidence. In the case of the *Fortune* list of centi-millionaires referred to in the previous chapter, it is estimated that about half had inherited the bulk of their wealth, including such well known names as Mellon, Rockefeller, du Pont, and Ford. The article suggested that inheritance had been declining as a source of great wealth, in that the heirs of those appearing in the earlier *Fortune* list in general failed to retain their position: of the twenty-two people on the 1957 list who had died, only one placed an heir on the list of 1968. The remaining half of the *Fortune* list were either self-made men or people who had considerably increased their inheritance. Examples of the second category were the two men at the very top, J. P. Getty and Howard Hughes, who both inherited substantial amounts but added very greatly to their inheritance. This illustrates the difficulty in distinguishing inherited from self-made wealth. Suppose that a person is now worth £200 000 and that he inherited £50 000 sixteen years ago. It would clearly not be correct to say that the difference of £150 000 represented accumulated wealth, since without the inheritance he would have been less well placed to accumulate. In order to make some allowance for this, we could postulate a certain rate of return on the inherited wealth; e.g., if the return were 7 per cent (in money terms), the inheritance would have trebled in sixteen years, so that the proportion of current wealth attributable to inheritance would be three-quarters rather than a quarter.

The *Fortune* approach is clearly subject to a great deal of error, and it is recognized in the article that many 'centi-millionaires' may be missing. This could well lead to a systematic bias. On the other hand, the alternative sources are far from ideal. The study by Barlow *et al.* (1966) of high-income individuals in the United States found, for example, that 'gifts and inheritances accounted for a relatively small fraction of aggregate wealth'. However, the treatment of saving made possible by inheritance was very approximate, and the authors recognize that the sampling of individuals according to income may not adequately reflect those with high wealth, who may be more likely to have inherited. Indeed, of those with wealth in excess of $½ million, 28 per cent said that half or more of their assets reflected gifts or inheritance. This latter finding was supported by the Federal Reserve Board (1966) study, which showed that a third of this group had inherited a 'substantial' part of their wealth, although the definition was not made explicit.

In Britain the most recent evidence about the importance of inheritance has been provided by the investigations of Harbury and Hitchens (1979) of those leaving wealth of £100 000 or more in 1956–7, 1965, and 1973. Taking a sample of male decedents, as in the earlier study of Wedgwood (1929) they traced the estates that had been left by the fathers, and thus examined the extent to which there were wealthy forebears. This method does not provide a fully adequate measure of the importance of inheritance. The *estates* left by the two generations are not necessarily a good indication of the total wealth transmitted, since they exclude wealth passed on in the form of gifts or settled in the form of trusts; for example there is one case in the sample where a person left £113 000 but is reported to have given away about £1 million during his lifetime. Some of those sons whose fathers apparently died leaving small estates may in fact have received from them substantial amounts in gifts or settled property. Moreover, while the father is the most likely person to have transmitted wealth, it may have come from other members of the family.

TABLE 8.2

Estates of fathers and sons, Britain 1956/7, 1965, and 1973

Percentage with father leaving at least*	Sons leaving estates of £100 000 or more in		
	1956/7	1965	1973
£1 million	9	4	7
£250 000	33	24	21
£100 000	51	45	36
£50 000	63	55	47
£25 000	68	68	58
£10 000	75	77	71

*At constant 1956–7 prices.
Source: Harbury and Hitchens (1979), Table 3.3.

The results of the study are summarized in Table 8.2. This shows first that a high proportion of those leaving more than £100 000 had fathers who themselves had been wealthy: over a fifth had left £250 000 or more (in real terms) and about a half had left more than £50 000. In their discussion of the results, Harbury and Hitchens suggest that sums of £50 000, £25 000, or even £10 000 'might be taken as lines of demarcation between the inheritors and the self-made' (1979, p. 45). (The last of these cut-off points, which would imply that only about a quarter would be classified as 'self-made', may appear very low, but it should be noted that the figures refer to 1956/7 prices.) Taking a cut-off of £25 000 for the estate of the father, Harbury and Hitchens conclude, from the pooled data for the three years, that two-thirds of top wealth-holders were 'inheritors' rather than 'self-made'. When account is taken of wealth received from other relatives (grandparents, uncles, aunts, brothers, etc.), the proportion is nearer three-quarters – and not all of these transfers could be traced.

From Table 8.2, it appears that there is a trend over time towards a diminished importance of inheritance: the percentage of inheritors in 1973 is 58 per cent rather than 68 per cent. But it will require a marked trend over a number of years to change the conclusion of Harbury and Hitchens that inheritance is a major determinant of wealth concentration.

8.5 The redistribution of wealth

One means by which the trend towards a reduced importance of inheritance could be accelerated is through taxes and other measures to redistribute wealth. Many countries, including Britain and the United States, employ a variety of measures: taxes on the ownership or on the transfer of wealth, measures to restrict the scope of property rights, and schemes to encourage wealth-holding at the lower end of the scale. In what follows, some of their main features are described, although the full implications clearly cannot be discussed in detail.

Taxes on the ownership of wealth

Taxes on the ownership of wealth may take two main forms. First, there are annual taxes on the value of wealth, usually referred to as wealth taxes. Second, there are taxes on the income from wealth in the course of the tax year. In the first case, the relevant consideration would be that a person was worth £X, in the second that he received an income of £Y on his wealth.

Although at present neither Britian nor the United States imposes a wealth tax, such taxes have been used in a number of other countries. In western Europe they have a long history, going back to the thirteenth century in some Swiss cantons, and in recent years they have been in force in Luxembourg, Norway, West Germany, the Netherlands, Denmark, and Sweden. The taxes have in general been progressive, with wealth below a certain level exempted and, in some cases, rates that increase with the level of wealth. In Sweden, in 1976 the tax started at some £100 000, and had rates rising from 1 per cent to 2½ per cent per annum. In Britain the Labour government announced in 1974 its intention to introduce such an annual wealth tax. The illustrative scales of tax began at £100 000 and involved rates rising to 2½ per cent or 5 per cent on wealth of £5 million or over. (The legislation was not introduced.)

The alternative system, that of taxing the income from wealth, is rather different, in that the tax liability depends on the form in which the wealth is held. A person owning paintings or yachts would not be subject to tax, since these yield no taxable income. In Britain, investment income in excess of a certain amount is subject to additional tax at the rate of 15 per cent over and above that payable on earned income. On the other hand, there also exist a number of avenues for avoidance, which are particularly important in the case of unearned income. The relatively generous treatment of capital gains, for example, could reduce the effective rate of tax substantially. A person building up a successful business may, as we have seen, obtain much of his financial reward in the form of capital gains when the company is floated publicly.

Taxation of the value of wealth, or the income from it, is directed at current ownership whatever its source. In terms of our earlier analysis, it may affect saving for life-cycle purposes, and it will fall on all those with substantial wealth, whether self-made or inherited. If the concern of the government is with inequality in inherited wealth, then the appropriate measures may be those linked to the transfer of wealth.

Taxes on the transfer of wealth

In Britain the main tax on the transfer of property is the capital transfer tax (up to 1974, estate duty). This is chargeable on a cumulative basis on the total transfers made by a person during his lifetime (in the March 1981 Budget, reduced to ten years before death) plus his estate at death. As such it is like a combined gift and estate tax, but with a lower scale for gifts. In 1982 the threshold was £55 000, with rates starting at 15 per cent for gifts and 30 per cent for estates, reaching 50 per cent over £2 million for gifts and 75 per cent for estates. The scale may appear progressive, but there are good reasons to doubt whether the capital transfer tax is going to be effective in reducing the concentration of wealth.

First of all, even if the nominal rates are paid, it may still be possible for a family to restore its position by new accumulation. Suppose that we consider a hypothetical family whose first generation died just as the 1894 budget took effect, leaving £500 000, which is equivalent to some £5 million today. The net estate was inherited by the eldest son who died in 1927, and then by his eldest son who died in 1960, in each case estate duty being paid at the full rates. Suppose also that they obtained a yield of 4½ per cent in real terms, and that they saved one-third of this income. The present representative of the family would still be worth some £2 million, even though estate duty had been paid three times. Despite the high nominal rates, the effect of the wealth transfer tax may be offset by accumulation coupled with the passing on of the estate intact from generation to generation.

Second, the effective rates of tax are reduced considerably below the nominal rates by a variety of special provisions. To begin with, there is an annual exemption, which means that a couple could pass £150 000 or more on to their children over a generation without paying any duty (together with £5000 each 'in consideration of marriage'). Then, there are concessions for agricultural land and property, for the assets of private business, for growing timber, and for works of art. For example, tax may be paid by instalments with no interest payable, or the tax base may be reduced.

Third, the original aim of the capital transfer tax was to tax all transfers, whether by gifts or at death, but this has been nullified by the changes made in the 1981 Budget, which mean that transfers outside the last ten years are ignored. The overall impact of that Budget has been described by Sutherland as follows:

the Chancellor made changes which will produce a dramatic reduction in the real burdens of most potential payers of Capital Transfer Tax (CTT). Even without sophisticated tax avoidance, over 99 per cent of wealth-owners will now be able to pay zero CTT when they hand on their assets. The burden to be borne by most of the remaining one per cent has also been greatly reduced. (1981, p. 37)

He goes on to comment that 'the scope for action by any future radical Chancellor of the Exchequer is clear' (p. 51).

The limited impact of capital taxation in practice is illustrated by the experiences of the Dukes of Westminster, as described by Kay and King:

It is generally believed that the largest sum ever paid in death duties . . . was the £11 m. paid on an estate estimated at between £40 and £60 m. on the death of the third Duke of Westminster in 1953. On the subsequent death of the fourth Duke, his reported estate was a little over £4 m., on which estate duty came to around £1 m. In fact not even this sum was paid, since . . . it was resolved that the Duke (who was partially disabled by war wounds received in 1942 and who died of cancer in 1967) was entitled to the benefit of an exemption . . . for those killed on active military service. The fifth Duke died in 1979, and press reports then estimated that the family fortune controlled by the new Duke of Westminster was between £300 m. and £800 m. (1980, p. 156)

It should be added that the sixth Duke married the granddaughter of millionaire Sir Harold Wernher.

The tax law in the United States is different, there being a federal estate tax supplemented by a gift tax, but there is similarly scope for reducing the effective tax liability; the use of trusts, the generous marital deductions, the establishment of charitable foundations. For example, John D. Rockefeller is reported to have paid virtually no estate tax when he died in 1960, since he had not only established trusts for his children earlier in life, but had also divided the final estate between a charitable foundation and his widow. Since the marital deduction permits half of the property of the deceased to be transferred to the surviving spouse tax-free, and since the transfer to the foundation is tax-exempt, he paid no tax. The establishment of a charitable foundation, such as the Rockefeller or Ford Foundation, means that the wealth does not pass to the heirs, but it may still allow them to enjoy considerable control over its use. The setting up of 'generation-skipping' trusts is another way of reducing the effective rate of tax. William Randolph Hearst Sr paid substantial estate tax in 1957, but it is estimated that no further tax will be payable until 2050 or later (Tuckman, 1973).

Wealth transfer taxes in Britain and the United States have the common feature that, apart from the provisions for the surviving spouse, tax liability is largely independent of the way in which the wealth is divided; they provide little inducement for donors to spread their wealth widely. It has therefore been proposed that they should be replaced by an inheritance tax levied on the amount received. In this way a million would bear less tax divided among ten heirs than if it was left intact to one person, and it would provide an incentive for, say, equal division to replace primogeniture.

The inheritance tax could take a variety of forms. It could be related to the individual bequest or gift, as is the case in a number of European countries. This, however, would provide no incentive for a person to leave wealth to those who had not previously inherited. The same tax would be payable if the money were left to a millionaire or to a person without a penny to his name. This would not accord with the objective of reducing inequality in the distribution of total inherited wealth. For this purpose, a much more effective alternative would be a tax based on the cumulated total of all wealth transfers, gifts, and bequests received by an individual over the course of his life in excess of a certain exemption level. The way in which such a tax would work has been described by Meade as follows:

Every gift or legacy received by any one individual would be recorded in a register against his name for tax purposes. He would then be taxed . . . according to the size of the total amount which he had received over the whole of his life by way of gift or inheritance. The rate of tax would be on a progressive scale according to the total of gifts or bequests recorded against his name in the tax register. (1964, p. 57)

Such a tax might appear at first sight like an administrative nightmare. The study by Sandford *et al.* (1973), however, showed that, although the administrative costs would be higher than with a straight estate tax, its operation was clearly feasible. The extra administrative burden might well be considered a small price for a tax that is explicitly directed at a major source of inequality of opportunity.

Other approaches

It is clear that there are many possible ways of making the taxation of wealth a more effective instrument for the redistribution of wealth. Fiscal measures are not, however, the only ones that can be adopted.

It would be possible to restrict the scope of private property. At present there are clearly limitations on the social and legal recognition of claims to ownership of property: one cannot, for example, claim a property right to a person, to the atmosphere, or to the sea. The scope of ownership could be further restricted in a variety of ways, ranging from relatively minor changes, such as the prohibition of certain types of trusts set up largely to avoid tax, to the more radical measures that might be found in a socialist economy, such as an absolute limit on the amount of property that could be passed from one generation to the next.

A second approach would be to take 'countervailing' measures, designed to offset the impact of the concentration of wealth. These could again take many forms. It would be possible to extend state ownership of wealth, for example through nationalization or a capital levy to redeem the national debt. In Britain, nationalization has long been a leading aim of Labour Party policy; but the motives for this have been concerned largely with control and the government's industrial objectives, rather than with redistribution. Indeed, with full compensation, nationalization would have no direct distributional effect. The state would acquire the physical assets, but would have to issue government bonds to the same value to pay the compensation, so that the net worth of the state would be unchanged. A capital levy, or a once-for-all tax on all wealth at rates comparable with those on estates, would lead to a substantial reduction in wealth at the top and, if the revenue were used to reduce the national debt, would change the balance between private and state capital. There are, however, a number of problems. The levy would catch saving for life-cycle reasons as well as inherited wealth. It would not provide a permanent solution, and fortunes accumulated after the levy would give rise to new inequality. The execution of the levy would be a major administrative task.

An alternative to the extension of state ownership is the increase of private wealth-holding by those who at present inherit nothing. Numerous measures have been proposed to encourage saving, but from the point of view of lifetime equity the important question is how far they serve to equalize the distribution of inherited wealth. This might be achieved through savings incentives, offering a return to small savers in excess of the market rate of interest: e.g. offering inflation-proofing of assets up to a certain sum per person. Many savings schemes in Britain, however, have tended to favour the higher-income groups through their tax-exempt status. A more direct approach is the idea of the state providing a guaranteed minimum inheritance, either as a 'coming of age' bonus or as a capital element in the state pension, payable on retirement. This would be in effect a 'negative capital tax', parallel to the negative income tax proposals for the redistribution of income discussed in Chapter 11.

Notes on sources and further reading

An excellent discussion of the forces underlying the distribution of wealth is given by Meade in his *Efficiency, equality and the ownership of property* (1964) and his more recent essay (1973). An extract from the latter is reprinted in Atkinson (1980b), as is the more technical article by Stiglitz (1969). An interesting − and again technical − treatment of the distribution as a whole is given in Conlisk (1977); and Becker has written extensively from a rather different standpoint − see in particular Becker (1981) and Becker and Tomes (1979). The role of inheritance has received particular attention from Blinder (1973), Pryor (1973), Ishikawa (1975) and Bevan (1979), Shorrocks (1979), Wolfson (1980), and Atkinson (1980a). (The last is reprinted in Atkinson, 1983.)

The empirical evidence about inheritance and bequests includes the classic study of Wedgwood (1928, 1929), and the more recent work of Harbury, described in Harbury and Hitchens (1979). For the work of historians in this area, see Rubinstein (1981). Evidence in the United States is covered by Brittain (1978), to whom I owe the quotation at the start of this chapter, Menchik (1979, 1980), and Tomes (1981). Evidence on France is provided by Kessler (1982) and on Sweden by Blomquist (1979).

The taxation of wealth in Britain is described in Prest and Barr (1979) and Sutherland (1981); and Sandford (1982) provides a useful review of capital taxation in different countries. Tax reform possibilities are dicussed by Kay and King (1980), and Pond, Burghes and Smith (1980). A wider view of redistributive policies is given in Atkinson (1972).

9

FACTOR SHARES

It has now become certain that the problem of distribution is much more difficult than it was thought to be . . . and that no solution of it which claims to be simple can be true.

(Alfred Marshall, 1890)

Inequality in the distribution of income depends on the distribution of earned incomes, on the concentration of wealth, and on the relative importance of income from earnings and capital. It is with this last aspect that the present chapter is concerned. As pointed out in Chapter 1, classical writing on the distribution of income was concerned primarily with the distribution among classes. Ricardo, for example, described 'the principal problem in Political Economy' as being to determine how 'the produce of the earth . . . is divided among three classes of the community, namely, the proprietor of the land, the owner of the stock or capital necessary for its cultivation, and the labourers by whose industry it is cultivated' (1821). At that time, it may have been reasonable to suppose that these three classes correspond to different positions on the income scale. Today, the relationship between the shares of factors of production and the distribution of income among persons is more complicated, but factor shares remain of considerable relevance. Although people may derive income from more than one source — they may, for example, receive interest on their savings in addition to their labour income — it is still broadly true that income from property (capital and land) is of greater importance at the top of the income scale. In this chapter we examine, therefore, the shares of land, labour, and capital in total income and how they are determined. Since fully adequate treatment of this question would require more space than one chapter, and there have been many books concerned solely with this subject, all that is attempted here is a brief survey of the principal features that need explanation and the theories that have been advanced.

9.1 The behaviour of aggregate factor shares

The share of wages or profits in national income may appear at first sight straightforward to measure: the national income accounts contain estimates of profits, rent, and wages, from which the required ratios may be derived. It is not, however, as simple as that, since one cannot readily allocate all income in a neat way between the three categories:

the study of the trends in the functional distribution of income is handicapped by the fact . . . that the nature of the components of income for which we have data has not been determined by the requirements of the economists but by the legal and institutional arrangements of our society. (Kravis, 1959, p. 918)

The kinds of problems that arise may be illustrated by reference to the figures for the United Kingdom and the United States in Tables 9.1 and 9.2. It should be noted that no attempt has been made to render these tables comparable — they are taken directly from the published national

TABLE 9.1
*Percentage shares of gross national product,
United Kingdom, 1860–1979*

	Wages and forces' pay	Salaries*	Self-employment income	Profits	Rents and property income from abroad	Adjusted share of labour†
1860–9	39	6	37		18	–
1870–9	39	6	37		18	–
1880–9	39	8	34		19	–
1890–9	39	9	33		19	–
1900–9	38	10	33		19	–
1910–14	37	11	16	17	19	55
1921–9	41	18	16	13	12	67
1930–8	40	19	14	14	13	68
1946–9	45	20	12	17	6	73
1950–9	44	22	10	18	6	73
1960–9	67		8	18	7	73
1970–9	68		9	15	8	75

* Including employers' contributions to pensions, etc.
† Including estimated labour component of self-employment income.
Sources: 1860–1959 calculated from Feinstein (1968), Tables 1, 2, and 5; 1970–9 from *National Income and Expenditure*, 1981, Table 1.2.

accounts. The UK figures, for example, relate to shares of gross national product, whereas the US figures relate to shares of national *income* (i.e., with an allowance for capital consumption). Also, the UK figures are averages for decades, whereas the US figures are for selected years. Among the items that cause difficulties are the following.

Rent In the case where rent is paid in cash to the landlord, measurement is straightforward, and where the property takes the form of owner-occupied housing, an imputed rent can be estimated. The main problems arise in the case of land and buildings occupied by companies, where it is almost impossible to separate the part of profit that represents a return to land from that which is the return to the capital employed. In view of this, many authors have chosen to discuss the distribution in terms of the twofold classification of labour and 'property', the latter including both profits and rents. This practice is followed in the final columns of both Table 9.1 and Table 9.2.

TABLE 9.2
Percentage shares of national income, United States, 1930-1950*

	Employee compensation	self-employment income**	Profits and interest**	Rent†	Adjusted share of labour‡
	%	%	%	%	%
1930	63	16	15	6	75
1935	66	19	12	3	81
1940	65	16	15	4	77
1945	68	18	12	2	83
1950	66	16	15	3	79
1955	69	13	15	3	79
1960	72	11	14	3	81
1965	70	10	17	3	78
1970	76	8	13	3	83
1975	77	7	14	2	83
1980	75	6	17	2	80

*   The figures have been rounded so that the shares add to 100 per cent.
** With stock appreciation and capital consumption adjustments.
†   With capital consumption adjustment.
‡   Calculated on basis of 'economy-wide' shares.
Sources: Statistical Abstract of the United States 1980, Table 734, and *Survey of Current Business*, December 1981, Table 1.11.

Self-employment income Problems of allocation arise even more acutely in the case of self-employment income, which represents a return both on the labour contributed by the self-employed and on their capital (or land). How is the income of the farmer, shopkeeper, or lawyer to be divided between 'wages' and 'property'? The method used by Feinstein in the estimates for 1860-1959 presented in Table 9.1 is to allocate to wages the income that the self-employed person would have received on average as a paid employee in the same sector of the economy and then to regard any residual as the return to capital (and the same method has been followed approximately for 1960-79). In the United States, Kravis

(1959) has examined the implications over the period 1900–57 of different methods. The first 'labour basis' is similar to that of Feinstein (although the earnings figure used was an average for the economy as a whole and was not broken down by sector). The second 'assets basis' is the reverse case, where the property employed by the self-employed is assumed to yield the same return as other property and the labour income is treated as the residual. The third method, the 'economy-wide' figures, assumes that the shares are the same as in the rest of the economy, so that the self-employed sector can in effect be ignored. The results from the three methods are rather different, particularly in the early part of the period; when self-employment accounted for nearly one-quarter of total income in 1900–09, the adjusted labour share ranged from 63 per cent on an 'assets basis' to 77 per cent on a 'labour basis' (Kravis, 1959, Table 1). But for more recent years the methods yield relatively similar results; and in Table 9.2 we take the 'economy-wide' approach.

Government capital and housework The national income accounts relate mainly to cash income, the only major imputed income taken into acount being the rents referred to above and farm produce for home production. The missing imputed income includes that accruing to capital employed in the home (consumer durables, cars, etc.) as well as the value of time spent on do-it-yourself, housework, etc. The last, as we saw in Chapter 4, could be quite substantial.

From Table 9.1 it appears that in broad terms the share in national income in Britain of employee compensation (wages plus salaries) is around two-thirds, and that the share of labour, including the return to self-employment (but not that to home production), is more like three-quarters. The ratio of the shares of labour and capital is broadly 3:1. There also appears to have been a rise in the share of labour over time. In Britain the ratio was more like 1:1 before the First World War, and in the interwar period it was 2:1. In the United States the pattern is similar for employee compensation, but the adjusted share of labour shows no apparent trend. On the other hand, the estimates of Kravis (1959) show the adjusted share of labour to have risen between 1900–9 and 1930–9.

Constant shares?

The evidence just described casts doubt on the common belief that the share of labour is constant over time. As we saw in Chapter 2, attention was drawn to the apparent stability by Keynes and subsequent Cambridge economists have continued the tradition:

No hypothesis as regards the forces determining distributive shares could be intellectually satisfying unless it succeeds in accounting for the relative stability of these shares in the advanced economies over the last 100 years or so, despite the phenomenal changes in the techniques of production, in the accumulation of capital relative to labour and in real income per head. (Kaldor, 1955b, p. 84)

The reference by Keynes to the statistical support for his statement was to the data for the share of wages in Britain. From Table 9.1 it can be seen that when he wrote, at the end of the 1930s, the share of wages was indeed at much the same level as it had been eighty years before; however, this ignores the secular increase that had taken place in *salaries*. The share of wages plus salaries had increased from 45 to 59 per cent, and this trend has continued, reaching 68 per cent in 1970-9.

A strong believer in the constancy of factor shares may still object to the evidence presented above by saying that he does not mean literal constancy and that the observed movements are still 'relatively small'. Kaldor, for example, referred not to constancy but to 'relative stability'. What does *relative* mean in this context? One interpretation might be in relation to the errors in the estimated components of national income; many of the figures are subject to quite considerable error, and it could be that the observed changes lie within these margins of error. However, even if the errors were all in the direction of understating labour's share in the early period, and of overstating it in the later period, it is unlikely that these would be sufficient to offset the trend (see Feinstein, 1968).

A second interpretation of relative stability has been advanced by Solow (1958): the relationship between the variation in the aggregate share of labour and the variation within individual industries. If the variation in the aggregate share is less than would be expected on the basis of the independent fluctuation of the shares in industrial sectors (food, textiles, chemicals, etc.), this suggests that a stabilizing force is operating at a macroeconomic level. As Solow puts it, 'if the calorie content of breakfast, lunch, and supper each varies widely, while the 24-hour total remains constant, we at once suspect a master hand at the control' (1958, p. 621). He tests this hypothesis using US data and concludes that the variation in the aggregate share is in fact no less than would be expected on the basis of independent fluctuations of the sectoral shares, so that no special explanation of *aggregate* stability is required — what stability there is in the share of labour is attributable to the individual sectors of the economy.

So far, we have taken a long-term perspective. What has been happening to profits and wage shares in recent years has been the subject of considerable discussion. This has focused particularly on the adjustment of profits for inflation. The national accounts figures in Table 9.1 need, for example, to be corrected for capital consumption. The standard procedure has been based on historic cost (original purchase price), but recent estimates have argued for use of replacement cost, which can make a major difference in times of rapid inflation. The calculations of the Bank of England *Quarterly Bulletin* (December 1978, p. 514) of the share of profits of industrial and commercial companies (excluding North Sea oil) show that historic cost profits fell only from 15½ per cent of income in 1965-9 to 13 per cent in 1974-7, whereas real profits fell from 12½ per cent of income to 5½ per cent.

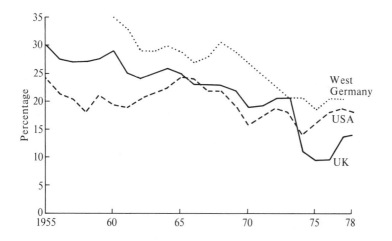

Fig. 9.1 The share of profits in manufacturing, 1955–1978: United Kingdom, United States, and West Germany (Source: Martin (1981), p. 35).

In Fig 9.1 we show the movement in the share of real profits (as percentage of value-added) in manufacturing over the period 1955–78 for the UK, United States, and West Germany. Once again we must stress the problems of comparability. Even where, as in the present case, the estimates are based on standard definitions, inconsistencies may arise because of the differences in the methods used to collect the raw data. All three countries show a downward trend, with the recent fall in the UK being particularly marked. It is also clear that there is considerable short-term fluctuation, and this warns us of the possible danger for a single year (as in some discussions of the 'profits crisis').

To sum up, there appears to have been a trend, viewed either over the course of the century or over the past two decades, for the share of profits to fall and the share of labour to rise. In the next two sections, we consider some of the main theories that have been advanced.

9.2 The orthodox competitive theory

The determination of the share of wages and profits in national income
is a difficult problem. The difficulty stems from a number of causes,
but one of the most important is that it involves the whole economic
system, and typically everything depends on everything else. In general,
to determine the factor shares we need to be able to describe the whole
state of the economy. Since a theory that can make predictions about
labour's share only on the basis of assumptions sufficiently detailed to
allow the determination of the wages paid to policemen in Cardiff or
Chicago is likely to be too cumbersome to provide any insight, economists
have commonly attempted to reduce the problem to a more manageable
form. These attempts have taken two, not necessarily exclusive, routes:

(i)   the formation of aggregate variables such as 'labour', 'capital', and
      'output', which may be treated as homogeneous for the purposes at
      hand;

(ii) the decomposition of the economic system, so that only a small
      number of the economic variables are considered as determinants
      of the factor shares.

In this section we examine the theory of factor shares presented in
most textbooks; this is presented with varying degrees of qualification
and caution, but can reasonably be described as the prevailing orthodoxy.
(It is often referred to as the 'neoclassical' theory.) The theory is usually
introduced as part of a general equilibrium analysis of the economy, the
factor shares being determined as part of an overall explanation of the
prices of factors and products: 'to build up a theory of distribution we
thus need a theory of factor prices and quantities. Such a theory is a
special case of the theory of price' (Lipsey, 1964, p. 407). This general
formulation is then reduced to a simpler form, through the first of the
two routes described in the previous paragraph: the assumption that the
aggregate production possibilities of the economy can be aggregated into
a single production function. This is the first of three key assumptions:

> *Assumption A* Output is determined by an aggregate function of
> total capital and total labour. This production function allows smooth
> substitutability between capital and labour with diminishing marginal
> returns to each factor, and exhibits constant returns to scale.

In this formulation, land is for simplicity ignored, so that the factor
shares considered are those of labour and 'property'. The assumption of
constant returns to scale means that, if both capital and labour are
increased by a given percentage, output will increase by the same
amount. A second important assumption made in the orthodox theory is:

> *Assumption B* All firms and consumers act as perfect competitors, that

is take prices, wages, and the cost of capital as given (they cannot exercise any bargaining power), and all firms aim to maximize profits.

These assumptions, while commonly made in economics, have naturally been subject to criticism and these criticisms are discussed below. Finally:

Assumption C The supplies of aggregate capital and labour are assumed to be given, a condition that may, for example, be secured by the full employment of a fixed stock of factors.

Given these assumptions, we can describe the equilibrium of the economy. If firms maximize profits at given product and factor prices, then this implies that they hire labour up to the point where the value marginal product of labour is equal to the cost of labour, and capital up to the point where its value marginal product is equal to the cost of capital. (The total paid out to the factors is guaranteed to add up to the total value of output by the assumption of constant returns to scale.) For this to work, the assumption made under A, that capital and labour are smoothly substitutable, is clearly necessary. If capital and labour were required in fixed proportions (one man could work with only one shovel), then the marginal products would not be defined. This problem worried Bertrand Russell: 'Consider a porter on a railway whose business it is to shunt goods trains: what proportion of the goods carried can be said to represent the produce of his own labour?' In part, the answer here is that we are concerned with aggregate production and not with production functions for individual industries (e.g. the railways), and that at an aggregate level the scope for substitution is greater, since there may be substitution between the different products. If we now write w for the wage rate and r for the return to capital, we have the conditions:

w = value marginal product of r = value marginal product of
          labour   capital

This gives a relationship between the relative shares of capital and labour and the supply of the two factors (since the marginal products depend on the factor supplies):

$$\frac{\text{Total profits}}{\text{Total wages}} = \frac{\text{capital} \times r}{\text{labour} \times w} = \frac{\text{capital} \times \text{marginal product of capital}}{\text{labour} \times \text{marginal product of labour}}$$

(Since the value marginal product = price × marginal product, the price term drops out (appearing on both top and bottom) when we substitute to obtain the final expression.)

In general, therefore, to provide a long-run theory of factor shares we need to explain how the factor supplies change over time. There is, however, one special case in which this is not necessary, and which played a leading role in early investigations. Where the aggregate production function takes a particular form, known as the Cobb–Douglas function, the shares of labour and capital are independent of the factor supplies. The theory would then be decomposable in the sense defined earlier. This function was employed by Douglas (1934) to explain the relationship between the growth of output and the growth of capital and labour: i.e., an investigation of the nature of the aggregate production function. He appreciated, none the less, that, with the further assumptions described earlier, the coefficients of his estimated production function would yield predictions about the factor shares. Douglas compared the shares implied by his measurements with those actually observed, and found a broad degree of agreement. More recently, however, studies have cast doubt on this conclusion (see below). Moreover, the Cobb–Douglas function implies that the relative shares remain constant over time, a prediction that is clearly not borne out by the evidence, as we saw in the previous section. This particularly simple resolution of the problem is not, therefore, one that can be sustained.

Except in the special Cobb–Douglas case, the factor shares depend on the relative supplies of capital and labour. This dependence may be represented in terms of the elasticity of substitution (denoted by σ), defined as the proportionate change in the ratio of capital to labour associated with a proportionate change in the relative factor rewards (r/w). It measures the ease of substitution, so that if the elasticity is low a change in r/w is associated with a small change in the capital intensity of production (by assumption the capital–labour ratio falls as r/w rises). The relevance of the elasticity of substitution may be seen from the fact that the relative shares of capital and labour may be written

$$\frac{\text{Total profits}}{\text{Total wages}} = \left(\frac{r}{w}\right) \times \left(\frac{\text{capital}}{\text{labour}}\right).$$

If the capital–labour ratio rises by y per cent, then the relative share of capital rises or falls, depending on whether the associated fall in r/w is less than or greater than y per cent, and this depends in turn on the value of the elasticity of substitution (σ). If σ is less than 1, then the associated change in r/w is more than y per cent and the share of capital falls; if σ is greater than 1, then the share of capital rises; and if $\sigma = 1$, the relative shares are unchanged (this is the Cobb–Douglas case). The proportionate change in the share of capital can in fact be shown to be:

$$(1 - \text{share of capital}) \times (1 - 1/\sigma) \times (y\%).$$

The application of this analysis to the trends in factor shares over time is illustrated by an example given by Solow (1958). He estimated that in broad terms the ratio of capital to labour in the United States had increased by 60 per cent over the first half of the twentieth century. If $\sigma = \frac{2}{3}$, which would be in line with some (but not all) empirical studies, and the initial share of capital were 30 per cent, then the proportionate change in the share of capital would have been:

$$0.7 \times (1 - 3/2) \times 60\% = -21\%$$

In other words, the share of capital would have gone down by about one-fifth, or from 30 to 24 per cent, and as Solow says, 'this is just the order of magnitude observed'. He does not, of course, mean by this that the issue is settled, but that the orthodox theory could at least be consistent with the evidence. (In order to conclude that it is consistent, we need of course to take into account the impact of technical progress, since technology clearly changed between 1900 and 1949. If technical progress is assumed to be labour- or capital-'augmenting', then the relevant consideration becomes the 'effective' capital–labour ratio, taking account of the increasing efficiency of the inputs over time. If labour- and capital-saving innovations had tended to balance each other, then the calculation described above would remain valid.)

The orthodox theory has been the subject of considerable criticism. It is not possible here to cover all the issues that have been raised in a long, and often bad-tempered, debate, and we focus on three areas that relate to the basic assumptions: the absence of perfect competition, the problems that arise in trying to derive an aggregate production function, and the implications of unemployment. Before turning to these criticisms, it should be noted that it is often referred to as the 'marginal productivity' theory. This term has been avoided here, since it is wrong to suggest, as some authors do, that the 'share of labour is *determined* by its marginal product'. First, the relationships between factor prices and marginal products are *derived* from more basic assumptions and are not themselves the primary postulates. Second, these relationships are consistent with a variety of assumptions about other aspects of the model – as we shall see.

The assumption of perfect competition is one of analytical convenience, but it does not accord with the market imperfections that appear to characterize most advanced economies. One way in which this assumption can be relaxed is through the straightforward introduction of a degree of monopoly. If a firm possesses monopoly power, it does not hire labour up to the point where the wage equals the value marginal product, but only to the point where the wage equals the marginal *revenue* product:

$$w = (1 - m) \times \text{value marginal product of labour.}$$

where m represents the degree of monopoly (and is the reciprocal of the elasticity of demand). In this way, if the monopoly profit is assumed to accrue to the owners of capital, the relative share of labour is reduced to only $(1 - m)$ times its previous value. (This explanation has some similarity with that put forward by Kalecki and discussed in the next section.)

An empirical test of this variation on the orthodox theory can be made simply by comparing the observed wage share with that predicted from the production function. As we have seen, Douglas claimed that the competitive case $(m = 0)$ provides a good fit with the evidence, but more recent studies cast doubt on this conclusion. Thurow (1968) has estimated a production relationship that is similar to that described earlier but allows for technical progress and unemployment, and from this obtained an estimate of the ratio between the wage and the value marginal product. In 1929 this ratio was 58 per cent and by 1965 it had risen to 63 per cent. Taken at its face value, this suggests that the share of labour may be reduced by the monopoly power of employers, although there are other factors that need to be taken into account, such as the impact of taxes. In the next section, the role of bargaining power, exercised both by employers and by trade unions, is discussed in greater detail.

The second set of difficulties, those associated with Assumption A of an aggregate production function, greatly occupied theoretical economists in the 1960s and led to a sustained attack on the orthodox theory. In some cases this attack has been rather indiscriminate, and it is necessary to isolate the issues involved. Most importantly, it is the *aggregate* nature of the theory of factor shares that is at stake, not the whole of orthodox theory. Hahn and Matthews sum up the situation as follows: 'As far as pure theory is concerned the "measurement of capital" is no problem at all because we never have to face it if we do not choose to. With our armchair omniscience we can take account of each machine separately' (1965, p. 110).

They go on, however, to point out that this is 'of little comfort to the empirically inclined', and this is well illustrated by the present case. The general neoclassical theory is too complex to allow straightforward statements to be made about the determinants of factor shares. For this purpose short-cuts have to be taken, and this is the role of the assumption of an aggregate production function; it is also, however, the source of serious objections to the orthodox approach. We have seen that the main prediction of the theory concerned the relationship between the factor share and the supply of factors, and the link between the increase in the capital-labour ratio and the fall in the ratio (r/w), via the elasticity of substitution. This assumed that r/w fell as the capital-labour ratio rose, but there is no need why this should necessarily happen in a more general model of production. As was demonstrated in early contributions by Robinson (1953) and Champernowne (1953), it is possible for a higher ratio r/w to be associated with a rise in an index of capital per worker and subsequent work has shown that this cannot be ruled out as an unlikely event.

What are the implications of this demonstration? Quite simply, they mean that there is little theoretical foundation for the aggregate production function used as a short-hand earlier in this section. The only justification that can be given is the *ad hoc* one that 'it works in practice'. If one does not accept this argument, there is no alternative way of predicting the behaviour of factors shares other than by solving the whole general equilibrium system. This is possible, but it means that no straightforward results can be obtained. In this form the theory is harder to refute but less useful at a global level.

The third criticism concerns the assumption of full employment. Assumption C does not, strictly interpreted, require *full* employment, but it does require a *fixed* level of employment, and cannot allow this to be endogenously determined. Yet the cyclical variation of factor shares is an aspect we need to study. In the United States attention was paid to the rise in labour's share during the Depression of the 1930s. Fig. 9.1 shows the cyclical movements in recent years; and the impact of the much higher unemployment of the early 1980s is an important question.

The incorporation of an endogenously determined level of employment poses a major challenge to the orthodox theory. The role of the assumption of fixed employment is to allow the decomposition of the economic system referred to above — the orthodox theory can by this device exclude a whole range of considerations. Some of these are discussed in the next section.

9.3 Alternative approaches

In this section we examine some of the alternative approaches to the determination of factor shares. For this purpose, they are grouped together under four headings.

Monopoly power theories

The bargaining power theories may be divided into those concerned with the monopoly power of firms and those concerned with collective bargaining and union power. The former have been stimulated particularly by the work of Kalecki, who argued that the share of labour depends inversely on the degree of monopoly. As Kalecki (1939) described it, the analysis begins at the level of the individual enterprise, where prices are set by equating marginal revenue and marginal cost. Marginal cost is assumed constant and taken here to include only wage costs. (Kalecki laid considerable stress on raw material costs, but these are omitted for ease of exposition.) Aggregating across enterprises, Kalecki concluded that the share of labour is governed by the average degree of monopoly. In assuming that the latter can be regarded as a macroeconomic concept, the Kalecki theory is in effect making the same leap as the orthodox theory from the microeconomic level to an aggregate representation. Just as in the orthodox case, there are problems with such a move; the aggregate degree of monopoly depends, for example, on the relative importance of different industries.

The Kalecki theory has been criticized on the grounds that the degree of monopoly is not related to the behaviour of the firm: 'the principal weakness in Kalecki's theory is that no satisfactory explanation is given for the size of individual mark-ups' (Lydall, 1979, p. 118). This aspect has recently been developed, notably in the work of Cowling (1982). Beginning with profit-maximizing behaviour by independent firms, he shows how the mark-up, and hence the degree of monopoly, is related to (a) the price elasticity of demand (present in Kalecki), (b) the Herfindahl measure of concentration (based on the squared market shares), and (c) the degree of collusion between firms. As with Kalecki, this mark-up is averaged across the economy, but we also need to take account of the ratio of imports to national income, the share of profits tending to increase with this ratio. The way in which the latter works is described by Cowling:

the substitution of Cologne Ford cars for Dagenham Ford cars by the Ford retailing network within the UK will in itself tend to raise the share of profits within the UK economy, i.e. part of the wage share in Ford cars will have been shifted from UK workers to German workers. (1982, p. 32)

Cowling goes further to point out that, where corporate managers enjoy a degree of discretion, the profit mark-up may fall short of that predicted by profit maximization, and that part of profits may be diverted to managerial remuneration.

The predictions of these oligopoly theories may be set against the historical record. In the case of the Kalecki theory, Phelps Brown has examined the long-run experiences of the UK, the United States, Sweden, and Germany from 1860 to 1965. This leads him to conclude that 'there is little to suggest that [the monopolistic pricing] theory has seized on a dominant factor in distribution' (1968, p. 27). For example, he points to the higher share of industrial profits in the United States in the latter part of the nineteenth century, but suggests that there were few grounds for holding that there was a higher degree of monopoly than in Germany or the United Kingdom. It is important to note, however, that he treats changes in international competition as an alternative to the Kalecki explanation, whereas these may well influence the monopoly power of domestic firms, an aspect that has been stressed in recent contributions.

Turning to the more recent postwar period, there are several reasons to suppose that the degree of monopoly may have increased. Industrial concentration in Britain has seen a fairly marked increase, especially via merger activity. Although the degree of collusion may have been reduced by legislation (such as that concerned with restrictive practices), the effectiveness of such measures has been doubted; and there has almost certainly been an increased degree of co-operation across national boundaries. What is more, the share of imports has increased substantially. All of these factors may have been expected to *increase* the share of profits — as opposed to the downward trend that we have observed — but it may well be that there have been countervailing forces. Cowling (1982) draws attention to the rise in the degree of managerial discretion, arguing that the share of profits is falling, despite the increased degree of monopoly, because of the rise of the power of management *vis à vis* shareholders. He also argues that the ways of mergers in Britain led to excess capacity which to date has not allowed monopoly profits to be realized. This would suggest that the trend in the profit share might be reversed in the future if the economy recovers.

Before leaving theories that relax the assumption of perfect competition, we should draw attention to the work of Lydall (1979). He assumes 'entry and product market competition', but allows for imperfect markets for knowledge (of techniques of production) and capital, as well as giving a central role to economies of scale. As a result,

the size of a firm in any industry will depend on its length of experience and its accumulated stock of internal funds. Hence the industry will usually contain . . . firms of every size . . . the firm with the highest costs will be the one-man firm. (1979, p. 144)

With the aid of some further simplifying assumptions, he shows how the share of profits is related to the degree of concentration in the industry, as discussed above, to the variation of wages with firm size (as considered in relation to the hierarchical theories of earnings in Chapter 6), and on the extent of economies of scale.

Trade union power theories

An alternative explanation for the fall in the share of profit is that there has been increased bargaining strength on the part of trade unions. This aspect has been stressed by a number of radical economists, including Glyn and Sutcliffe, who argued that in Britain in the 1950s and 1960s 'the basic reason for the decline in the profit share was the squeezing of profit margins between money wage increases on the one hand and progressively more severe international competition on the other' (1972, p. 65). The effect of the increased internationalization of the economy can be debated (for example, the car industry has seen a rise in the share of imports but also agreements between producers in different countries and an increased degree of state support), but the role of union power clearly warrants examination.

A theory of union monopoly power as a seller of labour, parallel to the theory of the firm described above, can readily be constructed. The impact of unionization would depend on the elasticity of demand for labour, which in turn would depend on the product demand and the technology of production. This is unsatisfactory, however, for at least two reasons. First, it requires a specification of the objectives of the union — the analogue of profit maximization — and simple assumptions like the maximization of the wage bill do not seem to capture the concerns of either leaders or members. Second, it is the *interaction* between the bargaining power of unions and that of employers that is of the essence; and the simultaneous treatment of these two elements poses difficult problems. Despite the advances in game theory, on the one hand, and our understanding of organizations, on the other, there is no widely accepted theory of union-employer bargaining. We are therefore left with general statements of the kind that the 'share of wages in the value of output varies, from one country and one period to another, with the strength and militancy of trade unions' (Robinson and Eatwell, 1973, p. 189).

Turning to the empirical evidence, we confront immediately the difficulty that there are problems in observing union power (as in Chapter 6). It may be measured by trade union membership or by more subjective measures: Phelps Brown and Hart (1952), for example, refer to the fall in the labour share in Britain following the Taff Vale court decision, which seriously restricted the scope for strikes, and in 1926-8 after the collapse of the General Strike.

The relationship between union membership and the share of labour is discussed by Fleisher (1970). He suggests that the level and growth of membership lead one to expect that the share would be relatively high and/or growing rapidly in 1910-19, 1930-9, and 1939-48, but that this is borne out only in the 1930s. He concludes that 'if one ignores the basic upward trend in both union membership and labour's share over the past sixty years, there is no observable stable relationship between the two series' (1970, p. 186). Rather similar conclusions are reached by Phelps Brown (1968), who points to the failure of the share of labour to rise in the twenty years before the First World War, despite the increased strength of trade unions, but draws attention to the successful resistance to wage cuts during 1921–2 and during the 1930s in the United States, which led to a rise in labour's share. The general conclusion drawn by him was that 'trade unions have taken little effect to narrow the share of profits when they have acted as the hammer' (1968, p. 21), although they have at least once had a permanent effect on labour's share by resisting wage cuts.

Accumulation and the share of profits

Associated with the names of Kaldor and other Cambridge (England) economists is a rather different theory of the determination of factor shares. This theory makes assumptions that permit both aggregation and decomposition of the economic system, in such a way as to allow a straightforward explanation of relative shares.

The main assumptions of this model, as set out in Kaldor (1955b), are described below.

Assumption a It is assumed that the aggregate production relationship may be summarized by a constant ratio of investment to incremental output denoted by v.

This assumption plays the same role as that of the aggregate production function in Assumption A of the orthodox theory. The second assumption is that usually regarded as central to the theory:

Assumption β Planned savings are a constant fraction (s_p) of profits and a constant fraction (s_w) of wages, where s_p is greater than s_w.

This has been described as a 'classical' savings hypothesis, in view of the link with classical economists, notably Ricardo, although it did not play a major role in their thinking. The extreme case where s_w is zero corresponds to the Marxian assumption that all accumulation is carried out by capitalists. Finally, the theory assumes:

Assumption γ The economy is on a long-run growth path with an exogenous rate of growth of output fixed in proportional terms.

This can most simply be interpreted in terms of a full employment constraint on output, with the effective labour force growing at a constant proportional rate (the only qualification being that the wage should be above the subsistence level).

For purposes of exposition, let us take the extreme case where s_w is zero. Planned savings are then s_p times profits, and if they are equal to planned investment, we have

$s_p \times$ profits = investment = $v \times$ (increase in output)

so that the share of profits is given by:

$$\frac{\text{Profits}}{\text{Output}} = \frac{v}{s_p} \times \text{(proportional growth rate of output)}.$$

We arrive therefore at the conclusion that the share of profits is deter-mined by the propensity to save out of profits, the exogenous rate of growth, and the investment-incremental output ratio. It is sometimes referred to as the 'widow's cruse', since any reduction in the savings of capitalists has to be offset by a corresponding rise in profits if equilibrium is to be maintained (if s_p is halved then profits must double).

This allows the factor shares to be determined from the equilibrium or planned savings and investment, without regard to the rest of the economic system. In this sense it is decomposable. This decomposition of the economic system is attractive, since it allows definite predictions about the share of profits to be derived from consideration of only a few elements of the economy. The share of profits is, other things being equal, higher when there is a higher ratio of investment to output, and if we compare countries with different propensities to accumulate out of profits (s_p), the share of profits is greater where the rate of savings is lower. The question is, however, whether this model is a plausible rep-resentation of the economy.

Two elements play a central role in allowing the decomposition of the economy: the assumption that the ratio v is constant, and the assumption of given savings propensities. These are considered in turn. According to Johnson, 'the crucial weakness in the Kaldor theory is that the [ratio v] is assumed not to be influenced by the rate of profit' (1973, p. 202). If we ask what difference it would make if the capital-output ratio became an endogenous variable, it can be shown that the ratio of profits to capital (the rate of profit) is determined by s_p and the rate of growth, independently of the level of v. The assumption is therefore crucial for the determination of the *share* of profit, but not for the *rate* of profit on capital. The importance of distinguishing between these two concepts is demonstrated by the fact that we can link the Kaldorian savings assumption to the earlier orthodox theory. With the assumption of competition made there, the equality of the marginal product of capital with this exogenous rate of profit determines the capital–labour ratio. The share of profits then depends on the properties of the production function: for example, if it is Cobb-Douglas in form then the shares remain constant over time. Although Kaldor would not accept the assumption of perfect competition, this shows how the classical savings function could be used to 'close' the orthodox system.

The assumption of an exogenous investment-incremental output ratio may be seen, therefore, as an alternative to the orthodox aggregate production function. Let us turn now to the second key assumption: the classical savings hypothesis. The plausibility of this assumption has been the subject of debate. The supporters argue that it captures an important feature of growth in capitalist economies — the role of capital accumulation out of profits — and reference has already been made to the classical antecedents. The critics, on the other hand, have asked why savings propensities should differ between classes of income.

In an early contribution, Pasinetti (1961) pointed to the need to distinguish between differential savings propensities according to source of income and different propensities by social classes. Where workers save, it becomes important to know whether they save a fraction s_p of the profits paid to them or whether they save the same fraction s_w as they save out of wages. Kaldor inclines to the former view, on the grounds that 'the high savings propensity out of profits attaches to the nature of business income, and not to the wealth (or other peculiarities) of the individuals who own property' (1966, p. 310). This raises the issue as to how far corporate behaviour can be viewed independently of personal savings decisions:

the addition to the real assets of corporations made possible by corporate savings must affect share values, and in the long run it is difficult to see how share values can diverge widely from the value of real assets. Change in share values is likely to have an influence on the saving behaviour of the owners of the shares. (Hahn and Matthews, 1965, p. 23)

Where corporate saving leads to a rise in share values of an equal amount, and where this capital gain is regarded by shareholders as fully equivalent to personal savings, the higher corporate saving is exactly offset by a corresponding reduction of personal saving. That firms are simply saving on behalf of the shareholders takes a rather extreme view of the behaviour of shareholders and the stock market. (We return to company finance below.)

The Pasinetti interpretation is based firmly on individual decisions, but here too the plausibility of the differential savings assumptions has been questioned. Some writers have asked why the savings propensities should differ between classes; others have suggested that it is not appropriate to a modern capitalist economy:

One can imagine an economy divided into two quite different distinct social classes . . . The labourers may be imagined . . . to have no need to save for the reason of making provision for old age . . . The capitalist class consists of those who are wealthy, interested in the accumulation of property and in passing it on to their offspring . . . This model, as stylized economic models go, may not be too bad as a representation of the state of England in the eighteenth or the early nineteenth century, but as an even stylized representation of a modern economy it is simply not adequate. (Bliss, 1975, Ch. 6)

Similarly, there are objections to the assumption that the savings propensity is uninfluenced by economic variables: 'why is it not influenced by the growth rate, or the rate of interest, or the price of champagne?' (Bliss, 1975, Ch. 6). The capitalist class may indeed accumulate without regard to the return, but if working-class saving is interpreted in life-cycle terms, then it is likely to be influenced by the rate of interest. The incorporation of such considerations is clearly a major requirement before the class savings theory can be accepted.

At an empirical level, the Kaldorian theory can be tested in a variety of ways. It is possible to investigate the evidence concerning particular assumptions, especially the classical saving hypothesis; alternatively, the predictions of the theory may be tested directly, by examining the relationship between the share of profits and the ratio of investment to total output (using the first equation on p. 216, or a modified version allowing for savings by workers). Since we observe actual rather than planned magnitudes, such a test is of limited value, but it may give some indication of whether the theory is at least consistent with the historical record. In the United States Reder showed that the evidence for full employment periods was 'not inconsistent with the acceptance of Kaldor's theory' (1959, p. 190) after 1921, but not in the period 1909–14. Phelps Brown (1968) has similarly pointed out that the shifts through the years of the First World War cast doubt on the theory, although he recognizes that the share of profits moved in parallel with the proportion of output invested at other times.

The role of accumulation in influencing the behaviour of the share of profit is also explored in the theory of Wood (1975), although in a rather different way, since he concentrates on capital formation by the company sector and on the sources of company finance. Over-simplifying, his approach may be seen as replacing s_p by $s_p/(1 + f - x)$, where f is the firm's target for the proportion of assets that it holds in liquid form and x is the target for the proportion of investment that is externally financed. (Wood goes on to develop the model in a different way from that described above.) Although the treatment of company financial behaviour may be questioned, the introduction of such features of real-world institutions is surely to be welcomed — and these are considerations relevant to the relation between factor shares and the personal distribution discussed in the next section.

Marxian theory and the share of profits

The Marxian scheme of analysis is both far-reaching in its implications and subject to a whole range of interpretations. It is not possible to do justice to it here, and we limit our discussion to those aspects most relevant to the factor share distribution.

The central concept for our purpose is the rate of exploitation, or the ratio of surplus value to variable capital. This ratio is often expressed in terms of the division of the working day into the time that a person works for himself and the time that he works for the capitalist: a ratio equal to 1 means, for example, that half the working day is 'paid' labour and the other half 'unpaid'. As it is described by Morishma, 'capitalists exploit workers by making them work longer than the hours required to produce the amounts of wage goods which they can buy with the wages they receive; thus surplus outputs are produced, which are the source of profits' (1973, p. 46). (For a discussion of the suggestive nature of the term 'exploitation', see Robinson (1966, p. 21), where she compares it with the alternative use of the term 'exploitation' by Pigou to denote the difference between wages under perfect competition and under imperfect competition, and argues that by the latter 'the reader is unconsciously lulled into the conclusion that, as long as competition prevails, labour receives all that it can rightly claim'.)

The distribution of income depends on the rate of exploitation, but there is no straightforward way in which this concept can be related to actual changes in money profits and wages, since the rate of exploitation is defined in terms of 'labour values' and not in terms of prices. Surplus value and profits cannot be equated, and to go from one to the other the 'transformation problem' has to be resolved. As a result,

A Marxian analysis cannot rely on data on wages or profits or on a 'capital–labour' ratio to prove exploitation; and as a corollary, the absence of exploitation is also not proven by any data on constancy of wage shares or of rising real wages or the ratio of wages to average product. (Desai, 1974, p. 57)

In view of this, we rely on a more heuristic account of the factors considered likely to influence the profit share in modern Marxian treatments (rather than attempt an explicit account of the transformation problem). We also refrain from entering the debate about the 'falling rate of profit' (in this respect, the title of this sub-section was carefully chosen). Particular attention is paid to the power of the working class. This brings us back to the considerations discussed earlier, under the heading of bargaining power, but the Marxian analysis has gone further in seeking to identify the *sources* of changes in the strength of labour. Mandel, for example, has stressed the role played by the 'reserve army of labour', as summarized below by Rowthorn:

Mandel points to the reserve army of labour, arguing that by the mid-sixties it had been severely depleted and could no longer perform its disciplinary role properly . . . He argues that the reserve army does not function primarily through supply and demand in the labour market, but through its effect on working-class bargaining power: a large reserve of unemployed or cheap labour demoralizes the working-class movement and undermines its organizational strength. (1980, p. 116)

The notion is developed by Weisskopf, who draws the distinction between the cyclical pattern ('as a cyclical expansion develops the demand for labour grows more rapidly than the supply' (1979, p. 345)) and the secular trend, where the 'reserve army would be replenished by [technological change], or by new sources of labour supply' (p. 345), and it is less obvious that the argument applies. Weisskopf further distinguishes between situations where workers are able to exercise 'defensive' power against adverse relative price movements and 'offensive' power, which permits real wage gains greater than the rate of productivity increase. He goes on to provide an empirical analysis of the US economy from 1949 to 1975, with results that are interesting but far from definitive — a description that applies to all of the empirical evidence we have cited in this and the previous section.

9.4 Factor shares and the personal distribution of income

After struggling with the preceding sections, the reader will probably agree with Marshall's pronouncement about the problem of distribution with which we began this chapter. We have seen that alternative theories have attempted to simplify the economic system so as to throw light on the determinants of the shares of wages and profits, but that this distillation brought with it many problems. The theories all emphasize aspects of the real world that are clearly important — the role of technology, the contribution of accumulation to growth, the strength of unions and employers, and the interests of workers and capitalists — but none by itself is probably fully adequate as an explanation of the observed pattern. In view of this, no attempt is made here at any kind of conclusion; instead, this final section considers briefly the relationship between factor shares and the personal distribution that is the main concern of the book.

At the beginning of this chapter, reference was made to the Ricardian identification of factor income with the three main classes of society:

$$
\begin{aligned}
\text{Labour income} &\longrightarrow \text{workers} \\
\text{Capital income} &\longrightarrow \text{capitalists} \\
\text{Rent} &\longrightarrow \text{landlords}
\end{aligned}
$$

While this class identification may still have relevance today, account must be taken of changes in the economic and social structure of society that have taken place since Ricardo wrote.

The first change concerns the ownership of capital. The Ricardian classification is based on the assumption that the working class owns no capital, but in a present-day advanced economy most workers have accumulated some savings for life-cycle reasons. The fact that people save for old age, either contractually or on their own account, means that part of the income from capital accrues to pensioners or members of the working population. Part of the profits of General Motors may be paid in dividends to an elderly widow with a few hundred dollars of savings or may go to a pension fund which in turn pays benefits to pensioners with low incomes. A closely related phenomenon is the spread of home ownership, which means that part of the share of rents accrues to occupiers rather than landlords.

The second change concerns the development of institutions that stand between the productive sector of the economy and the household sector. We referred just now to pension funds. These funds act as intermediaries, owning assets but having liabilities to the household sector, so that part of the income from capital is channelled through their hands. The entire company sector is indeed of this form. Profits accrue to companies, and they make decisions about their disposition, either paying them out as dividends or retaining them for investment in the company. (It is these financial decisions that are emphasized in the theory of Wood discussed above.) Where profits are retained, they do not immediately form part of personal income. On the other hand, as we have seen in the discussion of the Kaldor model, the shareholders may none the less benefit as a result of capital gains, these forming the counterpart in personal income of the retained profits that appear as part of national income.

A third major change has been the increase in the role of the state, which also acts as an intermediary between the productive sector and household incomes. Part of the wealth of the personal sector is held in the form of government bonds and other government liabilities. The interest paid on this national debt is a component of personal income, even though it has no counterpart in a return to a productive factor. While government taxes and transfers may be seen as redistributing a given pre-tax income, some transfers are commonly treated as 'original' income: for example, the *Blue Book* figures discussed in early chapters included state pensions as 'pre-tax' income. Taxes on companies must also be taken into account. As noted earlier, the share of profits in before-tax terms has fallen more sharply than profits after tax. Before-tax profits have received most attention in the literature, but it is profits after tax that are relevant to the personal distribution.

These considerations mean that total *national* income does not match up directly with the total *personal* income, as will be clear to anyone who has tried to do it from the national accounts. In broad terms, to go from gross national product to personal income as defined in earlier chapters, we have to take the following steps:

	Gross national product
−	Depreciation

=	National income

−	Retained company profits
−	Taxes on companies (e.g. corporation tax)
−	Profits accruing to government
+	Government transfers to persons (e.g. pensions)
+	Interest paid by government
+	Capital gains
+	Missing imputed income (e.g. home production)

=	Personal income before tax

In order to relate the distribution by factor shares to that by persons we have, therefore, to trace through these links and to take account of classes of income, such as government transfers, that did not appear in our earlier discussion.

The second consequence of the changes since the time of Ricardo is that the interests of different classes have become somewhat blurred. The worker may also be receiving profit income via his rights to a pension fund and may also benefit from (imputed) rent via the ownership of his house. It does not necessarily follow that a rise in the share of property is to the benefit of those at the top of the income distribution. At the same time, the concentration of wealth remains such that in general it is the rich for whom income from profits is important and the rest of the population who depend primarily on wage income or state benefits. If we regard earnings and transfers as 'labour' income, and the remainder as 'property' income, we may use the simple formula given by Meade (1964): if the top 5 per cent in the income distribution receive a per cent of the income from earnings and b per cent of the income from property, then their share in total income is given by

$$(a \times \text{share of earnings}) + (b \times \text{share of property}).$$

If a were 12½ per cent and b were 50 per cent (Meade takes rather higher figures for 1959), then the overall share in total income of the top 5 per cent would rise from 14 per cent, if the share of property were 5 per cent, to 22 per cent, if the share of property were 25 per cent. Changes in the share of earnings and property income may therefore still have a significant effect on the share of the top income groups.

Notes on sources and further reading

There are a relatively large number of books dealing with the subject of factor shares. Reference may be made to Johnson (1973) and Bronfenbrenner (1971). Ranadive (1978), Craven (1979), and Lydall (1979), which cover the field extensively. Phelps Brown (1968) provides a clear summary of the main features of different theories and comments on their relevance.

A useful collection of articles on trends in factor shares is Marchal and Ducros (1968), which includes studies by Feinstein of the United Kingdom, Haley of the United States, Ohkawa of Japan, and Jeck of West Germany. Phelps Brown and Browne (1968) contains data on France, Germany, Sweden, the United Kingdom, and the United States. Evidence on seventeen advanced countries is given by Heidensohn (1969). The study by Kravis (1959) brings out many of the methodological problems, as does that by Heidensohn and Zygmant (1974).

A clear statement of, and apology for, orthodox theory is given in Ferguson (1969), and it is also described in detail in the textbooks referred to earlier. There is a large volume of criticism, and for a selection the reader is referred to the readings edited by Hunt and Schwartz (1972): for example, the contributions by Robinson and Nuti. Particular mention should be made of Rowthorn (1980, Ch. 1). For a critique from a rather different perspective, see the preface to Hahn (1972).

Kalecki first presented his degree of monopoly theory in 1938-9 (Kalecki, 1939), and this is the version discussed in the text. In later writing the emphasis shifted, and he interpreted the index of monopoly power in a more general way. The modern application of the Kalecki theory is set out, and developed, in Cowling (1982). The role of power in determining changes in the distribution of income is the subject of Pen (1978).

The Kaldorian theory has been presented in a variety of forms. The text follows the original (Kaldor, 1955b); for a more recent statement of his views, see (1966). The reader should consult Pasinetti (1974) and Wood (1975).

Excellent introductions to Marxian economic theory are provided by Desai (1974), Fine (1975), Harrison (1978), and Junankar (1982). More difficult are Becker (1977) and Morishima (1973). Reference should also be made to Morishima and Catephores (1978), Rowthorn (1980), and Fine (1982).

10

POVERTY

A decent provision for the poor is the true test of civilisation

(Samuel Johnson, 1770)

In earlier chapters we have examined the distribution of income among the population as a whole; we now focus attention on the lower part of the income scale and the problem of poverty, with particular reference to Britain and the United States.

10.1 The definition of poverty

What exactly do we mean by poverty in countries such as Britain and the United States? This question has generated a great deal of controversy. Indeed, there are those who would argue that it is absurd to talk about poverty in present-day advanced countries, since those considered poor in the United States today have an income greater than the average per capita income of a hundred years ago, to say nothing of their being many times better off than the average Indian today. While it is true that low-income families in Britain and the United States would rank high on a world income scale, or in relation to the past, it is misleading to suggest that poverty may be seen simply in terms of an absolute standard that can be applied to all countries and at all times, independent of the social structure and level of development. The poverty line may depend on social conventions and the contemporary living standards of a particular society, and in this way somebody in the United States may be adjudged poor even though he has a higher income than the average person in India.

'Absolute' poverty

In order to bring out some of the problems in the definition of poverty, it may be useful to begin by considering the work of Rowntree (1901) in Britain and of Orshansky in the United States, to which reference was made in Chapter 3. Rowntree, in his study of poverty in York in 1899, was the first to consider in any detail the problems involved in defining poverty. The aspect of his work that has received most attention is his concept of 'primary' poverty, which applied to families whose income was 'insufficient to obtain the minimum necessaries for the maintenance of merely physical efficiency' (1922 ed., p. 117). His calculation of this absolute minimum was pioneering in its design, which involved using estimates by the American nutritionist Atwater to calculate the minimum requirements of protein and calories and then translating these into a 'diet containing the necessary nutrients at the lowest cost compatible with a certain amount of variety' (p. 129). The resulting menus were not ones that made the mouth water, as is shown by that for Tuesdays:

Breakfast	porridge and skim milk
Lunch	bread and cheese
Dinner	vegetable broth, bread, cheese, dumpling
Supper	bread and porridge

To the expenditure on food were added certain minimum amounts for clothing, fuel, and household sundries. This gave a poverty standard in 1899 of 5s 6d for a single person, 9s 2d for a couple and £1 0s 6d for a couple with four children, with the addition in each case of the rent paid. (These amounts are equivalent to 27½p, 46p, and £1.02½p in decimal currency. All amounts referred to subsequently have been converted to decimals.) This treatment of rent was based on the assumption that it was outside the control of the household. A similar approach was adopted in Rowntree's later studies in 1936 Rowntree (1941) and in 1950 (Rowntree and Lavers 1951).

The work of Orshansky, which provided the basis for much of the recent research on poverty in the United States, was similar to that of Rowntree, in that she took as her starting point estimates of minimum food expenditures. These were developed by the United States Department of Agriculture and were based on judgements regarding an acceptable trade-off between nutritional standards and consumption patterns. The calculation of total income requirements took a rather different form. On the basis of household budget data, Orshansky (1965) estimated the proportion of income spent on food in families of different sizes, and multiplied the minimum cost diet by the reciprocal of this proportion. If the cost of food requirements for a family of four was $1000 per annum and the proportion of income spent on food was one-third, this would give a poverty standard of $3000. The resulting poverty standard in 1962 ranged from $1900 for a couple with no children to $3130 for a family with two, and to over $5000 for a family of five children.

Attractive as this absolute poverty approach may be at first sight, it involves a number of serious conceptual difficulties, as has been pointed out by Townsend (1954), Rein (1970), and others. Most importantly, there is no single 'subsistence' level that can be used as a basis for the poverty line. Even in the case of food, which might appear to provide the firmest foundation, it is difficult to determine requirements with any precision. There is no one level of food intake required for subsistence, but rather a broad range where physical efficiency declines with a falling intake of calories and proteins. An individual's nutritional needs depend on a level of activity, the office worker requiring less than a miner or a farm worker. Moreover,

even for a specific group in a specific region, nutritional requirements are difficult to define precisely. People have been known to survive with incredibly little nutrition, and there seems to be a cumulative improvement of life expectation as the dietary limits are raised. (Sen, 1981, p. 12)

Where precisely the line is drawn depends, therefore, on the judgement of the investigator, and the idea of a purely physiological basis for the poverty criterion is lost.

Even if nutritional requirements could be determined in terms of calories, protein, etc., there would still be problems arising from the disparity between expert judgement and actual consumption behaviour. This disparity is highlighted by calculations like those of Stigler (1945), who showed that the minimum cost of a nutritively adequate diet for an adult male was some $200 a year (in current prices). Not only do housewives lack the dietary knowledge required to calculate the least-cost foods, not only are poor families forced to purchase food in uneconomical ways, but also eating habits are profoundly influenced by social conventions. This was recognized by Rowntree in his inclusion of items such as tea, which has little or no nutritional value, but which people will not go without (in this context he refers to the riot that took place in a Bradford workhouse when they tried to replace tea by a more nutritive gruel). Orshansky stated explicitly that 'social conscience and custom dictate that there be not only sufficient quantity but sufficient variety to meet recommended nutritional goals and conform to customary eating patterns. Calories alone are not enough' (1965, p. 5).

In the case of non-food items, there is an even greater degree of arbitrariness. Rowntree's 1950 standard included 2p a week for wireless, 3p for a daily newspaper, and 34p for beer, tobacco, presents, holidays, and books. It is hard to justify the inclusion of these items on an absolute subsistence definition. As Townsend (1962) has pointed out, 'a family might maintain its physical efficiency just as well in a caravan . . . as in a three-bedroom house. It could go to bed early and spend nothing on electricity.' The approach adopted by Orshansky avoided this kind of judgement, but has been criticized on other grounds. Friedman (1965) has argued that the proportion of income spent on food was underestimated, and hence the allowance for non-food needs *over*-estimated.

(In terms of the example given earlier, if the proportion of income spent on food were 40 per cent rather than 33½ per cent, this would give a poverty standard of $2500 rather than $3000.)

The existence of these difficulties does not mean that the notion of subsistence is irrelevant — concern with the risk of famine or other disasters is clearly central to distributional policy — but it points to the fact that any actual poverty line is likely to be influenced by contemporary living standards. It may therefore be quite reasonable to regard some people in the United States as poor even though, as Harrington (1962) put it, they live better than medieval knights or Asian peasants.

'Relative' poverty

The role of contemporary living standards has long been recognized. Adam Smith, for example, said in widely quoted passage:

> By necessaries, I understand not only the commodities which are indispensably necessary for the support of life but whatever the custom of the country renders it indecent for creditable people, even of the lowest order, to be without. A linen shirt, for example, is strictly speaking not a necessity of life. The Greeks and Romans lived, I suppose, very comfortably though they had no linen. But in the present time . . . a creditable day-labourer would be ashamed to appear in public without a linen shirt, the want of which would be supposed to denote that disgraceful state of poverty. (1776, p. 691)

In the same way, Marx referred to the fact that for the worker 'the number and extent of his so-called necessary wants . . . are themselves the product of historical development and depend, therefore, to a great extent on the degree of civilization of a country' (quoted by Coates and Silburn, 1970, p. 24). Moreover, Rowntree himself (1901) referred to the concept of 'secondary' poverty, based on the report by his investigator of 'evidences of poverty, i.e. obvious want and squalor' (1922 ed., p. 148). This concept was influenced by current living standards, as he explicitly recognized in 1936 when explaining why he had not sought to repeat the calculation of secondary poverty: 'ideas of what constitutes "obvious want and squalor" have changed profoundly since then' (1941, p. 461).

These considerations have led to the adoption of an explicitly relative standard of poverty. As it was put by Townsend, who has done most to develop this approach in recent times, 'individuals and families are in poverty whose resources, over time, fall seriously short of the resources commanded by the average individual or family in the community in which they live' (1973, p. 48). Or,

> People are 'poor' because they are deprived of the opportunities, comforts, and self-respect regarded as normal in the community to which

they belong. It is, therefore, the continually moving *average* standards of that community that are the starting points for an assessment of its poverty, and the poor are those who fall sufficiently far below these average standards. (Social Science Research Council, 1968)

Such a relative definition does not necessarily replace an absolute standard — like Rowntree, we may wish to employ two concepts in tandem. But it is not perhaps surprising that, as average incomes have risen, the relative approach has come to be widely used in countries such as Britain and the United States. At the same time, the adoption of a relative poverty standard does *not* mean that the poor are necessarily always with us. It is sometimes suggested that if, for example, we define the poverty line as half the average income, moving up with the general standard of living, then poverty cannot be abolished. On the contrary, it is quite possible to imagine a society in which no one has less than half the average income — in which there is no poverty according to this definition. The adoption of a relative concept of poverty does not prejudge the issue as to its extent. Nor does the fact that the poverty line may rise with the general level of incomes mean that it is a matter of 'keeping up with the Joneses'. It is a reflection of the interdependence of standards of living, as is well described by Jencks:

The goods and services that made it possible to live on $15 a week during the Depression were no longer available to a family with the same 'real' income in 1964 . . . many cheap foods had disappeared from the stores. Most people had enough money to buy an automobile, so public transportation had atrophied, and families without automobiles were much worse off than during the Depression . . . a person without a telephone could not get or keep many jobs . . . During the depression, many people could not afford indoor plumbing and 'got by' with a privy. By the 1960s, privies were illegal in most places. Those who could not afford an indoor toilet ended up in buildings which had broken toilets. (1972, p. 5)

The conversion of the relative poverty concept into a concrete measure is by no means straightforward. One approach has been to take the standard set by the government, either explicitly, as in the United States, or implicitly, as in Britain in the form of social security benefit levels (supplementary benefits and previously national assistance). The adoption of such a standard may be justified on the grounds that it represents an 'official' view of the minimum standard of income at a certain date. To quote Abel-Smith and Townsend, who used this definition in their study *The poor and the poorest*,

Whatever may be said about the adequacy of the National Assistance Board level of living as a just or publicly approved measure of 'poverty', it has at least the advantage of being in a sense the 'official' operational definition of the minimum level of living at any particular time. (1965, p. 17)

Or, as it was put by the National Board for Prices and Incomes (1971) in their report on low pay, 'Parliament has approved scales of supplementary benefits . . . with the result that it has *de facto* expressed a view as to the level of income below which families are in need.' In the United States, an official government poverty standard was set explicitly by the Council of Economic Advisers, who felt that it represented 'a consensus on an approximate standard'.

In what follows, we shall rely heavily on these official definitions of poverty, since much of the available evidence is presented in this form, but it should be stressed that they are open to objections. Social consensus is not necessarily the right way to define a poverty standard, and even if it is accepted, it is not clear that the Council of Economic Advisers have set the appropriate level. While the supplementary benefit scale has been approved by the British parliament as a minimum income level, it does not necessarily enjoy widespread social approval as a national minimum. The official poverty standards are based purely on money income and ignore other aspects of deprivation. No account is taken of poor-quality housing, schools, or health care, which may or may not be associated with low money incomes. No account is taken of the limited availability of community facilities, parks, playgrounds, transport, and of other environmental inequalities. Moreover, poverty may represent only one aspect of a more general powerlessness, an inability to influence one's environment. As described by Kincaid, 'lack of money is only one element in a complex of deprivations which make up the experience of poverty' (1973, p. 172).

The search for a measure that comes close to capturing the experience of poverty has led to the proposal of a 'participation' standard for poverty, taking account 'of the many roles people play as citizens, workers, parents, householders, neighbours and members of the local community' (Cripps, *et al.*, 1981, p. 184). The construction of such a participation criterion was one of the major innovations of Townsend's 1968-9 survey of poverty in Britain (Townsend, 1979). Townsend's aim was to investigate whether, below a certain income level, a significant number of families reduce their participation in the community's style of living. As he recognizes, there is no unitary and clear-cut national 'style of living', but he suggests that there are types of consumption and customs that may be indicative: for example, in operational terms, owning a refrigerator, having had a holiday away from home in the past year, having sole use of an indoor WC, having parties on children's birthdays, and having a cooked breakfast most days of the week. How far a definite cut-off emerges is a subject for debate, and differences in tastes remain a problem for the approach, but it is potentially of considerable interest.

10.2 The extent of poverty in Britain

In this section we describe the evidence about poverty in Britain, as measured by the official supplementary benefit scale. Before doing so, we should note certain implications of adopting this poverty standard. First, it means that poverty is being measured in terms of current money income defined on a weekly basis. As we saw in Chapter 3, such a short assessment period may indeed be considered appropriate when we are concerned with the extent of poverty. Second, supplementary benefits are assessed for a family unit. The payment is based on the income of an adult, dependent spouse, and children, but not on that of non-dependent members of the same household, such as a grown-up son or daughter. This means that all intra-household transfers (e.g. contributions to the housekeeping) should in theory be taken into account. Third, the supplementary benefit scale rates for families of different sizes embody equivalence scales, the rate for a single person being some 60 per cent of that for a couple, and so on. The rationale of these equivalence scales is not very clear, and it has been suggested by some writers, notably Wȳnn (1970), that they make inadequate allowance for the needs of older children. There is a higher 'long-term' scale for pensioners and certain other groups. A further feature of the supplementary benefit scale is that, like the Rowntree scale, it is defined exclusive of housing costs. The poverty standard consists therefore of a fixed scale – so much per adult, child, etc. – plus the rent or other housing outlay. In this way, the scale makes an approximate allowance for variatioñs in the cost of living, housing costs being the element with the greatest regional variation.

Supplementary benefit scale

The supplementary benefit fixed scale is shown in Table 10.1, expressed as a proportion of the net resources of a person in work with average earnings and the same family circumstances. For purposes of comparability, we have defined net resources to be net of housing outlay as well as tax, although it should be noted that this amount, like the allowance for travel to work costs, varies from one family to the next. For a single person, the supplementary benefit scale is some 30 per cent of the net resources of someone on average earnings. For a single pensioner (in this case the comparison is with a person of working age), the proportion is higher, since the long-term supplementary benefit scale is

TABLE 10.1
Supplementary benefit scale in Britain in relation to net resources of those in work, April 1982

	Supplementary benefit scale as % of net resources* of family of that type with one earner on average earnings
	%
Single person	29
Single pensioner aged 65†	37
Single parent with child aged 3	37
Married couple	44
Pensioner couple both aged 65†	55
Married couple and 1 child aged 3	55
Married couple and 2 children aged 4 and 6	63
Married couple and 3 children aged 3, 8, and 11	74

* Net resources = gross income − income tax − national insurance contributions + child benefit − rent − rates − fares to work. Supplementary benefit = scale rate + heating addition + free welfare milk + free school meals.
† Net resources in this case calculated for single or married employee under pension age.

Source: Calculated from tax and benefit rules on the basis of assumptions about rent and rates (average for council tenants), about travel-to-work costs (£5 a week), about other income (zero), and about heating additions (payable where child under 5).

applicable. For a couple, the scale rises to around a half of the net resources of an average earner; and for the family with three children it reaches three-quarters.

When Rowntree drew up the poverty standard described earlier, he stressed that:

the standards adopted . . . err on the side of stringency rather than extravagance . . . as I have pursued my investigation, I have been increasingly impressed by the fact that to keep a family of five in health on [£2.65] a week (in 1936) . . . needs constant watchfulness and a high degree of skill on the part of the housewife. (1941, p. 29)

In 1977 the Supplementary Benefits Commission (abolished in 1980, when the administration of the scheme became the direct responsibility of the Department of Health and Social Security) examined the evidence about the standards of living of those living on supplementary benefit. The commented on the 'tightness of supplementary benefit claimants' budgets' and noted that they 'in general have little cash to spare for non-essentials' (1977, p. 17). The Commission concluded that 'the supplementary benefits scheme provides, particularly for families with children, incomes that are barely adequate to meet their needs at a level that is consistent with normal participation in the life of the relatively wealthy society in which they live' (1977, p. 28). In 1980, Family Service Units and the Child Poverty Action Group studied the circumstances of sixty-five families with children living on supplementary benefit. They conclude that the 'families in our survey were not able to meet from their basic supplementary benefit all their normal day-to-day living requirements: their food, fuel, clothing, household and laundry expenses, their travel and leisure costs' (Burghes, 1980, p. 71). They go on to comment that

It is sometimes said that the problem with the supplementary benefit scheme is not that the rates are inadequate but that those who are dependent on the scheme cannot manage. However, a number of the interviewers, all experienced social workers and familiar with the families, still found themselves shaken by the grind and stress that the poverty of the scale rates imposes. Managing constantly and effectively over a long period [requires] personal security and strength. (1980, p. 73)

Number living below supplementary benefit scale

How many families in Britain live below this — far from generous — standard? In order to answer this question we need information about the lower part of the income distribution. In terms of the frequency distribution of incomes, described in earlier chapters, we want to know

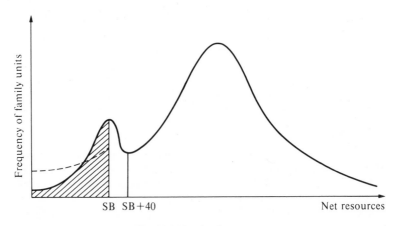

Fig. 10.1 Number in poverty

how many are in the left-hand tail – see Fig. 10.1, where the hatched area marks all those at or below the supplementary benefit level (the dashed line is discussed below). Two points should be noted about the diagram. The first is that the horizontal scale measures 'resources', that is income minus housing outlay, since this is the basis for the supplementary benefit assessment. The second is that we have drawn a (minor) peak in the frequency at the supplementary benefit scale level, to bring out the point that the recipients of benefit will tend to be clustered around this point. (The actual level of resources may depart from the scale because of payments for additional requirements, etc.) This means that the numbers in poverty may be quite sensitive to the precise poverty line chosen, depending on whether or not it includes the peak. Put another way, it may make quite a difference whether we take those strictly *below* the scale or those *at or below* the scale.

The evidence about the distribution of income in Britain discussed in Chapters 2 and 4 showed that there are two main sources: the *Blue Book* estimates and the *Family Expenditure Survey* (*FES*). Although the former source has been used (see Gough and Stark, 1968), it has a number of major limitations for the measurement of poverty according to the supplementary benefit standard. Most importantly, it does not contain information on housing outlay, so that 'net resources' cannot be directly calculated. Most recent studies of poverty in Britain have therefore been based on the *FES*, employing the data on household incomes and circumstances. In this respect, they may be seen as following in the tradition established by Rowntree in his surveys of York.

Use of the *FES* to measure the extent of poverty in Britain was pioneered by Abel-Smith and Townsend in their influential study *The poor and the poorest* (1965). They had access to the raw returns from the surveys of 1953–4 and 1960, and used these to estimate the proportion of households below the national assistance scale (in 1953–4 this was assessed in terms of expenditure and in 1960 in terms of income). The poverty standard adopted by Abel-Smith and Townsend was the national assistance scale (national assistance being the predecessor of supplementary benefit) plus 40 per cent. The purpose of the 40 per cent addition was to allow for the fact that the incomes of persons receiving assistance could be higher than the basic scale because of additional allowances (e.g. for heating, special diets, etc.) or items of income disregarded by the National Assistance Board (e.g. the first part of a disability pension). They found in 1960 that 3.8 per cent of the population had incomes below the national assistance (NA) scale. This shows that a substantial number of people – 2 million – were at or below the poverty line. A further 5½ million had incomes within 40 per cent of the assistance scale (Abel-Smith and Townsend, 1965, Table 15):

	Percentage of population	Numbers (approx.)
below 80% scale	0.9	½ million
below NA scale	3.8	2 million
below 140% scale	14.2	7½ million

The *FES* was subsequently employed by a number of academic investigators, and one of their achievements was to persuade the government to begin publishing official estimates of the numbers of low-income families, dating from 1972. Unfortunately, cutbacks in the Government Statistical Service made by the Conservative government mean that the figures are now produced only every other year, but this still represents a considerable advance in the information that is available. The most recent figures, those for 1979, are shown in Table 10.2, together with those for earlier years (although there is a break in the comparability of the series in 1977).

The official estimates indicate that in 1979 there were 2 million people living in families with incomes below the supplementary benefit level (and not receiving benefit). There were a further 5½ million living within 40 per cent of the scale, and some 4 million in receipt of supplementary benefit. The figures shown in the table are cumulative, so that there are in total 2130 + 5470 = 7600 below 140 per cent of the supplementary benefit scale. The overall total of 11½ million including those on benefit is quite a lot higher than found by Abel-Smith and Townsend for 1960 − it is 22 per cent of the population, compared with 14 per cent − but the figures are not directly comparable, since both the methods employed and the standard itself are different.

None the less, considering just the official figures, there is no evidence to suggest a downward trend in the size of the problem. Only limited weight can be attached to year-to-year variations in the figures, but it appears that in the early 1970s the number below the scale was 1½-1¾ million, compared with 2 million towards the end of the decade.

In what follows we examine more fully the position of the 2 million below the official low-income line, but first we need to consider the problems in the use of this statistical evidence.

Problems in the measurement of poverty

The problems in the measurement of poverty will be familiar from the discussion in earlier chapters, but there are certain aspects that are especially significant in the present context.

First, there are the shortcomings of the basic data source. The *FES* is derived from a small sample of the population (about 1 person in 2500), so that, for instance, year-to-year changes in the estimates may be attributable to sampling fluctuations. It does not cover people not living

TABLE 10.2

Official estimates of low-income families in Great Britain, 1972-1979

	Persons in families (thousands)*								
	Not receiving supplementary benefit (SB)						Including all those receiving supplementary benefit		
	below SB level			below 140 per cent of SB level					
	Over pension age	Under pension age	Total	Over pension age	Under pension age	Total	Over pension age	Under pension age	Total
1972	980	800	1780		—			—	
1973	850	740	1600		—			—	
1974	550	850	1410		—			—	
1975	740	1100	1840	3610	5220	8 830	5540	7000	12 540
1976	870	1410	2280	4050	6730	10 780	6000	8870	14 870
1977	760	1270	2020	3770	6100	9 860	5770	8260	14 020
1977†	760	1140	1900	3620	5250	8 870	5590	7400	12 990
1979†	1130	1000	2130	3900	3700	7 600	5890	5690	11 580

* The figures in the three sections of the table are cumulative. The figures relate only to people living in private households (excluding, for example, those in institutions). Finally, the figures are based on a small sample and are subject to sampling error. They have been rounded to the nearest 10 000 and for this reason the components do not necessarily add exactly to the totals shown.

† These figures are based on a comparison of incomes at the date of interview with the current scale; the estimates for earlier years adjust income to an end-of-year basis.

Source: Parliamentary answer to B. Sedgemore, MP (20 May 1974) and subsequent corrections; *Social Trends 1975*, Table 5.31; *Social Trends 1976*, Table 5.31; Department of Health and Social Security, *Low Income Families, 1979*, Tables 1, 2, and 5 and subsequent corrections.

in households, thus excluding groups who may be particularly vulnerable, such as the homeless and those in institutions. There is a sizeable degree of non-response (around 30 per cent), so that the estimates may be affected by differential non-response by different groups. There is evidence that certain types of income are understated when the survey totals are grossed up and compared with the national accounts aggregates. These considerations must be borne in mind when assessing the estimates. At the same time, the impact of these shortcomings should not be exaggerated. For example, a detailed investigation of the understatement of income (Atkinson and Micklewright, 1983) concluded that this was associated mainly with investment income and self-employment income, which may be less relevant to the low-income families considered here, and that for other more relevant types of income, such as earnings, social security benefits, and occupational pensions, the *FES* figures are relatively reliable.

Second, there is the question of the definition of the *unit*. As we have seen, the supplementary benefit assessment is based on the family unit, and this is the procedure followed in Table 10.2. On the other hand, a number of investigators, including Abel-Smith and Townsend, have used the household definition. With such a broader unit, the proportion in poverty will tend to be lower, and the choice between them depends on the degree of income-sharing that takes place. As it is put by Beckerman and Clark:

Whether the 'true' measure lies nearer one extreme or the other depends on the genuine amount of sharing of resources that takes place within any household or family unit. If there is none, for example, then the narrow unit would provide a correct estimate of poverty, since poor units would not be helped out by transfers of resources from richer units within the same household. If, on the other hand, there is full sharing, then the narrow unit would exaggerate poverty. (1982, p. 16)

Beckerman and Clark go on to argue that the household is 'probably preferable, since it is highly likely that in most multiple unit households there is enough intra-household sharing to prevent sub-units from falling below the poverty line' (1982, p. 16). There is however little concrete evidence, as we saw in Chapter 3, on which to base such a judgement. And the estimates of Beckerman and Clark show that it makes a substantial difference: using the *FES* for 1975, they find 3.2 per cent of the population below the supplementary benefit level on the basis of the family unit, compared with 2.3 per cent with a household unit (1982, p. 17).

Third, there are issues associated with the choice of *time period*. As argued in Chapter 3, when considering the incidence of poverty, we may want to take a short assessment period; we may be concerned with current weekly income. This is broadly the approach followed in the *FES*, but in one important instance the official estimates depart from current weekly income. Where the head of the family has been off work, through sickness or unemployment, for less than thirteen weeks, the official calculation is based not on their current income but on the family's normal income when the head is in work. This typically has the effect of reducing the number estimated to be in poverty, as is illustrated by the figures given by Beckerman and Clark − see Table 10.3. From a comparison of the two columns, it may be seen that the number of people estimated to be below the poverty line is increased by a third when current income is used. (Other aspects of the table are discussed below.)

The fourth question concerns the choice of *poverty measure*. To this point, we have referred solely to the number below the poverty line, or what has been called the 'head count' measure, and this is the indicator that has been almost universally employed. This may appear quite surprising in view of the extensive research on the choice of measures of income inequality (discussed in Chapter 3), but until the contribution of Sen (1976) there was almost a complete divorce between the two literatures. Once the question is asked, it is evident that the head-count ratio is not fully satisfactory. In particular, 'an unchanged number of people below the "poverty line" may go with a sharp rise in the extent of the short-fall of income from the poverty line' (Sen, 1976, p. 219). This is illustrated in Fig. 10.1 by the dashed line: the total number below the standard is unaltered, but more of them are at the lower levels of resources and fewer close to the supplementary benefit scale.

One way in which the extent of the short-fall can be incorporated is through the calculation of the 'poverty gap': in other words, to add the cash amounts by which people fall below the scale. So if there are 1 million old age pensioners, each £1 below the scale in weekly terms, this generates an annual poverty gap of £52 million. In Table 10.3, we show the estimates by Beckerman and Clark of the poverty gap in Britain in 1974-6, expressed both in absolute terms and as a percentage of the gross domestic product. Seen in the latter way, the problem appears smaller in size. Whether it is indeed quite 'cheap' to resolve will be discussed in Chapter 11.

Finally, there is the choice of *poverty standard*. The use of the supplementary benefit scale is open to question. For example, there are the issues raised by inflation. The official estimates for 1979 compare each family's income with the benefit scale applicable at the date of interview, taking no account of the fact that the scale is up-rated for inflation only once a year. Thus the Smith family interviewed on 5 November could be

TABLE 10.3

Alternative measures of poverty in Britain, 1974–1976

	'Normal' income*	Current income
Number of hundreds		
below poverty line† (thousands)	1551	1839
	(8.1%)	(9.6%)
Number of persons		
below poverty line (thousands)	2700	3690
	(5.0%)	(6.8%)
Poverty gap (£ million)	219	387
(% of gross domestic product)	(0.22%)	(0.39%)

* Normal income differs from current income in that those off work due to sickness or unemployment for less than 13 weeks are assumed to have income equal to the normal income of the family when at work.
† The poverty line is the supplementary benefit scale indexed to allow for the change in the retail price index.

Source: Beckerman and Clark (1982), Table 3.3.

above the poverty line, but the Jones family interviewed two weeks later could be 10 per cent below the line, even though they both had exactly the same income and circumstances. At times of relatively rapid inflation this could make quite a difference. In Table 10.2 we may compare the two official estimates for 1977. The lower is calculated in the manner just described; the upper adjusts all income to a common date (the end of the year). As may be seen, the latter gives figures that are some 5–10 per cent higher. The change was made because it was felt that the unadjusted figures gave 'a truer indication of the extent of low income', but this begs the question as to the appropriate choice of poverty standard. Do we want a poverty criterion that is fixed in real terms over time, or one that varies with the rate of inflation and the frequency of up-ratings?

More fundamentally, we must question the principles underlying the use of the supplementary benefit standard. One of the major objectives of Townsend's 1968/9 national survey of poverty (the main rival to the *FES* as a source of information about poverty in Britain in this period) was to investigate the implications of different approaches to the definition of poverty. It is not possible to do justice to the wealth of the material collected by Townsend, but in Table 10.4 we summarize the results on different definitions. The state's standard, or the supplementary benefit scale, shows rather more than 3 million people to have been below the poverty line, and this rises to 15 million if we include those 'on the margins' of poverty (i.e. less than 40 per cent above the scale). The 'relative income standard' is based simply on a comparison

TABLE 10.4

Alternative poverty standards in United Kingdom 1968/9

	Number below poverty line (thousands)	Percentage of population
		%
State's standard supplementary benefit scale	3 320	6.1
'On margins' of state's standard (140 per cent of supplementary benefit scale	11 860	21.8
Relative income standard*	5 000	9.2
Deprivation standard*	12 460	22.9

* See text for definition
Source: Townsend (1979), Table 7.1

with the mean income for a particular household type, a household being classified as 'poor' if its net disposable income falls below 50 per cent. On the basis of this − expressly relativistic − concept, the survey shows 5 million to be in poverty. Finally, there is Townsend's 'deprivation standard', the basis for which has been described earlier in the chapter. Application of this index leads to an estimate of 12½ million living below the poverty line.

10.3 The incidence of poverty in Britain

In Rowntree's original 1899 survey he found that the life of the labourer was marked 'by five alternating periods of want and comparative plenty' (1901, 1922 ed., pp. 169–70). The periods of want were his childhood, when he himself had children, and when he was too old to work. Poverty was seen as an expected part of the life-cycle of the working class, and not necessarily as a sign that the family had fallen on 'bad times'. This shows up in Rowntree's classification of the 'immediate' causes of poverty. In only 5 per cent of cases was it attributed to the chief wage-earner being out of work or having irregular work. In 16 per cent of cases, the cause was the death of the chief wage-earner, and in 22 per cent it was the size of the family (five or more children); but by far the largest category was those 'in regular work, but at low wages' (1922 ed., p. 153). By 1950, when Rowntree carried out his third, and final, survey of York, his classification of the causes was quite different; 'old age' now accounted for 68 per cent of poverty. But this can equally be regarded as part of the normal life-cycle, and the 'exceptional' circumstances of sickness, unemployment, and death of chief wage-earner still accounted altogether for only 28 per cent.

It is tempting to draw a comparison between these findings of Rowntree and the evidence for the 1960s and 1970s. After all, there is a direct line of descent from the Rowntree standard to the supplementary benefit scale (the Beveridge proposals for national assistance being based on similar calculations to those by Rowntree in his 1936 study). This is misleading, however, and the Rowntree poverty criterion differed in significant respects from the national assistance/supplementary benefit approach. Most importantly, Rowntree's assessment was much closer to the prewar household means test than to the family unit applied in assessing supplementary benefit, and at the time of his surveys this had considerably more impact than today (lodgers, for example, being much more common). In our re-analysis of the 1950 survey of York, Atkinson *et al.* (1981) show that, *if Rowntree had applied the national assistance standard*, he would have found between 5 and 10 per cent of the population to be below the poverty line, compared with the 2.8 per cent published in Rowntree and Lavers (1951). (It is interesting to speculate what would have happened if he had reported the existence of poverty on this scale — some 15 years before *The poor and the poorest* brought to public attention the persistence of poverty under the postwar welfare state.)

At the same time, Rowntree's description of the life-cycle of poverty may be of present-day relevance. Fig. 10.2 shows the pattern of family income and needs for a man whose earnings throughout his life are the lowest decile for his age group, and who has the following life history:

Age		
22	One child aged 1	Wife not working
27	Two children aged 3, 6	Wife not working
34	Three children aged 5, 10, 13	Wife not working
44	One dependent child aged 15	Wife at work part-time
54	—	Wife at work part-time
62	—	Wife retired
65	Retired	

The pattern of gross earnings is shown by the solid line in Fig. 10.2. Typically, the earnings of low paid workers reach a peak early in their lives and then decline, and this pattern is shown in the diagram, where earnings are at their highest in the 30s. In terms of the lowest decile of the overall distribution, earnings are above this level between the ages of 25 and 49 and below in the worker's 50s. The variation of earnings with age has to be viewed in the light of family needs at different stages of the life-cycle. For this purpose, needs have been assessed on the basis of the supplementary benefit scale plus 40 per cent (and rent), following the approach of Abel-Smith and Townsend (although for retirement we have taken just the long-term scale). The dashed line in the diagram shows

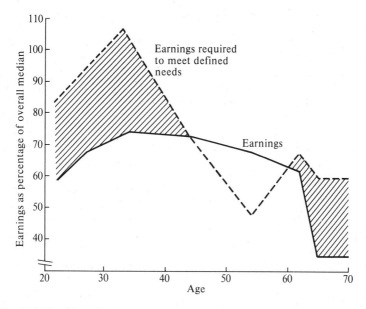

Fig. 10.2 The life-cycle of earnings and need, 1982. Based on earnings, taxes, and benefits as at April 1982. Person is assumed to be council tenant and to pay average rates and rent for family type. It is assumed also that rent/rate rebates are claimed where applicable. The work expenses deduction is that assumed by the DHSS in their tax/benefit model.

the gross earnings that the man would have to make for his family to reach this level, taking account of income tax, national insurance contributions, child benefit and family income supplement (if applicable), rent and rate rebates, and work expenses.

The variation of need with age has much the same pattern as earnings but is rather more accentuated. As a result, earnings at the lowest decile are less than sufficient to meet the supplementary benefit plus 40 per cent standard in earlier years; they are also insufficient as the man nears retirement, when his earnings drop and his wife's earnings cease. The hatched area in Fig. 10.2 shows the gap between earnings and needs, measured in 1982, and provides a modern version of the diagram used by Rowntree to illustrate the life-cycle of poverty.

Who is below the supplementary benefit standard?

From the official estimates, we can form some idea as to who is actually below the supplementary benefit scale. Table 10.2 shows that about half of the 2 million are over pension age, so that the last of Rowntrees's periods of 'want' is important. The remaining 1 million can be classified according to their family circumstances (from Department of Health and Social Security, *Low Income Families 1979*, Table 2):

Single with no children	350 000
Couple with no children	90 000
Single with children	110 000
Couple with children	450 000

This shows that the majority were families with children and that, despite the increase in the number of single-parent families, nearly a half were married couples with children. Of the families with children, 170 000 were as 'large' (interestingly, the official criterion is three or more children, compared with Rowntree's five or more) — or only just over a third. Poverty is certainly not just a question of large families.

The 1 million below pension age may also be classified according to the employment status of the family head (source as above):

Full-time work or self-employment	480 000
Sick or disabled for more than 3 months	60 000
Unemployed for more than 3 months	150 000
Other	310 000

These figures are less easy to interpret. The category 'full-time work' includes those off work for less than thirteen weeks, which is consistent with the definition of normal income but makes it difficult to isolate the effect of unemployment. However, even when allowance is made for this, it is clear that there is a substantial number of families below the poverty line where the head of the family is in work. The importance of the 'working poor' was one of the main findings of *The poor and the poorest*, a finding that ran counter to the prevailing wisdom since, as the authors say, 'for over a decade it has been generally assumed that such poverty as exists is found overwhelmingly among the aged' (Abel-Smith and Townsend, 1965, p. 65).

The pattern has definite similarity with that described by Rowntree. There are none the less significant differences, notably in the role played by the employment of married women. In Rowntree's case the improvement in the prospects of the family after the age of 40 was associated with the children going out to work and contributing to the income of the household. In the present case, the assessment is based on the family unit, so that the children growing up contribute only by reducing needs and not by increasing income (they are treated as a separate unit when they cease to be dependent). The main reason for the upturn is now the earnings of the wife. The importance of this factor has been stressed by Layard, Piachaud and Stewart in their analysis based on the General Household Survey for 1975:

whether a wife works is a crucial determinant of whether a family is financially speaking poor. Even when the husband has very low earnings, only 18 per cent of families have incomes below 140 per cent of SB [Supplementary Benefits] if the wife works, compared with 76 per cent if she does not. (1978, p. 129)

Poverty appears therefore to be particularly associated with three stages of the life-cycle: childhood, when one has children and the wife cannot work, and old age. These phases are all predictable, and one might have expected the social security legislation of the past eighty years to have led to a significant decline in the incidence of poverty among these groups. The reasons for this apparent failure are discussed in the next chapter.

At the same time, it would be quite misleading to suggest that poverty is the normal experience of all those at a certain stage in the life-cycle. There are more than 1 million pensioners below the supplementary benefit scale, but they are only 13½ per cent of the total number of persons in such families. There are 450 000 people below the line in families where there is a married couple and children, but they are less than 2 per cent of all families of that type. The reasons why these particular people fall below are to be found in the distribution of earnings, in differences in housing costs, in the unequal provision of pension benefits, and in limited investment opportunities.

Moreover, the figures are a 'snapshot' at one point in time and tell us nothing about individual life histories. Was the person growing up in a low-wage family in Rowntree's York in 1899 also among the unemployed when Rowntree came to carry out his 1936 inquiry? Was he one of the aged poor in 1960? There is very little known about the continuity of poverty throughout the lifetime, but one piece of evidence about *intergenerational* association is given by the study of Atkinson, Maynard and Trinder (1983) following up the children of the families interviewed by Rowntree in York in 1950. The findings need to be qualified in that it was not possible to trace all the children (some twenty-five years had elapsed when the tracing exercise began); the sample is not representative of York, let alone Britain; and so on. But while the results indicate that mobility is quite possible, they also show that it is far from perfect. Those children from 'low-income' (less than 140 per cent of the national assistance scale) families stood a 2.6 times higher chance of being in the same category themselves when interviewed in 1975–8 than of entering the 'comfortably off' (more than 200 per cent of the scale); whereas those children from comfortably off backgrounds in 1950 stood a 1.7 times chance of staying there than of having low incomes.

Finally, the references to unemployment may have suggested that it is relatively unimportant as a cause of poverty. It must however be remembered that the effect of a depressed labour market operates not just through the unemployment of the family head, and its consequences are felt not just at the time when he or she is out of work. Many of the elderly poor in the 1960s and 1970s were those whose ability to save for old age had been adversely affected by the 1930s Depression. The husband may be in work but the wife be unable to find employment, thus depressing family income below the poverty line. And one should not lose sight of the fact that the evidence set out above relates to the 1970s. In 1979 unemployment in Great Britain was 'only' 1.3 million, or well under half its 1982 level. At the time of writing (September 1982) it is not possible to assess the impact of the higher unemployment of the 1980s on the poverty figures; and on the basis of the delays with the previous statistics it will be some time before the first indication is available.

The experience of poverty

The picture of poverty presented so far has been purely statistical, and we end this section with a few family histories which may help make more immediate the problem with which we are concerned. The first two are taken from Townsend's 1968–9 survey:

Mr and Mrs Quick [the names are fictitious], 39 and 37, live in a privately rented four-roomed terraced house in a Lincolnshire village with their two children, aged 5 and 1 . . . Mr Quick is a packer in a cotton mill, and worked 52 weeks last year . . . He is not entitled to sick pay or an occupational pension . . . Mrs Quick gave up her work warping in the same mill just before the second child was born. His pay varies between £12.50 and £13.50 per week . . . There is a family allowance . . . but no other form of income, except that indirectly they appear to be subsidized by his employer, who owns the house and charges a rent of 90p a week . . . They lead a very spare existence, and have not had an evening out in the last fortnight or gone on a summer holiday because they couldn't afford to. (Townsend, 1979, p. 316–17)

This family were below 140 per cent of the supplementary benefit scale, and illustrate the position where the wife is not at work and the husband is low paid (in September 1968 the lowest decile for the earnings of full-time adult men was some £15 a week).

The second history shows the difficulty people face in making provision for old age:

Mr and Mrs Ellman, 81 and 70, have lived in a four-roomed cottage which they own in a village in Worcestershire, for forty-five years. It is very old and does not have mains sanitation . . . They do not have a television set, refrigerator or washing machine, but do have a radio. Mr Ellman had been a mining power-house attendant and had retired, at the age of 64, seventeen years previously. His wife had never worked. . . Their retirement pensions amount to £7.30 and a colliery pension another £1.10 . . . Their joint savings amount to £215 [and] they have been 'gradually eroding' their savings. (Townsend, 1979, pp. 328–9).

This couple, who had a number of disabilities, had an income below the supplementary benefit scale. They were however 'too independent' to apply for assistance.

Circumstances have undoubtedly changed since 1968-9, but whether they have improved is highly debatable, as is illustrated by the following letters:

We live in a village. We have two sons aged 11 and 13 . . . I have to put away £5 for each to cover bus and dinner money each week. That is my child benefit gone for a start . . . My husband, like thousands of others, is on short-time and has been for some few months now. He has worked for his firm for 16 years and has never before been faced with this situation. (McClelland, 1982, p. 10)

and

My husband earns a low wage and after deducting his expenses (which do not include drinking and smoking) he gives me £50. When I have taken account of rent, fuel bills, hire purchase and one or two others such as milk and insurance, I am left with £10 which has to buy the food. (McClelland, 1982, p. 20)

The impact of redundancy is illustrated by the following all-too-common story:

Five years ago we were a happy, contented family. My husband had a good job. I was working at North Tees Hospital. We were able to buy a nice house, we had annual holidays . . . Then my husband fell in ill health. He was made redundant, he was 54 then and because of his age was unable to find employment . . . As the years have gone on – our savings went, no more holidays, no social life at all . . . We receive £41.38 per week . . . My son is now 15 years old, he is a big boy with a big appetite. He seems to grow overnight. It is a nightmare trying to keep up with his clothes. (Unemployment Unit, 1981, p. 8)

Finally, we have concentrated on poverty as an individual experience, but this has to be seen against the background of the community in which they live. This is illustrated by the following description of one of the areas covered by a study of poverty in Belfast in 1978-9:

The Turf Lodge estate is situated on the edge of West Belfast at the bottom of a group of hills ... Built in the early sixties, the estate has a bleak, windswept appearance and ... much of the accommodation in the area is either unsuited to the needs of the tenants or of poor quality or both ... In addition to the problems of overcrowding and inherently unsuitable accommodation has been added the familiar curse of condensation [which] undermines health, increases heating costs, destroys clothing, produces food storage problems ... Few people would put up with such a poor-quality environment from choice but freedom of choice depends on stable work opportunities and adequate income. The majority of the people of Turf Lodge have neither. What they do have is a considerable amount of unemployment. (Evason, 1980, pp. 21–2)

10.4 Poverty in the United States

Poverty in the United States differs in a number of respects from poverty in Britain: in the nature of the problem, in the way it had been analysed, and in the policies adopted in the hope of securing its elimination. This reflects the dissimilarities in social and economic backgrounds, the variations in the institutions of social policy, and differences in the concerns of people and governments. At the same time, the problems in the two countries have much in common, not the least being the reawakening of interest in the early 1960s.

The official study of poverty in the United States which marked the opening of the War on Poverty was published in the *Economic report of the President* for 1964. The Council of Economic Advisers, which was responsible for the report, began by making clear that they were concerned with a relative standard of poverty:

society does not have a clear and unvarying concept of an acceptable minimum. By the standards of contemporary American society most of the population of the world is poor; and most Americans were poor a century ago. But for our society today a consensus on an approximate standard can be found. (1964, p. 57)

The 'consensus' standard adopted by the Council for the poverty line was a figure of $3000 per family in 1962 prices. This was based on estimates by the Social Security Administration of budgets for a non-farm family of four persons. The only allowance for differences in family size was that the poverty line for single persons was set at $1500. (It may be noted that in 1962 the median income was $6220.) On the basis of this poverty line, the Council estimated that, of the 47 million families in the United States, one-fifth were living in poverty in 1962. These families contained 30 million persons, of whom over 11 million were children. Moreover, over 10 per cent of families had total incomes below

$2000. This led President Johnson to declare that 'there are millions of Americans – one-fifth of our people – who have not shared the abundance which has been granted to most of us, and on whom the gates of opportunity have been closed'.

The definition of poverty employed by the Council of Economic Advisers was recognized by them as being crude. The index did not, for example, make adequate allowance for variation of need with family size. The fact that the $3000 standard was applied both to a childless couple and to a family with six children led to biased estimates of the composition of the poor, large families being relatively under-represented. Since that time, the poverty criterion has been refined, following the work of Orshansky referred to earlier, to take account of factors such as family size, the age of the head of the household, and income in kind for farm families. The more refined poverty standard is now used in the official estimates of the extent of poverty, published annually by the US Bureau of the Census, based on the Current Population Survey referred to in Chapter 4. In 1979, when the average cut-off for a non-farm family of four was $7412, the official estimates show 25.3 million people to be living below the poverty line, or 11.6 per cent of the total population. A further 10.2 million were living within 25 per cent of the poverty line (US Department of Commerce, *Characteristics of the Population Below the Poverty level: 1979*, Tables 1 and 2).

As in Britain, there has been considerable discussion of alternative approaches to the measurement of poverty. The official estimates include a variety of definitions. An important example is provided by the comparison of the results obtained using the census income definition and those with 'adjusted' income, where the latter includes government transfers in kind (such as food stamps and Medicaid), excludes taxes paid, and makes an allowance for under-reporting of income. In 1976 this had the effect of reducing the number of families below the poverty line from 10.7 million (13.5 per cent of the total) to 6.6 million (8.3 per cent). This same aspect is illustrated in columns (1) and (2) of Table 10.5, which relates to the proportion of persons, not families. But even with this adjustment, the proportion in poverty in 1980 is still 6 per cent.

Table 10.5 shows the estimates for a number of years. This introduces questions of the comparability of methods over time and the more fundamental issue of the way in which the poverty standard should be adjusted over time. The official standard has been increased in response to rising prices but has taken no account of the rise in real incomes. A different approach, and one closer in spirit to the views expressed by the Council of Economic Advisers, is that suggested by Fuchs (1969), who defined the poverty standard as half of the median income. This gives

TABLE 10.5
Poverty in the United States, 1965–1980

| | Persons below poverty line (% of total population) | | |
| | Official poverty threshold | | Relative poverty threshold* |
	Census income (1)	Adjusted income (2)	Census income (3)
1965	15.6	12.1	15.6
1968	12.8	10.1	14.6
1970	12.6	9.4	15.1
1972	11.9	6.2	15.7
1974	11.6	7.8	14.9
1976	11.8	6.7	15.4
1978	11.4	–	15.5
1980	13.0	6.1	–

*Relative threshold defined as 44 per cent of the median.
Source: Institute for Research on Poverty (1981), Tables 1 and 2

a figure for 1962 very close to the Council of Economic Advisers' definition ($3110), but quite different results for the trends over time: the proportion in poverty was 19 per cent in 1947 and exactly the same in 1970. Fuchs stresses that there is nothing inherent in his approach that leads to the proportions necessarily remaining stable: 'The stability is not now due to some mathematical property of the measure, or to some law of nature. It reflects the failure of twenty years of unprecedented prosperity and rapid economic growth to produce any significant change in the distribution of income, at least at the lower end' (1969, p. 202). The same picture is shown in column (3) of Table 10.5, which takes a slightly lower relative threshold (44 per cent of the median). On this basis, there is no evidence of amelioration.

The incidence of poverty

The Council of Economic Advisers devoted considerable attention to the composition of the low income population:

Some believe that most of the poor are found in the slums of the central city, while others believe that they are concentrated in areas of rural blight. Some have been impressed by poverty among the elderly, while others are convinced that it is primarily a problem of minority racial and ethnic groups. But objective evidence indicates that poverty is pervasive . . . the poor are found among all major groups in the population and in all parts of the country. (1964, pp. 61–2).

The first column of Table 10.6 confirms that in 1979 the 'high risk' groups identified by the Council did not account for the majority of

TABLE 10.6
Poverty in the United States, 1979

Persons	Percentage of total poor in group	Percentage of group below poverty line
Aged 65 and over	14	15
Black	31	31
In family with female head	52	32
Resident inside central city	37	16
		(All families 12 per cent)

Source: US Department of Commerce, Characteristics of the Population Below the Poverty level: 1979, Tables A and 1.

those below the poverty line. Those aged 65 and over made up only one in eight of the total in poverty; there were more than two whites in poverty for every black; nearly two out of three people in poverty did not live in central cities. The figures are not based on exclusive categories, and one person may appear in two or more rows of the table: for example, a black woman aged 65 living in New York. For this reason, we cannot add the figures in the first column. It can, however, be estimated from the Bureau of the Census source figures that the total number of persons in poverty who came into one or more of the three categories (aged, black, or in a family headed by a female) was 17 million out of a total in poverty of 25 million in 1979. There was a large number of people outside these high risk categories who were in poverty.

The Council of Economic Advisers were right, therefore, to stress that poverty is found among all major groups. Just as in Britain, poverty cannot be explained as 'exceptional', and this has important policy implications. At the same time, certain groups are clearly at much greater risk. This is brought out by the second column in Table 10.6. In 1979, 12 per cent of the total population were in poverty, but the proportion for families with a female head and for blacks was nearly three times as much. It is on this later aspect that the remainder of this section is focused.

Racial discrimination

In examining the difference between the incomes of whites and non-whites, we may (as in Chapter 6) distinguish between that part attributable to observed characteristics, such as age, education, geographical location, unemployment, and that part due to 'pure' discrimination. Is the higher proportion of blacks in poverty explained by their higher unemployment (the non-white unemployment rate has typically been

over twice that for whites), lower education, or the larger proportion
living in the south? Or is it the case that people in the same place, with
the same qualifications, get paid less on account of discrimination? This
is not to suggest that the differences in observed characteristics are unaffected by discrimination — the higher unemployment rate of non-
whites may well reflect discriminatory hiring practices, and young blacks
expecting to face labour market discrimination may well be less interested
in education — but the distinction does help to isolate the influence at
work.

This question has been examined by Thurow (1969), who used data
from the 1960 census for the incidence of poverty in different states to
estimate the contribution of different factors to the explanation of
poverty, measured according to the Council of Economic Advisers' definition. At that time, the proportion of white families in poverty was
18.6 per cent, compared with 47.9 per cent for non-white families, so
that the gap to be explained was 29.3 per cent (see table):

Sources of gap	Contribution
	%
Families living on farms	−0.3
Families with no one in labour force	1.3
Family heads with less than 8 years of education	12.7
Population aged 14 or over who worked 50 or more weeks per year	3.6
Index of industrial structure	0.8
Families headed by non-white	11.3

From these figures it is clear that other factors are important, primarily
education and unemployment, but that 'pure' discrimination appears to
be responsible for over one-third of the gap (although we must be
cautious in attributing all the unexplained difference to discrimination).

In the case of both education and 'pure' discrimination, there are
reasons to believe that their impact has declined in recent years. The
gap between the number of school years completed by whites and non-
whites has been narrowing; there has been some equalization of resources
in education; under the War on Poverty, there was a rapid increase in
compensatory education programmes; and the late 1960s saw a sharp
increase in the number of blacks entering college. The civil rights legislation of the 1960s and the operations of the Equal Employment Opportunity Commission may similarly have reduced the degree of pure
discrimination. Employers can no longer legally discriminate against
black employees: there are affirmative action programmes providing for
minimum quotas of black employees; unions can no longer restrict entry
to blacks (the Brotherhood of Railroad Trainmen, for example, had a
'Caucasian only' clause until 1959). How far such changes have affected

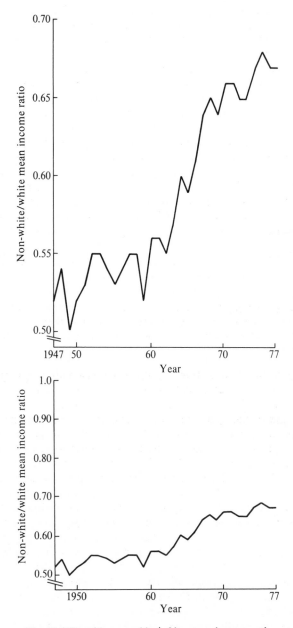

Fig. 10.3 Trend in non-white/white mean income ratio.

racial differences in income is less clear, and this has been the subject of debate.

In Fig. 10.3 we show the trend over the postwar period in the rates of mean incomes for non-white and white families. The upper part of the figure is taken from Blinder (1980), who concludes that there has been 'a substantial narrowing of the differential during the period' (p. 459). There are however several points that need to be noted. First, there is a simple matter of presentation. The upper part of Fig. 10.3 is drawn on the same scale as Blinder's diagram, the vertical axis corresponding to the range of the observations (0.50 to 0.68), but a more natural limit to the scale would be a ratio of 1.00, corresponding to parity between the mean incomes. The lower part of Fig. 10.3 shows the effect of taking the *same data* but changing the scale in this way. Certainly the visual impression is of a less dramatic increase.

The second point concerns the methods used to construct the data. During the period there were at least two occasions (1967 and 1974) when the Census Bureau modified the procedure for data handling. This had the effect of raising the non-white–white income ratio (Reich, 1981, p. 38). The difference was not large in an absolute sense, but 1 or 2 percentage points can have quite a significant impact on the *trend* over time.

Third, the movement of overall family income conceals the fact that the pattern was quite different for men and women. For women, the ratio of median incomes improved substantially over the period, reflecting in part an increase in full-time employment among non-white women. For men, on the other hand, the ratio fell between 1947 and 1959, and by 1965 had only returned to its previous level. In more recent years the ratio has risen, but the improvement for male incomes is considerably less.

Fourth, in examining the long-run trend in relative incomes, it is important to abstract from cyclical influences, since the position of non-whites tends to improve as unemployment falls. In 1958 unemployment was nearly 7 per cent, whereas by 1967 it had fallen to 4 per cent; during this period the relative income of black males rose from 50 to 60 per cent. This is a very substantial gain, but it represents a once-for-all effect: 'as the economy moves toward full employment, non-white incomes rise more than proportionately, but the equalization does not continue once unemployment stops falling' (Thurow, 1969, p. 61). According to the estimates of Reich (1981), a 3 per cent reduction in the employment rate would be expected to raise the relative income of black males by 5 per cent; when this is taken into account, the upward trend works out at about 4 per cent per decade. Reich comments that 'at that glacial rate the 0.63 ratio in 1977 would not increase to 1.0, the level of racial equality, until the year 2070' (Reich, 1981, p. 40).

Finally, it is important to bear in mind the effects of the migration from the south. Between 1940 and 1966, a net total of 3.7 million blacks in the metropolitan areas of the north and west rose from 20 per cent to nearly 40 per cent. There is marked regional variation in relative incomes: in 1959 the median income of black men in the south was a third of the white median income, compared with 70 per cent in other regions. To the extent that this is due to regional differences in discrimination, rather than to individual characteristics, the movement of blacks out of the south would tend to raise the national ratio. This in turn would mean that the gain was once-for-all, rather than continuing. On the other hand, the study by Freeman (1981) of the effects of anti-discrimination activity finds a significant impact in three of the four regions, and particularly in the south.

We have not space to give an exhaustive treatment, but it is clear that statements such as that by Moynihan, adviser to successive presidents, that 'the 1960s saw the great breakthrough for blacks' must be treated with caution. There are signs that the extent of discrimination may be declining over time, but it is important to ask how far it is due to structural changes that will not be repeated. It seems, in fact, from the experience of the postwar period, that the elimination of racial differences in income will be a slow process.

10.5 The future of concern

In many countries it was widely believed in the 1950s that poverty was no longer a problem. The impact of social legislation, Keynesian measures to maintain near-to-full employment, and rising wages, had, it was believed, ensured the abolition of poverty. In the early 1960s this was to change. In Britain the work of Abel-Smith and Townsend demonstrated the existence of a substantial minority living at or below the national assistance standard. In the United States, the writings of Galbraith and Harrington and the experiences of President Kennedy while campaigning in West Virginia contributed to the re-awakening of interest and to the War on Poverty. Poverty became a major political issue, which helped to win (Johnson in 1964) and lose (Wilson in 1970) elections.

The momentum carried through to the 1970s. New programmes for the poor continued to be enacted (e.g., family income supplement in Britain, supplemental security income in the United States). But doubts had begun to set in. The Office of Economic Opportunity in the United States was abolished in Nixon's second administration. The governments of the late 1970s became more concerned with budget cuts than with the abolition of poverty.

The 1980s finds the pendulum swung to the other extreme. The

Thatcher government in Britain and the Reagan administration in the United States have been willing to cut social security and other pro-grammes in a way that worsens the position of low-income groups. Indeed, such measures appear to have been welcomed on the grounds that they improve 'incentives'. But, although political fashions swing in this way, there can be little doubt that the problems discussed in this chapter will remain of continued importance unless far-reaching and broadly based anti-poverty policies are adopted. It is therefore essential to consider the measures that can be advocated by those who have not lost their concern for the position of the least advantaged.

Notes on sources and further reading

The concept and measurement of poverty is discussed in Townsend (1954, 1962, 1970, 1979), Social Science Research Council (1968), Friedman (1965), Rein (1970), Plotnick and Skidmore (1975), Depart-ment of Health and Social Security (1979), and Sen (1976, 1979, 1981).

The Rowntree studies of poverty in York are described in Rowntree (1922, first published in 1901; 1941) and Rowntree and Lavers (1951). The growth of concern in the 1960s was largely due to Wedderburn (1962) and Abel-Smith and Townsend (1965). A summary of the evi-dence available at the end of the 1960s is given in Atkinson (1969). More recent studies of poverty in Britain include Fiegehen, Lansley and Smith (1977), Van Slooten and Coverdale (1977), Supplementary Ben-efits Commission (1977), Layard, Piachaud and Stewart (1978), which was a background paper to the *Report No. 6: Lower Incomes* of the Royal Commission on the Distribution of Income and Wealth (1978), Berthoud and Brown (1981), and Beckerman and Clark (1982). The incomes of the elderly are examined in Townsend and Wedderburn (1965), Ministry of Pensions and National Insurance (1966), Parker (1980), and Altmann (1981) — see also Fogarty (1982). Family poverty is the subject of Ministry of Social Security (1967), Bull (1971), and Wynn (1970), and particular reference should be made to the publi-cations of the Child Poverty Action Group (for example, Burghes, 1980; Piachaud, 1981; and McClelland, 1982). Single-parent families are dis-cussed by Marsden (1969) and Finer (1974) (the Finer Report). The position of the disabled is described in Walker and Townsend (1981). Poverty and unemployment are considered in Showler and Sinfield (1980), Sinfield (1981), Burghes and Lister (1981), and Seabrook (1982). The problems of poverty in particular areas are well brought out in the study of St Ann's, Nottingham by Coates and Silburn (1970), in the study of Belfast by Evason (1980), and the comparison of the inner-city poverty in Paris and London by Madge and Willmott (1981).

For a broad treatment of deprivation in Britain, see the reviews of a wide range of evidence by Rutter and Madge (1976) and Brown and Madge (1982).

The revival of interest in poverty on the United States in the 1960s owed much to Harrington (1962). The official analysis of poverty began with the Council of Economic Advisers (1964), and the position in 1969 was summarized by the President's Commission on Income Maintenance Programs (1969). Government estimates of its extent and composition are published regularly by the US Bureau of the Census, in their series of Current Population Reports, under the title *Characteristics of the low income population*. More recent evidence is summarized in Plotnick and Skidmore (1975), Levitan (1980), and Institute for Research on Poverty (1981a). For accounts of the War on Poverty, see Kershaw (1970), Aaron (1978), and Danziger and Plotnick (1980). For the impact of the Reagan administration, see Institute for Research on Poverty (1981b) and Danziger and Haveman (1981). The relationship between racial discrimination and poverty is discussed by Thurow (1969). Evidence about recent trends in the black–white income ratio is contained in Blinder (1980), Reich (1981), and Freeman (1981).

A survey of the evidence about poverty in different countries (USA, UK, Canada, Australia, France, and Italy) is provided by Roberti (1979), reprinted in Atkinson (1980b), and case studies of Australia, Belgium, Norway, and Great Britain are presented by Beckerman (1979). Poverty in Europe is examined by Dennet *et al.* (1982). Particular reference should be made to the report of Commission of Inquiry into Poverty in Australia (Henderson, 1975), and of the summary of the evidence for Canada in Love and Oja (1977).

11

POLICIES FOR INCOME MAINTENANCE

Our task of reconstruction does not require the creation of new and
strange values. It is rather the finding of the way once more to known,
but to some degree forgotten, ideals and values.

(Message to US Congress by President Roosevelt, preceding passage of
Social Security Act, 1935)

This chapter examines the present policies for income maintenance in
Britain and the United States, the reasons why they have failed to
guarantee a minimum income to all according to the official poverty
standard, and the reforms that could be introduced.

The social security system in Britain owes much of its present form
to the Beveridge Plan, conceived during the Second World War and
translated into legislation by the Labour government in the immediate
postwar years. The fundamental aim of the Plan was 'to abolish want by
ensuring that every citizen willing to serve according to his powers has at
all times an income sufficient to meet his responsibilities' (Beveridge,
1942, p. 165). This 'national minimum' was to be guaranteed as of right,
through social insurance covering retirement and all major risks of loss
or interruption of earnings, and through family allowances. The scheme
was to cover everyone irrespective of income, and the benefits were to
be paid at the same flat rate for all.

The evidence of the previous chapter has demonstrated that the intentions of the Beveridge Plan have not been fulfilled. Despite the introduction of national insurance, there are still some two million people in
Britain below what the government considers to represent a minimum
standard of living. Similarly, in the United States the social insurance
system introduced under the Act of 1935 has not prevented many people
from falling below the official poverty line. In the first two sections, we
examine the reasons for this failure of social insurance.

11.1 Pensions and poverty in old age

The primary social security provision for old age in Britain at present is
the basic national insurance retirement pension. Virtually everyone
aged 65 or over (60 for women) who has retired from full-time work
receives such a basic pension, which, has averaged some 20 per cent of
average gross earnings for a single person and approximately 30 per cent

for a married couple, although there have been year-to-year variations. The total pension may be higher than this, on account of increments for deferred retirement, the graduated pension, and the age addition for those aged 80 or over, but many people receive little more than the basic rate.

The fundamental principle of the Beveridge Plan was that the social insurance benefits should be sufficient to guarantee subsistence, so that people should not have to resort to means-tested supplementation because of the inadequacy of the insurance benefits. In this respect, the postwar legislation departed from the Beveridge principles. The basic national insurance benefits were consistently below the minimum standard set for national assistance and later supplementary benefits. In 1948, the national insurance benefit for a married couple was £2.10, whereas the national assistance scale was £2 plus housing expenditure, so that a pensioner couple with a rent of more than 10p a week would have been below the poverty line if they had relied on national insurance alone. In 1982 the corresponding rates were equal, so that with *any* housing outlay a pensioner with no other income would have been below the poverty line. There has, therefore, been a consistent failure to provide basic state pensions that meet the government's own standards of adequacy.

The inadequacy of the national insurance pension would be less serious if old people could rely on alternative sources of income. However, a significant number may have *no income at all* from anything other than state sources. This very surprising fact was brought out by the government survey of 1965, which showed that one in five of all pensioners had no other income (Ministry of Pensions and National Insurance, 1966). Single women were particularly badly off in this respect, a third having no other income. The proportion with no other income was also very much higher for the older age groups, reaching 44 per cent for the group aged 85 and over. The very old were much less likely to be able to supplement their incomes by earnings, and many had exhausted their savings. In his 1968–9 survey, Townsend found that 24 per cent of the elderly not at work derived all their income from state benefits (1979, Table A91). (The position may have improved since the 1960s, and reference is made below to more recent sources.)

For those who do have other income, the principal sources are occupational pensions, interest on savings, and earnings. The 1965 survey showed that, for married couples and single men, pensions from previous employment were received in about half the cases and on average supplemented the national insurance pension by 50–70 per cent. Only 14 per cent of single women, however, were receiving occupational pensions. Occupational schemes have in the past granted relatively few pensions to the widows of deceased employees, and the proportion of women employees covered by occupational schemes is lower than that of men.

The position ten years later has been analysed by Layard, Piachaud and Stewart (1978), using the General Household Survey for 1975. They find that:

half the men in the sample received occupational pensions compared to one-third of spinsters, one-fifth of widows and only 4 per cent of married women. Among men there was little difference between age groups in the proportion . . . except in the oldest age group, for whom it was somewhat lower. Men who had formerly been in non-manual occupations were more often in receipt of occupational pensions . . . but the more striking difference was in the amounts of occupational pension received: this averaged £20 for those in receipt from professional and managerial occupations but only £5 for those from unskilled manual occupations. (1978, p. 124)

Savings may provide an additional source of cash income for pensioners, but for most the amounts involved are fairly small. About 30 per cent had no savings at all in 1965, and only a quarter had more than £600. But it should be noted that these amounts did not include the value of any owner-occupied property, and about one-third owned their own homes free of mortgage commitments. For these pensioners, housing costs were lower on average than for those in rented accommodation. The more recent government inquiry into retirement in 1977 showed that only some 40 per cent of those over pension age reported receipt of income from savings (Parker, 1980, Table 4.4.1).

Above we have referred almost interchangeably to the elderly and to the retired, but we must remember that not all those over the minimum retirement age have in fact stopped work, nor are all those who have retired over the minimum pension age. At the same time, the labour force participation by men over the age of 65 has fallen substantially over the postwar period, and the scope for part-time work has undoubtedly decreased with the worsening conditions in the labour market. What is more important, and much less fully investigated, is the position of those retiring early, who constitute a growing proportion of their age group. The popular stereotype of the early retirer is of someone who can afford to do so, financed by a generous pension from his employer and accumulated savings. The examination by Altmann (1981), based on the *Family Expenditure Survey* from 1970 to 1977, shows, however, that such people are a minority, and that many of the early retired have low incomes. She finds that the majority appear to be sick or disabled, with more than half being in receipt of sickness or indistrial injury benefit or of an invalidity pension.

Overall, it is clear that there are large differences in the circumstances of those at the end of their working lives. Moreover, these differences are related to those observed earlier in the life-cycle. The professional person retired on half his final salary, with the opportunity for part-time work and living in his own house, is in a quite different position from the person with only the basic national insurance pension who is living in rented accommodation. It was this kind of situation that Titmuss described as 'two nations in old age'. For the less privileged of these classes, the only recourse is to supplementary benefits, and the shortcomings of this means-tested scheme are described in Section 11.3.

The new state pension scheme

The evidence quoted above referred to the late 1970s or earlier, but 1978 saw the introduction of the new state earnings-related pension scheme, which is arguably the most important development in social security in Britain since the national insurance legislation of thirty years earlier. The aim is to provide earnings-related pensions to those not covered by adequate occupational schemes. When the scheme reaches full maturity, a person will receive, in addition to the basic state pension, a component related to his average earnings over the best twenty years of his working life. The formula is at present 25 per cent of earnings that lie between 20 per cent of overall average earnings and an upper limit. So a person with earnings equal to the overall average receives an additional pension of

$$0.25 \times (1 - 0.2) \times \text{average earnings.}$$

Taken together with the basic pension, this comes to 40 per cent of his averaged earnings — a doubling of the previous level of benefit. A married woman can receive a pension based on her own employment, so that for a married couple the improvement may be even more marked.

One of the major aims of the new scheme is to overcome the problems set out earlier. The White Paper, *Better pensions* (Cmnd 5713), took as its starting point the failure of the past system 'to guarantee all pensioners more than a low standard of living, or to prevent large numbers of them from having to rely on means-tested supplementary benefits'. As the figures given above indicate, the additional pension formula should ensure that this goal is met. Even a low paid worker, whose best twenty years come to only 60 per cent of the overall average, will receive a state pension equal to 30 per cent of average earnings — an increase of a half on the present basic pension. But it will take time. There is a twenty-year transition period, so that the formula described above will not apply until 1998. In the interim period, the additional pension will be a proportion of that amount, the proportion rising by a twentieth each year. Moreover, the scheme does nothing for those who retired before 1978. Given the long life expectancy of many pensioners today, especially women, there will be a long period before the scheme is fully mature. After all, a woman who retired at the age of 60 in 1978 could expect to be alive well into the next century.

Estimates have been made by Altmann and Atkinson (1982) of the number of pensioners likely to be below the supplementary benefit level in the future. These estimates are necessarily speculative and rest on a number of assumptions, including that supplementary benefits retains the same relationship with average earnings. The results show that the new scheme will transform the picture when pensions approach maturity. In the year 2031 very few pensioners will be below the poverty line, compared with the 1 100 000 who would be expected to fall below without the scheme. But the estimates confirm the fears that have been expressed with regard to the slow build-up of the new pension rights. At the turn of the century there will still be some 300 000–400 000 pensioners below the poverty line.

Pensions in the United States

In moving to an earnings-related scheme, Britain was coming into line with the United States (and a number of other countries). In the United States, the main social insurance provision for old age is the Old Age, Survivors, and Disability Insurance (OASDI). This programme has evolved more gradually than national insurance, its coverage being extended over the years, but the scheme now covers more than 90 per cent of those aged 65 and over. The pension depends on the age at retirement, the eligibility of the spouse for benefit, and the level of earnings before retirement. The formula was such that a man with median earnings retiring in the mid-1970s received a pension of some 40 per cent of his earnings at retirement, with an addition of half for his wife, which would have been broadly comparable with the benefits under the new additional pension in Britain if the latter had begun operation a generation earlier. The US formula is progressive, so that the replacement rate (pension as a fraction of earnings at retirement) was some 60 per cent for a worker at the level of the minimum wage.

The pension formula, coupled with indexation, means that, in the absence of legislative changes, those retiring now or in the future are likely to receive reasonable levels of pensions under the state scheme, but there remain a substantial number of people who retired earlier with lower amounts of benefit. This is illustrated by the average amounts paid, expressed as a proportion of the official poverty threshold for an aged couple. This has risen from around 50 per cent at the beginning of the 1960s to 75 per cent following the 1972 changes, reaching some 85 per cent in 1981 (Aaron, 1982, Fig. 9). But despite the rise, it is still below the poverty threshold. The low level of benefits actually being paid was one of the factors leading to the introduction of the means-tested Supplemental Security Income (SSI) programme in 1972. (This federal scheme was in part a replacement for earlier forms of assistance to the aged.)

The implications of the state pension payments being below the poverty threshold depend on the extent of income from other sources. As in Britain, there are employer pensions. According to Levitan,

it is estimated that over half of all employees in the private sector and most federal, state, and local government employees are covered by a pension or profit-sharing scheme. Eligibility requirements have been liberalised significantly over the last decade, increasing the proportion of covered workers ultimately qualifying for retirement benefits . . . Congress enacted the pension reform law in 1974 and has strengthened it since then to safeguard the integrity of private pension funds. (1980, pp. 47–8)

But he goes on to comment that 'the private retirement system is a way for middle- and upper-income families to insure against poverty in old age, rather than a way for low-income workers to protect themselves for the future' (1980, p. 48). A study of nearly 1000 private pension plans by the Bureau of Labor Statistics in 1974 led Schulz *et al.* to conclude that they:

had the potential of providing widely varying rates of preretirement earnings replacement for many covered workers. Moreover, when social security income was added, the combined benefit levels often fell short of providing income that would allow workers to maintain living standards into retirement without supplemental economic resources. Furthermore, the hypothetical replacement rates reported on in this analysis assume long periods of private pension coverage and retirement at the normal retirement age. Periods of noncoverage, early retirement, or both (common occurrences today) would significantly reduce the replacement rates provided by both private pensions and social security. (1979, p. 31)

The evidence about the actual receipt of income by the elderly in the United States suggests that quite a small proportion is derived from private pensions (see, for example, Moon, 1977). For those who continue working, earnings make a substantial contribution, but this applies to only a fraction of the aged. A larger proportion, around a half, have income from savings, but this provides on average considerably less in the way of income. The picture is, in fact, similar to that in Britain. Those who continue to work or are able to retire with a generous company pension are unlikely to find themselves below the poverty line;

those who have only the OASDI pension are much more likely to find themselves dependent on means-tested supplementation.

11.2 Family benefits: in and out of work

In Britain, many writers have referred to the 'rediscovery' of family poverty during the 1960s, but perhaps more important was the realization that family poverty was not due solely to family size. The Sunday newspaper supplement image of family poverty is typically of families with six or more children, and has no doubt affected attitudes to family policy. This was, of course, very much the view Beveridge took of the problem.

The social surveys of Britain between the two wars show that in the first thirty years of this century real wages rose by almost one-third without reducing want to insignificance, and that the want which remained was almost always due to two causes – interruption or loss of earnings power and large families (Beveridge, 1942, p. 154).

This belief led him to propose family allowances to provide for the subsistence needs of children, but to exclude the first child on the ground that 'very few men's wages are insufficient to cover at least two adults and one child' (p. 155).

In this respect Beveridge was wrong. The evidence in the previous chapter has demonstrated that large families account for only a small proportion: nearly two-thirds of the married couples with children below the supplementary benefit level had only one or two children. The reasons for this are two-fold. First, Beveridge was not necessarily right to assume that low pay would not be a problem. In April 1982 the lowest decile of earnings meant that a married man took home some £58 after income tax and national insurance contributions. If he had two children (aged 4 and 11), then the family would have received £10.50 in child benefit. From this total income of £68.50 has to be deducted work expenses and housing outlay to arrive at the net resources to be compared with the supplementary benefit scale for this family, which would have been £59.20. It is evident that there is unlikely to be much margin. The position may be moderated by means-tested benefits, such as the family income supplement and housing rebates, discussed in the next section, but this calculation illustrates the way in which earnings may be too low to support even an average-sized family.

The second cause of family poverty is the low level of child benefit. Following a long campaign, and the recommendation of Beveridge, family allowances were introduced after the Second World War for the second and subsequent children in the family. As in the case of the social insurance benefits, however, the level of the payment is below that which he recommended. Indeed, in 1966 the rate for the second child was the same in *cash* terms as that proposed by Beveridge in 1942, though prices had more than doubled. Increases in the rates of family allowances were infrequent: during the Conservative government of 1970-4, the allowances remained unchanged while prices rose by 40 per cent. In 1977, however, there came a major change, with the introduction of the new child benefit. This replaced both family allowances and the child allowances under the income tax, thus benefiting those who did not derive full advantage from the tax relief. It is payable at a uniform rate, tax-free, and with respect to all children. But the benefit remains below the supplementary benefit allowance for a child, as is demonstrated in Fig. 11.1, which shows the family allowance/child benefit for the second child in a family compared with the supplementary

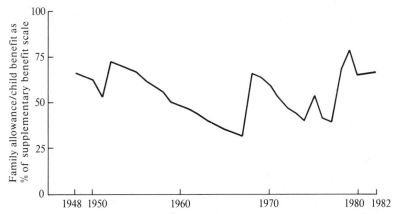

Fig. 11.1 Family allowance/child benefit as percentage of supplementary benefit scale for a child aged under 5. (*Source: Social Security Statistics 1981*, Tables 30.01 and 34.01)

benefit scale for a child aged under 5. Despite the jump associated with the introduction of child benefit (no account is taken in the diagram of the loss of tax allowance), it remains only some two-thirds of the amount required according to the scale. The aim of the family income supplement scheme, introduced in 1971, was to fill part of this gap, but the scheme has not enjoyed complete success, as we see in Section 11.3.

Single-parent families

The position is rather different for single-parent families, a group that includes widows and widowers, unmarried mothers, and mothers or fathers who are separated or divorced. This is a group that has grown rapidly in size, from about 570 000 families in 1971 to over 800 000 at the end of the 1970s. For widows there are national insurance benefits, payable as long as there are dependent children, and this may continue as a widow's pension (including an earnings-related benefit) if she is over 40 when the children have grown up. In certain cases this may be supplemented by a widow's pension paid by her husband's former employer. As a result, widows are less likely to fall below the poverty line than other single parents. They account, however, for only a minority of the fatherless families in Britain, a much greater number being women divorced or separated from their husbands. In these cases maintenance might be payable, but this depends on the ability and willingness of the father to pay. The only state benefit payable as of right in these circumstances is the one-parent benefit (in November 1981, £3.30 per family). This is not sufficient to prevent a large number of single-parent families (over 300 000 in 1980) from being dependent on means-tested supplementary benefit.

Incomes out of work

Interruption of earnings through sickness or unemployment does not necessarily lead to poverty. In Britain the national insurance scheme provides a flat-rate benefit (and between 1966 and 1982 there was an earnings-related supplement). But like the basic national insurance pension, the scheme does not provide an amount that is typically sufficient to ensure that the person reaches the supplementary benefit scale. Moreover, the conditions of entitlement are such that many of the unemployed do not in fact receive the insurance benefit. For a variety of reasons, including disallowance of benefit, waiting days and other delays, and exhaustion of entitlement, the proportion of the unemployed in receipt of national insurance benefit has been 50 per cent or lower – and has fallen still further as unemployment has risen in recent years. Of especial importance is the exhaustion of benefit. Not only is the insurance payment limited to twelve months in a spell, but also, spells may be 'linked' where the intervening period of work is short.

The implications of these short-falls in the insurance system depend on the other sources of income that are available to the unemployed. If unemployment came at random, then there would be a reasonable chance that those out of work would have some savings on which they could fall back, or that the wife would be in work. But the evidence from the DHSS cohort study of the unemployed in 1978–9 and other sources shows that unemployment tends to be concentrated on those already poor and disadvantaged in the labour market. The cohort study shows, for example, that, of those men still out of work after four weeks,

70 per cent reported having no income from a wife's earnings, having no cash investment income, and having savings of less than £500 (Supplementary Benefit Commission, 1980, p. 34). Once again, many are dependent on means-tested benefit.

The case of sickness is rather different — possibly because its incidence is more widely spread throughout the population. Employers' sick pay schemes have come to play an important role, notably with the statutory requirement introduced in 1982 for employers to provide coverage for the first period of sickness. This has had the effect of making coverage universal (previously, almost all non-manual workers had been covered, but less than three-quarters of manual men and less than 60 per cent of women manual workers). But employer's sick pay now replaces the state insurance benefit, and is subject to income tax, so that the position of those receiving the minimum statutory provision may well have worsened.

If we turn to the position of the disabled, we find that 'the piecemeal development of social security provision has created an extremely complex system, based on several different principles and a large number of different criteria for eligibility' (Walker, 1981, p. 45). There are a variety of insurance benefits, with preferential treatment being given to those covered by the industrial injury and war pension schemes, and with those in receipt of the non-contributory benefits introduced in the mid-1970s getting only 60 per cent of the contributory pension. The latter is clearly a major advance over the previous situation, where nothing was payable as of right, but it means that many of the recipients continue to rely on supplementary benefit.

The position in the United States

The income maintenance provisions for families in and out of work are different in a number of respects in the United States, and a detailed comparison is not possible here. The unemployment insurance programme, for example, is administered by state governments. There are minimum standards set by the US Congress, but there is considerable diversity of benefit provisions and eligibility criteria. Such geographical variation makes it more difficult to assess the adequacy of the social insurance scheme in meeting a national poverty target — and to make comparisons with Britain.

Of particular interest here is the treatment of working families with children. The United States, almost alone among advanced countries, has no general child benefit programme. At the same time, it has since 1976 used the tax system in reverse to achieve an income-related transfer. The Earned Income Tax Credit, operated through the tax machinery, provided (in 1981) a tax credit of up to $500 per year for families with dependent children, where this credit was tapered in such a way that it vanished at $10 000 a year. This scheme may be seen as a modest step in the direction of a negative income tax, which we discuss in Section 11.4.

11.3 The rise and failure of means-testing

Means-tested programmes are the oldest in the social security system; indeed, the supplementary benefit scheme in Britain can be traced back to the Elizabethan Acte for the Reliefe of the Poore of 1598. In more recent times, however, they have increased greatly in importance. Whereas Beveridge envisaged that 'the scope of assistance will be narrowed from the beginning and diminish throughout the transition period for pensions' (1942, p. 12), the number dependent on assistance has grown from 1 million in 1948 to more than 3 million in 1981. New means-tested benefits have been introduced: for example, rate rebates in 1966, prescription charge exemptions in 1968, family income supplement in 1971. In 1972, a national scheme for rent rebates replaced the previous schemes covering council tenants in certain local authorities, and the early rate rebate scheme, which largely benefited pensioners, was replaced by one with wider eligibility. These in turn were replaced in 1982 by a new 'unified' housing benefit.

The main feature of means-testing is that eligibility is determined by a family's income, in relation to its needs as defined for the purposes of the particular scheme. The definition of income differs from scheme to scheme. For family income supplement, it is gross income that is relevant (i.e. before tax and national insurance contributions); for exemption from prescription charges, on the other hand, a person may deduct not only tax and insurance contributions, but also working expenses, mortgage repayments, and hire purchase commitments. In some cases, a family is eligible either for full benefits or for none at all: for example, a family qualifies for free welfare milk if its income is below a certain level, but if its income rises above this level, eligibility is lost completely. In most cases, the withdrawal of the benefit is tapered as income rises. Under the family income supplement (FIS), a family receives, in addition to child benefit, a payment equal to half the gap between its income and a prescribed income level. In April 1982, the prescribed income level for a family with two children was £82 a week, so that if its income was £70 a week, a FIS payment of £6 a week was made, but if the income rose to £78, then the supplement would be cut to £2. In this way, the benefit falls to nothing as the family's income reaches the prescribed income level. In the case of FIS, the definition of needs relates only to family size; in other schemes, the definition involves other

Claim FIS on this form

- Answer every question in the boxes provided
- Answer in writing – don't use dashes or ticks
- Write your answers in BLOCK CAPITALS

1. Your names etc
- For a couple, fill in details for both man and woman

Surname	Other names	Date of birth	NI number
Mr			
Mrs/Miss			

Full address (including postcode)

Do either of you live at a different address? If YES write it down at question 11   Answer YES or NO

Is your permanent home in the UK? If NO write down why at question 11   Answer YES or NO

6. Do you work for an employer?   Answer YES or NO   Man   Woman

If YES, are you paid weekly, fortnightly, 4-weekly or monthly? Say which

- Fill in details of your last 5 paypackets if you're paid weekly; the last 3 if you're paid fortnightly; or the last 2 if you're paid 4-weekly or monthly.
- Enclose your pay slips as proof. If you don't have them (for example, if you have just started work), you can still claim now, and we will ask your employer for details. We won't tell him you're claiming FIS.

Employer's full name & address	What is your job?	Pay week/ month ending (fill in dates)	Hours worked each week	Gross earnings before deduction of tax & NI If none, write NONE	
				Man	Woman
				£	£
				£	£
				£	£
				£	£
				£	£

Are these earnings what you normally get? Answer YES or NO   If NO, give details of any which are higher or lower than normal at question 11, and say why.

How many hours each week (including overtime) do you normally work in this job?   **If you started this job less than 5 weeks ago, give the starting date**

9. If either of you has any other money coming in, fill in the details here
- Answer every question
- Do not include any income your children have – except maintenance payments

How much? If none, write NONE

Tips from your full-time or part-time job?   £   weekly average

Maintenance payments, for yourself or children, voluntary or by court order? If they are not regular, give details at question 11 instead   £   weekly

Pensions or other cash benefits (except child benefit)?   Name of benefit   Reference number   £   weekly

Interest from savings or capital?   £   total for past 12 months

Profit from boarders or sub tenants? Don't include your own family unless you make a profit from them. Here's how to estimate profit:

- **Boarders** Divide what you get from all boarders by 5, and write this in the box. But if this is your main income put the details at question 7 instead.   £   weekly
- **Sub-tenants** – fill in the total amount of rent you get. If you pay their heating, lighting or other expenses, give the details at question 11 instead.   £   weekly

How many sub-tenants do you have?

Declaration
- For a couple, both the man and the woman must sign
I/We declare that I/We have read the instructions on the form and to the best of my/our knowledge and belief the information given in this claim is true and complete. I/We claim family income supplement.
- Warning: to give false information may result in prosecution

Signed: Man   Woman   Date

Fig. 11.2 Extracts from application form for family income supplement in Britain. (*Source:* Department of Health and Social Security)

elements. For example, housing rebates depend on (i) income, (ii) family size, and (iii) rent and rates, according to a formula such as the following:

Rebate = 60% of (rent + rates) – 28% of excess of income over needs allowance

where the needs allowance depends on the number of dependants (the full formula is more complex). One consequence of this is that these schemes have become extremely complicated, as is illustrated by Fig. 11.2 showing *some* of the questions that have to be answered on the application form for the relatively simple family income supplement.

In the United States there has been a similar growth in the importance of the means-tested welfare system. As described by Aaron (1973, p.5),

Until the late sixties low-income Americans receiving federal, state, or local assistance were a small minority . . . only 7.1 million received public assistance, roughly 2 million lived in low-rent public housing . . . and 4.3 million received surplus agricultural commodities. Few households benefited from more than one of these programs.

By the early 1970s, this had changed:

The number of public assistance beneficiaries almost doubled to 13.8 million . . . Food and surplus agricultural commodities were used by more than 10 million persons . . . medicaid was providing largely free medical care for 18.2 million persons . . . a growing number of families received benefits under two, three or more programs.

These programmes all involved tests of income to determine eligibility and were in large part administered by separate authorities.

The growth of means-testing stems from an understandable desire to focus benefits on those considered to be in need. Faced with the inadequacy of social insurance and other benefits, successive governments in Britain and the United States have turned increasingly to income-related schemes as a low-cost means of helping low-income groups. This approach has not, however, succeeded in solving the problem of poverty, and means-tested schemes have been subject to two important criticisms: that they fail to reach all who are eligible, and that they involve high marginal rates of tax.

The first of these shortcomings was well recognized by Beveridge, who regarded 'the strength of popular objection to any kind of means test' as one of the main reasons for requiring that the social insurance benefits should be adequate in themselves and that people should not be forced to rely on means-tested assistance. The experience with national assistance and supplementary benefit bears out his misgivings. The inquiry by the Ministry of Pensions and National Insurance in 1965 showed that 47 per cent of pensioners had incomes below the national assistance scale (before taking account of the assistance in payment). Of these, slightly over half were actually receiving national assistance. Of the others, some were disqualified because they had savings in excess of the allowed limit, but nearly one-third were apparently entitled to benefit but not claiming. Checks by the Ministry on the accuracy of the information led to some reduction in the estimate, but they still concluded that 'rather more than 700 000 pensioner households (about 850 000 pensioners) could have received assistance if they had applied for it' (1966, p. 83). This confirmed the earlier findings of Cole and Utting (1962), and Abel-Smith and Townsend (1965). In its inquiry the Ministry explored the reasons why people did not claim. One clear reason was that people were ignorant or misinformed about the provisions. This was not, however, the only factor, and between a quarter and a third said they did not apply because they disliked charity or the national assistance board, or because their pride would not let them ask for help.

The Ministry inquiry was carried out before the replacement of national assistance by supplementary benefits, which had the aim of ensuring that 'the elderly will have no hesitation in claiming the new benefit to which they are entitled'. To this end, the Ministry of Social Security Act 1966 provided a specific *entitlement* to benefit, simplified the procedure for claiming, and made a number of other changes designed to increase the 'take-up rate'. (Further extensive changes were made in November 1980, with the scheme coming under the direct control of the Department of Health and Social Security and the Supplementary Benefit Commission being abolished. These changes did not have the express purpose of improving take-up.)

The introduction of supplementary benefits was claimed by the ministers concerned as a 'remarkable success' (Mr Houghton) and 'a tremendous social change' (Mr Crossman). These claims were based on the undoubted increase in the number of old people receiving assistance; however, they did not allow for the fact that a substantial part of the increase was attributable to the rise in the assistance scale, which increased the number eligible. Subsequent experience suggests that the optimism was misplaced. In Table 11.1 we show the official estimates of the take-up rate for 1979. These estimates are derived from the *Family Expenditure Survey* and need to be regarded with considerable caution. The number of families on which they are based is relatively small, and errors in the recording of income or needs will cause the estimates of the take-up rate to be biased downwards. Nevertheless, the official figures provide strong ground for believing that take-up falls significantly below 100 per cent. They show that a third of pensioners were apparently not claiming, with an average short-fall of £3 a week; for non-pensioners the take-up rate was rather higher, but the income lost by those not claiming was on average larger. The total estimated foregone benefit was £355 million.

TABLE 11.1

Estimated take-up of supplementary benefit in Britain, 1979

	Proportion of those entitled receiving benefit	Number eligible but not receiving	Average weekly amount unclaimed
	%		£
Pensioners	65	900 000	3.10
Non-pensioners including:	78	320 000	12.70
Sick and disabled	63	110 000	15.40
Unemployed	81	130 000	10.50
One-parent families*	85	60 000	10.20
Total	70	1 210 000	5.60

*Not included among the sick/disabled or unemployed.
Source: Hansard, 5 April 1982, col. 248

The experience of low 'take-up' rate has been repeated with other means-tested schemes. The inquiry into the circumstances of families (Ministry of Social Security, 1967) drew attention to the fact that only 10 per cent of ratepayers with incomes below the national assistance level had applied for rate rebates, although the great majority were eligible. Subsequent studies (e.g. Meacher, 1973) have concluded that, while an intensive advertising campaign improved the response, the problem of non-claiming still remained a major one. That problems persist for housing rebates is demonstrated by the following official estimates for England and Wales in 1980 (from *Hansard*, 21 April 1982, col. 117):

	Percentage take-up
Rent rebates (council tenants)	72.3
Rent allowances (private unfurnished tenants)	60.0
Rate rebates	69.9

When the family income supplement scheme was announced, the minister stated that a high take-up was vital for its success and the programme was budgeted on the basis of a take-up rate of 85 per cent. The new scheme was widely advertised on television and in newspapers, and its administration was designed with a great deal of care. None the less, the take-up rate has consistently fallen short of the target. Official estimates based on the family finances survey carried out in 1978/9 showed a take-up rate of approximately one-half. This result (which replaced an earlier estimate of around three-quarters) was described by the government spokesman as 'very disappointing and unsatisfactory' (*Hansard*, 10 June 1981, col. 134).

The problem of low take-up has received less attention in the United States, but its existence is clearly demonstrated in the case of the food stamp programme. This scheme allows low-income families to purchase food vouchers with a face value in excess of the purchase price, with eligibility for the programme and the size of the subsidy depending on income. Although the scheme was strongly supported by the Kennedy administration, it became clear after it had been in operation for less than five years that the stamps were not being taken up. A 1969 Senate report concluded that: 'nationally only 21.6 per cent of the poor people living in countries with food stamp programs participate in the program . . . Seven states have programs that reach less than 15 per cent of the poor' (quoted by Steiner, 1971, p. 213). According to MacDonald, in 1976 'less than half of all eligibles received stamps' (1977, p. 92). The experience with the incomes-tested Supplemental Security Income Program similarly indicates a participation rate during the first two years of operation of 50 per cent for the aged and 67 per cent for the blind and disabled (Warlick, 1981, p. 13).

The second objection to means-tested benefits is that they often involve high effective marginal rates of tax. As income rises benefits are withdrawn, and this has the same effect on disposable income as the taxation of income. A man receiving rebates for rent and rates might as a result of earning an extra £1 in April 1982, pay 30p in income tax and 8¾p in social security contributions, losing 17p off his rent rebate and 6p off his rate rebate, leaving him only 38¼p better off. The effective marginal tax rate in this case would have been 61¾ per cent. In certain cases he might actually have been worse off, the marginal tax rate exceeding 100 per cent, as would happen if his children had previously been receiving free school meals. In April 1982 the effective marginal tax rate on a permanent £1 increase in earnings for a one-child family varied between 75 and 200 per cent at the lower levels, and was then 61¾ per cent over a wide band – see Figure 11.3. Over a considerable range of earnings, therefore, a family claiming all the benefits to which it was entitled would have derived less than 40p benefit from a permanent £1 increase in income. This situation has been described as 'the poverty trap', since a family below the poverty line could raise itself above only with aid of a substantial increase in gross pay. The diagram assumes that the family claims the means-tested benefits for which it is eligible. If it did not claim, then the poverty trap would not arise (although this can scarcely be used as a defence!). Also, it has to be remembered that the calculations are for hypothetical families. The number actually in this position may well be quite small, although *Social Trends 1982* gives an official estimate of 370 000 families with marginal tax rates in excess of 50 per cent (p. 90).

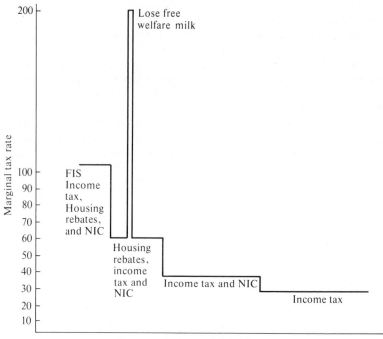

Fig. 11.3 Marginal tax rate on £1 additional earnings for family with one child in Britain, April 1982. The diagram takes account of income tax, national insurance contributions (NIC), family income supplement (FIS), housing rebates, and free welfare milk. It assumes that FIS is adjusted to the new level of earnings. The family is assumed to live in council property and to pay average rent and rates. The family is also assumed to take up its entitlement to FIS, housing rebates, and free welfare milk. Finally, it is assumed that the only source of family income is the husband's earnings.

At the top end of the income scale, high marginal rates of tax are often assumed to have adverse effects on the incentives to work and to save; and the existence of marginal rates as high, or even higher, at the lower end of the scale might be expected to have a similar effect. (Although the disincentive effect may be lessened by the fact that benefits such as the family income supplement may be re-assessed only some months later, and that people may have only very limited knowledge of the marginal tax arising from the withdrawal of benefits.) It is necessary to ask which aspects of labour supply are likely to be affected, and this in turn suggests that a £1 earnings increase by the husband may not be the most relevant case.

Not only are work decisions likely to involve discrete choices (for example, whether or not to work overtime, or to take a subsidiary job), but also, it may be decisions by other household members that are affected. The impact of taxes and the withdrawal of benefits may be different if we consider an increase in the earnings of the wife, her earnings being treated differently under the income tax and certain means-tested benefits. These, and other aspects of the poverty trap (such as the effect on wage claims), warrant fuller examination.

The high marginal tax rates arising from the overlap of means-tested programmes in the United States have been identified by Aaron as one of the principal factors leading to the failure of welfare reform during the Nixon administration. As described by the Chairman of the Senate Finance Committee, the President's family assistance plan

finds it necessary to sharply curtail the amount of earnings that a person can retain when he goes to work . . . In many cases, after one considers the increase in social security taxes paid, the loss of medicaid benefits, and especially if the family is enjoying the benefit of subsidized public housing, the family income would be reduced by more than 100 per cent of every dollar that a father or mother proceeded to earn. (quoted in Aaron, 1973, p. 3)

The family assistance plan foundered on the problem of maintaining incentives while securing an adequate level of benefits. In the next section we examine whether alternative approaches, involving more radical changes, can resolve the dilemma.

11.4 Negative income taxation, tax credits, and social dividends

The failure of the means-testing approach has led to a search for other methods of relating benefits to needs. There has been a wide variety of proposals for negative income taxes, for social dividends, and for tax credits. The schemes could be classified in a variety of ways, but one of the most important distinctions is in terms of the extent to which they would replace the present income maintenance system. In what follows, we describe three of the principal possibilities.

Social dividend or demogrant

The most far-reaching change would be the complete replacement of all present social security benefits, of the income tax, and of social security contributions by a single social dividend or demogrant scheme. In its simplest form, this scheme would involve the payment of a social dividend to everyone, dependent only on their family status; the revenue required to finance the scheme, and to replace the present income tax,

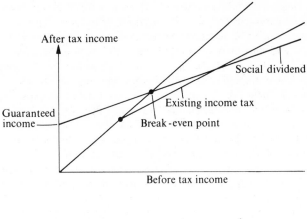

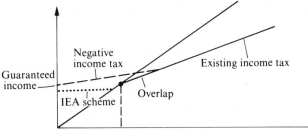

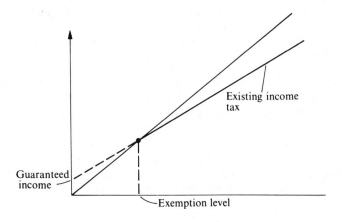

Fig. 11.4 Negative income tax schemes.

would be raised by a proportional tax on all income. The effect of this kind of scheme is illustrated in the top part of Fig. 11.4. The line marked 'social dividend' shows the income after allowing for tax and the social dividend. The point where the dividend is exactly offset by the tax payable is shown as the 'break-even' point. Those with low incomes would be net gainers and better off than with the existing income tax.

Such a scheme was first proposed in Britain by Lady Rhys Williams in 1942, and has been taken up by a succession of authors, a recent example being, Sir Brandon Rhys Williams MP (1982), who proposes a basic income of some 20 per cent of average earnings for a single householder, around a third of average earnings for a couple, and about a half for a couple with two children. The basic tax rate on all income would be in the range of 42–50 per cent. In the United States, the scheme was espoused by George McGovern in his presidential campaign, and he proposed a $1000 average per capita demogrant to be financed by a broad-based income tax (i.e. with fewer loopholes) at a rate of $33\frac{1}{3}$ per cent. This would have given a family of four a guaranteed income of $4000, with a break-even level of $12 000.

The attractions of this approach are clear. If the demogrant were set at a level sufficient to raise a family with no other income up to the poverty line, then it would be much more effective than the present system. There would be no gaps in the programme, and the problem of take-up would be eliminated. However, the main reason why this kind of scheme has failed to make progress so far was brought out in the McGovern campaign – that to pay an adequate demogrant (in terms of the poverty standard) would involve a substantial increase in taxation. The levels of payment proposed by McGovern were designed to meet the poverty line needs of a family of four; but critics soon pointed out that the proposed tax of $33\frac{1}{3}$ per cent was inadequate to raise the required revenue. The 1982 Rhys Williams proposal would involve an increase in the marginal tax rate (including national insurance contributions) of about 10 percentage points for most taxpayers. The essence of the problem may be seen quite simply from the following arithmetic. Suppose that the guaranteed minimum is set, for an average family, at x per cent of average incomes, and that the requirements of government revenue are such that the tax has to raise a further y per cent. This then determines the proportional rate of tax $x + y$ per cent. For any likely values of x and y, for example $x = 35$ per cent and $y = 15$ per cent, the tax will be around 50 per cent over the whole range.

Separate negative income tax schemes

The high rates of tax associated with the extreme social dividend approach and the fear that they would be politically unacceptable have led

to alternatives being proposed which would retain the main elements of
the present income tax and social security schemes. In particular, they
would retain the progressively increasing rates of tax of the present
income tax, allowing greater flexibility than a simple proportional rate,
and most of the present social security benefits, allowing the negative
tax payment to be set at a lower level. In the United States, the case for
a negative income tax as a supplement to the existing provisions has
been put in particular by Tobin: 'the merit of the negative income tax
approach is that a workable and equitable system of aiding the poor
can be introduced within the framework of present federal income
taxation' (1968, p. 118). As we have seen, the Earned Income Tax
Credit performs something of this function for low-income families.

These proposals have appeared in a variety of forms, but basically
involve a guaranteed payment and then the withdrawal of payment at a
rate of $33\frac{1}{3}$ or 50 per cent — see the dashed line in the middle part of
Fig. 11.4. As shown in the diagram, this leads to an overlap with the
present income tax, and the negative tax rate would continue to apply
until the after-tax income is the same as under the present 'positive' tax
schedule. Some people, therefore, would be both receiving negative tax
supplements and paying ordinary income tax.

Negative income tax schemes of this type have been put forward as a
means of channelling help to low-income familes without the disadvantages associated with means-tested benefits. They would be universal,
the coverage not being limited to people satisfying certain conditions,
and it has been argued that an automatic system of payment would be
possible, avoiding the need for people to apply and hence the problem
of low take-up. It has similarly been claimed that the negative income
tax would reduce the marginal rates of tax.

The impact of the introduction of negative income tax on marginal
rates of tax depends on its relation to other means-tested benefits. As
originally conceived in the United States, the negative income tax would
have replaced public assistance and all benefits in kind, such as housing
assistance and food stamps; but this would have meant setting the negative income tax payment at a considerably higher rate, to ensure that
no families close to the poverty line would lose from the introduction
of the scheme. (It is sometimes suggested that it is the necessary consequence of any reform that some people near the poverty line are made
worse off, but, even apart from the equity considerations involved, such
cases provide powerful ammunition for the opponents of reform.) If
the housing, food stamp, and medicaid programmes continued, with
only welfare being replaced by the negative income tax, then the contribution to reducing the marginal rates of tax could be smaller.

In Britain, the 'reverse income tax' (RIT) scheme proposed by the

Institute of Economic Affairs (1970) would have two important differences. The first is that the rate of tax would be 100 per cent, rather than 50 or $33\frac{1}{3}$ per cent. The scheme would guarantee to all households a minimum income at the supplementary benefit level, but would not provide any further payments above that level — see the dotted line marked 'IEA scheme' in the middle part of Fig. 11.4. The choice of a 100 per cent tax rate was dictated by a desire to minimize the cost of the scheme; it means, however, that the proposal can do little to alleviate the problem of the poverty trap. The best that can be claimed is that the marginal tax rate would not exceed 100 per cent.

The second difference is in the method of administration. Recognizing that the income tax system does not cover many of those in poverty, and that for these people the income tax procedure would not allow benefits to be paid until the end of the tax year, the Institute suggests that 'the agency administering a RIT may have to use separate procedures for assessment of means from those now used for income tax'. This would represent, however, a major departure from the principle of using the income tax machinery to eliminate the stigma attached to present means-tested programmes. If a separate application has to be made, then it seems likely that at least some of those eligible will not apply for the reverse income tax. It would be a benefit designed for the poor, and it has yet to be demonstrated that it could be administered more successfully than present means-tested benefits.

The tax credit scheme — an integrated negative income tax

The third type of scheme is that closest to what the main in the street might expect the term 'negative taxation' to mean: simply, setting the present income tax machinery in reverse and paying benefits to those below the tax threshold. The early versions of the scheme, notably that of Friedman (1962), were of this form. The scheme would operate through the existing tax machinery, the main new departure being that everyone would be required to file a tax return. On the basis of the information provided, a person would either pay tax as now or receive a negative tax supplement. In this way, the payment should be automatic and the problems of take-up should be avoided. The operation of the scheme is illustrated in the bottom part of Fig. 11.4. The level of benefit, shown by the dashed line, is determined by the income tax exemption level and the rate applied. The negative tax would be fully integrated into the positive tax, and there would be no overlap.

In the United States this variant has received less attention than the Tobin scheme discussed above; in Britain, however, an integrated negative income tax was proposed by the Conservative government under the title of a 'tax credit', and if they had been returned to power in the general election of February 1974, the scheme would have been in force by the end of the decade. Its main feature was the abolition of income tax allowances and their replacement by a weekly tax credit payable to all. This would have had the effect of helping those below the tax threshold who do not at present obtain full benefit from the tax allowances. At the same time, tax would have been payable at the basic rate from the first £1 of income.

The way in which the scheme would work may be illustrated by reference to the position of a married couple in the 1981/2 tax year, when the personal allowance for a married couple was £47 a week and the basic rate of tax, 30 per cent. The credit would therefore have been

$$30\% \times £47 = £14.10 \text{ per week.}$$

In the case of children, the principle of the tax credit has already been incorporated in the child benefit scheme (which turned the child tax allowances into cash).

The figures just given show that a straightforward replacement of tax allowances by credits would contribute little to solving the overall problem. According to the Treasury (Evidence to the Treasury and Civil Service Committee Sub-Committee, 12 May 1982), about 100 000 pensioners would be lifted off supplementary benefit (less than a tenth of the total) and the change would have little impact on the numbers receiving family income supplement. On the other hand, if the credits were made more generous, then the cost of the scheme would rise substantially for the reasons we have outlined earlier.

11.5 Alternative strategies

In the preceding sections we have described the inadequacies of existing social insurance systems in Britain and the United States, the failure of means-tested welfare programmes, and some of the problems with negative income taxation. What, then, should be done?

If it is accepted that the means-testing strategy of recent years has failed to provide a solution, then the choice lies between the replacement of means-tested benefits by some form of negative income tax and their displacement by the expansion of social insurance and other categorical programmes. Various types of negative income tax have been described earlier, but the social insurance alternative requires elaboration. Its main features would be the extension of social insurance to groups not at present covered and the raising of benefits to provide a guaranteed minimum income at a desired level. In the United States, this approach would be typified by the introduction of child allowances payable to all families irrespective of income (although if the allowances were taxable, the net benefit would be less for higher-income families). Within the existing social insurance programmes, the approach would involve, for example, the extension of coverage of OASDI. In Britain the social insurance approach would involve a substantial increase in basic national insurance benefits to bring them up to the average supplementary benefit payment, a significant increase in child benefit, the extension of social insurance to provide complete coverage of groups such as single-parent families and the disabled, and a raising of the tax threshold.

Opinion on the choice between these two approaches is often presented in polar terms, but this may well be misleading. Distinctions that appear clear-cut, such as between people who favour negative income taxation and those who do not, become less so in the face of the wide variety of schemes coming under this general label. The schemes favoured by the Conservative government in Britain and the McGovern campaign in the United States were, in fact, very different. Moreover, it is important to remember that the case for one type of approach may rest heavily on the institutional framework of a particular country. Given the differences between the existing income maintenance systems in Britain and the United States, it is not really surprising that the same policy may be espoused by Conservatives in one country and liberal Democrats in the other.

We can none the less distinguish between certain differences in emphasis:

Pattern of benefits Both approaches are concerned with guaranteeing adequate minimum income, but they differ in the extent to which they seek to *concentrate* benefit on those at the lowest income levels. Under the negative income tax proposals, benefits would be withdrawn at a rate of $33\frac{1}{3}$ per cent or more as income rose; under the social insurance approach, there would be less scope for such withdrawal, the main tapering of benefit being from their taxation under the income tax (although many supporters of this approach would favour re-introduction of a graduated tax rate structure, which, coupled with the 'taxation' of benefits, would reduce their value to the better-off). The concentration of benefit on the lowest income groups is seen as a major advantage of negative income taxation, and Tobin has claimed that, in the case of the alternative child allowance scheme, 'of the net benefits, nearly 80 per cent would go to families above the poverty line . . . the end result would be a modest but dubious redistribution from childless taxpayers to large families, and very little redistribution from rich to poor' (1968, p. 110). If we felt fully confident about the adequacy of the poverty standard and that no one above this level was in need, then the sharp cut-off of benefits at the poverty line might well be acceptable. However, it may be doubted whether we can be *that* confident about the choice of a poverty line, and we may feel that income redistribution towards those people not far above the poverty line may still be desirable. Moreover, the poverty line is defined for the purposes of analysis in terms of averages, and there may be people with incomes above the minimum who are, in fact, still in poverty because of individual variation in need.

Marginal tax rates and work incentives Associated with a particular benefit schedule is a pattern of marginal tax rates. The evidence concerning the effect of such differences in marginal rates on work incentives is limited, although more is becoming known, as the result of the negative income tax experiments in New Jersey and elsewhere. However, as Marmor has stressed, 'the absence of information about work incentives is no bar to the issue being politically important' (1971, p. 42). At a political level, concern about marginal rates is likely to focus on two issues: incentives for the poor not to work, and the increase in taxation for the middle classes. The negative income tax with a high rate of withdrawal of benefit will have high marginal tax rates at the lower end (although lower than the welfare programme it would replace), and to this extent it is likely to be less attractive on the former count. On the other hand, it provides benefits to those in work as well as to the unemployed, in contrast to the social insurance approach, which pays allowances for adults only when they are not working. Moreover, to the extent that the negative income tax has a lower cost, it will involve less increase in taxation for the middle-income ranges.

Measures to change pre-redistribution income A third difference concerns the relative importance of income maintenance as opposed to measures designed to change pre-redistribution incomes. Since the social insurance approach can provide no solution for the working man with no children, such measures must be accompanied by changes in labour market policy. The supporters of the social insurance approach typically favour the introduction of more effective minimum wage legislation, coupled with active steps to improve the employment prospects of the poor (such as the government acting as an employer of last resort). On the other hand, many of the proponents of negative income taxation see it as a means of eliminating government interferences in the working of the market and envisage the abolition of minimum wage legislation.

Take-up and stigma The supporters of the social insurance approach attach great importance to securing 100 per cent take-up, and to the fact that 'our insurance-type programs have worked better and gained greater acceptance than either our public assistance programs or those designed to aid the working poor' (US Department of Health, Education and

Welfare, 1969, p. 48). It seems safe to say that the social insurance approach would not encounter serious problems of incomplete take-up. On the other hand, with the negative income tax this is an open question, and it remains to be demonstrated that the scheme can be administered in a way that avoids the stigma of existing means-tested programmes.

Finally, whichever approach is adopted, it is clear that new initiatives in the field of income maintenance are required. There is no reason to suppose that economic development and macro-economic policy can by themselves eliminate poverty. Whatever the outcome of the 'supply side' experiments in Britain and the United States, it is likely to be a long time before any gains trickle down to the least advantaged. In the mean-time their plight can only have worsened. To say that the solution lies in substantially increased transfers of income, coupled with measures to create employment, is politically unfashionable − but it is clear that the nettle needs to be grasped.

Notes on sources and further reading

For a general discussion of income maintenance policy, see, among others, in the British context Titmuss (1958, 1974), George (1968), Gough (1979), Room (1979), Carter and Wilson (1980), Culyer (1980), Berthoud and Brown (1981), and Wilson and Wilson (1982). The current social security system in Britain is described in the Child Poverty Action Group's excellent guides, the *National welfare benefits handbook* and *Rights guide to non-means-tested benefits*. On supplementary benefits, Lynes (1981) is very helpful. A more technical, but valuable, account of social security law is given by Ogus and Barendt (1978) and Matthew-man and Lambert (1982). Income maintenance policy in the United States is discussed by Lampman (1971), Batchelder (1972), Schiller (1973), Barth *et al.* (1974), Schorr (1977), Levitan (1980), and Danziger, Haveman and Plotnick (1981).

Pensions policy in Britain is examined by Fogarty (1982), and a detailed study of the state earnings-related scheme is given by Creedy (1982) and Hemming and Kay (1982). The relationship between income taxation and pensions is discussed by Reddin (1980). Pensions in the United States are analysed in Munnell (1977) and the papers in Skidmore (1981). Valuable comparative studies on pensions in different countries are Schulz *et al.* (1974) and Wilson (1974).

Family benefits are discussed in Wynn (1970), Bull (1971), Bradshaw (1980), Bradshaw and Piachaud (1980), Study Commission on the Family (1981), and Piachaud (1981). On the interaction between tax-ation and benefits, see Field, Meacher and Pond (1977).

The problem with means-tested programmes in the United States are well described in Stein (1971), Steiner (1971), and Aaron (1973). The food stamp scheme is examined by MacDonald (1977). In Britain, see Meacher (1973) and Jordan (1973).

On negative income taxation, see Green (1967), Tobin (1968), Tobin, Pechman and Mieszkowski (1967), Institute of Economic Affairs (1970), Meade (1972), Atkinson (1973), Collard (1980), and Rhys Williams (1982).

12

THE APPROACH TO THE ISSUES

The aim of this chapter is not to draw conclusions about the extent of inequality, or about the need for changes in policy. Its purpose is rather to emphasize the main features of the approach, and to draw together the threads of a book whose subject matter has ranged from fringe benefits for executives to subsistence standards, from inheritance taxation to public assistance, from intelligence tests to trade union bargaining power.

The approach adopted to this wide range of topics has had certain common features. The first is the emphasis on quantitative aspects. Discussion of statistics may appear dull to students, and the activity of assembling and assessing data is often not highly regarded by academic economists. But it is an essential aspect. As it was put by Bowley many years ago,

> just as a theoretical chemist will have little or no power unless he fully appreciates experimental methods and difficulties . . . so no student of political economy can pretend to complete equipment unless he is master of the methods of statistics, knows its difficulties, can see when accurate figures are possible, can criticise the statistical evidence, and has an almost instinctive perception of the reliance that he may place on the estimates given him. (1937, p. 9)

Certainly, 'looking at the figures' seems very much preferable to the frequently employed alternative of consulting one's prejudices. This need for quantitative analysis is brought out clearly where, as often happens, the readily available evidence is seriously deficient. In many cases, writers have tended to point to the difficulties and then simply conclude that nothing can be said. To take two examples, Titmuss (1962) detailed with great care the shortcomings of the income distribution statistics in Britain, but did not indicate their likely quantitative importance, and Bauer (1971) argued that the problems in an international comparison of incomes were such that it was doubtful whether it had any meaning.

In contrast to this nihilistic outlook, the approach followed here has been to examine the extent to which the figures are deficient and to try and assess how far this affects the conclusions drawn. One has to ask whether the observed differences in incomes could be eliminated by making allowance for factors missing from the conventional picture, or whether the differences would be increased. As described by Kuznets, the approach adopted here 'is needed not only to warn against uncritical reliance on the estimates as they are usually shown but, perhaps even more, to counter their complete dismissal because of the serious errors and biases in them' (1966, p. 386).

Emphasis on quantification should not be interpreted as a blind faith in items that can be measured; rather, it reflects a concern with aspects of the distribution that are important. It is easy to point to features that are striking, even exotic, particularly at the upper tail of the distribution, but which are really relatively unimportant. Reference was made to the allowance for members of the House of Lords, and the high earnings of singers, film stars, and sportsmen probably come in the same category. In this book, the main focus has been on aspects of the distribution that affect a large number of people or substantial amounts of income and wealth. Chapter 8, for example, was concerned with a small fraction of the population, but on the grounds that they held a considerably larger proportion of total wealth.

The relative importance of different factors affects judgements about the equity or otherwise of the distribution. There is a tendency for it to be argued that the observed differences in income do not indicate inequity, since they reflect differences in individual decisions, in age, or in tastes. For this to be convincing, it would have to be established that the observed differences in income can in fact be explained in this way − just pointing to the possibility is not enough. In this book we have taken certain examples, examining the contribution of decisions about human capital (Chapter 5) and the role of life-cycle savings (Chapter 7). It appears from the evidence that earnings differentials do not simply reflect decisions about education; nor do age differences explain more than part of the concentration of wealth.

The interpretation of differences in income and wealth in effect requires an understanding of the determinants of the distribution, and a major part of the book has been concerned with seeking such an explanation. What are the forces governing movements in the share of profits? How far are earnings explained by the institutions of the labour market, rather than by personal characteristics of workers? Problems such as these are not only intellectually testing, but also must be resolved before we can make firm predictions about future developments or the impact of government policy. We have drawn attention to the danger of extrapolating from past trends without considering the underlying forces, and have stressed the dependence of policy recommendations (for example, minimum wage legislation) on particular views as to how the distribution is determined.

In seeking to understand the causes, however, we have time and time again come to phenomena for which no adequate explanation exists.

Governments are facing distributional problems whose causes are not well understood and for which there are often no agreed policies.

There has been a great deal of research in the past decade, but there are important issues still to be settled — and the questions have not remained the same. One of the aims of the book has been to demonstrate that far too little is known about this central subject. This is an indictment of economics, but it is also a challenge.

REFERENCES

Aaron, H.J. (1973), *Why is welfare so hard to reform?*, Brookings Institution, Washington, DC.

Aaron, H.J. (1978), *Politics and the professors, the Great Society in perspective*, Brookings Institution, Washington, DC.

Aaron, H.J. and McGuire, M. (1970), 'Public goods and income distribution', *Econometrica*, vol. 38.

Abel-Smith, B. and Townsend, P. (1965), *The poor and the poorest*, Occasional Papers on Social Administration, no. 17, Bell and Sons, London.

Alexander, A.J. (1974), 'Income, experience and the structure of internal labour markets', *Quarterly Journal of Economics*, vol. 88.

Allen, R.G.D. (1957), 'Changes in the distribution of higher incomes', *Economica*, vol. 24.

Althauser, R.P. and Kalleberg, A.L. (1981), 'Firms, occupations and the structure of labour markets, a conceptual analysis', in I. Berg (ed.), *Sociological perspectives on labour markets*, Academic Press, New York/London.

Altmann, R.M. (1981), 'The incomes of elderly men in Britain 1970–1977', PhD thesis, University of London.

Altmann, R.M. and Atkinson, A.B. (1982), 'State pensions, taxation and retirement income 1981-2031', in M. Fogarty (ed.), *Retirement policy, the next fifty years*, Heinemann, London.

Amsden, A.H. (ed.) (1980), *The economics of women and work*, Penguin Books, Harmondsworth.

Arrow, K.J. (1972), 'Models of job discrimination', in A.H. Pascal (ed.), *Racial discrimination in economic life*, D.C. Heath, Lexington, Massachusetts.

Arrow, K.J. (1973a), 'The theory of discrimination', in O. Ashenfelter and A. Rees (eds), *Discrimination in labor markets*, Princeton University Press, Princeton, NJ.

Arrow, K.J. (1973b), 'Higher education as a filter', *Journal of Public Economics*, vol. 2.

Ashenfelter, O. (1970), 'Changes in labor market discrimination over time', *Journal of Human Resources*, vol. 5.

Ashenfelter, O. (1978), 'Union relative wage effects', in R. Stone and W. Peterson (eds), *Econometric contributions to public polity*, Macmillan, London.

Ashenfelter, O. and Rees, A. (1973), *Discrimination in labor markets*, Princeton University Press, Princeton, NJ.

Astin, J.A. (1975), 'The distribution of wealth and the relevance of age', *Statistical News*.

Atkinson, A.B. (1969), *Poverty in Britain and the reform of social security*, Cambridge University Press, London.

Atkinson, A.B. (1970), 'On the measurement of inequality', *Journal of Economic Theory*, vol. 2.

Atkinson, A.B. (1971), 'The distribution of wealth and the individual life-cycle', *Oxford Economic Papers*, vol. 23.

Atkinson, A.B. (1972), *Unequal shares – the distribution of wealth in Britain*, Allen Lane, London.

Atkinson, A.B. (1973), *The tax credit scheme and the redistribution of income*, Institute for Fiscal Studies, London.

Atkinson, A.B. (1974), 'Poverty and income inequality in Britain', in D. Wedderburn (ed.), *Poverty, inequality and class structure*, Cambridge University Press, London.

Atkinson, A.B. (1980a), 'Inheritance and the redistribution of wealth', in G.A. Hughes and G.M. Heal (eds), *Public policy and the tax system*, Allen and Unwin, London.

Atkinson, A.B. (ed.) (1980b), *Wealth, income and inequality*, Oxford University Press, Oxford.

Atkinson, A.B. (1980c), 'Income distribution and inequality of opportunity', *Journal of the Institute for Advanced Studies* (Vienna).

Atkinson, A.B. (1983), *Social justice and public policy*, Harvester Press, Brighton.

Atkinson, A.B. and Harrison, A.J. (1978a), *Distribution of personal wealth in Britain*, Cambridge University Press, London.

Atkinson, A.B. and Harrison, A.J. (1978b), 'Wealth', *Reviews of United Kingdom Statistical Sources*, vol. 6, Pergamon Press, Oxford.

Atkinson, A.B. and Harrison, A.J. (1979), 'The analysis of trends over time in the distribution of personal wealth in Britain', *Annales de l'insee*, vol. 33–4.

Atkinson, A.B. and King, M.A. (1980), 'Housing policy, taxation and reform', *Midland Bank Review*.

Atkinson, A.B., Maynard, A.K. and Trinder, C.G. (1981), 'National assistance and low incomes', *Social Policy and Administration*. vol. 15.

Atkinson, A.B., Maynard, A.K. and Trinder, C.G. (1983), *Parents and children: incomes in two generations*, Heinemann, London.

Atkinson, A.B. and Micklewright, J. (1983), 'On the reliability of income data in the Family Expenditure Survey 1970–1977', *Journal of the Royal Statistical Society*, vol. 146.

Atkinson, A.B., Micklewright, J. and Sutherland, H. (1982), *Low pay: a preliminary look at the evidence from the family expenditure survey*, Low Pay Unit, London.

Bach, G. and Stephenson, J. (1974), 'Inflation and the redistribution of wealth', *Review of Economics and Statistics*, vol. 56.

Barlow, R., Brazer, H.E. and Morgan, J.N. (1966), *Economic Behaviour of the affluent*, Brookings Institution, Washington, DC.

Barr, N. and Roper, J. (1974), 'Tax credits', *Three Banks Review*, no. 101.

Barry, B. (1973), *The liberal theory of justice*, Clarendon Press, Oxford.

Barth, M.C., Carcagno, G.J., Palmer, J.L. and Garfinkel, I. (1974), *Toward an effective income support system*, Institute for Research on Poverty, Madison, Wisconsin.

Batchelder, A.B. (1972), *The economics of poverty* (2nd ed), John Wiley, New York.

Batten, P. *et al.* (1976), *Inequality within nations*, Open University unit 5, Patterns of inequality course, Milton Keynes.

Bauer, P.T. (1971), *Dissent on development*, Weidenfeld and Nicolson, London.

Bauer, P.T. and Prest, A.R. (1973), 'Income differences and inequalities', *Moorgate and Wall Street Journal*.

Beach, C.M. (1977), 'Cyclical sensitivity of aggregate income inequality', *Review of Economics and Statistics*, vol. 59.

Beach, C.M. with Card, D.E. and Flatters, F. (1981), *Distribution of wealth and income in Ontario: theory and evidence*, University of Toronto Press, Toronto.

Becker, G.S. (1957), *The economics of discrimination* (2nd ed. 1971), University of Chicago Press, Chicago.

Becker, G.S. (1964), *Human Capital* (2nd ed. 1975), National Bureau of Economic Research, New York.

Becker, G.S. (1967), *Human capital and the personal distribution of income*, University of Michigan, Ann Arbor, Michigan.

Becker, G.S. (1981), *A treatise on the family*, Harvard University Press, London.

Becker, G.S. and Tomes, N. (1979), 'An equilibrium theory of the distribution of income and intergenerational mobility', *Journal of Political Economy*, vol. 87.

Becker, J.F. (1977), *Marxian political economy*, Cambridge University Press, Cambridge.

Beckerman, W. (1979), *Poverty and the impact of income maintenance programmes*, International Labour Office, Geneva.

Beckerman, W. (1980), *National income analysis* (3rd ed.), Weidenfeld and Nicolson, London.

Beckerman, W. and Bacon, R. (1970), 'The international distribution of incomes', in P. Streeten (ed.), *Unfashionable economics*, Weidenfeld and Nicolson, London.

Beckerman, W. and Clark, S. (1982), *Poverty and social security in Britain since 1961*, Oxford University Press, Oxford.

Bégué, J. (1976), 'Remarques sur une étude de l'O.C.D.E. concernant la répartition des revenus dans divers pays', *Economie et Statistique*, no. 84.

Behrman, J.R., Hrubec, Z., Taubman, P. and Wales, T.J. (1980), *Socioeconomic success, a study of the effects of genetic endowment, family environment and schooling*, North Holland, Amsterdam/New York/London.

Bell, C.S. (1981), 'Minimum wages and personal incomes', in S. Rottenberg (ed.), *The economics of minimum wages*, American Enterprise Institute for Public Policy Research, Washington and London.

Ben-Porath, Y. (1980), 'The F-Connection', *Population and Development Review*, vol. 6.

Benus, J. and Morgan, J.N. (1975), 'Time period, unit of analysis and income concept in the analysis of income distribution', in J.D. Smith (ed.), *The personal distribution of income and wealth*, Columbia University Press, New York and London.

Berg, I. (1981), *Sociological perspectives on labor markets*, Academic Press, New York/London.

Bergmann, B.R. (1971), 'The effect on white incomes of discrimination in employment', *Journal of Political Economy*, vol. 89.

Bergmann, B. and Adelman, I. (1973), 'The economic role of women', *American Economic Review*, vol. 63.

Berry, A., Bourguignon, F. and Morrisson, C. (1983), 'The world distribution of incomes between 1950 and 1977', *Economic Journal*, vol. 93.

Berthoud, R. and Brown, J.C., with Cooper, S. (1981), *Poverty and the development of anti-poverty policy in the UK*, Heinemann, London.

Bevan, D.L. (1979), 'Inheritance and the distribution of wealth', *Economica*, vol. 46.

Beveridge, Lord (1942), *Social insurance and allied services*, HMSO, London.

Bhatia, K.B. (1974), 'Capital gains and the distribution of income', *Review of Income and Wealth*, vol. 20.

Blackburn, R.M. and Mann, M. (1979), *The working class in the labour market*, Macmillan, London.

Blau, F. and Jusenius, C. (1976), 'Economists' approaches to sex segregation in the labor market', *Signs*, vol. 1.

Blaug, M. (1976), 'The empirical status of human capital theory', *Journal of Economic Literature*, vol. 14.

Blaug, M., Dougherty, C. and Psacharopoulos, G. (1982), 'The distribution of schooling and the distribution of earnings', *Manchester School*, vol. 50.

Blinder, A.S. (1973), 'A model of inherited wealth', *Quarterly Journal of Economics*, vol. 88.

Blinder, A.S. (1974), *Toward an economic theory of income distribution*, MIT Press, Cambridge (Massachusetts) and London.

Blinder, A.S. (1980), 'The level and distribution of economic well-being', in M. Feldstein (ed.), *The American economy in transition*, University of Chicago Press, Chicago.

Blinder, A.S. (1982), 'On making the trade-off between equality and efficiency operational', in G.R. Feiwel (ed.), *Samuelson and neoclassical economics*, Kluwer-Nijhoff, Boston.

Blinder, A.S. and Esaki, H.Y. (1978), 'Macroeconomic activity and income distribution in the postwar United States', *Review of Economics and Statistics*, vol. 60.

Bliss, C.J. (1975), *Capital theory and the distribution of income*, North-Holland, Amsterdam.

Blomquist, N.S. (1979), 'The inheritance function', *Journal of Public Economics*, vol. 12.

Blowers, A., Braham, P., and Woollacott, J. (1976), *The importance of social inequality*, Open University Press, Milton Keynes.

Bluestone, B. (1968), 'Low wage industries and the working poor', *Poverty and Human Resources Abstracts*, vol. 3.

Bluestone, B. (1970), 'The tripartite economy: labor markets and the working poor', *Poverty and Human Resources Abstracts*, vol. 5.

Borjas, G.J. (1979), 'Job satisfaction, wages and unions', *Journal of Human Resources*, vol. 14.

Bosanquet, N. and Doeringer, P.B. (1973), 'Is there a dual labour market in Britain?', *Economic Journal*, vol. 83.

Boskin, M.J. (1972), 'Unions and relative real wages', *American Economic Review*, vol. 62.

Boulding, K.E. and Pfaff, M. (eds) (1972), *Redistribution to the rich and the poor*, Wadsworth, Belmont, California.

Bourguignon, F. and Morrisson, C. (1982), 'Earnings mobility over the life-cycle: a 30-year panel sample of French "Cadres"', paper presented at ICERD Conference on Panel Income Data.

Bowles, S. (1972), 'Schooling and inequality from generation to generation', *Journal of Political Economy*, vol. 80.

Bowles, S. (1973), 'Understanding unequal economic inequality', *American Economic Review, Papers and Proceedings*, vol. 63.

Bowles, S. and Gintis, H. (1973), 'IQ in the US class structure', *Social Policy*, vol. 3.

Bowles, S. and Nelson, V. (1974), 'The "inheritance of IQ" and the intergenerational reproduction of economic inequality', *Review of Economics and Statistics*, vol. 56.

Bowley, A.L. (1937), *Elements of Statistics*, P.S. King, London.

Bradshaw, J. (1980), *Equity and family incomes*, Study Commission on the Family, London.

Bradshaw, J. and Piachaud, D. (1980), *Child support in the European Community*, Bedford Square Press, London.

Braverman, H. (1974), *Labor and monopoly capital*, Monthly Review Press, New York.

Brittain, J.A. (1960), 'Some neglected features of Britain's income levelling', *American Economic Review, Papers and Proceedings*, vol. 50.

Brittain, J.A. (1978), *Inheritance and the inequality of material wealth*, Brookings Institution, Washington, DC.

Bronfenbrenner, M. (1971), *Income distribution theory*, Macmillan, London.

Brown, A. and Deaton, A. (1972), 'Models of consumer behaviour: a survey', *Economic Journal*, vol. 82.

Brown, C., Gilroy, C. and Kohen, A. (1982), 'The effect of the minimum wage on employment and unemployment', *Journal of Economic Literature*, vol. 20.

Brown, M.B. (1970), *What economics is about*, Weidenfeld and Nicolson, London.

Brown, M. and Madge, N. (1982), *Despite the welfare state*, Heinemann, London.

Browning, E.K. (1976), 'The trend toward equality in the distribution of net income', *Southern Economic Journal*, vol. 42.

Budd, E.C. (ed.) (1967), *Inequality and poverty*, Norton, New York.

Budd, E.C. (1970), 'Postwar changes in the size distribution of income in the US', *American Economic Review, Papers and Proceedings*, vol. 60.

Budd, E.C. and Seiders, D.F. (1971), 'The impact of inflation on the distribution of income and wealth', *American Economic Review, Papers and Proceedings*, vol. 61.

Bull, D. (ed.) (1971), *Family poverty*, Duckworth, London.

Burghes, L. (1980), *Living from hand to mouth*, Family Service Units and Child Poverty Action Group, London.

Burghes, L. and Lister, R. (eds) (1981), *Unemployment: who pays the price?*, Child Poverty Action Group, London.

Burkitt, B. (1975), *Trade unions and wages, implications for economic theory*, Bradford University Press with Crosby Lockwood Staples, London.

Cain, G.G. (1975), 'The challenge of dual and radical theories of the labor market to orthodox theory', *American Economic Review*, vol. 65.

Cain, G.G. (1976), 'The challenge of segmented labor market theories to orthodox theory', *Journal of Economic Literature*, vol. 14.

Cain, G.G. and Watts, H.W. (eds) (1973), *Econometric studies of labor supply*, Academic Press, New York.

Campion, H. (1939), *Public and private property in Great Britain*, Oxford University Press, London.

Cannan, E. (1914), *Wealth* (3rd ed. 1928), Staples Press, London.

Cappelli, P. (1981), *What people earn*, Macdonald, London.

Carley, M. (1981), *Social measurement and social indicators, issues of policy and theory*, Allen and Unwin, London.

Carter, C. and Wilson, T. (1980), *Discussing the welfare state*, Policy Studies Institute, London.

Champernowne, D.G. (1953), 'The production function and the theory of capital: a comment', *Review of Economic Studies*, vol. 21.

Champernowne, D.G. (1973), *Distribution of income*, Cambridge University Press, London.

Chenery, H. *et al.* (1974), *Redistribution with growth*, Oxford University Press, Oxford.

Chiplin, B. and Sloane, P.J. (1976), *Sex discrimination in the labour market*, Macmillan, London.

Chiswick, B.R. (1969), 'Minimum schooling legislation and the cross-sectional distribution of income', *Economic Journal*, vol. 79.

Chiswick, B.R. and Mincer, J. (1972), 'Time-series changes in personal income inequality in the United States from 1939, with projections to 1985', *Journal of Political Economy*, vol. 80.

Clay, H. (1925), 'The distribution of capital in England and Wales', *Transactions of the Manchester Statistical Society*, vol. 92.

Coale, A.J. and Stephan, F.F. (1962), 'The case of the Indians and teenage widows', *Journal of the American Statistical Association*, vol. 57.

Coates, K. and Silburn, R. (1970), *Poverty: the forgotten Englishmen*, Penguin, Harmondsworth.

Cole (Wedderburn), D. and Utting, J.E.G. (1962), *The economic circumstances of old people*, Codicote Press, London.

Collard, D. (1980), 'Social dividend and negative income tax', in C. Sandford, C. Pond and R. Walker (eds), *Taxation and social policy*, Heinemann, London.

Conlisk, J. (1977), 'An exploratory model of the size distribution of income', *Economic Inquiry*, vol. 15.

Copeman, G. and Rumble, T. (1972), *Capital as an incentive*, Leviathan House, London.

Council of Economic Advisers (1964), *Economic report of the President 1964*, US Government Printing Office, Washington DC.

Council of Economic Advisers (1973), *Economic report of the President 1973*, US Government Printing Office, Washington DC.

Cowell, F.A. (1977), *Measuring inequality*, Philip Allan, Oxford.

Cowell, F.A. (1979), 'The definition of lifetime income', Institute for Research on Poverty, Discussion Paper no. 566, University of Wisconsin, Madison.

Cowell, F.A. (1980), 'The structure of American income inequality', unpublished paper, London School of Economics.

Cowell, F.A. and Mehta, F. (1982), 'The estimation of inequality measures', *Review of Economic Studies*, vol. 49.

Cowling, K. (1981), 'Oligopoly, distribution and the rate of profit', *European Economic Review*, vol. 15.

Cowling, K. (1982), *Monopoly capitalism*, Macmillan Press, London.

Craig, C., Rubery, J., Tarling, R. and Wilkinson, F. (1982), *Labour market structures, industrial organisation and low pay*, Cambridge University Press, Cambridge.

Craven, J. (1979), *The distribution of the product*, Allen and Unwin, London.

Creedy, J. (1975), 'Aggregation and the income distribution', *Bulletin of the Oxford Institute of Economics and Statistics*, vol. 37.

Creedy, J. (1977), 'The distribution of lifetime earnings', *Oxford Economic Papers*, vol. 29.

Creedy, J. (1982), *State pensions in Britain*, Cambridge University Press, Cambridge.

Cripps, F., Griffith, J., Morrell, F., Reid, J., Townsend, P. and Weir, S. (1981), *Manifesto, a radical strategy for Britain's future*, Pan Books, London.

Crosland, C.A.R. (1964), *Future of socialism*, Jonathan Cape, London.

Culyer, A.J. (1980), *The political economy of social policy*, Martin Robertson, Oxford, London.

Dahrendorf, R. (1979), *Life chances, approaches to social and political theory*, Weidenfeld and Nicolson, London.

Dalton, H. (1920a), *The inequality of incomes*, Routledge and Kegan Paul, London.

Dalton, H. (1920b), The measurement of the inequality of incomes', *Economic Journal*, vol. 30.

Daniel, W.W. (1968), 'Personal taxation and occupational incentives', *Banker*, vol. 118.

Daniels, G.W. and Campion, H. (1936), *Distribution of national capital*, Manchester University Press, Manchester.

Daniels, N. (ed.) (1975), *Reading Rawls, critical studies of 'A Theory of justice'*, Basil Blackwell, Oxford.

Danziger, S. (1980), 'Do working wives increase family income inequality?', *Journal of Human Resources*, vol. 15.

Danziger, S. and Haveman, R. (1981), 'The Reagan Budget', *Challenge*, May/June.

Danziger, S., Haveman, R. and Plotnick, R. (1981), 'How income transfer programs affect work, savings and the income distribution: a critical review', *Journal of Economic Literature*, vol. 19.

Danziger, S., Haveman, R. and Smolensky, E. (1977), 'Comment on Paglin [1975]', *American Economic Review*, vol. 67.

Danziger, S. and Plotnick, R. (1977), 'Demographic change, government transfers, and income distribution', *Monthly Labor Review*, vol. 100.

Danziger, S. and Plotnick, R. (1980), 'The war on income poverty: achievements and failures', *Welfare Reform in America*, Institute for Research on Poverty, University of Wisconsin, Madison.

Danziger, S. and Taussig, M.K. (1979), 'The income unit and the anatomy of income distribution', *Review of Income and Wealth*, vol. 25.

Davies, J.B. (1979), 'On the size distribution of wealth in Canada', *Review of Income and Wealth*, vol. 25.

Davies, J.B. and Shorrocks, A.F. (1978), 'Assessing the quantitative importance of inheritance in the distribution of wealth', *Oxford Economic Papers*, vol. 30.

Deaton, A. (1981), 'On a method of measuring the costs of children', discussion paper, University of Bristol.

Deaton, A. and Muellbauer, J. (1980), *Economics and consumer behaviour*, Cambridge University Press, Cambridge.

Dennett, J., James, E., Room, G. and Watson, P. (1982), *Europe against poverty*, Bedford Square Press, London.

Department of Employment (1980), *Family expenditure survey 1979*, HMSO, London.

Department of Health and Social Security (1971), *Two-parent families*, HMSO, London.

Department of Health and Social Security (1972), *Families receiving supplementary benefit*, HMSO, London.

Department of Health and Social Security (1979), *The definition and measurement of poverty*, HMSO, London.

Desai, M. (1974), *Marxian economic theory*, (2nd ed. 1979), Gray-Mills, London.

Dickinson, H.D. (1932), *Institutional revenue*, Williams and Norgate, London.

Dilnot, A. and Morris, C.N. (1981), 'What do we know about the Black Economy?', *Fiscal Studies*, vol. 2.

Dinwiddy, R. (1980), 'The concept of personal income in the analysis of income distribution', Government Economic Service Working Paper no. 30, London.

Dinwiddy, R. and Reed, D. (1977), 'The effects of certain social and demographic changes on income distribution', *Royal Commission on the Distribution of Income and Wealth*, background paper no. 3, HMSO, London.

Doeringer, P.B. and Piore, M.J. (1971), *Internal labor markets and man-power analysis*, D.C. Heath, Lexington, Massachusetts.

Douglas, P.H. (1934), *Theory of wages*, Macmillan, London.

Douty, H.M. (1961), 'Sources of occupational wage and salary rate dispersions within labor markets', *Industrial and Labor Relations Review*, vol. 14.

Drago, G. del (1975), *International comparisons of levels of development*, Open University unit 15, Statistical sources course, Milton Keynes.

Duncan, C. (1981), *Low pay – its causes and the post-war trade union response*, Research Studies Press, Chicago, New York.

Dunlop, J.T. (1957), 'The task of contemporary wage theory', in J.T. Dunlop (ed.), *Theory of wage determination*, Macmillan, London.

Dunn, A.T. and Hoffman, P.D.R.B. (1978), 'The distribution of personal wealth', *Economic Trends*, issue 301.

Dunn, A.T. and Hoffman, P.D.R.B. (1981), 'Distribution of wealth in the United Kingdom: effect of including pension rights and analysis by age-group', 17th general conference of the International Association for Research in Income and Wealth, Chateau de Montvillargene, Gouvrieux, France.

Easterlin, R.A. (1980), *Birth and fortune*, Grant McIntyre, London.

Eccles, M. and Freeman, R.B. (1982), 'What! another minimum wage study?', *American Economic Review*, vol. 72.

Edgeworth, F.Y. (1922), 'Equal pay to men and women for equal work', *Economic Journal*, vol. 32.

Edwards, R.C. (1975), 'The social relations of production in the firm and labor market structure', in R.C. Edwards, M. Reich and D.M. Gordon (eds), *Labor market segmentation*, D.C. Heath & Co., Lexington, Mass., Toronto, and London.

Edwards, R., Reich, M. and Gordon, D.M. (1975), *Labor market segmentation*, D.C. Heath & Co., Lexington, Mass., Toronto and London.

Edwards, R., Reich, M. and Weisskopf, T. (eds) (1972), *The capitalist system*, Prentice-Hall, Englewood Cliffs, New Jersey.

Engels, F. (1892), *The condition of the working class in England*, Allen and Unwin, London.

Evason, E. (1980), *Ends that won't meet, a study of poverty in Belfast*, Child Poverty Action Group, London.

Fawcett, M. (1918), 'Equal pay for equal work', *Economic Journal*, vol. 28.

Federal Reserve Board (D.S. Projector and G.S. Weiss) (1966), *Survey of financial characteristics of consumers*, Board of Governors of the Federal Reserve System, Washington, DC.

Fei, J.C.H., Ranis, G., and Kuo, S.W.Y. (1979), *Growth with equity*, Oxford University Press, New York and London.

Feige, E. (1979), 'How big is the irregular economy?', *Challenge*, Nov–Dec.

Feinstein, C.H. (1968), 'Changes in the distribution of national income in the United Kingdom since 1860', in Marchal and Ducros (1968)

Feldstein, M.S. (1973), *Lowering the permanent rate of unemployment*, Joint Economic Committee, US Government Printing Office, Washington, DC.

Ferber, M.A. and Birnbaum, B.G. (1980), 'Housework: priceless or valueless?', *Review of Income and Wealth*, vol. 26.

Ferguson, C.E. (1969), *The neoclassical theory of production and distribution*, Cambridge University Press, London.

Ferguson, C.E. and Nell, E.J. (1972), 'Two books on the theory of income distribution: a review article', *Journal of Economic Literature*, vol. 10.

Fiegehen, G.C., Lansley, P.S. and Smith, A.D. (1977), *Poverty and progress in Britain 1953–73*, Cambridge University Press, Cambridge.

Field, F. (ed.) (1973), *Low pay*, Arrow Books, London.

Field, F. (1981), *Inequality in Britain: freedom, welfare and the state*, Fontana Paperbacks, Glasgow.

Field, F., Meacher, M. and Pond, C. (1977), *To him who hath*, Penguin, Harmondsworth.

Fields, G.S. (1980), *Poverty, inequality and development*, Cambridge University Press, Cambridge.

Fine, B. (1975), *Marx's Capital*, Macmillan, London.

Fine, B. (1982), *Theories of the capitalist economy*, Edward Arnold, London.

Finer, M. (1974), *Report of the committee on one-parent families*, HMSO, London.

Fisher, A. and Dix, B. (1974), *Low pay and how to end it, a union view*, Pitman, London.

Fisher, M.R. (1971), *The economic analysis of labour*, Weidenfeld and Nicolson, London.

Fleisher, B. (1970), *Labor economics: theory and evidence*, Prentice-Hall, Englewood Cliffs, New Jersey.

Flemming, J.S. (1979), 'The effects of earnings inequality, imperfect capital markets, and dynastic altruism on the distribution of wealth in life cycle models', *Economica*, vol. 46.

Flemming, J.S. and Little, I.M.D. (1974), *Why we need a wealth tax*, Methuen, London.

Fogarty, M. (ed.) (1982), *Retirement policy, the next fifty years*, Heinemann, London.

Freeman, R.B. (1973), 'Decline of labor market discrimination and economic analysis', *American Economic Review, Papers and Proceedings*, vol. 63.

Freeman, R.B. (1979), 'The effect of demographic factors on age–earnings profiles', *Journal of Human Resources*, vol. 14.

Freeman, R.B. (1980), 'The exit-voice tradeoff in the labor market', *Quarterly Journal of Economics*, vol. 94.

Freeman, R.B. (1980), 'Unionism and the dispersion of wages', *Industrial and Labor Relations Review*, vol. 34.

Freeman, R.B. (1981), 'Black economic progress after 1964: who has gained and why?', in S. Rosen (ed.), *Studies in Labor Markets*, University of Chicago Press, Chicago and London.

Friedman, M. (1954), 'Some comments on the significance of labor unions for economic policy', in D. McCord Wright (ed.), *The impact of the union*, Kelley and Millman, New York.

Friedman, M. (1957), *A theory of the consumption function*, Princeton University Press, Princeton, New Jersey.

Friedman, M. (1962), *Capitalism and freedom*, University of Chicago Press, Chicago.

Friedman, M. and Kuznets, S. (1945), *Income from independent professional practice*, National Bureau of Economic Research, New York.

Friedman, R.D. (1965), *Poverty: definition and perspective*, American Enterprise Institute for Public Policy Research, Washington, DC.

Fuchs, V. (1969), 'Comment on measuring the size of the low-income population', in L. Soltow (ed.), *Six papers on the size distribution of wealth and income*, National Bureau of Economic Research, New York.

Gastwirth, J.L. (1972), 'The estimation of the Lorenz curve and the Gini index', *Review of Economics and Statistics*, vol. 54.

George, V. (1968), *Social security: Beveridge and after*, Routledge and Kegan Paul, London.

George, V. (1973), *Social security and society*, Routledge and Kegan Paul, London.

Gillespie, W.I. (1965), 'The effect of public expenditures on the distribution of income', in R.A. Musgrave (ed.), *Essays on fiscal federalism*, Brookings Institution, Washington, DC.

Glyn, A. and Sutcliffe, B. (1972), *British capitalism, workers and the profits squeeze*, Penguin, Harmondsworth.

Goldberger, A.S. (1978a), 'Models and methods in the IQ debate', discussion paper, University of Wisconsin.

Goldberger, A.S. (1978b), 'The genetic determination of income: comment', *American Economic Review*, vol. 68.

Goldberger, A.S. (1979), 'Heritability', *Economica*, vol. 46.

Goldsmith, S.F. *et al.* (1954), 'Size distribution of income since the mid-thirties', *Review of Economics and Statistics*, vol. 36.

Goldthorpe, J. (1974), 'Social inequality and social integration in modern Britain', in D. Wedderburn (ed.), *Poverty, inequality and class structure*, Cambridge University Press, London.

Gordon, D.M. (1972), *Theories of poverty and underemployment*, D.C. Heath, Lexington, Mass.

Gordon, D.M., Edwards, R. and Reich, M. (1982), *Segmented work, divided workers*, Cambridge University Press, Cambridge.

Gordon, S. (1980), *Welfare, justice and freedom*, Columbia University Press, New York.

Gough, I. (1979), *The political economy of the welfare state*, Macmillan, London.

Gough, I. and Stark, T. (1968), 'Low incomes in the United Kingdom', *Manchester School*, vol. 36.

Gramlich, E.M. (1974), 'The distributional effects of higher unemployment', *Brookings Papers on Economic Activity*.

le Grand, J. (1982), *The strategy of equality, redistribution and the social services*, Allen and Unwin, London.

Green, C. (1967), *Negative taxes and the poverty problem*, Brookings Institution, Washington, DC.

Greenwood, D. (1982), 'A method of estimating the distribution of wealth among American families in 1973', *1981 Social Statistics Section, Proceedings of the American Statistical Association*.

Greve, J. (1978), *Low incomes in Sweden*, Royal Commission on the Distribution of Income and Wealth, Background Paper to Report no. 6, HMSO, London.

Griliches, Z. (1979), 'Sibling models and data in economics: beginnings of a survey', *Journal of Political Economy*, vol. 87.

Griliches, Z. and Mason, W.M. (1972), 'Education, income and ability', *Journal of Political Economy*, vol. 80.

Gurley, J. (1972), 'The state of political economics', *American Economic Review, Papers and Proceedings*, vol. 61.

Gutmann, A. (1980), *Liberal equality*, Cambridge University Press, Cambridge.

Hahn, F.H. (1972), *The share of wages in the national income*, Weidenfeld and Nicolson, London.

Hahn, F.H. and Matthews, R.C.O. (1965), 'The theory of economic growth: a survey', in *Surveys of economic theory* (vol. 2), Macmillan, London.

Haley, B.F. (1968), 'Changes in the distribution of income in the United States', in Marchal and Ducros (1968).

Hall, R.E. (1982), 'The importance of lifetime jobs in the US economy, *American Economic Review*, vol. 72.

Halsey, A.H. (1981), *Change in British society*, Oxford University Press, Oxford.

Hanoch, G. (1967), 'An economic analysis of earnings and schooling', *Journal of Human Resources*, vol. 2.

Harbury, C.D. and Hitchens, D.M.W.N. (1979), *Inheritance and wealth inequality in Britain*, Allen and Unwin, London.

Harrington, M. (1962), *The other America*, Macmillan and Penguin, London.

Harrison, A. (1979), 'The distribution of wealth in ten countries', *Royal Commission on the Distribution of Income and Wealth, Background Paper to Report no. 7*, HMSO, London.

Harrison, A. (1981), 'Earnings by size: a tale of two distributions', *Review of Economic Studies*, vol. 48.

Harrison, J. (1978), *Marxist economics for socialists, a critique of reformism*, Pluto Press, London.

Hart, P.E. (1981), 'The statics and dynamics of income distribution', in N.A. Klevmarken and J.A. Lybeck (eds), *The statics and dynamics of income*, Tieto, Bristol.

Hartog, J. (1976), 'Ability and age–income profiles', *Review of Income and Wealth*, vol. 22.

Hause, J.C. (1972), 'Earnings profile: ability and schooling', *Journal of Political Economy*, vol. 80.

Hawrylyshyn, O. (1976), 'The value of household services: a survey of empirical estimates', *Review of Income and Wealth*, vol. 22.

Hay-MSL Ltd. (1976), *Analysis of managerial remuneration in the United Kingdom and overseas*, Royal Commission on the Distribution of Income and Wealth, Background Paper to Report no. 5.

Health and Welfare Canada (1977), *The distribution of income in Canada: concepts, measures and issues*, Research report no. 04, Department of National Health and Welfare, Canada.

Heidensohn, K. (1969), 'Labour's share in national income – a constant?', *Manchester School*, vol. 37.

Heidensohn, K. and Zygmant, J. (1974), 'On some common fallacies in interpreting aggregate pay share figures', *Zeitschrift für die Gesamte Staatswissenschaft*, vol. 130.

Hemming, R. and Kay, J.A. (1981), 'Real rates of return', *Fiscal Studies*, vol. 2.

Hemming, R. and Kay, J.A. (1982), 'The costs of the state earnings related pension scheme', *Economic Journal*, vol. 92.

Henderson, A.M. (1949), 'The cost of children', Parts I–III, *Population Studies*, vols 3–4.

Henderson, R.F. (1975) (chairman), *Poverty in Australia*, Australian Government Publicity Service, Canberra.

Henle, P. and Ryscavage, P. (1980), 'The distribution of earned income among men and women, 1958–77', *Monthly Labor Review*, vol. 103.

Herriot, R.A. and Miller, H.P. (1972), 'Tax changes among income groups', *Business Horizons*, February 1972.

Hicks, J.R. (1971), *The social framework* (4th ed), Oxford University Press, London.

Hill, C.R. and Stafford, F.P. (1974), 'The allocation of time to pre-school children and educational opportunity', *Journal of Human Resources*, vol. 9.

Hill, C.R. and Stafford, F.P. (1977), 'Family background and lifetime earnings', in F.T. Juster (ed.), *The distribution of economic wellbeing*, Ballinger, Cambridge, Massachusetts.

Hindess, B. (1973), *The use of official statistics in sociology*, Macmillan. London.

Hollister, R.G. and Palmer, J.L. (1972), 'The impact of inflation on the poor', in Boulding and Pfaff (1972).

Houghton, R.W. (ed.) (1970), *Public finance*, Penguin, Harmondsworth.

Houthakker, H.S. (1974), 'The size distribution of labour incomes derived from the distribution of aptitudes', in W. Sellekaerts (ed.), *Econometrics and economic theory*, Macmillan, London.

Hunt, E.K. and Schwartz, J.G. (eds) (1972), *A critique of economic theory*, Penguin, Harmondsworth.

Hunt, E.K. and Sherman, H.J. (1972), *Economics: an introduction to traditional and radical views*, Harper and Row, New York.

Hunter, L.C. and Mulvey, C. (1981), *The economics of wages and labour*, Macmillan, London.

Hunter L.C. and Robertson, D.J. (1969), *Economics of wages and labour*, Macmillan, London.

Institute of Economic Affairs (1970), *Policy for poverty*, IEA, London.

Institute for Research on Poverty (1981a), 'Poverty in the United States: where do we stand?', *Focus*, Institute for Research on Poverty, University of Wisconsin, vol. 5.

Institute for Research on Poverty (1981b), 'The Reagan administration's budget cuts: their impact on the poor', *Focus*, Institute for Research on Poverty, University of Wisconsin, vol. 5.

Irvine, I.J. (1980), 'The distribution of income and wealth in Canada in a lifetime framework', *Canadian Journal of Economics*, vol. 13.

Irvine, I. and McCarthy, C. (1980), 'Further evidence on inflation and redistribution in the United Kingdom', *Economic Journal*, vol. 90.

Irvine, J., Miles, I. and Evans, J. (eds) (1979), *Demystifying social statistics*, Pluto Press, London.

Ishikawa, T. (1975), 'Family structures and family values in the theory of income distribution', *Journal of Political Economy*, vol. 83.

Ishikawa, T. (1981), 'Dual labor market hypothesis and long-run income distribution', *Journal of Development Economics*, vol. 9.

Jackson, D. (1972), *Poverty*, Macmillan, London.

Jain, S. (1975), *Size distribution of income: a compilation of data*, World Bank, Washington, DC.

Jencks, C. (1972), *Inequality*, Basic Books, New York.

Jencks, C. *et al.* (1979), *Who gets ahead?* Basic Books, New York.

Jensen, A. (1969), 'How much can we boost IQ and scholastic achievement? *Harvard Educational Review*, vol. 39.

Johnson, F. (1975), *Income distribution*, Open University unit 12, Statistical sources course, Milton Keynes.

Johnson, G.E. (1975), 'Economic analysis of trade unionism', *American Economic Review*, vol. 65.

Johnson, H.G. (1973), *The theory of income distribution*, Gray-Mills, London.

Jones, E. (1978), 'Estimation of the magnitude of accumulated and inherited wealth', *Journal of the Institute of Actuaries*, vol. 105.

Jordan, B. (1973), *Paupers*, Routledge and Kegan Paul, London.

Jorgenson, D.W. and Pachon, A. (1980), 'Lifetime income and human capital', in P. Streeken (ed.), *Human resources: concepts and measurements* Macmillan, London, forthcoming.

Joseph, K. and Sumption, J. (1979), *Equality*, John Murray, London.

Junankar, P.N. (1982), *Marx's economics*, Philip Allan, Oxford.

Kain, J.F. and Quigley, J.M. (1972), 'Housing market discrimination, home ownership and savings behaviour', *American Economic Review*, vol. 62.

Kakwani, N.C. (1980), *Income inequality and poverty: methods of estimation and policy applications*, World Bank Research Publication, Oxford University Press, Oxford.

Kaldor, N. (1955a), *An expenditure tax*, Allen and Unwin, London.

Kaldor, N. (1955b), 'Alternative theories of distribution', *Review of Economic Studies*, vol. 23.

Kaldor, N. (1966), 'Marginal productivity and the macro-economic theories of distribution', *Review of Economic Studies*, vol. 33.

Kalecki, M. (1939), *Essays in the theory of economic fluctuations*, Allen and Unwin, London.

Kay, J.A. and King, M.A. (1980), *The British tax system* (2nd ed), Oxford University Press, Oxford.

Kendrick, J.W. (1979), 'Expanding imputed values in the national income and product accounts', *Review of Income and Wealth*, vol. 25.

Kerr, C. (1950), 'Labor markets: their character and consequences', *American Economic Review, Papers and Proceedings*, vol. 40.

Kershaw, J.A. (1965), 'The attack on poverty', in M.S. Gordon (ed.) *Poverty in America*, Chandler, San Francisco.

Kershaw, J.A. (1970), *Government against poverty*, Brookings Institution, Washington, DC.

Kessler, D. (1982), 'Intergenerational wealth transfer', in D. Kessler, A. Masson, D. Strauss-Kahn (eds), *Accumulation et répartition des patrimoines*, Economica, Paris.

Kessler, D., Masson, A. and Strauss-Kahn, D. (1982), *Accumulation et répartition des patrimoines*, Economica, Paris.

Keynes, J.M. (1930), 'The income and fiscal potential of Great Britain', *Economic Journal*, vol. 49.

Kincaid, J.C. (1973), *Poverty and equality in Britain*, Penguin, Harmondsworth.

King, J.E. (ed.) (1980), *Readings in labour economics*, Oxford University Press, Oxford.

King, M.A. and Dicks-Mireaux, L-D.L. (1982), 'Asset holdings and the life-cycle', *Economic Journal*, vol. 92.

Kniesner, T.J. (1981), 'The low-wage workers: who are they?, in S. Rottenberg (ed.), *The economics of legal minimum wages*, American Enterprise Institute for Public Policy Research, Washington and London.

Knight, I. (1980), *The feasibility of conducting a national wealth survey in Great Britain*, Office of Population Censuses and Surveys, London.

Kohen, A.I., Parnes, H.S. and Shea, J.R. (1975), 'Income instability among young and middle-aged men', in J.D. Smith (ed.), *The personal distribution of income and wealth*, Columbia University Press, New York and London.

Kolko, G. (1962), *Wealth and power in America*, Praeger, New York.

Kolm, S.Ch. (1969), 'The optimal production of social justice', in J. Margolis and H. Guitton (eds), *Public economics*, Macmillan, London;

Kolm, S.Ch. (1972), *Justice et équité*, CNRS, Paris.

Kosters, M. and Welch, F. (1972), 'The effects of minimum wages on the distribution of changes in aggregate employment', *American Economic Review*, vol. 62.

Kravis, I.B. (1959), 'Relative income shares in fact and theory', *American Economic Review*, vol. 49.

Kravis, I.B. (1962), *The structure of income*, University of Pennsylvania Press, Philadelphia.

Kravis, I.B., Heston, A.W. and Summers, R. (1978), 'Real GDP per capita for more than one hundred countries', *Economic Journal*, vol. 88.

Kravis, I.B., Heston, A.W. and Summers, R. (1982), *World product and income*, Johns Hopkins University Press, Baltimore.

Krueger, A.O. (1963), 'The economics of discrimination', *Journal of Political Economy*, vol. 71.

Kuh, E. (1965), 'Cyclical and secular labor productivity in US manufacturing', *Review of Economics and Statistics*, vol. 47.

Kurien, C.J. (1977), 'Comment on "The measurement and trend of inequality"', *American Economic Review*, vol. 67.

Kuznets, S. (1953), *Share of upper income groups in income and savings*, National Bureau of Economic Research, New York.

Kuznets, S. (1955), 'Economic growth and income inequality', *American Economic Review*, vol. 45.

Kuznets, S. (1963), 'Quantitative aspects of the economic growth of nations: part VIII, distribution of income by size', *Economic Development and Cultural Change*, vol. 11.

Kuznets, S. (1966), *Modern economic growth*, Yale University Press, New Haven, Connecticut.

Kuznets, S. (1974), 'Demographic aspects of the distribution of income among families: recent trends in the United States', in W. Sellekaerts (ed.), *Econometrics and economic theory*, Macmillan, London.

Lampman, R.J. (1959), 'Changes in the share of wealth held by top wealth-holders, 1922–1956', *Review of Economics and Statistics*, vol. 41.

Lampman, R.J. (1962), *The share of top wealth-holders in national wealth 1922–1956*, Princeton University Press, Princeton, New Jersey.

Lampman, R.J. (1971), *Ends and means of reducing income poverty*, Markham, Chicago.

Land, H. (1977), 'Social security and the division of unpaid work in the home and paid employment in the labour market', *Social security research*, HMSO, London.

Langley, K.M. (1950), 'The distribution of capital in private hands in 1936–1938 and 1946–1947, Part I', *Bulletin of the Oxford Institute of Economics and Statistics*, vol. 12.

Langley, K.M. (1951), 'The distribution of capital in private hands in 1936–1938 and 1946–1947, Part II', *Bulletin of the Oxford Institute of Economics and Statistics*, vol. 13.

Lansley, S. (1980), 'Changes in inequality and poverty in the UK, 1971–1976', *Oxford Economic Papers*, vol. 32.

Layard, R. (1977), 'On measuring the redistribution of lifetime income', in M.S. Feldstein and R.P Inman (eds), *The economics of public services*, Macmillan, London.

Layard, R., Metcalf, D. and Nickell, S. (1978), 'The effect of collective bargaining on wages', in W. Krelle and A.F. Shorrocks (eds), *Personal income distribution*, North Holland, Amsterdam, New York and London.

Layard, R., Piachaud, D. and Stewart, M. (1978), *The causes of poverty*, Royal Commission on the Distribution of Income and Wealth, Background Paper to Report no. 5, HMSO, London.

Lazear, E.P. and Michael, R.T. (1980), 'Family size and the distribution of real per capita income', *American Economic Review*, vol. 70.

Leibowitz, A. (1977), 'Family background and economic success: a review of the evidence', in P. Taubman (ed.), *Konometrics: determinants of socioeconomic success within and between families*, North Holland, Amsterdam, New York, and Oxford.

Leighton, L. and Mincer, J. (1981), 'The effects of minimum wages on human capital formation', in S. Rottenberg (ed.), *The economics of legal minimum wages*, American Enterprise Institute for Public Policy Research, Washington and London.

Leser, C.E.V. (1976), 'Income, household size and price changes 1953–1973', *Oxford Bulletin of Economics and Statistics*, vol. 38.

Lester, R.A. (1964), *Economics of labour* (2nd ed), Macmillan, London.

Levitan, S.R. (1980), *Programs in aid of the poor for the 1980s*, Johns Hopkins University Press, London.

Levitt, M.S. (1976), 'The redistributive effects of taxation in the Report of the Royal Commission', *Economic Journal*, vol. 86.

Lewis, H.G. (1963), *Unionism and relative wages in the United States*, University of Chicago Press, Chicago.

Lillard, L.A. (1977a), 'Inequality: earnings vs. human wealth', *American Economic Review*, vol. 67.

Lillard, L.A. (1977b), 'The distribution of earnings and human wealth in a life-cycle context', in F.T. Juster (ed.), *The distribution of economic well-being*, Ballinger, Cambridge, Massachusetts.

Lindert, P.H. and Williamson, J.G. (1983), 'Reinterpreting Britain's social tables, 1688–1913', *Explorations in Economic History*, vol. 20.

Lipsey, R.G. (1964), *An introduction to positive economics*, Weidenfeld and Nicolson, London.

Lloyd, C. (1975), *Sex discrimination and the division of labour*, Columbia University Press, New York.

Love, R. and Oja, G. (1977), 'Low income in Canada', *Review of Income and Wealth*, vol. 23.

Loveridge, R. and Mok, A.L. (1979), *Theories of labour market segmentation*, Martinus Nijhoff Social Sciences, the Hague, Boston, and London.

Low Pay Unit (1978), 'Written evidence to the Royal Commission on Income and Wealth', *Selected evidence submitted to the Royal Commission for Report no. 6: lower incomes*, HMSO, London.

Low Pay Unit (1981), *Low pay – 1980s style*, Low Pay Review, London.

Lucas, R.E.B. (1977), 'Is there a human capital approach to income inequality?', *Journal of Human Resources*, vol. 12.

Lundberg, F. (1968), *The rich and the super rich*, Lyle Stuart, New York.

Lutz, M.A. (1976), 'The evolution of the industrial earnings structure: the geological theory', *Canadian Journal of Economics*, vol. 9.

Lydall, H.F. (1955), 'The life-cycle in income, saving and asset ownership', *Econometrica*, vol. 23.

Lydall, H.F. (1959), 'The long-term trend in the size distribution of income', *Journal of the Royal Statistical Society*, vol. 122, series A.

Lydall, H.F. (1968), *The structure of earnings*, Oxford University Press, Oxford.

Lydall, H.F. (1976), 'Theories of the distribution of earnings', in A.B. Atkinson (ed.), *The personal distribution of incomes*, Allen and Unwin, London.

Lydall, H.F. (1979), *A theory of income distribution*, Oxford University Press, Oxford.

Lydall, H.F. and Lansing, J.B. (1959), 'A comparison of the distribution of personal income and wealth in the United States and Great Britain', *American Economic Review*, vol. 49.

Lydall, H.F. and Tipping, D.G. (1961), 'The distribution of personal wealth in Britain', *Bulletin of the Oxford Institute of Economics and Statistics*, vol. 23.

Lynes, T. (1981), *The Penguin guide to supplementary benefits*, Penguin, Harmondsworth.

Lyons, P.M. (1972), 'The distribution of personal wealth in Northern Ireland', *Economic and Social Review*, vol. 3.

Lyons, P.M. (1974), 'The size distribution of personal wealth in the Republic of Ireland', *Review of Income and Wealth*, vol. 20.

MacAfee, K. (1980), 'A glimpse of the hidden economy in the national accounts', *Economic Trends*, February.

MacDonald, M. (1977), *Food, stamps, and income maintenance*, Academic Press, London.

Madge, C. and Willmott, P. (1981), *Inner city poverty in Paris and London*, Routledge and Kegan Paul, London.

Marchal, J. and Ducros, B. (eds) (1968), *The distribution of national income*, Macmillan, London.

Marin, A. and Psacharopoulos, G. (1976), 'Schooling and income distribution', *Review of Economics and Statistics*, vol. 58.

Marmor, T. (ed.) (1971), *Poverty policy*, Aldine, Chicago.

Marsden, D. (1969), *Mothers alone: poverty and the fatherless family*, Allen Lane, London.

Marshall, G.P. (1980), *Social goals and economic perspectives*, Penguin, Harmondsworth.

Martin, W.E. (ed.) (1981), *The economics of the profits crisis*, HMSO, London.

Matras, J. (1975), *Social inequality, stratification and mobility*, Prentice-Hall, Englewood Cliffs, New Jersey.

Matthewman, J. and Lambert, N. (1982), *Tolley's social security and state benefits*, Tolley, Croydon.

Mayer, T. (1960), 'The distribution of ability and earnings', *Review of Economics and Statistics*, vol. 42.

Mayhew, K. (1977), 'Earnings dispersal in local labour markets: implications for search behaviour', *Oxford Bulletin of Economics and Statistics*, vol. 39.

McClelland, J. (ed.) (1982), *A little pride and dignity*, Child Poverty Action Group, London.

McClements, L.D. (1977), 'Equivalence scales for children', *Journal of Public Economics*, vol. 8.

McClements, L.D. (1978), *The economics of social security*, Heinemann, London.

Meacher, M. (1973), *Rate rebates: a study of the effectiveness of means tests*, Child Poverty Action Group, London.

Meade, J.E. (1964), *Efficiency, equality and the ownership of property*, Allen and Unwin, London.

Meade, J.E. (1972), 'Poverty in the welfare state', *Oxford Economic Papers*, vol. 24.

Meade, J.E. (1973), 'The inheritance of inequalities', *Proceedings of British Academy*, vol. 59.

Meade, J.E. (1976), *The just economy*, Allen and Unwin, London.

Meier, G.M. (ed.) (1969), *Leading issues in development economics*, Oxford University Press, New York.

Menchik, P.L. (1979), 'Inter-generational transmission of inequality: an empirical study of wealth mobility', *Economica*, vol. 46.

Menchik, P.L. (1980), 'Primogeniture, equal sharing, and the US distribution of wealth', *Quarterly Journal of Economics*, vol. 94.

Mennemeyer, S.T. (1978), 'Really great returns to medical education?' *Journal of Human Resources*, vol. 13.

Metcalf, C.E. (1969), 'The size distribution of personal income during the business cycle', *American Economic Review*, vol. 59.

Metcalf, C.E. (1972), *An economic model of the income distribution*, Markham, Chicago.

Metcalf, D. (1977), 'Unions, incomes policy and relative wages in Britain', *British Journal of Industrial Relations*, vol. 15.

Metcalf, D. (1981), *Low pay, occupational mobility and minimum wage policy in Britain*, American Enterprise Institute, Washington.

Michelson, S. (1970), 'The economics of real income distribution', *Review of Radical Political Economics*, vol. 2.

Mill, J.S. (1891), *Principles of political economy*, Routledge, London.

Miller, H.P. (1964), *Rich man, poor man*, Signet Press, New York.

Miller, H.P. (1966), *Income distribution in the United States*, US Government Printing Office, Washington, DC.

Miller, S.M. and Roby, P. (1970), *The future of inequality*, Basic Books, New York.

Mincer, J. (1958), 'Investment in human capital and personal income distribution', *Journal of Political Economy*, vol. 66.

Mincer, J. (1970), 'The distribution of labor incomes – a survey', *Journal of Economic Literature*, vol. 8.

Mincer, J. (1974), *Schooling, experience and earnings*, Columbia University Press, New York.

Mincer, J. (1976), 'Unemployment effects of minimum wages', *Journal of Political Economy*, vol. 84.

Mincer, J. (1979), 'Human capital and earnings', in D. Windham (ed.), *Economic dimensions of education*, National Academy of Education, Washington, DC.

Mincer, J. and Polachek, S. (1974), 'Family investments in human capital: earnings of women', *Journal of Political Economy*, vol. 82.

Minimum Wage Study Commission (1981), *Report*, US Government Printing Office, Washington, DC.

Ministry of Pensions and National Insurance (1966), *Financial and other circumstances of retirement pensioners*, HMSO, London.

Ministry of Social Security (1967), *Circumstances of families*, HMSO, London.

Mirer, T.W. (1973a), 'The effects of macroeconomic fluctuations on the distribution of income', *Review of Income and Wealth*, December.

Mirer, T.W. (1973b), 'The distributional impact of the 1970 recession', *Review of Economics and Statistics*, vol. 55.

Mookherjee, D. and Shorrocks, A.F. (1982), 'An income decomposition analysis of the trend in UK income inequality', *Economic Journal*, vol. 92.

Moon, M. (1977), *The measurement of economic welfare, its application to the aged poor*, Academic Press, New York and London.

Moon, M. and Smolensky, E. (eds) (1977), *Improving measures of economic well-being*, Academic Press, New York.

Morgan, J.N. (1962), 'The anatomy of income distribution', *Review of Economics and Statistics*, vol. 44.

Morgan, J.N. (1965), 'Measuring the economic status of the aged', *International Economic Review*, vol. 6.

Morgan, J.N. (1974), *Five thousand American families*, University of Michigan Press, Ann Arbor.

Morgan, J.N., David, M.H., Cohen, W.J. and Brazer, H.E. (1962), *Income and welfare in the United States*, McGraw-Hill, New York.

Morgan, J.N. and Smith, J.D. (1969), 'Measures of economic well-offness and their correlates', *American Economic Review*, vol. 59.

Morishima, M. (1973), *Marx's economics*, Cambridge University Press, London.

Morishima, M. and Catephores, G. (1978), *Value, exploitation and growth*, McGraw-Hill, Maidenhead.

Mortimore, J. and Blackstone, T. (1982), *Disadvantage and education*, Heinemann, London.

Moylan, S. and Davies, B. (1980), 'The disadvantages of the unemployed', *Employment Gazette*, vol. 88.

Muellbauer, J. (1974), 'Prices and inequality: the United Kingdom experience', *Economic Journal*, vol. 84.

Muellbauer, J. (1977a), 'Testing the Barten model of household composition effects and the cost of children', *Economic Journal*, vol. 87.

Muellbauer, J. (1977b), 'The cost of living', in *Social security research*, HMSO, London.

Muellbauer, J. (1979), 'McClements on equivalence scales for children', *Journal of Public Economics*, vol. 12.

Muellbauer, J. (1980), 'The estimation of the Prais–Houthakker model of equivalence scales', *Econometrica*, vol. 48.

Mulvey, C. (1976), 'Collective agreements and relative earnings in UK manufacturing in 1973', *Economica*, vol. 43.

Mulvey, C. and Abowd, J.M. (1980), 'Estimating the union/non-union wage differential: a statistical issue', *Economica*, vol. 47.

Mulvey, C. and Foster, J.I. (1976), 'Occupational earnings in the UK and the effects of collective agreements', *Manchester School*, vol. 44.

Munnell, A.H. (1977), *The future of social security*, Brookings Institution, Washington, DC.

Musgrave, R.A., Case, K. and Leonard, H. (1974), 'The distribution of fiscal burdens and benefits', *Public Finance*, vol. 1.

Musgrave, R.A. and Musgrave, P.B. (1973), *Public finance in theory and practice*, McGraw-Hill, New York.

National Board for Prices and Incomes (1971), *General problems of low pay*, HMSO, London.

National Economic Development Office (1969), *Value added tax*, HMSO, London.

Natrella, V. (1975), 'Wealth of top wealth holders', paper presented to the 135th Annual Meeting of the American Statistical Association.

Nelson, E.R. (1977), 'Comment on "The measurement and trend of inequality"', *American Economic Review*, vol. 67.

Nicholson, J.L. (1949), 'Variations in working-class family expenditure', *Journal of Royal Statistical Society*, vol. 122, series A.

Nicholson, J.L. (1965), *Redistribution of income in the United Kingdom in 1959, 1957 and 1953*, Bowes and Bowes, Cambridge.

Nicholson, J.L. (1970), 'Redistribution of income: notes on some problems and puzzles', *Review of Income and Wealth*, vol. 16.

Nicholson, J.L. (1974), 'The distribution and redistribution of income in the United Kingdom', in D. Wedderburn (ed.), *Poverty, inequality and class structure*, Cambridge University Press, London.

Nicholson, J.L. (1975), 'Whose cost of living?', *Journal of the Royal Statistical Society*, vol. 138, series A.

Nicholson, J.L. (1976), 'Appraisal of different methods of estimating equivalence scales and their results', *Review of Income and Wealth*, vol. 22.

Nicholson, R.J. (1967), 'The distribution of personal income', *Lloyds Bank Review*, January.

Nordhaus, W.D. (1973), 'The effects of inflation on the distribution of economic welfare', *Journal of Money, Credit and Banking*, vol. 5.

Nordhaus, W.D. and Tobin, J. (1972), 'Is growth obsolete', in *Economic growth*, National Bureau of Economic Research Columbia University Press, New York.

Nozick, R. (1974), *Anarchy, state and utopia*, Basil Blackwell, Oxford.

Nygård, F. and Sandström, A. (1981), *Measuring income inequality*, Almqvist and Wiksell International, Stockholm.

Oaxaca, R. (1973), 'Male–female wage differentials in urban labor markets', *International Economic Review*, vol. 14.

Ogus, A.I. and Barendt, E.M. (1978), *The law of social security*, Butterworths, London.

O'Higgins, M. (1980), 'The distributive effects of public expenditure and taxation: an agnostic view of the CSO analysis', in C. Sandford, C. Pond, and R. Walker (eds), *Taxation and social policy*, Heinemann, London.

Okner, B.A. (1974), 'Individual taxes and the distribution of income', in J. Smith (ed.), *Personal distribution of income and wealth*, National Bureau of Economic Research, New York.

Okner, B.A. and Pechman, J.A. (1974), *Who bears the tax burden?*, Brookings Institution, Washington, DC.

Okun, A.M. (1975), *Equality and efficiency, the big tradeoff*, Brookings Institution, Washington, DC.

Orshansky, M. (1965), 'Counting the poor: another look at the poverty profile', *Social security Bulletines*, vol. 28.

Oulton, N. (1976), 'Inheritance and the distribution of wealth', *Oxford Economic Papers*, vol. 28.

Paglin, M. (1975), 'The measurement and trend of inequality: a basic revision', *American Economic Review*, vol. 65.

Pahl, J. (1980), 'Patterns of money management within marriage', *Journal of Social Policy*, vol. 9.

Paish, F.W. (1957), 'The real incidence of personal taxation', *Lloyds Bank Review*, no. 43.

Palmer, J.L. and Barth, M.C. (1977), 'The distributional effects of inflation and higher unemployment', in M. Moon and E. Smolensky (eds), *Improving measures of economic well-being*, Academic Press, New York.

Papanicolaou, J. and Psacharopoulos, G. (1979), 'Socioeconomic background, schooling and monetary rewards in the United Kingdom', *Economica*, vol. 46.

Parker, S. (1980), *Older workers and retirement*, HMSO, London.

Parsley, C.J. (1980), 'Labor unions and wages: a survey', *Journal of Economic Literature*, vol. 18.

Pasinetti, L. (1961), 'Rate of profit and income distribution in relation to the rate of economic growth', *Review of Economic Studies*, vol. 29.

Pasinetti, L.L. (1974), *Growth and income distribution*, Cambridge University Press, Cambridge.

Paukert, F. (1973), 'Income distribution: a survey of the evidence', *International Labour Review*, vol. 108.

Paukert, F., Skolka, J. and Maton, J. (1981), *Income distribution, structure of economy and employment*, Croom Helm, London.

Paul, J. (ed.) (1981), *Reading Nozick, essays on 'Anarchy, state and utopia'*, Basil Blackwell, Oxford.

Peacock, A.T. (1974), 'The treatment of government expenditure in studies of income redistribution', in W.L. Smith and J.M. Cuthbertson (eds) *Public Finance and stabilisation policy*, North-Holland, Amsterdam.

Pechman, J. (ed.) (1977), *Comprehensive income taxation*, Brookings Institution, Washington, DC.

Pen, J. (1971), *Income distribution*, Allen Lane, London.

Pen, J. (1978), 'The role of power in the distribution of personal income: some illustrative numbers', in W. Krelle and A.F. Shorrocks (eds), *Personal income distribution*, North-Holland, Amsterdam.

Pencavel, J.H. (1974), 'Relative wages and trade union in the United Kingdom', *Economica*, vol. 41.

Phelps Brown, E.H. (1962), *The economics of labor*, Yale University Press, New Haven, Connecticut.

Phelps Brown, E.H. (1968), *Pay and profits*, Manchester University Press, Manchester.

Phelps Brown, E.H. (1977), *The inequality of pay*, Oxford University Press, Oxford.

Phelps Brown, E.H. and Browne, M.H. (1968), *A century of pay*, Macmillan, London.

Phelps Brown, E.H. and Hart, P.E. (1952), 'Share of wages in the national income', *Economic Journal*, vol. 62.

Phelps Brown, E.H. and Hopkins, S.V. (1981), *A perspective of wages and prices*, Methuen, London and New York.

Piachaud, D. (1974), *Do the poor pay more?* Child Poverty Action Group, Poverty Research Series 3, London.

Piachaud, D. (1981), *Children and poverty*, Child Poverty Action Group, London.

Piachaud, D. (1982), *Family incomes since the War*, Study Commission on the Family, London.

Pigou, A.C. (1952), *The economics of welfare* (1952 ed), Macmillan, London.

Plotnick, R.D. and Skidmore, F. (1975), *Progress against poverty*, Academic Press, New York, San Francisco, and London.

Podder, N. and Kakwani, N.C. (1976), 'Distribution of wealth in Australia', *Review of Income and Wealth*, vol. 22.

Polanyi, G. and Wood, J.B. (1974), *How much inequality?* Institute of Economic Affairs, London.

Pollak, R.A. and Wales, T.J. (1979), 'Welfare comparisons and equivalence scales', *American Economic Review*, Papers and Proceedings, vol. 69.

Pond, C., Burghes, L. and Smith, B. (1980), *Taxing wealth inequalities*, Fabian Tract 466.

President's Commission on Income Maintenance Programs (1969), *Poverty amid plenty*, US Government Printing Office, Washington, DC.

Prest, A.R. (1963), 'Review of Titmuss [1962]', *British Tax Review*.

Prest, A.R. and Barr, N.A. (1979), *Public finance in theory and practice* (6th ed.), Weidenfeld and Nicolson, London.

Prest, A.R. and Stark, T. (1967), 'Some aspects of income distribution in the UK since World War II', *Manchester School*, vol. 35.

Projector, D.S. (1968), *Survey of changes in family finances*, Board of Governors of the Federal Reserve System, Washington, DC.

Pryor, F.L. (1973), 'Simulation of the impact of social and economic institutions on the size distribution of income and wealth', *American Economic Review*, vol. 63.

Psacharopoulos, G. (1977), 'Family background, education and achievement', *British Journal of Sociology*, vol. 28.

Psacharopoulos, G. (1978), 'Labour market duality and income distribution: the case of the UK', in W. Krelle and A.F. Shorrocks (eds), *Personal income distribution*, North-Holland, Amsterdam, New York, and Oxford.

Psacharopoulos, G. and Layard, R. (1979), 'Human capital and earnings: British evidence and a critique', *Review of Economic Studies*, vol. 46.

Radical Statistics Education Group (1982), *Reading between the numbers*, BSSRS Publications Ltd, London.

Rainwater, L. (ed.) (1974), *Inequality and justice*, Aldine, Chicago.

Ranadive, K.R. (1978), *Income distribution, the unsolved puzzle*, Oxford University Press, Oxford.

Ranis, G. (ed.) (1972), *The gap between rich and poor nations*, Macmillan, London.

Rawls, J. (1972), *A theory of justice*, Clarendon Press, Oxford.

Reddin, M. (1980), 'Taxation and pensions', in C. Sandford, C. Pond, and R. Walker (eds), *Taxation and social policy*, Heinemann, London.

Reder, M.W. (1959), 'Alternative theories of labor's share', in M. Abramovitz *et al.* (eds), *The allocation of economic resources*, Stanford University Press, Stanford, California.

Rees, A. (1973), *The economics of work and pay*, Harper and Row, New York.

Rees, A. and Schultz, G. (1970), *Workers and wages in an urban labor market*, University of Chicago, Chicago.

Reich, M. (1981), *Racial inequality, a political–economic analysis*, Princeton University Press, Princeton.

Rein, M. (1970), 'Problems in the definition and measurement of poverty', in Townsend (1970).

Revell, J.R.S. (1965), 'Changes in the social distribution of property in Britain during the twentieth century', *Actes du troisième congrès d'histoire economique.*

Revell, J.R.S. (1967), *The wealth of the nation*, Cambridge University Press, London.

Reynolds, L. (1982), *Labour economics and labour relations*, eighth edition, Prentice-Hall, Englewood Cliffs.

Reynolds, M. and Smolensky, E. (1977a), *Public expenditure, taxes and the distribution of income, the United States, 1950, 1961, 1970*, Academic Press, New York.

Reynolds M. and Smolensky, E. (1977b), 'Post-fisc distributions of income in 1950, 1961, and 1970', *Public Finance Quarterly*, vol. 5.

Reynolds, M. and Smolensky, E. (1978), 'The fading effect of government on inequality', *Challenge*, July–August.

Rhys Williams, Sir B. (1982), 'Evidence' to House of Commons Select Committee on the Treasury and the Civil Service, Sub-Committee on Personal Taxation and Income Support.

Ricardo, D. (1821), *The principles of taxation and political economy*, J.M. Dent, London.

Roberti, P. (1979), 'Counting the poor: a review of the situation existing in six industrial nations', in Department of Health and Social Security, *The definition and measurement of poverty*, HMSO, London.

Robinson, J. (1933), *Economics of imperfect competition*, Macmillan, London.

Robinson, J. (1953), 'The production function and the theory of capital', *Review of Economic Studies*, vol. 21.

Robinson, J. (1966), *An essay on Marxian economics* (2nd ed), Macmillan, London.

Robinson, J. and Eatwell, J. (1973), *An introduction to modern economics*, McGraw-Hill, London.

Room, G. (1979), *The sociology of welfare*, Basil Blackwell/Martin Robertson, Oxford.

Rosen, S. (1969), 'Trade union power, threat effects and the extent of organisation', *Review of Economic Studies*, vol. 36.

Rosen, S. (1970), 'Unionism and the occupational wage structure in the United States', *International Economic Review*, vol. 11.

Rosen, S. (1977), 'Human capital: a survey of empirical research', in R.G. Ehrenberg, *Research in Labor Economics*, vol. 1, JAI Press, Greenwich, Connecticut.

Rothbarth, E. (1943), 'Note on a method of determining equivalent income for families of different composition', in C. Madge (ed.), *Wartime pattern of saving and spending*, Macmillan, London.

Rottenberg, S. (ed.) (1981), *The economics of legal minimum wages*, American Enterprise Institute for Public Policy Research, Washington, DC, and London.

Routh, G. (1980), *Occupation and pay in Great Britain 1906–79*, Macmillan Press, London.

Rowntree, B.S. (1901), *Poverty – a study of town life* (1922 ed), Macmillan, London.

Rowntree, B.S. (1941), *Poverty and progress*, Longmans, London.

Rowntree, B.S. and Lavers, G.R. (1951), *Poverty and the welfare state*, Longmans, London.

Rowthorn, B. (1980), *Capitalism, conflict and inflation*, Lawrence and Wishart, London.

Roy, A.D. (1950), 'The distribution of earnings and of individual output', *Economic Journal*, vol. 60.

Royal Commission on the Distribution of Income and Wealth (1975a), *Report no. 1. Initial report on the standing reference*, HMSO, London.

Royal Commission on the Distribution of Income and Wealth (1975b), *Report no. 2. Income from companies and its distribution*, HMSO, London.

Royal Commission on the Distribution of Income and Wealth (1976a), *Report no. 3. Higher incomes from employment*, HMSO, London.

Royal Commission on the Distribution of Income and Wealth (1976b), *Report no. 4. Second report on the standing reference*, HMSO, London.

Royal Commission on the Distribution of Income and Wealth (1977), *Report no. 5. Third report on the standing reference*, HMSO, London.

Royal Commission on the Distribution of Income and Wealth (1978), *Report no. 6. Lower incomes*, HMSO, London.

Royal Commission on the Distribution of Income and Wealth (1979a), *Report no. 7. Fourth report on the standing reference*, HMSO, London.

Royal Commission on the Distribution of Income and Wealth (1979b), *Report no. 8. Fifth report on the standing reference*, HMSO, London.

Royal Commission on the Taxation of Profits and Income (1955), *Final Report*, HMSO, London.

Rubery, J. (1978), 'Structured labour markets, worker organisation and low pay', *Cambridge Journal of Economics*, vol. 2.

Rubinstein, W.D. (1971), 'Occupations among British millionaires, 1857–1969', *Review of Income and Wealth*, vol. 17.

Rubinstein, W.D. (1974), 'Men of property: some aspects of occupation, inheritance and power among top British wealth-holders', in P. Stanworth and A. Giddens (eds), *Elites and power in British society*, Cambridge University Press, London.

Rubinstein, W.D. (1980), *Wealth and the wealthy in the modern world*, Croom Helm, London.

Rubinstein, W.D. (1981), *Men of property*, Croom Helm, London.

Ruggles, P. and O'Higgins, M. (1981), 'The distribution of public expenditure among households in the United States', *Review of Income and Wealth*, series 27.

Runciman, W.G. (1966), *Relative deprivation and social justice*, Routledge and Kegan Paul, London.

Runciman, W.G. (1974), 'Occupational class and the assessment of economic inequality in Britain' in D. Wedderburn (ed.), *Poverty, inequality and class structure*, Cambridge University Press, London.

Russell, T. (1982), 'The share of top wealth holders: the life cycle, inheritance and efficient markets', in D. Kessler, A. Masson and D. Strauss-Kahn (eds), *Accumulation et répartition des patrimoines*, Economica, Paris.

Rutter, M. and Madge, N. (1976), *Cycles of disadvantage*, Heinemann, London.

Samuelson, P.A. (1967)/1973), *Economics* (7th and 9th eds), McGraw-Hill, New York.

Sandford, C.T. (1971), *Taxing personal wealth*, Allen and Unwin, London.

Sandford, C.T. (1982), 'International trends in the taxation of capital', in D. Kessler, A. Masson, D. Strauss-Kahn (eds), *Accumulation et répartition des patrimoines*, Economica, Paris.

Sandford, C.T., Willis, J.R.M. and Ironside, D.J. (1973), *An accessions tax*, Institute for Fiscal Studies, London.

Sattinger, M. (1980), *Capital and the distribution of labor earnings*, North-Holland, Amsterdam.

Saunders, C. and Marsden, D. (1979), *A six-country comparison of the distribution of industrial earnings in the 1970s*, Royal Commission on the Distribution of Income and Wealth, Background Paper to Report no. 8, HMSO, London.

Sawyer, M. (1976), 'Income distribution in OECD countries', *OECD Economic Outlook*, OECD, Paris.

Schiller, B. (1973), *The economics of poverty and discrimination*, Prentice-Hall, Englewood Cliffs, New Jersey.

Schmähl, W. (1982), 'Income analysis based on longidudinal data from social security earnings records: relative earnings-position (age-earnings-profile) and individual replacement rate of German workers', paper presented at ICERD Conference on Panel Income Data.

Schorr, A.L. (ed.) (1977), *Jubilee for our times, a practical program for income inequality*, Columbia University Press, New York.

Schultz, T.P. (1964), *The distribution of personal income*, US Government Printing Office, Washington, DC.

Schultz, T.P. (1969), 'Secular trends and cyclical behaviour of income distribution in the United States: 1944–1965', in L. Soltow (ed.), *Six papers on the size distribution of wealth and income*, Columbia University Press, New York.

Schultz, T.P. (1975), 'Long-term change in personal income distribution: theoretical approaches, evidence and explanations', in D.M. Levine and M.J. Bane (eds), *The Inequality Controversy*, Basic Books, New York.

Schulz, J., Camir, G., Krupp, H., Peschke, M., Sclar, E. and Van Steenberge, J. (1974), *Providing adequate retirement income, pension reform in the United States and abroad*, Brandeis University Press, Hanover, New Hampshire.

Schulz, J.H., Leavitt, J.D. and Kelly, L. (1979), 'Private pensions fall short of pre-retirement income levels', *Monthly Labour Review*, vol. 102.

Scitovsky, T. (1973), 'Inequalities: open and hidden, measured and immeasurable', *Annals of the American Academy of Political and Social Science*, vol. 409.

Seabrook, J. (1982), *Unemployment*, Quartet Books, London.

Semple, M. (1975), 'The effect of changes in household composition on the distribution of income 1961–73', *Economic Trends*, December.

Sen, A.K. (1973), *On economic inequality*, Clarendon Press, Oxford.

Sen, A.K. (1976), 'Poverty: an ordinal approach to measurement', *Econometrica*, vol. 44.

Sen, A.K. (1978), 'Ethical measurement of inequality: some difficulties', in W. Krelle and A.F. Shorrocks (eds), *Personal income distribution*, North-Holland, Amsterdam, New York, Oxford.

Sen, A.K. (1979), 'Issues in the measurement of poverty', *Scandinavian Journal of Economics*, vol. 81; reprinted in S. Strøm (ed.), *Measurement in public choice*, Macmillan, London.

Sen, A.K. (1981), *Poverty and famines, an essay on entitlement and deprivation*, Clarendon Press, Oxford.

Sherman, H.J. (1972), *Radical political economy*, Basic Books, New York.

Shorrocks, A.F. (1975), 'The age–wealth relationship', *Review of Economics and Statistics*, vol. 57.

Shorrocks, A.F. (1979), 'On the structure of inter-generational transfers between families', *Economica*, vol. 46.

Shorrocks, A.F. (1981), 'Income stability in the United States', in N.A. Klevmarken and J.A. Lybeck (eds), *The statics and dynamics of income*, Tieto, Bristol.

Showler, B. and Sinfield, A. (eds) (1980), *The workless state*, Martin Robertson, Oxford.

Simon, H.A. (1957), 'The compensation of executives', *Sociometry*, vol. 20.

Simons, H. (1938), *Personal income taxation*, University of Chicago Press, Chicago.

Sinfield, A. (1970), 'Poor and out of work in Shields', in Townsend (1970).

Sinfield, A. (1978), 'Analyses in the social division of welfare', *Journal of Social Policy*, vol. 7.

Sinfield, A. (1981), *What unemployment means*, Martin Robertson, Oxford.

Skidmore, F. (ed.) (1981), *Social security financing*, MIT Press, Cambridge, Massachusetts.

Sloan, F.A. (1970), 'Lifetime earnings and physicians' choice of speciality', *Industrial and Labor Relations Review*, vol. 24.

Sloane, P.J. (ed.) (1980), *Women and low pay*, Macmillan, London.

Smeeding, T. (1979), 'On the distribution of net income: comment', *Southern Economic Journal*, vol. 45.

Smith, A. (1776), *An inquiry into the nature and causes of the wealth of nations* (1892 ed.), Routledge, London.

Smith, J.D. (1974), 'The concentration of personal wealth in America 1969', *Review of Income and Wealth*, vol. 20.

Smith, J.D. (1982), 'Estimates of the trend and current concentration of wealth', in D. Kessler, A. Masson, D. Strauss-Kahn (eds), *Accumulation et répartition des patrimoines*, Economica, Paris.

Smith, J.D. and Franklin, S.D. (1974), 'The concentration of personal wealth 1922–1969', *American Economic Review, Papers and Proceedings*, vol. 64.

Social Science Research Council (1968), *Research on poverty*, Heinemann, London.

Solow, R.M. (1958), 'A skeptical note on the constancy of relative shares', *American Economic Review*, vol. 48.

Solow, R.M. (1960), 'Income inequality since the war', in R.E. Freeman (ed.), *Postwar economic trends in the United States*, Harper, New York.

Soltow, L. (1965), *Toward income inequality in Norway*, University of Wisconsin Press, Madison.

Soltow, L. (1968), 'Long-run changes in British income inequality', *Economic History Review*, vol. 21.

Spence, M. (1974), *Market signalling*, Harvard University Press, Cambridge, Massachusetts.

Spence, M. (1976), 'Competition in salaries and signalling pre-requisites for jobs', *Quarterly Journal of Economics*, vol. 90.

Spence, M. (1981), 'Signalling screening and information', in S. Rosen (ed.), *Studies in Labor Markets*, University of Chicago Press, Chicago and London.

Stark, T. (1972), *The distribution of personal income in the United Kingdom 1949–1963*, Cambridge University Press, London.

Stark, T. (1977), *The distribution of income in eight countries*, Royal Commission on the Distribution of Income and Wealth, Background Paper to Report no. 5.

Stark, T. (1978), 'Personal incomes', in *Reviews of United Kingdom Statistical Sources*, vol. VI, Pergammon Press, Oxford.

Starrett, D. (1976), 'Social institutions, imperfect information and the distribution of income', *Quarterly Journal of Economics*, vol. 90.

Steele, R. (1981), 'Incomes policies and low pay', in J. L. Fallick and R.F. Elliott (eds), *Incomes policies, inflation and relative pay*, Allen and Unwin, London and Boston.

Stein, B. (1971), *On relief*, Basic Books, New York.

Steiner, G. (1971), *The state of welfare*, Brookings Institution, Washington, DC.

Stephenson, G. (1980), 'Taxes, benefits and the redistribution of incomes', in C. Sandford, C. Pond, and R. Walker (eds), *Taxation and social policy*, Heinemann, London.

Stewart, M. (1972), 'The distribution of income', in W. Beckerman (ed.), *Labour's economic record*, Duckworth, London.

Stewart, M.B. (1981), 'Relative earnings and individual union membership in the UK', Centre for Labour Economics, London School of Economics, Discussion Paper no. 100.

Stigler, G.J. (1945), 'The cost of subsistence', *Journal of Farm Economics*, vol. 27.

Stigler, G.J. (1946), 'The economics of minimum wage legislation', *American Economic Review*, vol. 36.

Stiglitz, J.E. (1969), 'Distribution of income and wealth among individuals', *Econometrica*, vol. 37.

Stiglitz, J.E. (1973), 'Approaches to the economics of discrimination', *American Economic Review, Papers and Proceedings*, vol. 63.

Stiglitz, J.E. (1975), 'The theory of "screening", education, and the distribution of income', *American Economic Review*, vol. 65.

Study Commission on the Family (1981), *Family finances*, Study Commission on the Family, London.

Summers, R., Kravis, I.B. and Heston, A. (1980), 'International comparison of real product and its composition: 1950–77', *Review of Income and Wealth*, vol. 26.

Summers, R., Kravis, I.B. and Heston, A.W. (1981), 'Changes in the world income distribution', discussion paper, University of Pennsylvania.

Supplementary Benefits Commission (1977), *Low incomes*, HMSO, London.

Supplementary Benefits Commission (1980), *Annual Report 1979*, HMSO, London.

Sutherland, A. (1981), 'Capital transfer tax: an obituary', *Fiscal Studies*, vo. 2.

Taubman, P. (1975), *Schooling, ability, nonpecuniary rewards, socioeconomic background and the lifetime distribution of earnings*, North-Holland, Amsterdam.

Taubman, P. (1976), 'The determinants of earnings', *American Economic Review*, vol. 66.

Taubman, P. (ed.) (1977), *Kinometrics: determinants of socioeconomic success within and between families*, North-Holland, Amsterdam, New York, Oxford.

Taubman, P. (1978a), *Income distribution and redistribution*, Addison-Wesley, Reading, Massachusetts.

Taubman, P. (1978b), 'The relative influence of inheritable and environmental factors and the importance of intelligence in earnings functions', in W. Krelle and A.F. Shorrocks (eds), *Personal income distribution*, North-Holland, Amsterdam, New York, Oxford.

Taussig, M.K. (1973), *Alternative measures of the distribution of economic welfare*, Industrial Relations Section, Princeton University, Princeton, New Jersey.

Taussig, M.K. (1976), 'Trends in inequality of well-offness in the United States since World War II', in S. Danziger and M.K. Taussig (eds), *Conference on the trend in economic inequality in the US*, Institute for Research on Poverty, Madison, Wisconsin.

Taussig, M.K. (1982), 'Wealth inequalities in the US', in D. Kessler, A. Masson, D. Strauss-Kahn (eds), *Accumulation et répartition des patrimoines*, Economica, Paris.

Tawney, R.H. (1964), *Equality* (new edition with Introduction by R.M. Titmuss), Allen and Unwin, London.

Thatcher, A.R. (1968), 'The distribution of earnings of employees in Great Britain', *Journal of the Royal Statistical Society*, vol. 131, series A.

Thomas, C. (1981), 'Low pay and income policy', in R.E.J. Chater, A. Dean and R.F. Elliott (eds), *Incomes policy*, Clarendon Press, Oxford.

Thorndike, R. and Hagen, E. (1959), *Ten thousand careers*, John Wiley, New York.

Thurow, L. (1968), 'Disequilibrium and the marginal productivity of capital and labor', *Review of Economics and Statistics*, vol. 50.

Thurow, L. (1969), *Poverty and discrimination*, Brookings Institution, Washington, DC.

Thurow, L.C. (1971), *The impact of taxes on the American economy*, Praeger, New York.

Thurow, L. (1973), 'Toward a definition of economic justice', *Public Interest*, no. 31.

Thurow, L. (1976), *Generating inequality*, Macmillan, London.

Thurow, L.C. and Lucas, R.E.B. (1972), *The American distribution of income: a structural problem*, US Government Printing Office, Washington, DC.

Tinbergen, J. (1975), *Income distribution, analysis and policies*, North-Holland, Amsterdam, Oxford, New York.

Tipping, D.G. (1970), 'Price changes and income distribution', *Applied Statistics*, vol. 19.

Titmuss, R.M. (1958), *Essays on 'the welfare state'*, Allen and Unwin, London.

Titmuss, R.M. (1962), *Income distribution and social change*, Allen and Unwin, London.

Titmuss, R.M. (1974), *Social policy, an introduction*, Allen and Unwin, London.

Tobin, J. (1968), 'Raising the incomes of the poor', in K. Gordon (ed.), *Agenda for the nation*, Brookings Institution, Washington, DC.

Tobin, J. (1970), 'On limiting the domain of inequality', *Journal of Law and Economics*, vol. 13.

Tobin, J., Pechman, J. and Mieszkowski, P. (1967), 'Is a negative income tax practical?', *Yale Law Journal*, vol. 77.

Tomes, N. (1981), 'The family, inheritance, and the intergenerational transmission of inequality', *Journal of Political Economy*, vol. 89.

Townsend, P. (1954), 'Measuring poverty', *British Journal of Sociology*, vol. 5, reprinted in Townsend (1973).

Townsend, P. (1962), 'The meaning of poverty', *British Journal of Sociology*, vol. 13: reprinted in Townsend (1973).

Townsend, P. (ed.) (1970), *The concept of poverty*, Heinemann, London.

Townsend, P. (1973), *The social minority*, Allen Lane, London.

Townsend, P. (1979), *Poverty in the United Kingdom*, Allen Lane, London.

Townsend, P. and Davidson, N. (ed.) (1982), *Inequalities in health, the Black report*, Penguin, Harmondsworth.

Townsend, P. and Wedderburn, D. (1965), *The aged in the welfare state*, Bell, London.

Tuckman, H.P. (1973), *The economics of the rich*, Random House, New York.

Turner, H.A. (1957), 'Inflation and wage differentials in Great Britain', in J. Dunlop (ed.), *Theory of wage determination*, Macmillan, London.

Unemployment Unit (1981), *A dossier of despair, experiences of unemployment in the North East*, Unemployment Unit, London.

US Department of Health, Education and Welfare (1969), *Toward a social report*, US Government Printing Office, Washington, DC.

US Department of Health, Education and Welfare (1976), *The measure of poverty*, US Government Printing Office, Washington DC.

US Department of Labor (1970), *Manpower report of the President 1970*, US Government Printing Office, Washington, DC.

US Department of Labor (1971), *Black Americans: a chartbook*, US Government Printing Office, Washington DC.

Usher, D. (1966), *Rich and poor countries*, Institute of Economic Affairs, London.

Usher, D. (1980), *The measurement of economic growth*, Basil Blackwell, Oxford.

van Slooten, R. and Coverdale, A.G. (1977), 'The characteristics of low income households', *Social Trends*, vol. 8.

Vickrey, W. (1947), *Agenda for progressive taxation*, Ronald Press, New York.

Wabe, S. and Leech, D. (1978), 'Relative earnings in U.K. manufacturing — a reconsideration of the evidence', *Economic Journal*, vol. 88.

Wachtel, H.M. and Betsy, C. (1972), 'Employment at low wages', *Review of Economics and Statistics*, vol. 54.

Wachter, M.L. (1974), 'Primary and secondary labor markets: a critique of the dual approach', *Brookings Papers on Economic Activity*, vol. 3.

Walker, A. (1981), 'Disability and Income', in A. Walker and P. Townsend (eds), *Disability in Britain, a manifesto of rights*, Martin Robertson, Oxford.

Walker, A. and Townsend, P. (ed.) (1981), *Disability in Britain, a manifesto of rights*, Martin Robertson, Oxford.

Warlick, J.L. (1981), 'Participation as a measure of program success', *Focus*, Institute for Research on Poverty, University of Wisconsin, vol. 5.

Watts, H.W. (1969), 'Graduated work incentives: an experiment in negative income taxation', *American Economic Review, Papers and Proceedings*, vol. 59.

Webb, A. and Sieve, J. (1971), *Income redistribution and the welfare state*, Bell, London.

Webb, S. and Webb, B. (1902), *Industrial democracy*, Longman's Green, London.

Wedderburn, D. (1962), 'Poverty in Britain today – the evidence', *Sociological Review*, vol. 10.

Wedgwood, J. (1928), 'The influence of inheritance on the distribution of wealth', *Economic Journal*, vol. 38.

Wedgwood, J. (1929), *The economics of inheritance*, Routledge, London.

Weisbrod, B.A. and Hansen, W.L. (1968), 'An income-net worth approach to measuring economic welfare', *American Economic Review*, vol. 58.

Weiss, L. (1966), 'Concentration and labor earnings', *American Economic Review*, vol. 56.

Weisskopf, T.E. (1979), 'Marxian crisis theory and the rate of profit in the postwar US economy', *Cambridge Journal of Economics*, vol. 3.

von Weizsäcker, C.C. (1978), 'Annual income, lifetime income and other concepts in measuring income distribution', in W. Krelle and A.F. Shorrocks (eds), *Personal income distribution*, North-Holland, Amsterdam, New York, Oxford.

Welch, F. (1978), *Minimum wages*, American Enterprise Institute, Washington, DC.

Welch, F. (1979), 'Effects of cohort size on earnings: the Baby Boom babies' financial bust', *Journal of Political Economy*, vol. 87.

Whalley, J. (1979), 'The world income distribution', *Review of Income and Wealth*, vol. 25.

Wiles, P.J.D. (1974), *Income distribution, East and West*, North-Holland, Amsterdam.

Wiles, P.J.D. and Markowski, S. (1971), 'Income distribution under Communism and Capitalism', *Soviet Studies*, vol. 22.

Wilkinson, F. (ed.) (1981), *The dynamics of labour market segmentation*, Academic Press, London.

Williamson, J.G. (1976), 'The sources of American inequality, 1896–1948', *Review of Economics and Statistics*, vol. 58.

Williamson, J.G. (1977), '"Strategic" wage goods, prices and inequality', *American Economic Review*, vol. 67.

Williamson, J.G. (1980), 'Earnings inequality in nineteenth century Britain', *Journal of Economic History*, vol. 40.

Williamson, J.G. (1981), 'The structure of pay in Britain 1710–1911', in P. Uselding (ed.), *Research in economic history*, vol. 5, Johnson, Greenwich, Connecticut.

Williamson, J.G. and Lindert, P.H. (1980), *American inequality, a macroeconomic history*, Academic Press, New York London.

Wilson, J. (1966), *Equality*, Hutchinson, London.

Wilson, T. (ed.) (1974), *Pensions, inflation and growth*, Heinemann, London.

Wilson, T. and Wilson, D.J. (1982), *The political economy of the welfare state*, Allen and Unwin, London.

Wise, D.A. (1975), 'Personal attributes, job performance and probability of promotion', *Econometrica*, vol. 43.

Wolff, E.N. (1980), 'Estimates of the 1969 size distribution of wealth in the US', in J.D. Smith (ed.), *Modelling the distribution and intergenerational transmission of wealth*, University of Chicago Press, Chicago.

Wolff, E.N. (1981), 'The accumulation of household wealth over the life-cycle', *Review of Income and Wealth*, vol. 27.

Wolfson, M.C. (1979), 'Wealth and the distribution of income', *Review of Income and Wealth*, vol. 25.

Wolfson, M.C. (1980), 'The bequest process and the causes of inequality in the distribution of wealth', in J.D. Smith (ed.), *Modelling the distribution and intergenerational transmission of wealth*, University of Chicago Press, Chicago.

Wood, A. (1975), *A theory of profits*, Cambridge University Press, Cambridge.

Wootton, B. (1962), *The social foundations of wage policy* (2nd ed), Allen and Unwin, London.

World Bank (1982), *World development report 1982*, Oxford University Press, Oxford.

Wynn, M. (1970), *Family policy*, Michael Joseph, London.

AUTHOR INDEX

SUBJECT INDEX